CARTHAGE AND TUNIS,

PAST AND PRESENT:

In Two Parts.

BY

AMOS PERRY,
LATE UNITED STATES CONSUL FOR THE CITY AND REGENCY OF TUNIS.

PROVIDENCE, R. I.:
PROVIDENCE PRESS COMPANY, PRINTERS.
1869.

DT
245
.P46
cop 2

Entered according to an Act of Congress, in the year 1868,
By AMOS PERRY,
In the Clerk's Office of the District Court of the United States for the District of
Rhode Island.

PREFACE.

During the leisure of a prolonged residence where I was often reminded of the name and glory of Carthage, I naturally pursued trains of thought and courses of study suggested by the scenes around me. I read the history and observed the actual condition of the country, without, however, any thought of communicating through the press in regard to the subjects that engaged my attention. But in the course of time, communications were received from gentlemen and societies, asking for such a variety of information as could be furnished only by one acquainted with the geography, history, races, antiquities, commerce, institutions, and even the poetry and legends pertaining to the land of DIDO and of HANNIBAL. This manifestation of interest, together with some official and personal expressions from the honored head of the Department of State at Washington, served to quicken my efforts, leading me to study and observe, as well to answer the inquiries of others, as to gratify my individual taste.

The idea of this work was thus suggested, and its preparation was at length undertaken with a view of supplying a public want. I would not, however, have the inference drawn from this remark, that I failed to appreciate the efforts of my predecessors in this field of labor. Messrs. SHAW, TEMPLE,

TABLE OF CONTENTS.

PART FIRST.

General History, from the Ninth Century, B. C., to the Last Half of the Nineteenth Century, A. D.

CHAPTER I.
Summary Description of the Tunisian Territory.—Brief Sketch of its Political Revolutions. 3–7.

CHAPTER II.
Ancient History, from the Ninth Century B. C., to the Seventh Century A. D. 8–154.

SECTION I.—The Country before the arrival of the Phœnicians. 8–13.—Rise and Progress of the Punic Power. 13–41.

SECTION II.—Carthage and Rome. 42–46.—First Punic War. 46–66.—War of the Mercenaries. 66–71.—Conquests in Spain.—Second Punic War, 71–97.—Hannibal. 97–109.

SECTION III.—Third Punic War.—Taking and ruin of Carthage. 109–117.—Carthage under Rome.—Massinissa and Jugurtha. 117–125.

SECTION IV.—Cæsar in Africa.—Cato of Utica. 125–134.—Christianity in Africa. 134–149.

SECTION V.—The Vandals and Byzantines in Africa.—First Arab Invasion. 149–154.

CHAPTER III.
History of the Middle Age, from the Seventh to the Sixteenth Century. 155–167.

SECTION I.—The Arab Conquest and the Country under the Lieutenants of the Oriental Califs and under the first Independent Princes. 155–159.

SECTION II.—Dynasty of the Hafsites.—Expedition of St. Louis. 159–167.

TABLE OF CONTENTS.

CHAPTER IV.

Modern History, from the Sixteenth Century to the last half of the Nineteenth Century. 168-222.

SECTION I.— Fall of the Hafsites.— Expedition of Charles V.— The Spanish Domination. 168-181.

SECTION II.—Turkish Domination and the Deys. 181-188.

SECTION III.—The Beys. 188-208.

SECTION IV.—Relations of Barbary in general and of Tunis in particular with different Christian Nations.—Corsairs and Slavery. 208-222.

PART SECOND.
Actual State of the Country.

CHAPTER I.
Natural Divisions, Extent and General Aspect of the Country. 225-234.

CHAPTER II.
Population.— Races.— Religious Creeds, Rites and Ceremonies.— Pilgrimages to Mecca.—Manners, Customs and Superstitions. 235-333.

CHAPTER III.
The Mussulman Woman and the Mussulman Problem. 333-360.

CHAPTER IV.
Climate.— Products of the Soil.— Manufactures.— Arts and Trades. 361-384.

CHAPTER V.
Principal Cities.—Their Characteristics and Peculiarities. 385-427.

CHAPTER VI.
Archeological Sketch of the Country.—Monuments and Traces of the Past.—Carthage, Utica, Hadrumetum, etc. 428-461.

CHAPTER VII.
Government and Administration.—Army.—Navy.—Finances.—Public Instruction.— Benevolent Institutions.— Revenues and Burdens of the State. 462-482.

CHAPTER VIII.
The Israelites in Tunisia. 483-504.

CHAPTER IX.
The Europeans in Tunisia.—Comparative Importance of their Colonies and Influence.—Foreign Representatives at the Tunisian Court. 505-517.

CHAPTER X.
General Considerations upon the Present Condition of Tunis, compared with the Past, and Inferences in regard to the Future. 518-528.

Appendix and Index.

Part First.

GENERAL HISTORY.

CHAPTER I.

Summary Description of the Tunisian Territory.—Brief Sketch of its Political Revolutions.

THE Mediterranean sea, around which have been accomplished so many phases of history, becomes narrow in its centre by the approach of Europe and Africa, so as to present in its ensemble the irregular form of an immense figure eight reversed thus, ∞.

At the point of the union of the two parts of this ∞, projects out towards Europe, in the face of Sicily, a territory whose coast is comparatively sinuous and indented, which territory now constitutes the regency of Tunis, (Africa Propria, Zeugitania, Byzacium.) Bounded by the Mediterranean on the north and east, by Algeria on the west, by the desert on the south, and Tripoli on the southeast, it extends between 33° and 37° 20′ north latitude, and between 7° 40′ and 11° 40′ east from the meridian of Greenwich, having an area of sixty thousand square miles, and a sea coast five hundred and fifty miles in length.

Geologically connected with Algeria and Morocco (Numidia and Mauritania) by the last links, and formed by the last table lands of that Atlas which is, as it were, the back-bone of northern Africa, Tunisia opens to the north, between cape Blanc and cape Bon, its gulfs of Bizerta and Tunis into the western basin of the Mediterranean where it faces Italy, France, Spain and the Intermediate islands. On the east, from cape Bon to the island of Gerba, it opens out into the eastern basin of the same sea, its gulfs of Hommamet and Gabes towards Sicily and Malta, Tripoli and Greece, Egypt and Asiatic Turkey.

It is the finest position of north Africa. Commercial preponderance and the control of the Mediterranean are its attractions for the powers which dispute with each other for its possession or for its neutralization.

To the advantages of general topography, Tunis possesses also important conditions of natural riches. It has a soil admirably fertile, furrowed by streams of water which run at present almost like torrents, but which were once navigable or ingeniously employed for purposes of irrigation. It has numerous sources of living water in rare abundance. It has mountains covered towards the north with proud forests, and containing mines of iron, lead, argentiferous lead, quicksilver and antimony, and rich quarries of marble It has many mineral springs of singular medicinal efficacy. Its vicinity to the interior of Africa made it once the most important market and commercial country of the African continent, and, under favorable circumstances, it might again become distinguished for its commerce. Such are the privileges, which, with its admirable maritime position, we shall study more in detail further on,—privileges which necessarily predestined Tunis for long and glorious annals, which are not wanting, as we shall see as we proceed in our studies.

Occupied at first by a primitive population of which we know scarcely the names and still less the history, its social and political existence commences in fact only at the arrival of the Phœnicians.

These incomparable navigators, who scented, so to speak, and discovered upon all the shores of the ancient world stations capable of strengthening and developing their mercantile power, could not long remain unacquainted with this gulf of Tunis, worthy one day to shelter the daughter and the rival of Tyre, the Superb.

They built there Carthage. At first a modest colony, then flourishing, it became rapidly independent of its mother country; and at length assuming the rule that belonged to its declining metropolis in the East, it inherited its empire and enlarged its horizon.

Rome, already preponderant in its peninsula, could not advance further without striking against this Punic colossus which projected its shade menacingly from the coast of Sicily.

There was to take place the first shock. Between such adversaries as fatally excluded each other, since each aimed at supremacy, the struggle was of necessity long and terrible. Carthage fell. The balance of the ancient world lost its most powerful counterpoise until the universal equilibrium was broken definitely in favor of Rome, and the centre of gravity of every known people was established under its sway.

Rome inherited from Carthage as the latter from the Phœnicians. Fruitful Africa (*Africa ferax*) became the granary of Italy and its chief source of supply at the end of the republic and under the empire.

At the beginning of Christianity, it became one of its bright centres; and this is not the least attractive period of its history.

In the fall of the Roman empire, it formed naturally a general quarter and stragetic point for the victorious Barbars.

Then while the Byzantine Cæsar was laboriously re-conquering this best of all the provinces which broke away from him in every part of the empire, behold Islamism and its furious propagandists, drawn in their turn by the renown and the importance of this country, came to heap up still other ruins and create new institutions.

The Mohammedan conquests once organized, the Moslem governments of the middle age succeeded not without éclat in this lieutenantcy of the supreme califate.

The sword of the crusaders came there to be broken in the hands of St. Louis. That of Spain and the Holy Empire glistened for a moment in the grasp of Charles V, and of the ephemeral guardians of his conquest.

Then flocked thither the Osmanlis, that *rear ban* of the great army of the Prophet. To their domination, now violent and now feeble from decay, succeeds through the struggles of the Turkish pretorians and the prowess of the pirates, a government almost native and national, which continues to this day.

In all these vicissitudes, the country of Carthage has been able to regain neither its agricultural and commercial importance nor the splendor of its first days.

From the Punic epoch to our own, in point of prosperity and grandeur, it can be said that for Tunis there is *decreasing* progression.

Long, curious and touching is its history of more than twenty-seven centuries, whose tableau we shall attempt briefly to retrace before studying in detail the actual state (so interesting in all respects) of the country that has been the theatre of it. Why, then, should not its future, prepared by the gradual amelioration of the present, recall something of its magnificent past?

CHAPTER II.

Ancient History from the Ninth Century, B. C., to the Seventh, A. D.

SECTION I.

THE COUNTRY BEFORE THE ARRIVAL OF THE PHŒNICIANS.—RISE
AND PROGRESS OF THE PUNIC POWER.

HISTORIANS speak only very vaguely of North Africa during the period previous to the arrival of the Phœnicians. Herodotus gives the names of numerous peoples or nations situated between Egypt and lake Triton; but he says nothing of the inhabitants along the Atlas, and he sums up his information upon Africa thus: "There are only two great native peoples, the Libyans and the Ethiopians."

Leaving aside the Ethiopians, (whether they were really blacks or simply a people of a very swarthy complexion,) since authors place them altogether towards the interior, there remain for the general primitive people of North Africa only the Libyans.

Sallust, who attempted to trace back the origin of this people in the Numidian books of Hiempsal, written out according to ancient traditions, says that after the death of Hercules in Spain, the Persians, the

Medes, and the Armenians who had followed him, came again into Africa and mixed up with the ancient inhabitants of the country, the Libyans and the Getulians. From the union of the Persians and the Getulians sprang the Numidians; and from the union of the Medes and Armenians with the Libyans sprang the Moors.

The Byzantine historian, Procopius, speaks of the Moors as Canaanites expelled from Palestine at the epoch of the invasion by Joshua. Admitting this, let us observe that the Getulians, Numidians and Moors enter into the unity of the Libyan race vaguely indicated by Herodotus.

In fact, Sallust speaks of the Getulians as having the same manners and the same traits of character as the Libyans; and Strabo considers them as a branch of that people. Herodotus regards the Numidians as a simple variety of the Libyans, and Strabo regards the Moors in the same light. According to Sallust, Moors and Numidians are, it is true, mixed races, but are attached to a more numerous and predominant primitive population, with which they were necessarily confounded.

From that which precedes, we can, I think, infer, first, the existence of a single primitive population, whose origin the Latin and Greek authors scarcely specify, and which they regarded, according to their habits, as purely aboriginal and indigenous; second, successive foreign immigrations, which became amalgamated with this native population.

And, first, this population itself, like that of the whole world, is of oriental origin; for humanity, like civilization, has followed the light of the rising sun from east to west. The identity or the similarity of the language and of the general characteristics of this population and of the primitive inhabitants of western Arabia, Palestine and Egypt indicates their common origin. The Libyans, like the ancient Egyptians and the Phœnicians, are of a stock slightly mixed, in which predominates the blood of Ham.

According to the Bible, Mizraim, Canaan, Cush and Phut were brothers, and modern philology has found a striking analogy between the very name of the Lehabim descendants of Mizraim, and the Libyans of antiquity, (in Greek, $\Lambda\iota\beta\upsilon\eta$, Libya; $\Lambda\iota\beta\upsilon o\iota$, Libyans).

The Arab historians who speak of Africa agree with ethnographers and modern travellers in affirming the identity of the Libyans or primitive Africans, and of the actual Berbers.

These Berbers, who are scattered over the whole north of Africa, from the valleys of the Atlas to the desert of Sahara, and from Egypt to the Atlantic ocean, and who are called Amasighs in Morocco; Cabyls in Algeria, Tunisia and Tripoli; Tibboos in Fezzan and in Egypt, and Touaregs in the north of the Sahara;—these Berbers, are regarded to-day as one of the types of that primitive family which science calls Egypto-Berber, and of which they are the most numerous and the most persistent branch.

What were the condition and physiognomy of this Libyan or Berber race, spread *ab antiquo* over all North Africa? It appears that from Egypt to the end of the Syrtis Minor, (gulf of Gabes), it led the wandering life of the Nomads; from lake Triton to the ocean, *i. e.*, from the southeast to the northwest, it had fixed habitations and lived by the tillage of the ground. Back of these maritime and agricultural Libyans, lived the Getulians, a people of the same race, as we have said, but more rude and nomadic. The very nature of the soil explains these differences of life. From the columns of Hercules to the Syrtis Minor, the territory sustained and divided by mountains, extends towards the Mediterranean some narrow but fertile valleys. Beyond these, the continent is depressed; it is the sandy plain, the immense desert, which widens out from the ocean to Egypt, reaching almost to the orient towards the shores of the eastern Mediterranean. Nothing, then, is more natural than that the Libyans, modifying their habits, and at length their manners, according to surrounding circumstances, should become subdivided, while at the same time preserving the general character of their race.

What was that character? "The men are robust and active," says Sallust, "and capable of enduring all fatigues; their constitution, almost always more powerful than disease, yields only to the burden of old age, unless by chance they fall under the tooth of the wild beast or by fire." "Happy to lie upon the ground," says Procopius, "they have for all seasons only one thick dress, a tunic with a long nap, which they wear around them. They have no knowledge of bread or wine; wheat and barley in their natural state are sufficient for their nourishment."

Such was, and such is still, fundamentally, the physical character of the Libyans or Berbers: force, sobriety, activity, and thence a proud spirit and dauntless valor.

Which are the eastern peoples that in the course of centuries immigrated into North Africa? Nothing truly historic exists upon this subject. Traditions transmitted by authors, or even orally from one generation to another, preserve dark souvenirs of these immigrations without indicating either their epoch, their nature or their exact name. Probably the facility with which the immigrants became assimilated and incorporated by virtue of a common origin, contributed to this obscurity of history.

The Phœnicians and the Greeks are the only peoples of historic antiquity whose invasions are well known and traced back in their consequences. Sailors and merchants, they came to establish themselves upon the two large promontories, which face, one of them towards Greece, and the other towards Sicily: the Greeks in the country of Cyrene; the Phœnicians in that of Carthage. We need not occupy ourselves with the Greeks; a word only about the Phœnicians will suffice.

Their history is essentially that of their voyages and of their colonies. The Tyrian Hercules is the symbol of that history. "His march," says the illustrious German, Heeren, "is not marked by the sacking of the cities and the devastation of the country; but by a long suite of flourishing colonies, which introduced agriculture and the arts to a gross and barbarous people."

The Phœnician establishments had naturally to extend from east to west upon the shores of the

Mediterranean. From the Hellespont and the isles of the Archipelago to the strait of the Columns, they dotted the coasts of Africa, of Spain and of the great intermediate islands, especially during the brilliant period of the navigation and of the commerce of the Phœnicians, which was from the tenth to the sixth century, B. C.

The admirable position and the fertility of the country which constitutes the actual regency of Tunis had the effect to early attract the attention of this essentially mercantile and utilitarian people. They flocked there and founded successively Utica, Carthage, Hadrumetum, Thysdrus, Leptis Parva, etc. But Carthage speedily inherited power from the Phœnicians and so developed it as to eclipse the glory of the Phœnician metropolis. It must then engage our attention for a while at this point of the course which we propose to take from the past to the present of Tunisia.

RISE AND PROGRESS OF THE PUNIC POWER.

It appears certain that in the twelfth century, B. C., the Phœnicians had founded upon the Libyan coast numerous colonies; some of them dependent upon their respective oriental metropolis, whose voluntary and purely commercial immigrations had peopled them; others established by citizens exiled on account of civil wars; and all of them become powerful by the development of the nautical skill and commercial enterprise of their race.

The first or rather the most important of the Phœnician cities founded in Africa before Carthage, was Utica, situated twenty-five miles to the northwest of Tunis, upon the territory of the actual Bou-Shahter on the ancient western shore of the gulf of Tunis, from which it is at present removed several miles.

I say *ancient shore*, for it is certain that the actual western bank of this gulf has been slowly formed by the alluvium of the Majerda, (ancient Bagrada), which has changed its channel. It once flowed much nearer Carthage into the sea, while at present it empties into the lake of Porto Farina (Ghar el Melh). We shall, in speaking of the present state of the country, enter into some details on this subject.

Utica was founded, according to all the historians, two or three centuries before Carthage. But across the vague indications of these distant and confused epochs, how can we attain precision and certainty? How dissipate the shades that envelope the origin of the Phœnician power in Africa and the cradle of Carthage?

"Carthage," says the learned Dureau de la Malle, "had the sad destiny to shed forth a great light only at the moment of its ruin, and to see the care of its glory entrusted to foreign writers. All knowledge of Carthaginian writers has long since been lost; and of foreign authors not one has written consecutively the history of this republic."

According to the common poetic tradition, Carthage, a Tyrian colony was founded by Dido or Elissa, great-grand-daughter of that Ithabel, king of Tyre, who was, according to the Scriptures, the father of the famous Jezebel. She had married one of her relatives, Sichæus or Sicharbas, one of the most opulent citizens of Tyre. Pygmalion, brother of Dido, a cruel and covetous tyrant, assassinated Sichæus. in the hope of enjoying his immense possessions. But Elissa, thwarting his plans, secretly seized the treasures of her murdered husband and escaped by sea in company with a few courageous partisans; and, after sailing about a long time in the eastern Mediterranean, she arrived in Africa on the western coast of the gulf of Tunis, according to Strabo, one hundred and twenty stadias (ten or twelve miles) from the city of Tunis.

Virgil explains in the Æneid, as rendered by Dryden, the foundation of Carthage. The beautiful Venus is represented as standing upon a prominent hill, now Sidi Bou Said, and enlightening the pious Æneas with the following narration, which has come to be a part of the history or rather poetry of the country:—

"The rising city, which from far you see,
Is Carthage, and a Tyrian colony.
Phœnician Dido rules the growing state,
Who fled from Tyre, to shun her brother's hate:
Great were her wrongs, her story full of fate;
Which I will sum in short. Sichæus, known
For wealth, and brother to the Punic throne,
Possessed fair Dido's bed; and either heart
At once was wounded with an equal dart.
Her father gave her, yet a spotless maid;
Pygmalion then the Tyrian sceptre swayed—
One who contemn'd divine and human laws.
Then strife ensued, and cursed gold the cause.
The monarch, blinded, with desire of wealth,
With steel invades his brother's life by stealth;
Before the sacred altar made him bleed,
And long from her concealed the cruel deed.
Some tale, some new pretence, he daily coined,

> To soothe his sister and delude her mind.
> At length, in dead of night, the ghost appears
> Of her unhappy lord: the spectre stares,
> And with erected eyes his bloody bosom bares.
> The cruel altars and his fate he tells,
> And the dire secret of his house reveals:
> Then warns the widow and her household gods
> To seek a refuge in remote abodes.
> Last, to support her in so long a way,
> He shows her where his hidden treasure lay.
> Admonished thus, and seized with mortal fright,
> The Queen provides companions of her flight:
> They meet and all combine to leave the state,
> Who hate the tyrant, or who fear his hate.
> They seize a fleet, which ready rigged they find,
> Nor is Pygmalion's treasure left behind.
> The vessels, heavy laden, put to sea
> With prosperous winds: a woman leads the way.
> I know not, if by stress of weather driv'n,
> Or was their fatal course disposed by Heav'n;
> At last they landed, where from far your eyes
> May view the turrets of New Carthage rise;
> There bought a space of ground, which (Byrsa called
> From the bull's hide) they first inclosed, and walled."

According to a well-known legend, Dido asked the natives of the country for as much land as she could enclose with an ox-hide. This apparently small favor once obtained, the shrewd princess had an ox-hide cut into narrow strips, and fastening them together at the ends, she in that way enclosed a large tract of land around the hill where afterwards arose the citadel called the *Byrsa* on account of the stratagem employed by Dido; for Βυρσα (Byrsa) in Greek signifies skin or hide.

But this singular etymological explanation loses its value beside an observation long since made, that in the Syriac, as in the Hebrew, (and the Phœnician strongly resembles these two tongues), the word

Bosra signifies citadel, and thus this word, copied and slightly altered by the Greeks, becomes *Byrsa*.

Other historians, such as Philistus, Appian and St. Jerome, maintain, on the contrary, that the real founders of Carthage were Zoros and Karchedon, and that Elissa only enlarged it. In each case, they agree to date its foundation long before that of Rome, and at least 870 years before the Christian era; and this is the date generally adopted.

Some critics, however, date the foundation of Carthage as far back as 1250 years B. C., which epoch corresponds very nearly to that of the Trojan war. This opinion has the advantage of justifying Virgil, who has been so much reproached with the anachronism of representing at the court of Dido a hero who lived three centuries before. According to this hypothesis, Dido and Æneas were contemporaries, and the accounts of the Æneid are substantially historic.

But we cannot know the name of the veritable founder of Carthage; for the authors who think it founded 1250 years B. C., regard Zoros and Karchedon only as having enlarged it before the arrival of Dido.

From various causes, the history of the first centuries of Carthage is even less known and more confused than that of Rome. It is sufficient to admit, as marking points, that Carthage was probably founded in the course of the ninth century B. C., and that if the honor of founding it does not belong to Dido, that princess had at least the honor of enlarging it and of commencing its career of prosperity.

It is related that in laying the foundations of the *New City*, (in the Phœnician tongue, *Kartha-hadtha*, from which the Greeks make out *Karchedon*, and the Latins, *Carthago*), they found imbedded in the soil the head of an ox. This emblem of servitude, having been regarded by the Phœnician priests as a bad omen, they proceeded to dig a little further on, and found the head of a horse, which is the symbol of ardor, courage and conquest. This legend, without doubt, caused the horse to be selected as the emblem of Carthage; and the symbol of this great mercantile power, became henceforth either *a spirited winged horse in the act of leaping*, (a pegasus), *a horse in the shade of a palm tree,* or simply *the head of a horse.**

Built upon a peninsula joined to the main land by an isthmus, which is found at the present time considerably widened by the continuous alluvium of the Majerda, Carthage extended around the Byrsa, which is the actual hill of St. Louis, so as to touch the furthest slopes of cape Cammart on the northeast, and the shores of the lake of Tunis on the southwest. When we reach, in the course of this narration, the last period in its history, we shall give some essential details upon its topography and upon its ruins.

In order to enlarge the limits of her empire, at first very contracted, Carthage had to struggle for a long time against the surrounding tribes, to which at the origin she paid tribute. She had to conquer, little by little, that territory on which she afterwards succeeded in establishing many new centres of power

---

* The engraving on the title page represents the two sides of a Carthaginian coin.

and points of support. She threw off her dependence, ceased to pay tribute, invaded, point by point, all the Tunisian coast of the Mediterranean, and gradually advanced towards the interior. She became the centre of attraction for all these Phœnician colonies, — her elders, her rivals, her sisters, or her daughters, Utica, Hadrumetum, Leptis Parva, Hippo-Zarytos, etc., — and disseminating in the midst of the Libyans her establishments, by degrees she enveloped them as in a Punic net strongly fastened to the shore, and speedily extended her power from the present Algerine frontier to the remote borders of Tripoli.

Thus was definitely formed, by the mixture of two races, that Libyo-Phœnician people, whose primitive Phœnician colonies, recruited and enlarged by natives, had been their cradle, and who were going to act in the ancient world under the name of Carthaginians, and under the sole impulsion of Carthage, a part similar to that acted at a somewhat later period by the people of Latium under the name of Romans and under the conduct of Rome.

But history gives no definite information about these struggles, which lasted at least two or three centuries, and resulted in the supremacy of Carthage. It speaks of them vaguely, and dwells with distinctness only on the contest between Carthage and Cyrene in regard to the boundary line between their territories.

Cyrene was, as is known, a very powerful city, situated on the shore of the Mediterranean to the east of the Syrtis Major, and it was originally a colony founded by the Lacedemonians. After unavailing combats, the parties agreed upon a truce, and that two deputies should set off from the cities of Carthage and Cyrene at the same time, and that the place where they should meet should become the boundary line between the two states.

The Carthaginian brothers, Phileni, leaving Carthage, passed through all the country of Syrtis Minor and entered the confines of Cyrenaica on the border of Syrtis Major. The Cyrenian deputies protested on meeting the Carthaginians so soon; accused them of setting off before the time agreed upon, and would not consent to thus draw back their frontier to the detriment of Cyrene and to the advantage of Carthage. They offered, however, to credit the word of the Phileni and establish the frontier at the place of their meeting on the condition of burying alive their rival deputies on the spot. The Phileni magnanimously sacrificed their lives for the aggrandizement of their country, whose territory was thereby immensely extended. The Carthaginians lauded them as benefactors, and soon rendered them divine honors, erecting on the place of their devotion *the Altars of the Phileni,* (aræ Philœnorum), which became henceforth the eastern boundary of their empire. They received in this way under their jurisdiction the Lotophagi and the Nasamons, powerful native tribes which afterwards became the agents of the commerce carried on between Carthage and Central Africa.

Tranquil on the side of Cyrene; victorious over the Numidians and the Moors, and dominant, by reason of her force and skill, and the superiority of her comparative civilization, over all the African tribes near which she had once humbly begged a little nook of land, Carthage turned her attention and her ambition towards the Mediterranean. Once sovereign over this sea, she would rule the ancient world.

At this epoch, (540 B. C.), the Phocians were a formidable maritime nation. Carthage united her growing fleet to that of the Etrurians and gave them battle in the waters of the great island of Cyrnos, (Corsica). The Phocians were defeated, and the island came under the dominion of the victors.

This was the first station gained by Carthage in the Mediterranean, and it was maintained only by means of great efforts and sacrifices. But the commanding position of this sea being Sicily, this ambitious colony coveted it, and Malchus, a general greatly distinguished by his successes over the Africans, invaded and seized most of this island in the year 536 B. C.[*]

A frightful plague, however, came to moderate the joy of Carthage in this success, and in spite of numerous human sacrifices to appease the anger of the gods, the scourge redoubled its fury and desolated the city. To this misfortune was added the defeat of Malchus in his attempt to land in Sardinia. He was accused and banished with his army; but, irritated, he marched upon Carthage, took possession of it, put to death ten senators and seized the power. Soon accused of aspiring to the throne, he was himself put to death.

It was several years later when the first treaty

---

[*] Malchus was the first sufet (chief magistrate) of which history speaks. It was probably in his time that the monarchy, the first government of Carthage, was replaced by a complex republican government of which we shall speak further on.

between Carthage and Rome was concluded, (509 B. C.), a year after the fall of the Tarquins and during the consulship of Junius Brutus and Marcus Horatius. This document, whose object was to establish a kind of alliance between these two republics by means of fixed limits to the navigation of the Romans, and of obstacles along the Italian coast to the ambition of the Carthaginians, shows, on the one hand, that as early as the consulship of the first Brutus, the commerce of Rome had already become sufficiently flourishing to attract attention; and, on the other hand, that the Carthaginians had then become masters of the sea and of the island of Sicily, and of almost all of Sardinia. The Carthaginians had also carried their commerce to the maritime cities which were under Roman jurisdiction on the southwest coast of Italy, and had probably menaced them with arms.

This extension of the Carthaginian power over the Mediterranean was due especially to Mago, the successor of Malchus, who was a great captain and a superior magistrate and statesman. This second sufet of Carthage organized and disciplined her armies, removed far back the frontiers of her territory, developed her commerce, and left at his death this great work to be continued by his two sons, Hasdrubal and Hamilcar, who proved to be worthy heirs of his talents and of his noble and patriotic ambition.

They invaded anew Sardinia. Hasdrubal perished there after having been clothed eleven times with the dignity of sufet in honor of his victories and other services, and after having four times received the honor of a triumph. His brother Hamilcar succeeded him in command.

This was the period when Xerxes, the king of the Persians, began his gigantic and disastrous expedition against the Greeks. He wished to exterminate the Greeks. The Carthaginians burned to achieve the conquest of Sicily. They then seized this occasion to make an alliance with the Persians, and it was agreed that while the latter were marching against Greece, the Carthaginians should crush the Greeks of Sicily. They landed there 300,000 men by means of a fleet of 2,000 ships.

After landing at Panormus (Palermo) and giving several days of repose to his army, Hamilcar invested Himera, a neighboring city. Heron, governor of the place, having in vain solicited and awaited aid from Leonidas, king of Lacedemonia, invoked the aid of Gelon, king of Gela, and then master of Syracuse, who hastened to him with 50,000 infantry and 5,000 cavalry.

Gelon did not, however, give battle at once; for he would have been outnumbered and overpowered. He employed a ruse. Hamilcar was expecting a deputation from Selinus, his ally. Gelon despatched to the Punic camp some horsemen, who succeeded in passing themselves off as the expected delegation, and who, massacring Hamilcar, astonished and terrified the Carthaginians, and then profited by the consequent disorder to burn their fleet.

Gelon, who followed not far from his emissaries, forthwith attacked the Punic camp. Vigorously repulsed at first, he soon succeeded in breaking the ranks and destroying large numbers of the enemy. As soon as the Carthaginians learned of the death of

Hamilcar and saw the flames rising from their burning ships, they lost courage and fled. The confusion and carnage were terrible; half of the Carthaginian army perished upon the field of battle. The rest attempted in vain to entrench themselves in a place where they were in utter destitution; hemmed in and starving, they surrendered at discretion. The battle of Himera took place, according to some authorities, on the same day as that of Thermopylæ, (480 B. C.); but Herodotus and Aristotle say, on the contrary, that it occurred on the same day as that of Salamis, which was a few days later than that of Thermopylæ, and Dureau de la Malle adopts their opinion.

At the news of the disaster of Himera, Carthage, in a state of consternation, seemed to see the enemy already at her gates. She exiled at first, in stupid vengeance, Gisco, son of Hamilcar. She then sent in great haste to Gelon an humble embassy. The conqueror, moderate and modest, courteously received the embassy, and made peace on terms which were regarded as favorable to the vanquished. Carthage was to pay the expenses of the war, (about $2,500,000), and erect two temples to transmit to posterity the conditions of the peace written upon tables of marble. Some historians add that Gelon also stipulated that Carthage should abolish the custom of human sacrifices.*

---

*This act would correspond well with the character of Gelon. It is known that after the important victory which saved his country, he called a general meeting of his fellow-citizens in arms. He went there unarmed and without escort, and offered to give account of all his conduct. The entire people applauded him as a glorious liberator, and far from reproaching him with a power which he had so well used, they confirmed it to him and proclaimed him king. Two of his brothers succeeded him in office.

It was to prevent the dangers incurred to the cause of civil liberty by the union of all these powers in the hands of this family of generals, that the Carthaginians established the *Centumvirate*, or tribunal of one hundred senators, to whom the chiefs of the army had to render account of their conduct.

Meanwhile Carthage had not renounced her projects in Sicily. Neither the disaster which befell the army of Hamilcar, nor the plague which devoured that of Himilco, his son and successor, who had gained there important advantages, could discourage her ambitious views. Though obliged to relinquish power, she clung to the hope of regaining and enlarging her dominions. A new occasion offered for the realization of her hopes was joyfully seized.

After the destruction of the Athenian fleet, commanded by Nicias, before Syracuse, the Segestans, who were allies of the vanquished, fearing the resentment of the conquerors, sought the protection of Carthage, and promised to put themselves under her guidance and direction. The Carthaginians desired nothing better than to occupy Segeste. They knew, on the one hand, the strength the Syracusans had acquired by their recent victory. They therefore hesitated and deliberated a long time. On the other hand, national ambition and the counsel of the sufet Hannibal, son of Gisco, spurred them on to take the decisive step; and thus, under the pretext of protecting Segeste, an army of more than one hundred thousand Carthaginians and mercenaries invaded Sicily.

Hannibal, grandson of the vanquished commander

at Himera, was eager to vindicate the military renown of his family and the honor of his country. He attacked Selinus. (409 B. C.) The defence was, like the attack, terrible. Women, children and enfeebled old men came forth and fought like lions against the besiegers, whose fury they thus exasperated. Selinus, carried by assault, was given over to the brutish vengeance of the soldiery. Then Hannibal permitted, as a special favor, some unfortunate survivors to establish themselves as tributaries of Carthage amidst the ruins of their city.

The victorious general soon turned his force against Himera; took the town by assault, and razing it to the ground, delivered its inhabitants over to fire and sword, sparing only 3,000 prisoners, whom he subjected to cruel torments and debasing ignomy. Then making them languish on the very spot where the horsemen of Gelon had assassinated Hamilcar, he had them all massacred together as an expiatory hecatomb to the manes of his grandfather.

Hannibal returned to Carthage laden with the spoils of war. The entire population came forth to meet him with acclamations of joy and gratitude. This great success intensely stimulated the Punic ambition, which could henceforth be allayed only by the complete conquest of Sicily.

But before beginning on a vast scale a war, which was to be this time decisive and final, the Carthaginians wished to prepare for themselves a solid and sure point of support. Doubtful allies not answering their purpose, they founded upon the north coast of Sicily, near a thermal spring, a city thence called

Thermæ, (baths, at present Termini,) which they peopled with Carthaginians and other African colonists.

Then they apponted again Hannibal to the command of a new army of 150,000 men. This general, not wishing on account of his great age to bear alone this responsibility, they assigned as his lieutenant his cousin Himilco, son of Hanno.

They soon attacked Agrigentum, a powerful and rich city, situated, like Selinus, on the side of Sicily facing Africa. Besieging it at its weakest point, Hannibal elevated, as high as the ramparts, a formidable terrace constructed with the ruins of a vast necropolis which he had demolished; and thus he fought the enemy as on a plain.

But all at once the plague breaks out in his camp. His soldiers, regarding this casualty as the chastisement of heaven for the violation of the tombs, will touch no more the work; and to calm the outraged manes, they multiply their prayers and sacrifices according to Punic rites. They immolate an infant to the sombre god Moloch, and cast into the sea many living and many strangled men to satisfy the god of the deep.

Agrigentum being one of the bulwarks of Sicily, the Syracusans and the people of the island flock under its walls, fight the Carthaginians, and hold them blocked up and menaced with famine in their camp. The mercenaries were already speaking of passing over to the enemy, when Himilco, learning that a convoy of provisions would arrive from Syracuse at Agrigentum by sea, lays in wait for it with forty galleys, destroys the Syracusan fleet which was escorting it, and brings abundance and encouragement to his soldiers, and want and consternation to the inhabitants of Agrigentum.

The besieged abandoned their walls, leaving to the mercy of the enemy their houses, their riches, and what distressed them most, their wounded, their sick, and their old men. A few of these unfortunate creatures effected their flight to Gela; the rest were massacred at the entrance of Himilco, who spared no one, and he carried away magnificent spoils, pictures, precious vases, objects of art and ornaments of every sort, which he speedily sent to Carthage. Among the spoils, was the famous *Bull of Phalaris*.

He took then Gela, in spite of the support afforded by Dionysius, the tyrant of Syracuse. But the state of his army induced him to propose terms of peace, which Dionysius, fearing that further resistance would result in the loss of his power, promptly subscribed. The Carthaginians, besides their former conquests in Sicily, kept Selinus, Agrigentum, Himera, Gela and Camarina. The Leontins, Messenians, and the rest of the unconquered people of the island, preserved their independence, and Dionysius continued to reign at Syracuse, (405 B. C.)

But this peace could not last. Dionysius and Carthage were rivals for the supreme control of Sicily, to possess which one of them had naturally to destroy the other. Dionysius, having first strengthened his power, made immense war preparations, which he superintended himself, complimenting and rewarding the meritorious in person. Syracuse became like a vast arsenal, and was filled with troops recruited from every quarter.

Profiting by the consternation prevailing at Carthage on account of the ravages of the plague propagated there by the army of Himilco on its return, Dionysius harangues the Syracusans, and calls upon them to put forth their energies and crush with one blow that Punic power which was threatening to invade the entire island. A general massacre is begun at Syracuse, and gradually extending, reddens the soil of Sicily with Carthaginian blood.

Then Dionysius summons Carthage to give up all her establishments in Sicily or to accept war, and, without waiting for a reply, he invests the city of Motya with an imposing army and fleet. The defence was obstinate, but the city was taken and the inhabitants massacred. Dionysius left there a garrison and returned to Syracuse, where a skilful *coup de main* of a little Carthaginian squadron had annihilated by night all his vessels which were in the harbor.

There the sufet Hanno soon appeared with 100,000 men and 400 ships. He ravages the territory of Syracuse; sends admiral Mago to seize some of the ports of the city; takes possession of a suburb where he pillages the temples of Ceres and Proserpine, then fortifies his camp with the materials of the tombs which were about the city, and among them that of the late king Gelon, and he constructs three forts for defence. But a frightful plague breaks out and destroys nearly all his army, and the remains of it are annihilated by fire, famine and the enemy.

Himilco shamefully capitulated and fled to Carthage with a small company of his fellow-citizens, abandoning to the enemy all his companions in arms who did not belong to Carthage. But soon stung with remorse and abashed with shame, he ended his life by starvation.

Meanwhile, the African subjects of Carthage, tired of oppression and indignant at the cruelty inflicted by Himilco on their brethren in Sicily, rise in rebellion to avenge their wrongs and free themselves from bondage. Marching towards the capital, they take Tunis, and soon press around the walls of the great city to whose ambition and cruelty they attribute all their ills. The besieged, believing in a new chastisement inflicted by the offended gods, adopt solemnly the worship of Ceres and Proserpine, whose temples at Syracuse Himilco had profaned; and gaining confidence by their devotion and sacrifices, they prepare themselves for resistance. But famine, disorder and bloody dissension appear in the camps of the rebels, who, diminished and demoralized, raise the seige and disperse. (395 B. C.)

In the year 383 B. C., Mago returned into Sicily with another army. After various successes, which restored the Carthaginians to power, a truce of nine years was concluded. But Dionysius induces the cities subjected by Mago to revolt anew, and the latter, hastening back, is beaten and killed in the great battle of Cabala. Carthage implores peace, and the conqueror replies that he will accord it when the suppliant shall have evacuated Sicily and paid all the expenses of the war.

Carthage gained time; then sent young Mago II, who speedily changed the relative position of the two powers, and forced Dionysius, vanquished in his turn, to sue for peace. The Punic general, moderate and prudent, acceded to his request. But he soon renewed the struggle, and was defeated in a naval engagement. A new treaty was then concluded. Finally, in the year 365 B. C., the death of Dionysius, the elder, aged sixty-three years, delivered Carthage from her most formidable enemy. During his long reign of thirty-eight years, he held in check the proud and formidable heir of Tyre with her immense armies and fleets.

The second treaty between Carthage and Rome was concluded about this time. (352 B. C.) It differs from the first only that its provisions apply also to the cities of Tyre and Utica.

At the death of Dionysius, the elder, civil war broke out in Syracuse. Dionysius, the younger, had all the faults of his father without having his good qualities. He was soon driven away, though he afterwards succeeded in reëntering and holding the city. Carthage, profiting by these disorders, attempted to introduce her forces into Syracuse. Mago took possession of the harbor and landed there 60,000 men. But the famous Greek general, Timoleon, sent by Corinth to protect her colony, destroys, first, the army of Icetas, usurper of Leontini, which was an ally of Carthage. He then causes divisions to spring up among the Sicilian enemies of Syracuse, and establishes himself in the citadel while Dionysius departs for Corinth, and succeeds, by his position and influence, in striking Mago with so great fear of being betrayed and annihilated that he sails for Carthage. Accused of treason, he anticipates the punishment prepared for him, and, to escape the terrible infliction, commits suicide. Foiled in their efforts to seize and torture their unfortunate general, his countrymen gratified their revengeful sentiments by suspending his lifeless body from a cross.

Hamilcar II and Hannibal II soon land in Sicily with 70,000 soldiers. Timoleon, with 5,000 foot and 1,000 horse, boldly encounters them and gains a complete victory over them in the midst of a storm on the banks of the river Camicus. The victorious soldiers enter and repose in the Punic camps, which are given them as their share of the spoils.

Carthage was still suffering from this reverse, when the conspiracy of Hanno occurred. Hanno was by his riches and influence her foremost citizen. He wished to reign. With this view, he plotted to poison all the senators, whom he invited to the marriage of his daughter. Already he had ordered tables to be spread in the public porticos for numerous citizens, who were probably most of them his accomplices; also a sumptuous banquet was preparing in his palace for the chiefs of the republic. But the latter, who were secretly warned of his projects, successfully foiled the odious plan of Hanno, by passing a decree which definitely regulated henceforth the expenses and ceremonies of marriage, and thus rendered useless all the preparations of the traitor. The latter then excites the slaves to revolt, and fixes the day for the outbreak. Then discovered anew, he entrenches himself in a strong castle at the head of several thousand partisans, and then appeals for aid to the king of Mauritania and other African princes.

But the Carthaginians succeed in seizing him; have him scourged, his eyes torn out, his arms and legs broken, and after executing him in the presence of the people, hang his disfigured body to a cross. His sons and all his relatives, even those who were strangers to his conspiracy, were unmercifully massacred, so that there might remain neither an imitator nor an avenger of Hanno.

Meanwhile Timoleon had imposed on the Carthaginians a treaty which limited their territory to the river Halycus, and by which the Carthaginians should grant to all Sicilians the right to establish themselves at Syracuse, and should never make an alliance with the regal enemies of this city.

Syracuse had just fallen under the power of Agathocles. This son of a potter, fearfully depraved, but of superior intelligence, rose from the post of a brigand and simple soldier to that of a chiliarch (commander of 1,000 men) and general at Syracuse. Then, driven from this city on account of his ambition, he becomes prætor and general among the Mugatins, in the name of which people he takes possession of Leontini, and menaces the Syracusans, who implore and obtain the aid of the Carthaginian general, Hamilcar. Agathocles also solicits the mediation of Hamilcar, promising his services in return. The Punic general foreseeing the advantage of an alliance with this formidable adventurer, obtains for him not only peace and the right to reënter Syracuse, but the dignity of prætor in this city which had driven him out and which he had just besieged. He enters with a guard of 50,000 Africans. Soon he massacres the principal patricians; then the senate; then the notable plebeians, and reigns supreme. He attacks afterwards the neighboring cities with the assent of Hamilcar. The latter was accused before the senate by the Sicilian allies of Carthage, who had been menaced by Agathocles. He was secretly condemned to death, but it so happened that he died a natural death without any knowledge of his sentence. Agathocles was so irritated by this judgment which showed him in what light he was held by the Punic senate, that he boldly declared war against Carthage.

Hamilcar, son of Gisco, had an engagement with Agathocles near Himera, and drove him back into Syracuse. Another battle is fought, and another defeat is suffered. Syracuse is reduced to extremities. Agathocles, fearing the hatred of his fellow-citizens; seeing Sicily completely in the hands of the Carthagenians, and himself without the means to resist them, conceives the extraordinary idea of invading Africa and reducing Carthage to an extremity as great as that of himself at Syracuse.

Counting upon the ill-concealed hatred of the African subjects at Carthage, and upon the absence of the best Carthaginian troops then stationed in Sicily, he leaves a little band of brave men in the besieged city; takes with him his best soldiers; embarks upon sixty vessels; cuts his way through the enemy's squadron, which seeks to hem him in without knowing who he is, and finally lands not far from cape Bon before any person at Syracuse even suspects his astonishing project, which he executes with wonderful secrecy and tact, none of his companions even understanding his design. As soon as he is fairly disembarked upon this land for whose conquest he is come, calling a meeting of his companions-in-arms, he explains his plans with electrifying eloquence, and then boldly burns his vessels so that there may be no chance for the safety of his troops except in the execution of his orders. The army soon marches through fertile and well cultivated plains covered with country houses. This sight, together with the sympathy of disaffected Carthaginian subjects, animates its failing courage. Swollen with recruits, this army sweeps on with resistless force.

Carthage, which soon learns of all that is passing, is stricken with terror. One party within the walls fearing a siege, demands that the senate treat with the enemy. But after the first shock is passed, they put weapons into the hands of all citizens within the fortifications, and speedily raise an army of 40,000 foot, flanked by 1,000 horse and 2,000 war chariots, which go forth under the orders of Hanno and Bomilcar, to encounter Agathocles. The latter, with only 14,000 men, gained the victory through the treason of Bomilcar, who, hoping after the defeat of his colleague, to come into power by the aid of his troops, left the army commanded by Hanno to fight alone, and its general to perish in the disorder and defeat occasioned by the misconduct of the traitor himself. Agathocles encamps at Tunis, and the Carthaginians see at a distance their country ravaged and their villages burned. Terror awakens superstition. They repent of having until then, by a sacrilegious avarice, gradually diminished their annual offerings sent *ab antiquo* to the god Melkharth, the Tyrian Hercules, who was protector of the Phœnician metropolis and of all its colonies. They send this time splendid gifts. To make reparation also to the god Moloch (Saturn) whom they had defrauded, sacrificing the sons of slaves instead of patrician children according to the rite, they now sacrifice 200 young victims chosen from among the first families; and to complete the expiation, 300 persons voluntarily lay bare their throats to the accursed knife, happy to give up their lives for the safety of their country.

Meanwhile Agathocles, supported by the Africans who sought to throw off the yoke of Carthage, was master of Hadrumetum, Thapsus, Leptis Parva, and of more than 200 other secondary places, and by force or by strategy he had twice repulsed the enemy from his fortified camp at Tunis.

Hamilcar is recalled from Sicily. Before his departure, he discourages Syracuse by a false report of a disaster befallen Agathocles in Africa, and gains some advantages; but the truth is soon known from the mouth of a messenger sent by Agathocles himself. Hamilcar, returning to the charge, is beaten, taken and killed.

Agathocles, everywhere triumphant, subdues by his presence of spirit and by his eloquence and firmness, a sedition which breaks out in his army, and which the Carthaginians seek to encourage; and he makes overtures of alliance to Ophellas, king of Cyrenaica, former lieutenant of Alexander the Great, and husband of a descendant of Miltiades. Ophellas was entertaining ambitious views in regard to acquiring the control of Africa. Agathocles proposed uniting together to annihilate Carthage, the sole obstacle to this project; then to divide the west between the two; Ophellas taking Africa, and Agathocles Sicily. Ophellas, pleased with the proposition, came with 20,000 men to join the victorious Sicilian. The latter received him at first graciously, but, soon repenting of his agreement, assassinated in his camp the unfortunate Cyrenian king, and then succeeded, by means of magnificent presents and promises, in retaining his army in his service.

The dangers to Carthage from a foreign foe were on the increase, and civil dissensions came to aggravate them. Bomilcar, at the head of 8,000 partisans, had attained the position of an autocrat, shedding the blood of his fellow-citizens. Terror and consternation gain full sway. The Carthaginians believe in the presence, or in the speedy arrival, of Agathocles. But soon they come to their senses. Some courageous young men organize resistance. Bomilcar and his partisans, impelled by a storm of arrows and stones, leave the city in disorder and go forth to entrench themselves upon a neighboring hill, which is called Gebel Khawee or Catacomb Hill, where the citizens, arms in hand, molest and distress them. The senate put an end to the struggle by proclaiming a general amnesty. Bomilcar reënters the city. He is seized, subjected to horrible tortures, and is finally crucified in the centre of that forum where but recently he was received and applauded as a king.

Fortunately for Carthage, Agathocles had no

knowledge of this interior disorder; for he would doubtless have turned it to his advantage; and fortunately for Agathocles, Carthage had no knowledge of his relations with the unfortunate Ophellas; for she would have gladly leagued herself with the latter to defeat the former, thus greatly changing the current of events and the relative position of the parties intriguing for power.

And now the conquering Syracusan takes Utica and Hippo-Zarytos, and gives them over to his brutal soldiery for deeds of cruelty and death; and having subjected most of the maritime cities and a great number of the tribes in the interior, and made an alliance offensive and defensive with the Numidians, he judges his authority so well established in Africa that he need not deign to take any reprisals from Carthage, which seems too feeble to be feared. He takes 2,000 soldiers alone, leaving the rest to his son, Archagathos, and returns into Sicily.

While the new general effeminately pursues some expeditions, Carthage resolves to rise from her humiliation or to perish in the effort. She puts into the field three armies, under Adherbal, Hanno and Himilco; and to oblige the enemy to divide his force, she sends them in three different directions. Hanno and Himilco attack and kill Eschrion and Eumachus, lieutenants of Archagathos; destroy nearly all their army; and, uniting with Adherbal, they drive back and besiege in Tunis the son of Agathocles, who is so cast down by these reverses that he sends in haste, entreating his father to come and save him.

Agathocles, though tottering on his throne in Sicily, hesitates not to throw himself once more into Africa. He again forces his way out of the harbor of Syracuse, which is still blockaded by a little though persistent Carthaginian squadron; he repulses a fleet that tries to block up his way. In fine, he lands in Africa, fights a drawn battle with the three Carthaginian generals, and retires roughly handled into his camp. During one night the Punic camp takes fire; disorder prevails there; several thousand Africans, having lost faith in Agathocles, quit him at this moment to pass over to the Carthaginians; the latter, seeing them coming at a distance, believe it an attack of the enemy; the confusion is such that 5,000 Carthaginians, embarrassing each other in their flight, perish in the flames and by the precipices, or kill each other in their blind terror.

The African deserters, retracing their steps, cause the same panic and a similar disaster in the camp of Agathocles. At length, after various vicissitudes of fortune, this wonderful adventurer, fatigued with this long and painful war; feeling himself too weak longer to continue it; seeing also the sea in the power of the enemy, and himself without vessels for embarking his troops, lost all courage and energy, and embarked secretly by night upon a light vessel for Sicily. His son and his small army remained exposed to the vengeance of the Carthaginians. The army, indignant, revolted, and massacred Archagathos, and then was forced to treat with the enemy on the following terms: The Sicilians were to give up to the Carthaginians all their African conquests for the sum of 300 talents, and as to the remainder of the army, those who wished were to be incorporated into the Punic army, and the rest were to be sent into Sicily. Some municipal chiefs, who resisted the execution of this treaty, were crucified, and their soldiers, reduced to slavery, were compelled to work as serfs of the soil in the same fields, which they had ravaged under their Syracusan chieftan. Thus, after a four years struggle which had failed to annihilate her, Carthage rose up and became more powerful than ever.

The following year a new treaty with Agathocles reëstablished the possessions of the two parties in Sicily, as they were before the war; and Carthage agreed to pay on this occasion to her old enemy, whom she still feared, 300 talents, (a little less than $500,000), and 200,000 measures of wheat.

Agathocles died after a reign of twenty-eight years, in his ninety-fifth year. The democracy rose again in Syracuse and civil war broke out, which lasted nine years, at the expiration of which the Carthaginians came again to besiege that city with 100 vessels and 50,000 men.

At this epoch, (278 B. C.) the Carthaginians and the Romans renewed their old treaty, adding to it a clause offensive and defensive against Pyrrhus, king of Epirus, who was menacing at the same time Italy and Sicily. When this prince, having gained a foothold in Magna Grecia (southeastern Italy), had defeated many Roman armies, the Carthaginians sent to their allies a fleet of 120 ships, commanded by Mago, with offers of assistance. The Roman senate thanked them, but declined to accept the proffered aid.

About this time Pyrrhus, who was a son-in-law of Agathocles and was moreover invited by the Syracusans, passed the straits of Messina and landed upon the island. The Sicilians opened to him the gates of their city and gave up the key to their treasury. The king of Epirus with his allies had soon reduced to his subjection all the possessions of Carthage in Sicily, except alone the city of Lilybeum. The Carthaginians in these circumstances desired terms for an accommodation. Pyrrhus replied with the demand that they should evacuate Sicily as the sole condition of peace. They refused; and, as he had besieged Lilybeum, they repulsed him with heavy losses. Soon his arrogance and cruelties disgusted the Sicilian cities. The Carthaginians augmented their troops. Pyrrhus, beset with dangers and losing confidence in his ability to maintain himself there, left to its former masters that beautiful and flourishing country, which he lost more rapidly than he gained. At the moment of his embarkation for Tarentum, drawing a deep sigh, he exclaimed: "Oh! the beautiful battle-fields we leave for the Carthaginians and the Romans!"

SECTION II.

CARTHAGE AND ROME.—FIRST PUNIC WAR.—WAR OF THE MERCE-
NARIES.—SECOND PUNIC WAR.—HANNIBAL.

The remark of Pyrrhus was speedily verified. Carthage and Rome soon met face to face. They were the two greatest powers of the west; that is, of the so-called ancient world, which each wished to rule alone.

The identity of their ambition was enough to constitute their rivalry and bring on their struggle: the opposition and the antipathy of their national and political character necessarily precipitated, aggravated and rendered more terrible that struggle.

The contest lasted nearly 120 years, upon various fields of battle, and with numerous pretexts and turns of fortune; but always with the same end; the same earnest efforts, and the same tenacity of purpose on both sides: for in disputing with each other, at first for the possession of Sicily; then of Spain; then of Africa itself, it is the empire of the Mediterranean and the control of the ancient world, which Rome and Carthage wished each to wrest from the other, exercising universal and undisputed sway.

To realize this vast ambition to which both were impelled by the very force of things, each of them will bear the greatest sacrifices; will face the most terrible dangers; will courageously put in peril the very independence and even the political existence of her own city; and it is solely in losing both, that is, in surrendering her right to live, that Carthage will acknowledge herself conquered in this long and bloody competition; since it would have been solely by the annihilation of Rome that she would have believed herself victorious, had fortune smiled on her efforts for supremacy and life.

"The wars between Rome and Carthage," says the learned Heeren, "being the inevitable consequence of rivalry for aggrandizement between two conquering powers, as soon as they approached each other in their conquests, it matters not to know which was the aggressor. While we cannot see how to clear Rome from reproach, we cannot but remark that, according to the laws of sound policy, it would be difficult to reconcile the safety of Italy with the absolute rule of Carthage over Sicily."

If we remark, from another point, that in the contrary supposition, the consequences would have been the same; in other words, that if instead of the Carthaginians, the Romans had ruled Sicily, the security of Africa, or rather the maritime empire of Carthage would have been endangered, we are led to infer what in fact occurred, that the cause and the arena of the first encounter of the two rivals would have been found in Sicily.

At the beginning of the Punic wars, the superiority of Carthage is manifest. She ruled from the Syrtis Major to Hippo Regia (near Bona) in Africa. Two-thirds of Sicily, Corsica and Sardinia, supported in the western Mediterranean her formidable navy, and her great armies, recruited among twenty different peoples, secured her sway. Rome extended, it is true, by her possessions, her colonies and her *municipia* in almost all peninsular Italy, to the straits of

Messina, but she was poor in comparison with Carthage; she had no fleet to command respect, and her commerce as well as her maritime importance was comparatively small.

But if territorial importance, exterior force and apparent power gave the superiority to Carthage, how many considerations show that the preparations for the final issue of the struggle were far from being in her favor. The aristocracy governed at Carthage as at Rome. But at Rome the patricians held it an honor to justify their rank as the first citizens by their virtues and patriotism. At Carthage, enervated, corrupted, avaricious, selfish, tyrannical and contemptuous towards the rest of the people, they formed an isolated caste rather than a class which crowned all the others. Love of glory, ambition to combat, to conquer or to die for country, such were the aims and motives of Rome. To aggrandize commerce, to accumulate riches, to enjoy them even viciously, such was the tendency of Carthage. Here the defence of country was an odious burden imposed for money on strangers. At Rome, the soldiers were only citizens armed. The Carthaginian troops being mostly mercenaries, could have neither discipline, devotion to country, nor veritable courage; and the irregularity of the payments and the bad chances of war made many foes, and caused serious embarrassments. On the other hand, rigid discipline, deliberate, patient and unlimited devotion, courage and energy in the face of danger, and noble patriotism were the characteristics of the Roman legions. In a word, Rome in all the vigor of her youth, had a spirit and a heart national: her army was a part of herself, animated with the views and sentiments of the country. Carthage already in full corruption, had only an eager desire to aggrandize or at least preserve her mercantile empire: her army was imported and paid for. At Rome, the sentiment of honor predominated: at Carthage, that of utility.

They were unlike also in religion and in politics. At Carthage, the divinity, evil-doing, terrible, and gross, like the races descended from Ham, was manifested to worshippers only in striking them with calamities, and claimed from them as homage only cruel and unnatural sacrifices or abominable ceremonies and orgies. Massacre and prostitution were the two aspects of this brutifying worship; terror and wantonness the two forms of piety.

At Rome, in spite of the aberrations of paganism, the ideas of meekness, goodness, mercy, justice and beneficence pervaded the public religion and its national manifestations, and the gods were regarded as the supreme protectors of goodness and of the good, and the eternal punishers of wickedness and of the wicked.

It was the policy of Rome, it is true, to extend her empire by conquest; but the conquered peoples promptly accepted her rule either from a consciousness of its superiority or on account of its direct benefits; they were admitted to the rights and shared the hopes of the metropolis, from which, in fact, they differed little in language, manners and character.

Carthage, planted in the midst of the natives of Africa, who little resembled her in language and manners; for the lapse of centuries and diversity of circumstances and influences had deepened the chasm between the Syro-Phœnicians and the Libyans, peoples originally similar; Carthage, we say, rendered herself odious to her subjects and her tributaries by her severely mercantile spirit, and by the cupidity, injustice and cruelty of her agents.

Also, while Rome, loyal and trustful, had fortified her colonies and her *municipia*, which were always at the moment of danger her advanced posts against her enemies; Carthage, scarcely expecting the loyalty, of which she had not given the example, left, in her distrust, all the cities of her terrritory open and without defence that they might not become centres of revolt; and these same cities were always, after the invasion by Agathocles, points of support prepared for foreign conquerors in advance of their arrival.

"To Rome, then," we say with the historian of Julius Cæsar, "to Rome belonged the future. On the one side, a people of soldiers restrained by discipline, religion and purity of morals, animated by love of country and surrounded by devoted allies; on the other side, a people of dissolute merchants, refractory mercenaries, and restless, discontented subjects.

THE FIRST PUNIC WAR. (264—241 B. C.)

The struggle began in Sicily. The Mamertines[*] of Campania, former mercenaries of Agathocles, see-

---

[*] The word Mamertines comes from *Mamers*, which in the Campanian dialect signified Mars.

ing themselves menaced in Messina, where they had established themselves by treachery and maintained themselves by violence, invoked the aid of Rome against their aggressors, Hiero II of Syracuse and Hannibal, general of the Carthaginians.

The senate deliberated long. On the one hand, it appeared unworthy of the majesty of the Roman people to aid brigands whose imitators and allies they had just chastised without pity;* on the other hand, it was urgent to arrest the progress of the Carthaginians in Sicily, and this was an excellent occasion. The matter was sent for the decision of the people. The latter, excited by the consuls, declared in favor of aiding the Mamertines.

The consul Appius Claudius passed first the straits almost alone; and introduced into Messina by the aid of the Mamertines, succeeded in exciting the inhabitants against the Carthaginian masters of the citadel, who were soon driven off. But the commander of the Punic forces was crucified for cowardice and treachery by his indignant fellow patriots, and the city was invested by them more energetically than before. Meanwhile Appius Claudius returned to Regium, where his legions were awaiting him; he put them upon large ships, which were repulsed by the Punic fleet; he then feigned a retreat; but soon, in the obscurity of the night, came back with all his forces upon rafts which could not attract the attention of

---

* A Roman Legion, wholly composed of Campanians, profited by the troubles of the war of Pyrrhus to treacherously take possession of the city of Regium, and commit there deeds of horror. After the departure of Pyrrhus, the senate drove the invaders out of the city, and severely chastised them.

the enemy from a distance.* Landing in Messina, (264 B. C.) and finding himself pressed by the Syracusans and Carthaginians, he offered them peace, which they refused on his terms. Appius then attacked them separately, and defeated Hiero, who, dissatisfied with the Carthaginians because they neglected to watch the Romans, withdrew to his capital. The legions assaulted the Punic entrenchment and were driven back with terrible slaughter. Pursued in their retreat by the Carthaginians, who were drawn forward by the presumption of success and by the ardor of their zeal, the Romans returned to the charge, overwhelmed the Africans, and drove them back in confusion to their camp, which they did not dare leave so long as Appius remained in Sicily. The latter soon repassed into Italy, not, however, without leaving a strong garrison in Messina, and ravaging the territory of Syracuse with the view of withdrawing Hiero from the Punic alliance.

The following year, the new consuls, Marcus Valerius and Marcus Otacilius came to prosecute and accomplish the work of Appius at the head of an army of 32,000 foot soldiers and 3,600 cavalry, including four legions.

The superiority of the tactics and discipline of the Roman soldiers, and the skill, moderation and austere dignity of the chiefs struck the Sicilians so much the more, as the Carthaginians and the Mamertines had subjected them to much tyranny and cruelty. Hiero, on his side, already foreseeing the issue of the struggle

---

* After the accomplishment of this enterprise, Appius received the surname *Caudex*, which signifies raft or vessel.

from the progress of the Roman power; observing the sympathies or the discouragement of the Sicilians, and remarking that his allies had lost successively three-score places, among which were Catania and Taurominium, declared himself for the Romans, and demanded peace of the victorious consuls. They accorded it on easy terms, for in making an ally of the king of Syracuse, they acquired another considerable point of support and the means of supplying themselves with provisions in the richest provinces of Sicily; since until then they were often short of provisions, receiving them only from Italy, while the Punic fleet was mistress of the sea.

It was agreed then that Hiero should be reëstablished in the possession of all his ancient kingdom; that he should pay a sum equivalent to $100,000 for the expenses of the war, and that prisoners on each side should be restored. Hiero observed faithfully during half a century an alliance which was of the highest advantage to the Roman people.

At the news of the defection of Hiero, and of the consequent consolidation of the Romans in Sicily by means of that alliance, Carthage enlarged her army of occupation with mercenaries from Gaul, Spain and Liguria, and selected Agrigentum for her principal armory and base of operations. The position and fortifications of this city rendered it almost impregnable. The Romans besieged it immediately; suffered a repulse and recovered from it; blockaded the besieged during five months, and reduced them to famine. Then Hannibal, son of Gisco, commander of the place, having solicited and finally obtained reënforcements and provisions, which the aged Hanno brings, the Romans find themselves, in their turn, in distress, and their cavalry suffer a defeat, which serves to discourage them. But in a decisive battle, they defeat Hanno and Hannibal. Nevertheless, the latter succeed in leaving Agrigentum, crossing the Roman entrenchments during the night with all their garrison, the rear guard of which alone attracts their attention and arouses the vengeance of the victors. The Romans enter the city the following day; give it up to pillage, and sell as slaves 25,000 of its inhabitants. Then, satisfied with this conquest, and wearied with the pains and sacrifices which it had cost them, they retire to Messina.

Carthage, irritated by the loss of Agrigentum, dismissed Hanno from office, imposed upon him a heavy fine, and sent Hamilcar into Sicily in command of a fleet which succeeded in taking most of the maritime cities conquered by the Romans.

The latter, continuing their hostilities, became masters of all the cities of the interior, and were eager to drive out of Sicily the Carthaginians still established on the coast. They wished also to protect Italy from the incursions of the Punic fleet. To effect this two-fold object, it was necessary to dispute for the empire of the sea, and to actually wrest it from Carthage. Rome conceived this idea and magnanimously resolved to realize it.

She had not a single vessel of war capable of encountering those of Carthage. At most, her allies furnished her some triremes (vessels with three rows of oars) which the Punic quinqueremes, altogether

VICTORY OF DUILLIUS.

heavier and swifter, would have sunk without difficulty. Ship-builders and rowers were also in demand. But whatever was wanting, the energy of Rome would create and have at any price. A Carthaginian quinquereme, providentially stranded upon the coast, served as a model. The shore was covered with timber and with earnest workmen: 120 galleys with five rows of oars were built, armed and equipped in sixty days, and in this same interval, soldiers exercising themselves with enthusiasm, in naval manœuvres and tactics, became rowers and sailors.

The consul, Cornelius, forthwith exposes by an act of imprudence seventeen Roman vessels, which Admiral Boodes, lieutenant of Hannibal, surrounds. Forced to surrender, he is conducted in triumph to Carthage.

But Duillius, the colleague of Cornelius, leaving to the tribunes the command of the legions, embarks and goes proudly forth in search of the Carthaginians, whom he encounters off Mylæ (Milazzo on the northeast of Sicily). While he was getting ready for the combat, the inferiority of his ships strikes him suddenly, and he promptly conceives an ingenious means of obviating a real difficulty. He elevates upon the prow of each ship his famous *corvus*, a kind of machine resembling a drawbridge, sliding along from a solid mast on his own vessels, and grappling, by means of powerful iron hooks, the deck of the enemy's vessels where it falls down, thus forcing upon the foe a hand-to-hand encounter.

The Carthaginian admiral, mounted upon a formidable seven-banked galley, once taken from Pyrrhus, advanced disdainfully with his 130 ships, in the confident expectation of overwhelming with the first blow this upstart navy, with movement so unwieldy and awkward. The machines upon the prows preöccupied a little the Carthaginians; but, soon reässured upon this invention, which seemed to them puerile and clumsy, they attack furiously the vessels of Duilius. The *corvi*, falling suddenly upon the galleys within reach, hold them fast, and force the frightened crew to a terrible combat. Thirty galleys were speedily sunk or captured. Hannibal, dismayed, takes flight. The rest of his fleet hold out, and try to make the Romans pay dearly for the easy victory over their advance guard. But the prodigious energy, skill and agility shown in the management of the Punic galleys prove of no avail. When they approach the heavy ships of Duillius, the terrible *corvi* seize them, and changing the form of the combat, render illusive the superiority of the Punic evolutions and manœuvres. The courage, arms, discipline and vigor of the Roman soldiers speedily triumph over their enemies, ill-prepared for such a struggle upon the decks of their ships, and relying solely for victory upon advantages and movements purely maritime. Duillius, profiting by the enthusiastic confidence of his forces and by the terror of the enemy, landed in Sicily, delivered Segeste from a siege, and took Macella without Hamilcar's daring to show himself.

Hannibal, vanquished and fearing the anger of the senate, sent a friend to save him by a skilful artifice. He asks the senators, if Hannibal, to whom Duillius offers battle, ought to accept it or not. With one

voice they cry: "Let him give battle without delay."
"Very good," replies the envoy, "he has given battle
and lost it." The senators were dismayed at the
news, but they could not think of punishing Hannibal. Duillius, on his return to Rome, was received
with extraordinary honors. They raised to his glory
a rostral column, with an inscription, which monument is preserved to our day.

After the departure of Duillius, there arose between
the soldiers of the legions and the auxiliary troops
some dissensions, which came near ruining the Roman
army. Hamilcar's force destroyed 4,000 men and
retook a number of cities.

Soon Hannibal, the Carthaginian admiral vanquished off Mylæ, reäppeared with a new fleet
against the consul, Cornelius Scipio, who was taking
measures for the conquest of Sardinia and Corsica.
Mistress of these two islands, Carthage drew from
Sardinia, whose soil was fertile, cereal products, sheep,
cattle and metals; Corsica, poorer, yielded only wax
and honey. But in these two provinces, especially
in Corsica, Punic domination was odious and but partially established. To tame these insular savages
and habituate them to submission, Carthage had laid
waste their country and committed deeds of cruelty.

Favored by this hatred, Cornelius easily took possession, first of Corsica and then of Sardinia, and
inflicted a disastrous defeat upon the unfortunate
Hannibal, who this time was a victim of the indignation and ferocity of his own soldiers; they nailed
him, while living, to a cross, and then tortured him
for their pleasure before killing him.

In Sicily, Hamilcar, master of Enna, Camarina, Eryx and Drepanium, held in check the legions of Florus; but the new consuls, after having menaced Palermo, take by assault Hippanum and enter by capitulation Mytistratum, which they destroy with fire and sword.

In marching upon Camarina, they were enclosed in a defile by the Carthaginian army, which occupied all the commanding heights and cut off the chances of escape. The tribune, Calpurnius Flamma, and 400 companions saved the legions by an act of self-devotion. They dashed furiously upon the Carthaginian army, causing the latter to concentrate all their efforts upon them, and thus giving an opportunity for the Romans to escape in an opposite direction. Calpurnius survived this heroic hecatomb. His body was drawn from among the dead almost riddled with wounds, and the senate honored him with the *obsidional crown.*

The consul Atilius Calatinus then invested Camarina; took it by means of the famous war machines of Hiero, and sold most of its inhabitants as slaves. Master of Enna, Camarina, Sittana, and of a great number of other Punic places, he invested Liperi, whence Hamilcar, who had secretly entered it, vigorously repulsed him.

The struggle, which was thus prolonged with various turns of fortune, would have lasted indefinitely; but each of the belligerents resolved by a decisive blow to seize the empire of the sea, on which the final victory depended. Three hundred and fifty Carthaginian galleys, commanded by Hamilcar and provided with 147,000 men, encountered (256 B. C.) off cape Ecnoma, near Agrigentum, 130 Roman ships of the same force, under the orders of the consuls Manlius and Regulus, and provided with 138,000 men.

The action was long, complex and terrible. Twice upon the point of conquering by the superiority of their ships and manœuvres, Hamilcar and his lieutenant Hanno had finally to yield to the tenacity of the consuls and to the heroism of the Roman soldiers in boarding their ships as soon as the famous *corvi* fell upon them. Thirty Carthaginian galleys were sunk, and sixty-four were captured; the Romans lost twenty-four ships, but left none in the hands of the enemy.

Africa was henceforth open to the Romans. While awaiting the reply of the senate, whose orders they had asked, the victorious consuls rallied their fleet at cape Bon (Hermeum) and then took possession of Clypea (Kalibia) where they erected strong fortifications. They then ravaged the rich and magnificent country around, forced many places to capitulate, and made 20,000 prisoners. At length, the reply arrived from the senate. Manlius was recalled with a part of the fleet and of the army. Regulus was maintained in Africa with 40 vessels and with 15,000 foot soldiers and 500 horsemen.

He remained alone charged with continuing the victories of Rome under the title of pro-consul; but he was oppressed by this honor, and wrote the senate that, "since the manager of the seven acres of land which he owned was dead, and his day laborer had absconded, carrying away all his farming tools, he could not leave his fields uncultivated, for they were his only means of supporting his wife and children." The senate had the fields of Regulus leased and cultivated, and his family supported at the expense of the state. We see by this that the manners as well as the virtues of the age of Cincinnatus had not then fallen into dishonor at Rome.

Carthage, in a state of consternation, recalls Hamilcar from Sicily and gives him Hasdrubal, Hanno and Bostar as his lieutenants, at the head of an army raised in great haste. The frightened people flocked to the capital, or revolted: Regulus, master of 200 places, was marching upon Carthage, that seemed on the eve of ruin.*

Regulus began the siege of Ades (Rades), when forthwith the Punic generals took possession with their cavalry and elephants of a hill which commanded the camps of the Romans, hoping to overwhelm them by a descent. But the Roman general observing the unevenness of the ground, turns this movement of the enemy to his advantage; his troops rush up both sides of the hill at the same time. Horses and elephants in their efforts to descend are thrown into disorder, and end by breaking the solid ranks of the mercenaries in the rear. The whole Punic army is hurled pell-mell down the open side of the hill into the plain below, followed speedily by the Romans who fall upon the broken ranks with merciless fury. Regulus immediately profits by the

---

* It is related that Regulus found near the river Bagrada a serpent of such enormous size that it was necessary to employ machines of war to kill it, and that its skin, sent to Rome, measured forty yards.

victory to ravage with impunity the country around, and takes possession of Tunis which he fortifies and makes his head-quarters.

Beaten by land and by sea, frightened at the progress of Regulus and at the revolt *en masse* of the Numidians in the interior, who were destroying the country with fire and sword and showing a disposition to aid the legions and share with them the spoils of the vanquished, the Carthaginians sent senatorial deputies to Regulus to treat for peace. He received them haughtily, and laid down the following hard conditions: "Give up all Sicily, Sardinia and Corsica; restore all prisoners without ransom; pay all the expenses of the war; submit to an annual tribute; engage to have as friends and as enemies only those of Rome; possess only one vessel of war, and furnish the Romans fifty triremes whenever they shall require them."

The embassadors, deeply moved and wounded, entreated Regulus to show more moderation. They obtained only this arrogant reply: "Those who know not how to conquer must know how to obey conquerors." The senate of Carthage was shocked, and declared that they must suffer everything rather than submit to the shame of those conditions.

At this critical moment, an important arrival was announced at Carthage. The ships which had been long before sent into Greece for the enlistment of mercenary troops, came laden with fighting men. Of that number, was the Lacedemonian Xanthippus, a rough soldier well skilled in military tactics. Informed of the deplorable situation of Carthage and of the mode of warfare employed by her generals, he hesitates not to promise not only the safety of the city, but a prompt victory, provided they will submit to his direction; for, in his opinion, the past defeats are solely due to errors in the military art. Dignitaries and generals showed themselves on that occasion magnanimous; they sacrificed their rights and their *amour propre*, entrusting to this stranger, so severe in his judgment and so self-confident, the defence, safety and honor of their country.

He marches out of Carthage at once; subjects the army during several days to exercise to acquire a knowledge of military evolutions and manœuvres, and then offers battle to the Romans. Regulus is at first surprised to see the Carthaginians change their ordinary method, but he is sure that he shall conquer once more these enemies whom he has so often defeated.

Nothing of the kind however occurred. Through the able generalship of Xanthippus, and the appropriate use of the cavalry and the elephants, which this time had a firm footing on a level plain, the Romans suffered a disastrous rout. Two thousand of them only succeeded in escaping and taking refuge at Kalibia. The victorious army, having lost only 1,000 men, triumphantly reëntered Carthage, drawing the Roman pro-consul in chains and 500 picked soldiers made prisoners with him. (255 B. C.)

Carthage was intoxicated with joy. Religious festivals, banquets, and rejoicings of every kind celebrated the victory of Xanthippus. As to himself, he took a wise part. That he might not be exposed to the ingratitude and jealousy of those whom he had saved, he sailed for Greece.*

The news of the disaster of Regulus did not discourage the Romans. They sent into Africa a new fleet. The Carthaginians, who had just subdued the Numidians, attacked in vain Kalibia, and, launching upon the sea 200 new-built ships, encountered at cape Bon the Roman fleet, consisting of 350 vessels. They were overpowered. The Romans, though conquerors, evacuated Kalibia and turned towards Sicily. On the way thither, a violent tempest dispersed the fleet, and reduced it to eighty ships.

The Carthaginians, profiting by this loss, increased their forces in Sicily and retook Agrigentum. But in three months time, Rome had repaired her fleet, and the consuls Cneius Scipio Asina and Atilius Calatinus brought to Messina the vessels which had escaped being wrecked; uniting them to 220 vessels just built, they took Cephalodium and menaced Drepanum, and then invested Panormus, the capital of the Punic possessions in Sicily. The siege and the defense were obstinate. The city, however, was taken, and 10,000 citizens redeemed themselves by paying a ransom equivalent to $400,000; 13,000 were sold at auction together with the spoils. The conquerors left at Panormus a garrison and returned to Rome. During the passage, a Carthaginian squadron lying in wait captured some of the vessels laden with spoils.

* Some authors say that the Carthaginians treacherously put him to death during his returning voyage;. but neither Polybius, nor the Latin historians speak of this.

The following year, the consuls Cœpio and Blosus ravaged the coasts of Africa, but at cape Palinurum their entire fleet was lost in a tempest. Rome, discouraged this time, gave up the supremacy upon the sea and relied solely upon her legions. But in their turn, the legionaries were seized, after the defeat at Tunis, with a fear of encountering the elephants, so terrible in an open country. They avoided then every battle where they would have to encounter these warlike beasts.

Carthage wished then to make a last effort to drive the Romans from Sicily. But, having an exhausted treasury, she sent an embassy to solicit a loan of more than $2,000,000 of Ptolemy Philadelphus, king of Egypt, who, as an ally of both powers, refused to grant it, and interposed in vain his mediatorial efforts to terminate the struggle. The Carthaginians raised by great sacrifices 200 vessels, 140 elephants and 20,000 soldiers, and sent them, under the command of Hasdrubal, to attack Panormus which was defended by Metellus. The latter pretended at first to avoid an engagement, only to draw the enemy into difficulty. When Hasdrubal had advanced under the walls of the city, some light-armed troops attacked him furiously. The elephants, frightened, wounded and irritated, turned against the Carthaginians, who, attacked by the legions of Metellus in their turn, were speedily overcome. Hasdrubal lost 20,000 men and all his elephants, twenty-six of which were sent to Rome to grace the triumph of the victorious general.

Carthage then made overtures of peace, and joined

to her ambassadors the unfortunate Regulus, in the hope that his influence would render the Romans more conciliatory. Regulus, received without the walls by the senate and consulted by it, would speak neither as a senator nor as a Roman, but simply as a private person. Regardless of his own fate and confident of a successful issue, he encouraged his fellow-citizens to continue the war, and not consent to the exchange of prisoners. For, he said, "the best part of the Punic army is in your power, while the enemy have at their mercy only some infirm and useless Romans like myself." The senate adopted the counsel of Regulus, regretting that the good of the republic required the sacrifice of so great a citizen.

It was in vain that his family, friends and fellow-citizens united their efforts to retain him at Rome. Regulus regarded only his promise to return to Carthage. At the news of what had taken place, Punic vengeance knew no bounds. This generous and venerable old man was subjected to the most heart-rending cruelty; his eyelids were cut off; he was rolled in a cask bristling with points, and then exposed, bleeding and with mutilated eyes, to the African sun upon the burning sand. In that state he was hung upon a cross. Greater by his captivity and death than by his virtues, Regulus is one of the most affecting types of that sublime devotion to country and of that heroism in misfortune, with which the history of the Roman republic is filled.

But a painful cloud obscures this admirable picture. The Roman senate, and Marcia, the widow of Regulus, were not worthy of him. They subjected many

Punic prisoners to the most atrocious tortures and prolonged this odious vengeance upon numerous innocent victims. Here we are almost led to question whether compassion and forgiveness were regarded as virtues among the ancients.

The war continued; and the city of Lilybeum, a fortified town of the Carthaginians in Sicily, was invested by four legions and 200 sail, and was manfully defended by Himilco. This general, vigilant and firm, defeated a plot formed by some mercenary officers to deliver the city over to the Romans; he conciliated by his eloquence, promises and rewards of honor the refractory soldiers, and resisted the besiegers until Hannibal, son of Hamilcar, by a bold manœuvre penetrated through the surprised and disconcerted Roman fleet, and landed 10,000 fresh troops in the city. Soon Himilco, making a furious sally, attempted to burn the war machines of the Roman army; he ended only in a furious fray, and turned back, leaving the Romans wearied and exhausted. Hannibal seized this occasion to go out of the harbor and join Adherbal at Drepanum.

In another sally, Himilco succeeded in burning the Roman machines, and the besiegers then turned the siege into a blockade. Another Hannibal, styled *the Rhodian*, who had several times audaciously entered Lilybeum through the Roman fleet, was finally captured with his vessel; but this success was completely effaced by the disaster at Drepanum, where the consul Claudius, while trying to destroy the fleet of Adherbal, allowed himself to be blocked up in an enclosure of the harbor, from which only 30 vessels out of 200 escaped, and 20,000 sailors and soldiers were left prisoners and 8,000 were killed or drowned. Adherbal completed this victory by supplying Lilybeum with provisions conveyed in barks which had been captured from the Romans near Panormus.

The other consul, Junius, saw a part of his formidable fleet sunk in the very harbor of Lilybeum at the moment of provisioning the Roman camp. While the legionaries were hastening to defend their ships, Himilco overcame them by a sudden sally. The rest of the Roman fleet succeeded in escaping, pursued by the victorious Carthalo; but a tempest destroyed even the last ship, and Rome was found once more obliged for the want of a fleet to leave to Carthage the empire of the sea.

Junius, hastening the operations of the siege to repair for past errors, succeeded in taking possession, by means of treachery, of the mountain and city of Eryx, situated between Trapani and Palermo. At this epoch (248 B. C.), begins to appear upon the scene the famous Hamilcar Barca, the father of the great Hannibal. He takes possession of the strong post of Ercta between Eryx and Palermo, and there maintaining himself three years in spite of all the efforts of the Romans, succeeds in provisioning Lilybeum. He ravages the coasts of Italy and thus excites the rage of the Romans, who, while waiting for the refitting of their fleet, turn pirates. While attracting the attention of the enemy on different coasts, he seizes the city of Eryx, and there maintains himself two years between two Roman armies, with which he struggles with perseverance, skill, courage and magnanimity in the midst of great privations and sufferings.

Rome, perceiving that with such an adversary she must put forth her utmost efforts, fitted out a new fleet, which speedily gained over the Carthaginians, near the isle of Ægimuri (Zembra), a victory whose fruits were lost by a tempest. Still another fleet is raised by the voluntary contributions of her citizens, and manned by skilful sailors. This attacks forthwith Drepanum under the conduct of Lutatius, who, though wounded in the first combat, succeeds in taking the ports of Drepanum and Lilybeum. Then, while admiral Hanno is hastening from Carthage with 400 galleys to supply Eryx with provisions, and embark upon his ships some of Hamilcar's veterans with a view to boarding Roman ships, Lutatius encounters him near the group Ægades and gains a brilliant victory. (242 B. C.)

Carthage then believes herself menaced with an invasion, as after the battle of Ecnoma: Hanno is put upon a cross, and Hamilcar Barca is charged to treat for peace with the Romans. Lutatius, more prudent than Regulus, and also wearied, like all his compatriots, with this interminable war, avoids harshness in the conditions for settlement. Honoring the noble bearing of Hamilcar with his worthy companions at Eryx, he requires no surrender of arms and offers the following terms of peace:

1. Carthage and Rome to be independent powers.

2. The Carthaginians to cede to the Romans their possessions in Sicily.

3. The Carthaginians not to make war upon the

allies of the Roman people, and each party to give up their prisoners without ransom.

4. To pay to Rome in the course of ten years a sum equivalent to $3,500,000.

This treaty was not at-first ratified by the Roman people; but commissioners were sent into Sicily to modify some of its provisions. They made no important changes, but simply added a clause requiring the Carthaginians to pay for war expenses also 1,000 talents ($1,000,000), and give up all the islands situated between Sicily and Italy except Corsica and Sardinia.

Carthage lost with the supremacy of the sea the foundation of her power, and then began her fatal decline.

Thus was terminated the first Punic war, one of the longest wars of history; since it lasted nearly twenty-four years. These two peoples endured the greatest sacrifices and losses, and we can form some idea of their efforts by seeing them each, after immense disasters, combine to build hundreds of quinqueremes (five banked galleys) for one last battle. The Romans lost materially more than their rivals; but with better organization and temperament, they triumphed in the end because they possessed more power of resistance.

Carthage was superior to Rome in respect to her navy and the skill of her generals. No Roman chief can be compared with the wonderful Hamilcar, worthy father of a worthy son, who during five years held in check all the forces of Rome in Sicily, and had the sole glory of not being conquered; for he marched out of Eryx with all the honors of war.

The superiority of Rome was in her constitution and in her national virtues. The first Punic war was a duel between two peoples, which with different forces and characters aspired to the same end,—to play the first *role* in the world. That *role* the force of nature and the providence of God secured, as it always does secure in the final analysis, to the most worthy.

WAR OF THE MERCENARIES. (240—237 B. C.)

After the war of Sicily, Gisco, lieutenant of Hamilcar, sent into Africa the mercenary troops, company by company, so as to give time for the republic to pay and disband them in successive order.*

Then, however, the treasury was exhausted; and the senate, unable to decide upon new sacrifices, lost much time in deliberation, and thus the entire army was amassed at Carthage, discontented and ready to revolt. The senate, fearing an outbreak, requested the officers of the mercenaries to conduct all their troops to Sicca (Kef), paying each man on account a piece of gold. They removed with them their baggage and their families, which the senate, in its trouble, did not wish to keep at Carthage, where they would have been pledges of fidelity.

Arrived at Sicca, they began to make exaggerated estimates of the sums due them and of the bounties promised on various occasions. Hanno, sent to calm them, humbly confessed the distress of the republic and asked of them a delay. At this language, the

---

* These mercenaries were Spaniards, Gauls, Greeks, Ligurians and especially Africans.

discontent increased and broke out into violence. Twenty thousand of these desperadoes marched upon Carthage, seizing and occupying Tunis.

The senators, trembling with fear, deputed each day some one to quiet their terrible neighbors, sending food in abundance without any fixed price. The fear prevailing at Carthage encouraged the insolence of the insurgents. After having agreed upon the balance of their arrears, they demanded an indemnity for their lost horses; then satisfaction for the extra cost of provisions during the war. Gisco, whom they knew well and who had succeeded in gaining their confidence, leaves Carthage with the necessary money, and, after a conference with their chiefs, he calls together the soldiers, each nation by itself; he addresses them; succeeds in allaying the turbulence of their passion and effecting a settlement; when all at once two seditious officers, Spendius and Mathos, raise their voices and declare within hearing of the African mercenaries that the plan is to pay off the other subjects and then send those who are paid to fall upon the Africans and take revenge for their revolt. A tumult breaks out. Many officers are stoned. The word *revenge*, the only one perhaps which was understood by all, was caught up in twenty different dialects and repeated from all parts of the camp. Victims fell. Such scenes ended only in being renewed at each parley. Gisco, always calm and unmoved, resisted the storm with benevolence and firmness. But one day he yielded to his indignation. Pressed by the Africans who were calling for their pay, he replied in an unguarded moment:

"Go to Mathos, your general." Furiously excited by this remark, they instantly rushed upon Gisco, pillaged all the money which he had with him and loaded him and his companions with chains.

Mathos immediately excited the cities and the tribes of the interior to revolt, and began at the head of 70,000 men that terrible war of Africa which lasted more than three years and suspended Carthage over a new abyss. The rebellion was of vast extent and enlisted the fiercest passions of a motley crew of vulgar and brutified desperadoes. The women as well as the men, full of spite on account of the withholding of the treasure and the oppression exercised by the Punic agents, sacrificed all their precious objects for the expenses of the war, which they sought to make general and terrible. Utica and Hippo-Zarytos, menaced by the rebels, massacred their Punic garrisons and threw the mutilated dead into the streets. Sardinia, excited in its turn, crucified Hanno and offered allegiance to Rome.

Hamilcar Barca, until then in disfavor, was reëstablished in the command of the army. His great ambition was to save his country. He routed forthwith the mercenaries and drove them back far from Utica; then, with the aid of the Numidians returned to their allegiance, he inflicted a new check on them, killing 10,000 and making 4,000 prisoners, whom he treated generously. Mathos, Spendius and Antarites, fearing that the magnanimity of Hamilcar might encourage defections from their ranks and desiring to check a growing sentiment in favor of the Carthaginians, spread the report that letters received from Sardinia and Carthage exhorted them to distrust Gisco and his unfortunate companions and the feigned humanity of Hamilcar. Antarites, commander of the Gauls, proclaimed a complete rupture with Carthage, and to render it definite and without remedy, he favored the massacre of Gisco and of the other prisoners. Spendius had 700 of them leave the camp; their hands and ears were cut off; their legs broken, and then they were thrown, while living, together into a pit. Hamilcar implored the mercenaries to give up the dead bodies; the reply was that every envoy should share the same fate and that they would cut off the hands of every ally of Carthage.

Hamilcar, shocked, cast to the beasts his prisoners, and resolved on horrid reprisals. Yet he could not prevent Utica and Hippo-Zarytos from entering into alliance with the rebels, nor the latter from besieging Carthage. This city asked the aid of her allies, and Hiero of Syracuse, understanding that the ruin of Carthage would cause such a preponderance of Rome as to endanger his safety, sent important aid, and the Romans facilitated the provisioning of the besieged, forbade the Italians aiding the rebels and rejected the overtures of Sardinia and Utica. Carthage breathed again; and Hamilcar, after patient struggles and successful encounters, succeeded in driving back a part of the mercenaries between the mountains and enclosing them in the defile of the Axe where, being unable either to escape or to fight, they were reduced to such a state of starvation as to hideously devour each other. A fierce quarrel arose between their chiefs. Antarites, Spendius and many others demanded a *safe conduct* and came into the camp of Hamilcar to treat. The latter exacted of them *ten rebels* of his choosing, and that all the others should withdraw without arms and clothed only with one tunic. The treaty having been signed, Hamilcar declared to the envoys that they themselves were the *ten rebels* of his choice, and he retained them. On receiving this news, the mercenaries in despair renewed the warfare. But they were so hemmed in on every side that the army of Hamilcar massacred them to the last of 40,000 men.

The army of Mathos was besieged in Tunis. But Hannibal, lieutenant of Hamilcar, allowed himself to be surprised and captured. Mathos had him nailed to the same cross on which Spendius had hung. The senate sent immediately to the aid of Hamilcar the rest of the citizens in a state to bear arms under the command of Hanno. These two generals, hitherto mortal enemies, were reconciled by patriotism, and acting in concert, they harrassed and beat the mercenaries in detachments, and finally routed them in a general engagement in an open field. Mathos was delivered over to the cowardly vengeance of the Carthaginian populace. All the towns submitted except Utica and Hippo-Zarytos, which were too much compromised in the revolt to hope for mercy. Hamilcar exercised great severity in bringing them to terms.

Thus ended this disastrous war, which soon had an unexpected consequence for Carthage. She lost Sardinia; for the Romans, who at first refused the offers of the mercenaries encamped in this island, ended by accepting them. Carthage protested and sent an army into Sardinia. Rome, pretending to be attacked by Carthage, declared war. Carthage, too much exhausted to sustain it, abandoned Sardinia, and seeing Roman ambition and greediness still unsatisfied, consented to a large increase of the tribute which the last treaty imposed. This is neither the first nor the last time that the *Majestas populi Romani* found itself disputing with Carthage for the monopoly of the famous "Fides Punica," which, though it may not have been formally engrafted into the *Roman code*, has become singularly characteristic of modern diplomacy.

CONQUESTS IN SPAIN. (237—219 B. C.)

When Carthage had recovered from pressing danger and embarrassment, she sought to indemnify herself for her losses by conquests in Africa and in Spain. Hamilcar, the hero of the preceding wars, became naturally the chief of those which were planned. The senate, besides, was not unwilling to remove him; for it feared his influence and popularity in the capital. Hamilcar began by vigorously attacking the Numidians who were at best rebellious subjects. Promptly subduing them, he passed victoriously along all the African coast of the western Mediterranean, and extended the empire of Carthage to the shores of the Atlantic; and then undertook his expedition into Spain.

We know neither the date nor the history of the first entrance of the Carthaginians into that country.

We know only that they went there under the pretext of protecting Gades (Cadiz), a city of Phœnician origin, menaced by a neighboring people jealous of its greatness.

The Carthaginians soon delivered Cadiz and established themselves in the provinces around without our knowing either the extent or the limits of their conquests. They had soon to encounter the warlike Celtiberians or Gallic Spaniards, commanded at first by two heroic brothers, whose names are not known, and after their death by Indortes. The brothers were successively defeated, and Indortes lost 50,000 men. Hamilcar, wishing at the same time to frighten and gain over the barbarians, had the chief put to death and 10,000 prisoners set at liberty. He pursued during nine years his aggressive measures in Spain, subduing all the western coast and a part of the interior. But after having always triumphed in long and terrible combats, he became a victim to a stratagem, like that which probably saved the life of his son at a later period in Italy. The natives attached oxen to burning carriages; as the flames burst forth the beasts, furious from fright and pain, dashed forward into the Punic army, putting it into disorder. Hamilcar perished fighting in the thickest of a fray brought on in this extraordinary manner.

The faction of Barca, which was opposed to that of Hanno, and which, through its increasing glory and riches, had become more influential than ever at Carthage, succeeded in appointing as successor of Hamilcar, his son-in-law, Hasdrubal, who was then the leader of the popular party at the capital. Hasdrubal set off for Spain, and being more of a statesman than warrior, had the tact and power to draw a multitude of chiefs and tribes under the sway of Carthage. His most important service, however, and that on which his glory most depends, was the founding of Carthagena, which became the emporium of Carthage and the bulwark of her domination in Spain.

Hasdrubal in his progressive march finally encountered the Romans in the valley of the Iberus (Ebro); for not far south of this river, was their ally, Saguntum. A treaty was signed by which the Carthaginians were forbidden to cross this river, and they engaged also to respect Saguntum.

Hasdrubal was during nine years the governor of Spain, where he was suspected of entertaining plans to become an independent ruler, when he was assassinated, as he knelt at the foot of the altar, by a Gallic slave, who sought thus to revenge the recent treacherous death of his master.

As soon as the news of his death reached Carthage, that city became the scene of animated and angry debates. The question was, who shall be the successor of Hasdrubal. The latter had, sometime before his death, asked the senate to name as his lieutenant the young Hannibal, his brother-in-law and beloved pupil, who was then twenty-four years old. The Barca party warmly supported this nomination; but Hanno, the leader of the opposition, strenuously opposed it, setting forth in strong terms the danger of thus increasing the power of a single family by putting into the hands of this warlike and enterprising young man the buckler and sword of the republic.

The nomination of Hannibal was nevertheless confirmed with enthusiasm. The sympathy and confidence of the officers and soldiers were extended to him in advance of his appointment. They knew the affection which Hasdrubal had for him, and they seemed to see relive in him at the same time his brother-in-law Hasdrubal, for whom they still mourned, and the magnanimous Hamilcar, his father, whom they could never forget.

He had a mind elevated to command the entire situation; a courage ready for any danger, and a body proof against fatigue and hardship. Firmness and *sang froid* were the foundation of that earnest character, and increased its power a hundred-fold. Like all great men, he was the personification of his time and the incarnate genius of his country, appearing to avenge the past and assure the future.

SECOND PUNIC WAR. (219—201 B. C.)

Carthage had lost in the first Punic war her magnificent establishments in Sicily; and the Romans, profiting by her embarrassments at the close of the rebellion of the mercenaries, had seized Sardinia in contempt of law, justice and honor. Revenge was the chosen part of Carthage. She yearned to conquer and humiliate Rome; to re-conquer Sicily and Sardinia; and, in fine, to change the *roles* of the two great republics, bringing down the soaring eagle to the humble condition in which the winged horse was then found. Such was also the thought and ambition of Hannibal, who deliberately planned to accomplish this object by the invasion and conquest of Italy.

While yet a child, he had shared the resentment of his country, and divined, as by instinct, that he should one day become her avenger. When Hamilcar, his father, was on the eve of his departure for Spain, he expressed warm filial affection and desired to be his companion in that campaign. The father promised to grant his request, provided he would breathe upon the altar implacable hatred to the Romans. Hannibal, who was then scarcely nine years old, took that oath with the resolution and energy of a man. The opportunity of keeping it was afterwards afforded him.

He sought, first of all, to strengthen the Punic power in Spain. Three formidable nations there, the Ocladi, Carpetani and Vaccæi, resisted his sway. He promptly took their strongholds one after the other, and then marched upon the banks of the Tagus, where he routed their united army of 100,000 men. He then invested Saguntum contrary to the wishes of the senate and in violation of treaty stipulations. To justify his conduct, he declared that the Saguntians were the aggressors, since they were making war upon the Torboletes, who were allies of Carthage.

During this siege (219 B. C.), embassadors came from Rome into Spain to complain to Hannibal. He would not, however, even listen to their remonstrances. They then passed over to Carthage and demanded, without result, the surrender of Hannibal into their hands.

After eight months siege, Saguntum fell. The resistance was heroic, and the inhabitants would not then consent to the dishonor of becoming prisoners. An immense funeral pile was erected upon the public square, and the senators and notable persons cast upon it first their treasures and then themselves, choosing a speedy death by fire rather than await the chances of ignominious captivity or cruel murder. The rest of the inhabitants defended themselves in their houses, and disputed with the conquerors, street by street, for the possession of the city. They were all massacred, and nothing was left upon the ground but smouldering ruins.

Rome, indignant, sent a new deputation to the senate of Carthage, which, being divided into two parties, hesitated how to reply. Then Fabius, the chief of the embassy, raising a fold in his toga: "I bring you peace or war," said he, "choose ye." "Choose yourself," retorted the chief of the senate. "I give you then," rejoined Fabius, shaking the fold from his toga, "I give you war." "We will accept it; we will sustain it," was the united, sober and earnest response of that deliberative body.

Hannibal was then free to realize his scheme; the way was open for him; and we shall soon see how he pursued it.

While Rome was preparing for the war with her habitual promptitude and energy, ordering one of her consuls to pass into Sicily and thence into Africa, and the other to reach Spain by sea and drive out the Carthaginians; Hannibal, getting ready to march upon Italy, wishes first to leave Spain and Carthage invulnerable. He sends into Africa 15,000 picked soldiers; he places 30,000 mountaineers, taken from the Pyrenees, at Gades under the orders of Hasdrubal and Hanno, to whom he also leaves twenty-four elephants and sixty galleys; he charges this army to defend the country in case of attack and to form a reserve force for time of need; he secures by presents and promises the good will and confidence of his own troops which had been chosen from among the best; lets them rest at Carthagena during the entire winter; goes to the temple of Hercules in Gades; spreads a report far and wide that the national god promises him victory; brings together for his expedition vast sums of money and stores of provisions, and at the opening of spring begins his march with 90,000 infantry, 12,000 cavalry and 40 elephants, and crosses the Ebro in the month of June.

Rome had in vain sought allies in the north of Spain. They reproached her bitterly with abandoning Saguntum. The Gauls also rejected her overtures and reminded her of her wars against their brethren in Italy (Cis-Alpine Gaul). Left to rely upon herself, Rome showed no signs of weakness. The army of Scipio sailed for Marseilles. When it arrived there, Hannibal had already passed the Pyrenees and the Rhone, winning by his address or his arms all the Celtiberian and Gallic tribes. A squad of Roman cavalry assaulted his rear guard without arresting its progress. He hastened to reach his new ally, Cis-Alpine Gaul, and pursued his march towards the Alps, protected on his rear by the Allobrogians who abundantly supplied his army with provisions and secured it against the light troops of Scipio.

At length Hannibal pointed out the Alps to his soldiers with expressions of hope and confidence. Coming from a warm climate, he had to pass through a bleak, icy region, often combating barbarians amid rocks, precipices and snow-drifts. It was then the month of October.*

It took nine whole days to climb those colossal mountains,—nine days of fatigue, suffering and cruel combats upon steep and slippery slopes; over chasms filled with snow, which would suddenly give way under the force of rocks hurled from above by fierce mountaineers, who repeatedly succeeded in crushing entire groups of soldiers; through dangers or ambuscades into which it was led by the ignorance or treachery of the guides: the Punic army overcame all difficulties, scaling to the summit of the mountain and covering immense declivities with its dead. From these heights, pointing to the beautiful country and splendid horizon on the Cis-Alpine side, Hannibal reanimated the drooping courage of the army, and after a little repose, began his descent, which was much wilder and, by reason of its steepness, glaciers and abysses, much more difficult than the ascent. They filled up the openings of rocks, dug out paths, improved or made roads, and built bridges. It required five days of herculean labor to conduct the army into the plains below. In marching from Carthagena to

---

*Leaving Carthagena, Hannibal passed by Emporia, Jungaria (Junquera), Narbo (*Narbonne*) and Nemassus (Nimes). He crossed the Rhone between Orange and Avignon, near Roquemaure, at the place called at present the *Passage of Ardoise*. He went up this river, passing by Asunum (Montelimart); crossed the Isere near its confluence; followed it up to its source; climbed up the Little St. Bernard; descended by the valley of Aosta, and came into the country of the Insubres and thence to Turin.

the Rhone, the army lost 30,000 men. In crossing the Alps, 36,000 more perished. There remained then only 36,000 men to challenge and conquer on the vast fields of Italy the Roman people who, to save their country could, in arming all their able-bodied citizens, put in line of battle, 300,000 combatants.*

While Scipio was seeking in vain along the Rhone to cut off the army of Hannibal, his colleague, Sempronius, was awaiting in Sicily the occasion to pass into Africa, and the prætor Manlius was occupying with 20,000 men Cis-Alpine Gaul, to prevent its revolt. But the Cis-Alpines speedily overcame Manlius; whereupon Scipio, leaving to his brother, Cneius, the conduct of the expedition into Spain, hastened to take command of the remains of Manlius' army and await Hannibal at the foot of the Alps.

The Punic army rested several days; then took Turin (Augusta Taurinorum), which remained faithful to Rome; tried in vain to win over the Cis-Alpines who remained neutral in spite of their engagements with Hannibal, and it finally encountered and routed the Roman army on the banks of the Ticinus (Tesino) in Transpadan Gaul. In this conflict (218 B. C.), the consul was wounded, and his life was saved only by the extraordinary valor of his young son.

Rome hastily recalled Sempronius, notwithstanding his successes in Sicily, where under the prætor Æmilius he had destroyed at Lilybeum a Punic fleet. He had just taken possession of Malta when he received the

---

* Hannibal began his expedition with 102,000 men, including 12,000 cavalry. After passing the Rhone, he had only 64,000 infantry and 8,000 cavalry. After crossing the Alps, he had only 30,000 infantry and 6,000 cavalry. Most of his elephants also perished.

order of the senate to come to the aid of Scipio. He joins the latter upon the Trebbia and seeks an engagement contrary to the advice of his colleague. The Roman army crosses the icy waters of the river without refreshment and shivering with cold; on reaching the other side of the stream, it finds the enemy in battle array, after having been well cared for during the night and warmed and refreshed by their morning repast. The soldiers of Sempronius could scarcely fight. Hannibal overcame them without difficulty and killed or took as prisoners 30,000 men. Cis-Alpine Gaul and Liguria then revolted and took sides with the conqueror, whose army, filled up with these belligerent allies, amounted to 90,000 men.

Hannibal thinks then of penetrating like a wedge, the heart of Italy, so as to separate and annihilate the Roman power. Forced back by a violent storm, he turns towards Placentia and has two deadly encounters suddenly brought on by Sempronius. In one of these, Hannibal is wounded; in the other, he is surprised in his camp. These two actions, of slight importance in themselves and without result, are unnoticed by most historians; but they show on the one side the tenacity of Hannibal, and on the other the intrepid confidence of Rome and her consuls,—a confidence which the defeat at Trebbia could not impair.

Hannibal then came into Etruria to encounter the rash and impetuous Caius Flaminius, recently named consul by the people against the wishes of the senate. In trying to reach his foe by a short route, he became involved in the marshes of Clusium, which were enlarged and rendered almost impassable by the over-flowing of the Arno. His army suffered severely, and he himself lost an eye. But escaping from this embarrassing position, he enticed and fell upon the Roman army on the borders of Lake Thrasymenus, (Perugia) and there, in the midst of a thick fog, with repeated shocks of an earthquake, cut it in pieces (217 B. C.).

He passed thence into Umbria and Picenum, declaring that he came into Italy only to subdue the arrogance of Rome and free her neighbors from tyranny. To support this declaration, he proposed to retain only Roman prisoners and to send others back without ransom, and he ravaged the country only to punish open hostilities and supply his army with provisions. He marched then by Samnium towards the coasts of Apulia. Arriving in the centre of Italy, without communication with Africa, without machines of war, and menaced upon his rear by enemies, he wished to have the Appenines between himself and Rome, hoping by his alliance with the southern provinces to establish himself there, and thus be enabled to open communication with Carthage. But he improved every occasion to again overpower the Romans; and with this view he watched all their movements.

Rome in a state of alarm had just named Quintus Fabius Maximus as pro-dictator. He was a general as remarkable for his skill and prudence, as his predecessors were for their want of skill and for rashness. He divined the means of overcoming Hannibal. He knew him to be without relations with Carthage;

repulsed by most of the allies of Rome; separated from the Cis-Alpines, and his army fatigued by long marches and already suffering from privations. He resolved to temporize as much as possible; to harass the Punic army by incessant partial combats, and to accept no set battle without the victory being assured by the previous exhaustion of the enemy. Thus, placing himself upon some heights, after enclosing the inhabitants in the cities, he made frequent sudden attacks and ravaged the country far around. In fine, wearying the army of Hannibal with frequent skirmishes and the employment of all the artifices common to partisan warfare, Fabius effectually reduced it and made it incapable of continuing its victories. He thus merited the glorious surnames: the *Temporizer and Buckler of the Republic*, (Cunctator, et Scutum Reipublicæ). He succeeded in enclosing Hannibal in a defile, where he hoped to overwhelm him; but the cunning African let loose during the night against the Roman army a herd of oxen with lighted fagots fastened to their horns; these animals, becoming furious from fright and pain, dashed against the Roman battalions, breaking their ranks and giving the Carthaginians opportunity to escape from their perilous position.

The people of Rome, becoming dissatisfied with the delays and especially with the failure of the last plan of Fabius, and suspecting him even of treason, joined to him as colleague Minutius, whose imprudence and impetuosity came near losing the army. Fabius saved it; and Minutius, displaying true greatness of soul, came humbly to implore pardon of the dictator and lay at his feet the ensigns of his command. The war then continued with the same ability and plan of operations until Hannibal, beginning to despair of conquering the Romans, already thought of turning back towards Gaul.

But the military tactics of Fabius and of his successors Servilius and Attilius Regulus, ended by wounding the *amour propre*, and exciting the impatience and hostility, of the senate and popular party at Rome. They named as consul Terentius Varro, the son of a butcher, an obscure, incompetent and rash man, with whom by a little foresight they associated Paulus Emilius,* a pupil of Fabius. At the same time, four prætors were appointed, two to guard Rome, one for Gaul and the fourth for Sicily. The last one was the famous Marcellus; the troops in Spain were under the orders of the two Scipios and were reïnforced.

The two consular armies, composed of eight legions and of an equal number of allies, in all 87,000 men, met, near Cannæ in Apulia, the Carthaginian army strong with 50,000 soldiers.

Hannibal, short of provisions, was upon the point of being abandoned by a part of his allies. Varro, instead of waiting to reduce him by famine, foolishly persisted in giving him battle, sustained as he was in this course of action by the senate, whose views were in strict accord with his own. Paulus Emilius opposed and resisted this measure in vain. His presumptuous colleague, on the very day of his becoming command-

---

* Paulus Emilius was the father of the famous Paulus Emilius, the conqueror of Perseus, king of Macedonia.

er-in-chief of the two united armies, crosses the river Aufidus (Ofanto) and places himself in a disadvantageous situation, where his whole army is pelted in the face by volumes of sand raised up by a violent wind. At this sight, Hannibal, notwithstanding the inequality of the number, seeing the Romans crowded together in bad order, extends out his line of battle as at Trebia and Thrasymenus, flanks Varro's soldiers with his cavalry, and finally by a bold movement hems in his whole army. The Romans were pitifully defeated and butchered. Paulus Emilius died a hero, while Varro withdrew in haste, leaving the field of battle covered with 40,000 citizens and 30,000 allies. Two questors, eighty senators and twenty-one military tribunes were among the dead (216 B. C.).

From the unlucky day of the battle of Allia,* when the sword of the Gauls became so terrible on the banks of the Tiber, no such crushing disaster had befallen Rome. And nothing equalled the consternation of the first moment except the magnanimity with which she resolved to save herself and vindicate her honor. The senate met at the gates of the city those who had escaped from Cannæ, and, instead of uttering reproaches for the defeat, voted thanks to Varro for not despairing of the republic. A dictator was then named. They consulted the Sybilline books. They buried alive, to conciliate the gods, two Gauls and two Greeks of both sexes, and gruffly sent back the Carthaginian envoy with an imperious order for Hannibal immediately to leave the territory of the republic.

* A river near Rome.

New legions were hastily levied. Eight thousand slaves were enrolled with the promise of their liberty after their first combat. Citizens of all orders submitted to the greatest sacrifices; some giving up their slaves; others their salaries or incomes; the women contributing their jewels, and everybody doing something for the safety of his imperilled country. It was a magnificent display of devotion, confidence and patriotism;—a glorious uprising of a great people, superior to defeat, as to victory,—of a people who intuitively perceived their destiny, and moved with a proud will to resist every obstacle to their aggrandizement.

But Hannibal marched not upon Rome. Historians are wont to speak of this as a great mistake, and to cite the remark which Livy attributes to Maherbal: "You know how to conquer, O Hannibal, but not how to profit by your victories." If we reflect, nevertheless, on the exhaustion of the Punic army by the succession even of its victories; by its prolonged sojourn in Italy without receiving any aid from Carthage; obtaining some reïnforcements from certain parts of Italy, but obliged to challenge or fight all the rest of the peninsular inhabitants; if we observe that the principal superiority of the Carthaginians was in their cavalry, which would become useless in a siege, and that the want of machines had already been the cause of Hannibal's failure in the attack on several places: if we consider, in fine, that with his genius and experience, Hannibal was in this case the best of judges, since no one knew better than himself his own soldiers, and what the Romans could do, whose preparations and means of resistance he understood: if we weigh well all these matters, we shall appreciate, I think, the wisdom of Hannibal, in refusing to risk losing all by imprudently enlisting in an enterprise so difficult and doubtful as the siege of Rome. Let us add that, after the battle of Cannæ, the conquerors were twice as far from Rome as at Thrasymenus.

Hannibal entered into Campania, and received by his brother Mago the submission of numerous inhabitants of Southern Italy. The occupants of Central Italy remained always faithful to Rome. He failed at the siege of Naples, but Capua opened to him her gates. He established himself there with his army, and sent Mago to Carthage, to render account to the senate of all that he had done, and obtain aid to continue his victories.

Mago spread out before the astonished senate three bushels of gold rings taken from Roman knights and senators killed at Cannæ; and giving a glowing account of the successes of the Punic arms in Italy, insisted, at the conclusion of his address, on the necessity of gloriously terminating this struggle by granting some indispensable reïnforcements. Himilco, also of the Barca party, rose in his turn, jeered the opposition, and, turning to Hanno, its leader, asked him what he thought then of the war against the Romans, and of the necessity of surrendering Hannibal to them. "Let us see," concluded he, turning to Hanno, "what this *Roman senator* will say in the midst of the senate of Carthage." Hanno replied, with as much irony as haughtiness, that he was neither proud nor repentant, and that he regretted more than ever the war, and should not cease to blame the invincible Hannibal for breaking a precious peace until he had obtained another on more honorable and advantageous conditions. Calling upon Mago, he tauntingly asked: "Since Rome is on the eve of her ruin, what people of Latium, what Roman citizens have taken sides with Hannibal? What propositions for peace has Rome made? If nothing of this kind has taken place," added Hanno, "we have the war upon us now as hard as at first. After so many victories, demands are made upon us the same as if we had been defeated. I conclude, then, that if Hannibal is really victorious, we ought not to send him aid because he must have no need of it; if he is conquered, we ought not to grant it because he does not merit it."

Notwithstanding this plausible and ingenious reasoning, showing the party politician or rather the adroit demagogue in the guise of the patriot and statesman, the senate decreed by acclamation to send Hannibal 4,000 Numidians, 40 elephants and a large sum of money. But the opposition speech had its effect. There was so much delay and negligence about sending these reïnforcements, in themselves so inadequate, that Hannibal had to rely on himself alone for his maintenance in Italy. Marcellus, *the Sword of the Republic*, seconded by Fabius, who was its *Shield*, holds Hannibal in check in the quadrilateral formed by Capua, Arpi, Regium and Tarentum, and force him to shut himself up in Capua, which he makes his winter quarters, and, contrary to common opinion, does not allow his soldiers to become effeminate and demoralized; and there he anxiously waits for promised supplies from Carthage, with which he hopes to put himself in communication by sea; but these supplies, either refused, badly directed or intercepted, never reach him.

The following spring he marches towards the extremity of the peninsula to form some alliances there, and then returns into Campania. Marcellus and Fabius, avoiding every set battle, inflict upon him partial defeats which, in their accumulated influence, are more disastrous than one great defeat.

Hannibal then applied to Philip, king of Macedonia, who, fearing the ambition of Rome, hesitated not to contract an alliance offensive and defensive with the Punic general, an alliance which engaged reciprocally Macedonia and her allies, and Carthage and hers. But Philip was dilatory in his movements, and the prætor, Marcus Valerius Levinus, soon forced him to burn at the mouth of the river Aoüs, the fleet with which he had designed to transport his army into Italy.

Meanwhile Marcellus defeats Hannibal before Nola and Casilinum, and drives him out of Campania (215–214 B. C.). Hannibal, drawing back, attempts then to take possession of Tarentum with a view of securing his communications with Macedonia. The taking of this city and the defection of Syracuse, which at the death of Hiero declared itself for the Carthaginians, restored for a moment his courage and fortune. He killed 15,000 Roman soldiers in Lucania, and advanced to the aid of Capua, besieged by the foe during his absence; he delivered it the first time and then in a second effort failed, when suddenly he resolved to make a diversion upon Rome. He appeared under her walls, but was discouraged by her means of resistance, and especially by the attitude of the senate, which, to defy him, put up at auction the ground on which he was encamped. He then marched into Brutium, definitely abandoning Capua to the Romans (211 B. C.). Syracuse had also just fallen under the arms of Marcellus in spite of the learned defense organized by the great Archimedes. Soon the Libyan Mutine delivered up Agrigentum, and the Carthaginians quit for the last time Sicily, which became henceforth a Roman province. (210 B. C.)

Tarentum is retaken from Hannibal, but Marcellus perishes in an ambuscade. Hannibal makes for this worthy adversary a great funeral, weeps over his remains, and sends his ring and ashes to his son.

Carthage finally decides to send aid to her admirable general, who, tracked like a lion from one retreat to another, returns to the charge and defends himself. Withdrawing once more into Brutium, he exhausts the resources of military tactics and, proving the valor of his veterans, maintains himself there for years with alternations of success and reverse, but always equal to himself in fruitfulness of invention and firmness of purpose. Passing to the foot of that Italy which he had pierced to the quick and reduced to extremity, he awaited with lofty bearing the stunning blows which Rome, recovering from her humiliation and gathering up her strength, was to deal out upon him and his devoted country.

Hasdrubal, his brother, who was a commander in Spain, received orders to join him with 50,000 men. He succeeds in avoiding a Roman army which pursues him; passes the Ebro and the Pyrenees; marches through Gaul; crosses the Alps; enters Cis-Alpine Gaul and then loses all by stopping to besiege Placentia. The consul Claudius Nero, learning of the plan of Hasdrubal, leaves a part of his army to watch Hannibal; then hastens with the rest of it up through Italy; unites with his colleague Livius Salinator, on the banks of the Metaurus, where he encounters and routs the Punic army, killing Hasdrubal. Then, retracing his steps, he has the bloody head of the vanquished brother cast into the camp of Hannibal. The conqueror of Cannæ, touched to the heart, recognizes in this sad event the fate of Carthage (207 B. C.), and shuts himself up among the mountains and fastnesses of Brutium.

The affairs of Carthage were no more flourishing in Spain. Cneius and Cornelius Scipio had taken in a few months 120 fortified places, and had gradually extended Roman jurisdiction from the Ebro towards the south, and had made an alliance with Syphax, king of a part of Numidia, who furnished them a body of excellent cavalry. After the battle of Cannæ, Hasdrubal wished to leave the command to Himilco and cross over into Italy. He was conquered twice, and almost all the Spaniards declared themselves for the Romans. Four other victories over Hasdrubal, Mago and Gisco opened to the Scipios Saguntum, which had been eight years in the power of the Carthaginians. But fortune changed all at once. Cneius and Cornelius were vanquished and killed. Marcius, simply a knight, took command of the army and defeated Mago. But the senate not confirming him in command, he was succeeded by the consul Nero, who, after having entrapped Hasdrubal in a defile, let him out on conditions which were immediately violated. Finally, Publius Cornelius Scipio, son of Cornelius, was called to succeed Nero. He joins to himself the valiant and skilful Marcius, and, though but twenty-five years old, shows himself equal to the occasion. He meditates, and resolves to strike a blow at the very heart of Carthaginian power in Spain,— at New Carthage, which as a fortress was deemed to be impregnable, and was the centre of extensive commerce and riches. He besieged it, took it, and found there, with an immense booty, hostages from all parts of Spain. He was merciful, moderate, benevolent and generous. Sympathy and gratitude drew towards him all hearts. All the Spanish chiefs became his allies, and at length the last Punic troops commanded by Mago were driven from Cadiz.

After Spain was subjected and pacified, he returned to Rome and was made consul. He requested permission immediately to pass over into Africa. Fabius, the Temporizer, strongly opposed this request, saying that it was necessary first to annihilate Hannibal in Italy itself. Scipio, on the contrary, thought that in carrying the war into Africa, he would finally force him out of Italy, and, drawing him upon Punic territory, would destroy at the same blow the great enemy of Rome and her formidable rival. As to his victory, he did not entertain a doubt; for it was needful for his glory and the safety of Rome, and Scipio had confidence in his country and in himself.

Lælius, after having ravaged the African coasts, wrote his friend Scipio that Massinissa, king of the Massylian Numidians and a very useful ally of Rome during the wars in Spain, desired him to pass without delay into Africa, where Syphax, taking sides with Carthage, had turned his arms against him. Scipio at length obtained permission (204 B. C.) to pass over into Africa with 30,000 men and a numerous fleet. Though his project had been for a long time known at Carthage, he landed without obstacle at Beautiful Promontory, situated northwest of Carthage. He besieged Utica. Sixty thousand men came to defend it under the command of Hasdrubal and Syphax. Winter suspends hostilities. In the following spring, rejecting the propositions for an accommodation with Syphax, he surprises the two camps of the enemy and burns them; and in another great battle which takes place five days from Carthage on the great plains south of Testour, he almost annihilates their united army. Having possession of Tunis himself, he sends a part of his army to the aid of Massinissa, who is soon enthroned at Cirta (Constantine), the former capital of Syphax. Massinissa finds in Cirta the famous Sophonisba, the daughter of Hasdrubal and the wife of Syphax, who, more successful than Dido with Æneas, induced her husband to forsake the cause of Rome and enlist for Carthage. Forgetting his former disdain and perhaps touched by her beauty and tears, Massinissa wishes to marry her, but Scipio claims her as a prisoner of Rome, and Massinissa, to manage his allies and save Sophonisba from the ignominy of a triumph, sends her some poison, which she courageously takes and dies.

About this time, the senate recalled Hannibal, who always remained quartered in Brutium, and also Mago, who was in the north of Italy unable to hold any communication with him. Mago died on his way home by sea. "Hannibal," says Livy, "gnashed with his teeth and shed tears of rage," as he tore himself from that Italy which he had for sixteen years inflicted with such evils as only extraordinary genius envenomed by hatred could effect. He landed at Leptis; then came to Hadrumetum, and from there went near Zama to take command of 50,000 men.

Before any encounter, Scipio and Hannibal had an interview, at which the services of an interpreter seem to have been necessary. They came together with generous emotion, and conversed with calmness and dignity; but had to separate, though personally admiring each the other, without any conclusion of terms. Hannibal reminded Scipio with sadness of the inconstancy of fortune, of which he himself presented a striking illustration; but the young conqueror of Spain, being unable to yield that which he demanded, declared that for a settlement they must appeal to the arbitration of arms.

Some skirmishes took place at first between the advanced guards at Zama, but the great battle that took the name of Zama and became illustrious in the annals of history, was fought a little distance from that city between Killa and Naragarra. (202 B. C.)

Scipio places the spearmen (hastati) upon the first line of his army, leaving intervals between each cohort. Upon the second line he places the princes (an order of soldiers), whose cohorts he does not range opposite the intervals of the first line according to Roman usage, but behind each other, with intervals between the ranks on account of the great number of elephants belonging to the enemy. The triarii (soldiers of the third line) constitute the reserve force. Upon the left, Lælius commands the Italian cavalry, and upon the right, Massinissa is placed over the Numidian horsemen. Some light armed troops (velites) are introduced into the open space of the first line to bring on the combat. If their ranks are broken in the onset, they have orders to withdraw by the open space to the rear of the main army, which, remaining intact and isolated, will not be likely to suffer from the defeat.

Hannibal places in front of his troops eighty elephants; the first line is composed of the mercenaries Ligurians, Gauls, Balearians and Moors. Behind these, he stations the Africans and the Carthaginians; finally he forms the third line, removed from the second line more than two hundred yards, and introduces here the veteran troops which had accompanied him in his Italian campaign.

The Numidians on both sides and the light armed troops of each army begin the combat by bloody and vain skirmishes. Then the Carthaginian elephants move heavily against the Roman infantry, throwing

the front ranks into disorder and crushing them.
But the elephants speedily reach an open space,
where by order of Scipio they are attacked by three
lines of troops and are thus driven far away, pierced
with spears and javelins. Many of the elephants,
maddened and furious with their wounds, retrace
their steps with cries of rage. The Romans no
longer fearing the "monster oxen of Lucania,"* force
back in disorder these huge beasts, which in their
frenzy rush away into the midst of the Carthaginian
army, bearing tumult and death in their course.

Lœlius and Massinissa then fall upon the cavalry
opposite to them, and break, disperse, pursue and cut
it in pieces.

The infantry of the two armies now engage each
other. The mercenaries of Hannibal make a furious
onset against the opposing force, but shortly afterwards, perceiving that the second line of their own
army, instead of coming to their support, remains
in a state of inactivity, their indignation is so aroused
that they turn their arms fiercely against it. Thus
encountered by their own mercenaries and by the
Romans, the second line succumbs under the double
shock. Driven back, the soldiers of the second line
rush tumultuously towards the third line, whose javelins and pikes are suddenly thrust at them, like the
quills of porcupines, checking their course and dispersing them along the wings of the army in the
open plain.

* At the time of the invasion of Italy by Pyrrhus, the Roman soldiers
were frightened by the elephants of his army, which in their simplicity
they styled the monster oxen of Lucania.

This third line of Hannibal's army remains still unmoved and threatening. It is composed of the consecrated battalions of Carthage and now constitutes the sole hope of the state.

Scipio unites all his forces against it and urges them forward in person, showing himself by turns, at this decisive moment of the battle, a great general, orator and soldier.

These old companions of Hannibal, valiant men who had subdued the Alps, humbled the pride of Roman legions and consuls, measured by the bushel rings from the fingers of Roman knights slain at Cannæ, and hovered like birds of prey around the Eternal City; these veterans, hitherto invincible, can neither sully their fame nor disregard their duty. The conflict for supremacy is fierce and bloody; the victory wavers for a long time. But all at once Lœlius and Massinissa return from the pursuit of their immediate antagonists and, with the multitude of their horsemen upon the gallop, dash with irresistible force upon the rear of the valiant Carthaginian infantry, cutting down the soldiers with their sabres and trampling them under the feet of their horses. The army of Hannibal is shaken, broken and utterly overpowered by the shock.

Hannibal himself, finally yielding to destiny and drawn away, as it were in a sweeping tornado, escapes from the field with only fifty chosen horsemen, as once escaped the consul Varro from him in Italy; and thus in sadness he reaches the road to Hadrumetum (Susa).

And now by the side of fifteen hundred Romans,

twenty thousand Carthaginians lie weltering in their blood upon the plains of Zama, and still another twenty thousand are prisoners of war. Carthage has here her slaughter of Cannæ; but it is a slaughter from which she will never recover as did Rome from her humiliation fourteen years before.

Hannibal fled precipitately to Hadrumetum. Invited to Carthage, he returned there after thirty-six years' absence, and advised the senate to ask for peace. Scipio, with his head-quarters at Tunis, thought for a time of besieging Carthage, but renouncing this plan, accorded peace on the following conditions, viz.: "Carthage to give up Spain, Sicily, and all the islands of the western Mediterranean to the Romans; to deliver up her prisoners and deserters, her elephants, and her entire fleet with the exception of ten galleys; to pay in the course of fifty years 10,000 talents (about $10,833,000 in intrinsic value, and ten times that sum if we take account of the relative value of gold and silver); to make no war without the consent of Rome; and to reëstablish Massinissa in all the possessions of his ancestors."

When the Punic senate read these conditions, there was much hesitation and a long pause. Gisco rose to utter his protest, when Hannibal leaped from his place and forcibly drew Gisco back to his seat. To calm the indignation aroused by this rudeness and violence, Hannibal said that having left his country at the age of nine years, he had forgotten the usages of the senate, assuring his colleagues that he had no other intentions than to serve the public good. He added that the rejection of the terms offered would, in his view, result in the complete annihilation of Carthage. The peace was then concluded.

Thus sadly ended the second Punic war. Carthage lost her magnificent colony in Spain, and, by the hard conditions of the treaty of peace, the very spring of her force,—her fleet, and consequently her national personality; for in fact she became the humble subject of Rome. The latter was aggrandized by the humiliation of her rival. *Hinc populus late rex.* The people thus greatly extended their rule. Queen of the western Mediterranean, Rome had soon to turn towards the east. Carthage alone had been able to restrain her, and now that city, awaiting her destruction, which was only a question of time, was reduced not only to weakness, but to the humiliating condition of a vassal, a slave of Rome in that same Africa which she wished to make the centre of the ancient world. Rome was henceforth that centre. Superiority of national character and arms was going to make all countries successively converge there. The Roman empire was thus formed.

Carthage gave up 500 vessels, which Scipio burnt upon the sea in plain sight of the frightened city. It was like an illumination of rejoicing at the victory of Rome. When the first instalment of the tribute became due, many senators wept. Hannibal burst into a laugh,—a hideous laugh, that was the highest expression of despair.

The Romans speedily exercised the tyrannic supremacy which the treaty secured. They summoned Carthage to recall and deliver up to them General Hamilcar, who, at the head of an army of

Gauls and Ligurians, was making war upon the northern part of Italy. Carthage humbly declared that Hamilcar acted on his own responsibility without her knowledge or consent. She disowned and severely reproached him, and finally exiled him, as if this last champion of her cause were a public enemy; and further to appease the anger of Rome, she sent her in great haste 200,000 measures of wheat, and the same quantity to the Macedonian legions.

Hannibal thought only of preparing his country for a new term of life, with a view of effecting a terrible revenge. He strove with all the power of his genius to secure important reforms in the administration of the government. Sustained by the popular party, he took strong ground against a kind of judicial oligarchy that had for a long time monopolized the control of state affairs. All its members were bound to act as a unit, and the influence of all protected the abuses of each. Hannibal dared to raise his protest against this association of corrupt officials; and, to effect a change, he secured the enactment of a law to elect new judges each year, and that no person should under any pretext continue in office two successive years. He then turned his attention to the department of finance, and exercised there pitiless severity. There were at that time in the country official plunderers of public property,—overseers of imposts and directors of finance,—who lived in luxury and ruined the people by abominable extortions. He scrutinized and controlled their conduct, and in general regulated the financial administration with so much rigor and success, that his astonished countrymen soon found themselves prepared to pay the tribute imposed by the Romans without additional taxes.

He revived agriculture, which was in a declining state. Knowing that the cultivation of the soil was the great source of riches and power for his country, he devoted to it his best energies. He employed the leisure of his troops in raising on large tracts of land olive trees, which served to introduce an important branch of business and means of wealth. But while he healed the wounds of his country by devoting it first of all to works of peace, he did not entirely neglect the military art, nor fail to give his troops healthy exercise in frequent expeditions against rebellious tribes. He raised up thus gently and skilfully the great power vanquished at Zama; for though borne down by destiny, he still hoped that Carthage would become the head and heart of a universal league against the accursed tyranny of Rome.

He knew and secretly encouraged the movement which was preparing in the east. Antiochus III, king of Syria, excited by the Ætolians, was planning an expedition into Greece to destroy there Roman domination and then invade Italy. Philip III, of Macedonia, on his side, had not changed his views since the disaster on the Aoüs. But if Hannibal was occupied with the east, awaiting an opportunity to play a part in the events which were preparing there, Rome watched him, observing with the clairvoyance of hatred and jealousy his minutest acts. His enemies at Carthage, who were spies paid by the Roman senate, at length denounced the great man as a traitor, and the Roman senate demanded his immediate surrender. Hannibal foresaw and anticipated the consequence of these measures. He left by night, with two faithful companions, and travelled on horseback to Thapsus,* on the eastern coast, where he sailed in a galley which had been a long time in readiness for him. He touched at Kerkenna and thence proceeded direct to Asia. From Tyre, where he landed and was received with honor, he departed for Antioch; he then visited at Ephesus king Antiochus, whom he found in the midst of his preparations for war. He speedily gained his confidence. He represented to him how important it was for the peace and liberty of the world to crush Rome, and that this object could be accomplished only in Italy. He offered himself to command the expedition, and promised the concurrence of Carthage, where he had already sent an emissary, Aristo, to have an understanding with the Barca party. But the mission of Aristo became known. The aristocratic party, the party of peace and servility, became restless; the senators, whose souls had been bought up by Rome, forced Aristo to appear before the magistrates. Aristo succeeded in escaping after some lists had been posted in the streets indicating the complicity of the most illustrious families. The senate, trembling with fear, sent an embassador to Rome to tell the whole story and acquit itself of blame.

* Some writers say that Hannibal sailed from *Africa* near Thapsus, a city subsequently named Torris Hannibalis by the Romans, and at present called *Media*.

In a little while, Antiochus, influenced by envious courtiers, became cool in his relations with Hannibal. His distrust was increased by several conversations that were held between the Roman embassadors just arrived at Ephesus and the illustrious exile. In this connection occurred a familiar incident. Publius Scipio was one of those embassadors. He saw Hannibal, and asked him which of all the generals, living or dead, he would place in the first rank. "Alexander," replied Hannibal. "In the second?" "Pyrrhus." "In the third?" "Myself." "And in which class would you place me," continued Scipio, smiling, "if you had conquered me?" "Then," replied Hannibal, with animation, "I would place myself before Alexander even." Scipio was touched by this noble and delicate praise, which placed him beyond comparison.

Antiochus, passing into Greece, found there scarcely any partisans; and after losing much precious time, was at length routed at Thermopylæ; he returned to his kingdom a fugitive, realizing and acknowledging, unfortunately too late, the wisdom of the counsels and plan of Hannibal. The Romans then passing over into Asia, defeated Antiochus at Magnesia, and demanded of him the surrender of Hannibal (190 B. C.). The latter fled at first into Crete, then took refuge with Prusias, king of Bithynia. He commanded many times with success the troops and navy of this prince in a war against Eumenes, king of Pergamos and an ally of the Romans. Flaminius came in the name of the senate to demand the surrender of Hannibal. The latter tried to escape, but the soldiers of Prusias guarded the seven doors which he had arranged leading out of his apartment. "Deliver," cried he, "deliver the Roman people from their long restlessness; for they have not patience to await the death of an old man. The Romans have sadly degenerated! The fathers warned Pyrrhus to be on his guard against a traitor that sought to poison him; the sons now send a consul to force Prusias to secure the death of his guest and friend by the most abominable treachery." Then, invoking upon the perfidious Prusias the wrath of the gods who avenge violated hospitality, he swallowed a subtle poison, which he always carried with him, and died aged about sixty-five years, 183 B. C.

The same year died in voluntary exile at Linternum, cursing his ungrateful country, Scipio, the conqueror at Zama; also Philopœmen, the soul of the Achæan league and the last of the Greeks, died in the city of Messina, poisoned by traitors sold to Rome.

Thus perished obscurely and wretchedly that man who would have saved the greatness of Carthage if it had been possible. As general, administrator and politician, in traits of character, as in functions the most opposite, he was always equal to himself. In assuming at the age of twenty-four the command of the army in Spain, he prepares with extraordinary ability, sagacity and success for his prodigious invasion of Italy. Infusing new life, and rendering that army worthy of himself and of his object, he draws it forth and hurls it from Carthagena to the Campania of Rome, 1,200 miles, through fatigues and dangers, and encounters with enemies, and with nature, more formidable still. A conqueror of the Alps and of the legions of Rome, he reduces to extremity the Eternal City, and needs to consummate her ruin only to be understood and supported by Carthage. Abandoned by her, he sees with grief snatched from him that Italy which he had held bound as a prey for sixteen years; and, recalled in haste to the aid of his imperilled country, he returns into Africa only to see it fall irrecoverable upon the plains of Zama. Vanquished, still glorious, he advises Carthage to yield to destiny, and, transforming himself into a statesman and magistrate, prepares for it a revenge by an admirable administration and an extended correspondence with allies. Exiled in order to escape the vengeance of Rome, he goes to the east to raise there a tempest, whose thunderbolts he would direct; and when he becomes a slighted, betrayed guest, ready to fall by the perfidy of his host into the cruel hands of his eternal enemies, he dies bequeathing the opprobrium of his death to Prusias and the Roman senate. He is himself to the last;—always and everywhere the Great Hannibal.

The wonderful part which he played in life supposes powers and traits of character which explain it, and which are sufficiently manifest in the foregoing recitals. An African, Hannibal had, with all the impetuosity and, in some sort, violence of his race, that will, firmness and self-possession, which are so rare in all men, and are ordinarily incompatible with ardor and bounding energy. He was at the same time a man of passion, and of reason; of enthusiasm,

and of sober calculation. He exalted his army by
his word and example. But the exaltation which
he inspired and shared never troubled his head, nor
produced a tremulous hand. Like all superior men,
he was especially powerful by the economy and
direction of his forces, and by that imperturbable
self-balance, that harmoniously united them and
wonderfully increased their effect. His vigilance,
penetration, activity and valor as a general, enabled
him to secure his ascendancy over his soldiers.
Twenty different nationalities were represented in
his army, and yet he never had to suppress a
sedition, notwithstanding the frequent want of food
and great sufferings of various kinds. A soldier
himself, of superior courage, address and skill, he
shared all the soldier's labors, dangers and trials.
A general worthy of his title, after having attached
to himself his soldiers by a fraternal participation in
their hardships and their glory, he exercised his
superior mind and rank in elevating their spirit and
encouraging their heart by kindly words and proofs
of benevolent interest, which in their turn relieved
him of the necessity of frequent demonstrations of
severe justice, firmness and inflexibility in the maintenance of discipline. By securing the attachment
of his army, he succeeded in maintaining it without
revolt or serious loss for many years in a hostile
country, without aid from Carthage, where, on the
contrary, he was opposed by malignant partisans;
and his allies in Italy were devoted to him only because he never failed to show himself moderate and
loyal towards them. It is in vain that Livy, biased

by his Roman rancor, accuses him of impiety, of the violation of his oath, of dishonesty, avarice and cruelty, without giving any proofs; and it is but just to relate that Polybius praises him for having rejected with horror the proposition to live on human flesh, butchering his prisoners, because he was short of provisions; that Diodorus, of Sicily, reports the honors which he rendered to the dead body of the consul Sempronius, instead of profaning it, as he was urged to do; and that Justinus commends his temperance and the almost austere wisdom of his conduct and manners. His impiety would be proved only by the pillage of some temples; but did he order this himself? And would not the antagonism of the national religions explain this? We see him, on the contrary, make vows to Hercules, and invoke at his death the avenging gods. As to his avarice, he never took his share of the spoils, was always nobly generous towards his soldiers, and did not become rich during the four years of his almost supreme control at Carthage.

Polybius tell us, it is true, that Hannibal was regarded as avaricious at Carthage and cruel at Rome; but he is careful to add that there was a difference of opinion, and that it would not be astonishing if his enemies had spread these reports. As to ourselves, these reports seem to us as natural as they are ill-founded, and easily explained, if we consider that there must have been at Rome, not to speak of the public hatred towards a common enemy, a multitude of relatives of the victims at Tesino, Trebia, Thrasimenus and Cannæ; and at Carthage, a great many families embittered against him on account of his financial reforms, which affected injuriously their private interests. Now he who kills our relatives is in our eyes cruel, as he who takes from them the control of the public funds seems avaricious, especially if he takes it for himself; but if he has simply killed upon the field of battle, and deprived extortioners of office for the good of the state, what then do such cruelty and avarice become?

The sobriety of Hannibal was proverbial. He ate hastily and drank very little wine, without ever reclining at table according to the custom of the ancients. Temperance is a commanding virtue wherever it may be found, but is specially important for a general; and it serves in this case to contradict the story about military voluptuousness (deliciæ) at Capua; for sober and inflexible in discipline, would Hannibal have permitted his troops to become effeminate and demoralized?

He was remarkable for his mental culture; and in the midst of his interminable enterprises and labors, he seems to have found time to cultivate letters and to write in the Greek language several books, which have been lost. Sophilos and Philenius, both Lacedemonians, were his secretaries and faithful companions. They labored to write his history, which has also been lost.

It would be peculiarly interesting to possess, for the want of Punic documents, some account of this great man given by his two secretaries, who had the best opportunity to know and judge him, and transmit to posterity his complete historic portrait.

But, in the absence of their statements, we may, by means of all the sketches found in Greek and Latin authors who have spoken of him, draw a noble and commanding figure, which, if it be not his veritable image, is at least a shadow of it sufficient to give an idea of him; and so in the midst of the events in which he was an actor and a hero, we can imagine and admire his full character, after having considered him in detail as a general, a citizen and a man.

Cannæ and Zama date back more than twenty centuries, but the glory of Hannibal has not yet faded, nor has his physiognomy lost any of its originality, nobleness or grandeur. He stands forth majestically in the history of Carthage, and is the highest expression of Carthaginian greatness. Superior to his countrymen, who little understood him, and abandoned him when he was on the point of triumphing almost single handed, he equals the entire Roman people, who conquered him, and whom he alone resisted. We can readily fancy Roman legions victorious without Fabius, Marcellus or even Scipio; but it is impossible to imagine a handful of Carthaginians for fifteen years victorious in Italy without Hannibal. Behind the Italian legions, almost all composed of Roman citizens, was Rome itself, their indestructible soul and strength. Of the Punic armies, mostly composed of mercenaries, the soul and strength was not Carthage, but Hannibal. Now a man, be he ever so great, cannot contend, for an indefinite time, against a manly people that wishes not to perish, unless he is supported by another people of equal valor. Hannibal had then to yield; because Carthage in the end failed him, and he could not save her and make her a nation of the first class without her own active and earnest coöperation. But the honor remains to him —and how great that honor!—of having for a long time retarded the victory of Rome and the fall of his country, of which he never despaired; since he attempted to resuscitate her, so to speak, after she had by her own faults fallen dying upon the field of Zama.

But he was not solely the great champion of Carthage. With the independence and liberty of his country, were indissolubly connected the independence and liberty of the ancient world, of which Carthage was the last bulwark. He thus had the consciousness of defending a great cause, and he defended it with a character and glory that associate him, in the memory and admiration of men, with those colossuses of genius, which, towering above the ruins of empires, withstand the force of time and age.

SECTION III.

Third Punic War.—Taking and Ruin of Carthage.—Carthage under Rome.—Massinissa and Jugurtha.

Massinissa, king of eastern Numidia, whose capital was Zama Regia, and at a later period Cirta (Constantine), was an ancient ally of Carthage, and gave her important aid in her wars in Spain. He was won over to the Roman cause by Scipio Africanus I, as was also Syphax, king of the western Numidians, whose capital was *Siga* (in the province of Oran). The latter lost his estates at the beginning of the second Punic war.

The very terms of the treaty at the close of that war sealed the inexorable fate of Carthage. She was despoiled of her richest colonies and of her fleet; inflicted with a tribute less crushing in itself, than deadly in its moral effect; and deprived of all national personality. But this was not enough: in addition to all these causes, slowly but surely leading to ruin, she needed another means as sure, but more prompt, to destroy her. This means was the ambition of Massinissa, who resided on the very confines of Carthage, which was to become his victim.

The hatred and the calculations of Rome were used by her protegé for his own purposes. Massinissa encroached upon the territory of Carthage. Carthage protested against his encroachments. Rome being invoked, gave her decision in favor of the Numidian king, who then continued his aggressions and usurpations of power. On the further complaints of Carthage, the senate sent into Africa Scipio Nasica. The decision was given in favor of Massinissa, who continued to aggrandize himself at the expense of his enemy.

Cato, the Censor, the incorruptible, the wise, the just, in his turn came to Africa to show himself unjust towards Carthage. The latter refused him as an arbiter in her affairs; hence his fiat, "*delenda est Carthago*," urged on his return to Rome. The senate, less impatient to arrive at an end of which it was certain, adopted the advice of Scipio Nasica, who, for the time, only wished to humiliate yet more the ancient rival of Rome. It was substantially the same thing. "Let us kill the sick man," Cato brutally cried. Let us have him die wisely, little by little, thought Scipio and the senate.

Massinissa usurped power so extensively, with the knowledge and official consent of Rome, that Carthage in despair reached the point sought by her enemies. She violated the clause of the treaty forbidding her to make war without the permission of Rome. She took up arms against the insatiable Numidian king. The latter, having wrong and force on his side, two excellent conditions for a ferocious triumph, encountered a great army commanded by Hasdrubal, while he was awaiting aid from Rome, who, instead of succoring a suppliant, was not slow in her turn to rush upon her miserable rival. In vain Carthage entreated by means of three humble embassies. The senate in its feigned clemency promised to spare the city (*civitas*), anticipating in its bad faith, a misunderstanding about the word which it employed. The Carthaginians naturally understood the word *civitas* to include the city (urbs) as well as the citizens; the senate rejected this interpretation, quibbling and prevaricating in the most ignoble manner.

Arms, machines, ships, hostages; Carthage delivered up all without hesitation upon the injunction of the senate, thus expecting at least to save her existence. But, at last, the senate declared to the inhabitants that they must leave the city; for they alone were to be spared. Upon this announcement, their despair was roused to indignation, and they revolted. They rose in arms to save their homes and their country, or to perish with them. The consuls Censorinus, Manillus and Piso, were successively sent and failed to take the town by siege (149-147 B. C.). At last Scipio Æmilianus, tightening his grasp on the place, closed the port by a gigantic dike and reduced the city to extremities. The besieged, to the number of about 700,000, dug into the rock, making another entrance to their port, where they constructed from the wood of their buildings a new fleet. But soon the Côthon (harbor) was occupied; the Romans penetrated into Carthage, fought for a week from street to street and from house to house, and took possession of the Byrsa, whose garrison with Hasdrubal was spared. A destructive fire occurred which lasted several days. The city was plundered, dismantled and essentially ruined, and the Carthaginian state was reduced to a Roman province under the name of Africa, having Utica for its capital (146 B. C.).

Instead of giving a detailed account of the military events connected with the last days of Phœnician Carthage, as they are set forth by Roman and Grecian authors, we will dwell a moment on a single character that appears in the closing scenes. We are wont to hear of the devotion and heroism of Roman matrons; but we doubt whether any country has furnished a more striking illustration of fidelity, loyalty and patriotism, than Carthage furnishes in the conduct of the wife of Hasdrubal. The example of this woman appears to us the more worthy of note, as it stands out in bold contrast with that of her husband. Mr. Guérin, in his admirable work entitled " Voyage Archéologique dans la Régence de Tunis,"

HASDRUBAL'S BASENESS.

draws a parallel between two remarkable women, one of whom perished on a funeral pile at the foundation of Carthage from disappointed love, and the other perished in the same way at the destruction of that city, as an act of devotion to her country. The facts are as follows:

At the period of the taking and destruction of Carthage, to which we have just given our attention, after the ports and the city had fallen into the power of the conqueror, and the Byrsa, where 50,000 men, women and children had taken refuge, was surrendered; the temple of Æsculapius, which was erected on the summit of that citadel, held out against the besiegers for some time. There the Roman deserters entrenched themselves to the number of 900. They were commanded by Hasdrubal, who, influenced by the love of life and seeing all resistance vain, secretly left his wife, children and soldiers, and hastened with an olive branch in his hand to cast himself humbly at the feet of Scipio. The Roman general, as a means of inducing a complete surrender, showed to the defenders of the sanctuary this husband, father and warrior who blushed not to dishonor himself by such baseness. The little band in the sacred enclosure, betrayed by their chief but not discouraged by his desertion, and hoping for no pity from the conqueror, took in their despair the heroic resolution to deprive Scipio of the honor of their capture; and applying the torch to the temple in which after being driven from the open square they took refuge, they buried themselves living under the smoking ruins of that edifice, and thus escaped by a free and voluntary death the tortures which they knew were reserved for them. It was then that the wife of Hasdrubal, protected by the feebleness of her sex and by her maternity, showed a magnanimity which must have moved the great heart of Scipio to compassion. Instead of fleeing from the fire which was ready to devour her and accepting the protection which was proffered, she precipitated herself with her two children into it, pronouncing on the occasion eloquent and pathetic words which history has preserved and consecrated.

Another woman immortalized by Virgil, had in the same place, if we may believe poetry, perished upon a funeral pile seven centuries before. This woman, who has been at all times known under the name of Dido, and whose passion and poetic misfortunes have given an interest to the African coast, is represented by Virgil as yielding to the violence of unrequited love, and committing suicide because of the ingratitude of Æneas, thus forgetting that she was a queen and the founder of an empire, and that the good of her rising state required that she should survive the infidelity of the Trojan hero. Nevertheless, her misfortunes awaken our commiseration, and it is not without tender emotion that we read the complaints, regrets and imprecations which Virgil puts into her mouth at the moment when upon the funeral pile she gives the fatal blow that ends her agonies. But I will avow frankly, that, despite the verses of the Latin poet and the eloquence and groans of Dido at the moment of expiring, I prefer the energetic simplicity of the words which are attributed to the wife of Hasdrubal, when in view of the shameful conduct of her husband, holding up her two children and casting a defiant look from the circuit of the flames beginning to crackle around her, she turns to the enemy, refusing to surrender, and addresses Scipio in the following terms transmitted to us by Appian: "Roman, the gods favor thee, since they accord thee victory. But remember thou, to punish Hasdrubal, who has betrayed his country, his gods, his wife and his children. The genii which once protected Carthage, will aid thee in this work of vengeance." Then turning towards Hasdrubal, she cried: "O basest of wretches and most infamous of men! Thou wilt see me die here with my two children! But soon thou wilt know that my lot is less dreadful than thine own! Illustrious chief of once powerful Carthage, thou shalt honor the triumph of him at whose feet thou crouchest! and after that triumph, thou shalt receive the chastisement which thou meritest!"

History here seems to me to surpass in grandeur poetry, and the wife of Hasdrubal, in my opinion, eclipses the Dido of Virgil. These two women, one at the origin and the other at the fall of the same city, appear on the summit of the Byrsa, expiring upon a funeral pile; but the one who ought to have lived for her subjects and for the development of the colony which she founded, kills herself because a lover abandons her and wounds the heart and rejects the throne which she offers him, going, as he professes, under the auspices of the gods, to lay upon the banks of the Tiber the foundations of the city which was to destroy Carthage. She concludes her touching imprecations by the prophetic announcement of the great avenger which the future reserves in the person of Hannibal. The other also sacrifices herself and her children, that neither she nor they may survive her dear country, whose last sanctuary she defends to the end; she dies, and in dying sustains, so far as in her power, the honor of the Carthaginian name, whose stains by her husband had alone roused her highest indignation.

The impression has generally prevailed that Carthage was, like Jerusalem at a later period, razed to the ground. But Mr. Dureau brings together conclusive testimony to show that only that part of it was destroyed which was necessary as a means of warfare; that other parts were simply injured by fire, and the whole city dismantled and plundered of its objects of value. Mr. Dureau concludes his discussion of this subject thus: "An evident proof that the whole city was not destroyed by fire is that the Sicilians and Italians, at the invitation of Scipio, came to claim the ornaments of their cities and temples which the Carthaginians had carried off to decorate their capital." These were, says Diodorus Siculus, portraits of their illustrious men, statues executed with remarkable talent, and offerings in gold and silver, which they had made to their gods. Himera found there her statue, representing her as a woman; and the statue of the poet Stersichorus; Segeste found her Diana; Gela many objects of art; and Agrigentum the famous Bull of Phalaris. Many cities of Italy and Africa recovered by the liberality of Scipio the precious objects of which they had been robbed by the Carthaginians.

"The destiny of these admirable works from Sicily is altogether remarkable. Transported from Sicily to Carthage by one victory, another victory restores them to Sicily; by the pillage of Verres they are taken to Rome, whence by another pillage under the Vandal general, Genseric, they are taken back to Carthage, six centuries after their removal from there."

Appian concludes his account of the taking and ruin of Carthage, by saying that "Scipio had the booty sold; and the arms, machines and useless vessels burned; then making a province of the territory, he embarked with his army for Rome." The impression is clearly left that Carthage was stripped and dismantled, but not razed to the ground.

CARTHAGE UNDER ROME.

After the close of the third Punic war, Carthage was abandoned by the Romans for upwards of twenty years. Then Caius Gracchus (124–122 B. C.), giving no heed to the imprecations pronounced against those who should try to build up and inhabit the Punic city, established there a Roman colony, which was successively enlarged by Julius Cæsar, after his victories in Africa (46 B. C.) over the partisans of Pompey, and then by Augustus; and subsequently by other emperors, such as Hadrian and the Antonines, so that Carthage became at length, according to the expression of Pomponius Mela, "rich and flourishing for the second time."

Embellished under the long pro-consulate of Gordian the elder, Carthage was in 420 A. D., fortified anew by Theodosius the younger. "Carthage," says a writer of the fourth century, "is the second city of the world;" and the poet Ausonius, a contemporary of Gratian, considered Rome and Constantinople alone as superior to her. She was, according to the representation of Salvian: "The African Rome, having establishments for all public offices, schools for all the liberal arts, and academies for philosophy and learning." She became the centre of the renowned Christian Church of Africa, the seat of more than twenty councils, and a focus of light by means of her learned men who resided there in large numbers from 100 to 429 of the Christian era.

The African province served as a source of supply under Rome, and was by many writers styled the granary of Italy. Its rich soil and genial climate attracted colonists from abroad, and its population was variously estimated between the first century and the fourth from 12,000,000 to 18,000,000 souls. The productiveness of the soil and the riches of the country are represented to have been very great.

Salvian says that Carthage was always the rival of Rome, at first by her arms and courage, and latterly by her grandeur and magnificence. The mere list of her remarkable monuments in the Roman period sufficiently indicates her greatness and splendor. The magnificent aqueduct, the amphitheatre, the theatre, the circus, the gymnasium, the pretorium, the temples of Æsculapius, Cælestis, Saturn and Apollo, the public squares, the basilicas, churches and many other buildings are made known to us by contemporary writers.

After the battle of Zama, Massinissa, the faithful and efficient ally of Rome, received from the hands of Scipio Africanus, the investiture of all Numidia with the title of king. We have seen how he afterwards showed his gratitude for that honor, by harassing Carthage in her misfortune and drawing upon her the Third Punic War. But he had a higher aim than to serve Rome as a mere instrument of her vengeance. The successive enlargement of his territory, which was sanctioned by the senate, was not the ultimate object of his ambition. He aspired to become the sovereign ruler of all North Africa. The senate understood his projects and, after having shrewdly employed him to effect the overthrow of Carthage, seized that occasion to intervene in his affairs for the aggrandizement of the republic. The Numidian king did not at first conceal his disappointment and chagrin. But having intelligence as well as ambition, he understood that henceforth he must content himself with enjoying the vast dominions which he owed to his alliance with Rome, and that it would be folly for him to engage in any enterprise against the great republic. Besides, at his advanced age, the fatigues of war and the responsibilities of administering the government doubtless prevented his attempting to realize the vast projects which he had early conceived and fondly entertained. He thought then only of securing his possessions to his children. His former friendly relations with the family of the Scipios, and the rising renown of the young Scipio Æmilianus, then a simple legionary tribune, induced him to invite the latter to come and aid him in his final arrangements. But perceiving the approach of death before the arrival of Scipio, he called to his side his family, and declared that he made Scipio Æmilianus responsible for dividing his kingdom and his effects between his sons, and that he wished them to conform just as fully to the decisions of Scipio, as if he himself had made them by express will. He recommended to his sons to persevere in the maintenance of the Roman alliance, and to have unbounded confidence in the senate. He then died in the year 148 B. C., aged ninety-eight years. He had passed his ring to his eldest son, Micipsa. He left forty-four children, only three of whom were legitimate heirs to his throne, viz.: Micipsa, Gulussa and Manastabal. Scipio soon came to Cirta, and divided as follows the heritage of Massinissa: Micipsa had the supreme government and the capital; Gulussa the command of the army, and Manastabal the administration of justice. Each took the title of king and a third of the vast treasures left by their father. Æmilianus then left with a body of Numidians to continue the hostilities begun long before against Carthage. He was artful in dividing the authority among the three brothers in such a manner that each could restrain the other and all of them be retained by mutual distrust or defiance in the alliance of Rome.

The remarkable part, which Massinissa played in Numidian history, makes some notice of him peculiarly appropriate in this place. He reigned nearly seventy years, and labored always for the prosperity of his kingdom, encouraging among his subjects agricultural and industrial habits, and training his army according to the military tactics of the Romans. He was also firm and energetic in his efforts to repress the thieving propensities of the Numidians. Acquainted with the delicacies of the Greek civilization which then flourished at Rome, he retained only its virtues, disdaining its effeminacy and vices to such a degree as to maintain, notwithstanding his own refined tastes and culture, the almost savage habits of his country, which he contracted in his youth. He had his companions at table served with the choicest articles in dishes and plates of gold, while he himself partook of ordinary food, served in coarse earthern ware. The day after the combined victory over the Carthaginians at Zama, he was seen at the door of his tent, taking for his repast a piece of coarse brown bread, while his soldiers celebrated the event with luxuries and delicacies. Always simply clad, temperate, energetic and indefatigable, he accustomed himself until he arrived at extreme old age to the rudest exercises, and retained to the end extraordinary force and agility. He was esteemed the best horseman of all Numidia, and at ninety years of age was regularly seen, with bare head, mounted without saddle upon a fiery steed; and thus he passed the entire day, riding back and forth to direct and superintend in all their details the manœuvres of his army. An eminent warrior, a shrewd politician, and a wise, generous and just king, Massinissa is justly esteemed the hero of his time, and the most unique and remarkable specimen of Numidian character on record.

Micipsa, his eldest son, reigned thirty years, and at his death (119 B. C.) divided his states between his sons, Adherbal and Hiempsal I, and his nephew Jugurtha, who had become his son by adoption. Jugurtha had a commanding figure, a penetrating mind, a pleasing address, unusual energy, and a courage of which he gave the amplest proof at the siege of Numantia in Spain, where Micipsa had sent him at the head of Numidian auxiliaries. On his return into Numidia, he handed to Micipsa a letter, in which Scipio complimented in strong terms the superior qualities of the young commander. The Numidian king, already anxious for the future of his sons, was saddened by this letter; but he strove to overcome his fears, making no difference between his two sons and Jugurtha. On his death-bed, he called to him the three, and, after having recommended to them harmony and union, addressed to Jugurtha generous and fitting words, and proposed him as a model for his sons. But soon there was trouble. To reign alone, Jugurtha shrank not from assassinating Hiempsal, who, in his arrogance had seized every occasion to wound his pride. Adherbal having taken up arms in self-defense, Jugurtha pursued him to Cirta, obliged him to capitulate, and then put him to death. Adherbal had in vain implored the intervention of Rome. But the senate was no longer incorruptible, and Jugurtha was left to pursue his own way.

Soon, however, the tribune Caius Memmius aroused public indignation against Jugurtha, and the senate was constrained in the year 112 B. C., to declare war against him. Calpurnius Piso landed in Africa; but, influenced by Numidian gold, accorded to the enemy an advantageous peace. Memmius protested again in the name of ancient Roman honor. Jugurtha was summoned to the capitol, and appeared there with an air of haughtiness and disdain; and as if to defy his pretended judges, he caused to be assassinated, in the city itself, Massiva, a nephew of Micipsa, who came there to press his claims to the Numidian throne.

On his departure, Jugurtha spoke in terms of sarcasm and contempt of "that venal city that waited only for a purchaser." Returning with impunity to Africa, he bribed the consul Albinus, and cunningly drawing the army of Aulus, the consul's brother, into a difficult pass, he subjected it to the dishonor of passing *under the yoke* near Calama. Æmilius Metellus, a good general and an incorruptible man, was then sent to avenge this affront to the republic. His many victories acquired for him the epithet of the Numidian. Soon he was succeeded by his lieutenant Marius, who, becoming consul, replaced him in the command. Marius, continuing the war with vigor, invested and took Capsa (Gafsa), the capital of Jugurtha, and then, in an engagement which lasted three days, he defeated his army united to that of Bocchus, his father-in-law, who was the king of Mauritania. The latter speedily treated with the Romans, and, influenced by the insinuating language of Cornelius Sylla, the questor of Marius, treacherously drew Jugurtha aside for an interview, where, appearing unarmed, he was bound and delivered over to the Romans. Jugurtha was then conducted to

Rome and honored the triumph of Marius; he was afterwards cast into the Mamertine prison, where he died of starvation in the year 106 B. C.

Several years afterwards, Marius, having been five times named consul, overcame the Cimbrians and the Teutons, and was called *the third founder of Rome* after Romulus and Camillus. Then at the end of *the Social War*, in which his rival, Sylla, was especially distinguished, he began with the latter that fierce struggle, of which the sovereign command was the object, and Rome the victim. A fugitive at Minturnum, he disarmed by that terrible look and by that voice well known among the Cimbrians, the slave of that nation sent to kill him. Then wandering lonely upon the coast of that Africa which he once left for the honor of a triumph, he proudly replied to the messenger of the prætor of Utica, who ordered him to depart: "Go, tell your master that you have seen Caius Marius an exile amid the ruins of Carthage."*

A truly remarkable and significant sight! The ruin of a great city and that of a great man, each a comment on the other! But more happy than Carthage, Marius rose again; made a bloody entrance into the city of Rome; was named consul for the seventh time and died of his excesses; while Sylla, conqueror of the east, hastened to seize the dictatorship, terrified Rome by his revenge, and after having abdicated, descended alone and unarmed to the forum,

---

* The poet Lucan says:
 * * * * * Solatia fati
 Carthago Mariusque tulit, pariterque jacentes
 Ignovere deis. * * * * *

declaring himself, with insulting haughtiness, ready to give account of his conduct and government to the people.

After the death of Jugurtha, Numidia was divided between Bocchus and two grandsons of Massinissa, Iarbas and Hiempsal II.

SECTION IV.

Cæsar in Africa.—Cato of Utica.—Christianity in Africa.

When Sylla had triumphed in Italy, he sent Pompey to pacify Africa, where Domitius Ænobarbus, a partisan of Marius, had taken refuge with Iarbus, a competitor of Hiempsal, king of Numidia, who was also an opponent of Sylla. Near Utica, Domitius and Iarbas were defeated in the year 81 B. C.; and Hiempsal was reëstablished in his kingdom, enlarged by the provinces of his vanquished rival.

Juba, son of Hiempsal, embraced then naturally the party of Pompey in his struggle with Cæsar, and in the civil war between the aristocracy and democracy of Rome. The partisans of Cæsar in Africa commanded by Curio, were at first, unlike those in Italy, unsuccessful. Juba, uniting his troops to those of Attius Varrus, a lieutenant of Pompey, succeeded, by means of elephants and of Gallic and Spanish horsemen, in overpowering near Utica a considerable force under Curio; and, to the injury of the cause of Pompey, he treated his prisoners without mercy.

In consequence of this victory, and while Cæsar was completely occupied with the war in the east, king Juba, surrounded by several chiefs of the Pompeian party, viz.: Labienus, Petreius, Afranius and Metellus Scipio, the latter of whom was the father-in-law of Pompey, assumed airs of haughtiness very humiliating to the Roman generals, and exercised his power without restraint. When the wreck of the Pompeian army, which had escaped the disaster at Pharsalia, arrived in Africa, and it became a serious question how to organize the forces so as to successfully resist the menaced invasion by Cæsar, a fierce rivalry sprang up between Varrus and Scipio for the supreme command, neither of whom especially merited the honor.

In that trying crisis and emergency appeared Marcus Porcius Cato, called Cato of Utica, a grandnephew of Cato the censor, and a worthy heir and representative of his sterling qualities and manly character. At fourteen years of age, seeing in the streets the dead bodies of those whom Sylla had proscribed and murdered, he called for a dagger to deliver Rome from her oppressor. At a later period he conquered Ptolemy Auletes, king of Egypt and an enemy of the republic, and declined the honors of his victory. Thoroughly distrusting Pompey, he combated the ambition of Cæsar, whose results he foresaw. At the period of the civil war, he declared himself for Pompey, and gained important advantages at Dyrrachium. After the defeat of Pompey at Pharsalia and his assassination in Egypt, Cato conducted the remains of the conquered army into

Africa proper, to join there the other chiefs of his party. He reached Tunisia, coming through Barca and along the extended coast of Libya, and fortified on his route Cyrene. In his first interview with the Pompeian leaders and Juba, he combated the arrogant pretensions of the latter, with a firmness and dignity worthy of Cato, the elder. The Numidian king took the place of honor between Scipio and Cato; the latter promptly changed his seat, leaving Scipio in the centre. Urged to assume the chief command, he declined the honor because he had been only a prætor, and he gave it to Scipio because he had been a consul. Harmony was thus restored among the partisans of Pompey, and Juba found himself checked in the exercise of his tyrannic influence.

It was important for the Pompeians to secure Utica, then the capital of the African province. The inhabitants of that city strongly favored Cæsar, because Juba, a partisan of Pompey, had brutally treated them when he victoriously entered the city after the defeat of Curio. In deliberating upon the measures to be adopted, Juba, in accordance with his ordinary violence, favored the destruction of the city and the extermination of its inhabitants. This aroused the indignation of Cato, who severely reproached the cruelty and brutality of the Numidian king, and then voluntarily undertook himself to maintain Utica against Cæsar. He shut himself up there, happy thus to establish a last bulwark to Roman liberty, and no longer to be in immediate contact with those chiefs, who in their weak subserviency to Juba or in their petty rivalries and personal disputes, often excited his pity or contempt.

Meanwhile Cæsar landed at Hadrumetum (Susa) on the 1st of January in the year 46 B. C., with only 3,000 men and 150 horses, the rest of his forces having been separated by a storm at sea. Trying in vain to take Hadrumetum by assault, he encamped at Ruspina (Monastir) situated about fifteen miles southeast of Hadrumetum, and there entered upon his third term as consul and dictator. He then brought under his jurisdiction Leptis Parva and other cities of less importance, and sought to unite all his forces before marching against the enemy. But suddenly Labienus attacked him with 8,000 Numidian horsemen. Cæsar succeeded in escaping from his embarrassing position only after a murderous combat of seven hours. Then Scipio came with eight legions and 4,000 horsemen. Cæsar withdrew to the shore, and his situation became the more dangerous on account of his want of provisions and forage. Juba, informed of his distresses, hastened to strike him a blow with the combined forces of his states. If the Pompeian generals and the Numidian king had effected a union of their forces according to their plan, they would probably have accomplished the ruin of Cæsar. But Cæsar was not to be caught thus. With that extraordinary penetration for which he was remarkable, he had anticipated this very danger; and thus, at the moment when he seemed fated to suffer a defeat, he gained a victory.

A desperado named Sittius, who had played a conspicuous part in the Catalinian conspiracy and then passed over into Africa, became there an adventurous filibuster. He sometimes carried on a guerrilla warfare on his own account, and sometimes sold himself to the party or chieftain that proposed the best terms. He had gained great military renown by his singular good fortune in always being on the winning side. Cæsar understood the value of this man, and readily drew him with his motley crew into his service, and then threw him with a strong force into Numidia, at the very moment when Juba was coming out of it. At the same time, two Moorish kings, Bocchus and Bogud, partisans of Cæsar, hastened in their turn to take possession of the states of Juba, which Cæsar had audaciously assigned them in the name of the republic. Juba, frightened by these demonstrations, retraced his steps; but the other two armies pressed hard upon Cæsar. He succeeded, however, by employing the name of Marius, always popular in Africa, and by the influence of Sittius, in winning over the Gætulians and a part of the Numidians from the cause of Pompey; and after having finally received by sea the reïnforcements so long expected, he encountered and defeated Scipio in a cavalry engagement.

In the meantime Juba had entrusted the defence of his states to Saburra, and was returning in all haste to the aid of Scipio. On receiving this news, the army of Cæsar, greatly inferior in numbers, was alarmed and dismayed. Cæsar resolved to exaggerate still more the rumors that depressed his soldiers, and, calling his troops together, he thus addressed them: "King Juba is upon us with ten legions, 30,000 horsemen, 100,000 light-armed troops, and 300 elephants. Let newsmongers then cease to make troublesome inquiries and reports. What I tell you is based upon positive information. I am decided to put refractory babblers upon the oldest of my ships and abandon them to the mercy of the sea."

These words fell with crushing weight, confirming the worst fears of his soldiers; but the courage of the men was speedily aroused when, on the approach of Juba, they learned how very small was his force in comparison with that which Cæsar had attributed to him. Juba had in fact but three legions, 800 cavalry and 30 elephants. The soldiers of Cæsar then, instead of entertaining fears about the union of the armies of Juba and Scipio, took courage and became eager for a combat.

Cæsar finally received the rest of his legions, and especially the tenth legion, which he held in high esteem. He renewed the discipline of his troops, exercised them in combats against the elephants and Numidian cavalry; then he resolved to terminate the war, according to his habit, by terrible blows. He defeated Varrus by sea and Labienus by land. Juba's army suffered by the defection of many Numidians. His soldiers that tried to escape were seized and crucified, and the infatuated king fell upon the city of Vacca (Baja) with all his force, massacring its inhabitants and producing an utter ruin of their place because they had proposed terms of submission to Cæsar. After having for a long time avoided a decisive engagement, Scipio and Juba were at length constrained to encounter Cæsar near Thapsus (cape Dimas). The rout of the Pompeians was begun by the elephants, which became unmanageable and vented their rage against the army they were designed to aid. In their furious flight, these beasts attacked the barriers of the Pompeian camps, and were urged on in their work of destruction by the soldiers of Cæsar. The camps were then penetrated and the victory won. This was the last great action in Africa for the cause of the republic. Ten thousand Pompeians laid down their lives upon the field of battle. Cæsar left three legions to govern Thapsus; he sent a force to besiege Thysdrus, thirty-five miles distant, and then set off on his expedition against Utica, one hundred and fifty miles distant, where Cato remained to the vanquished to raise his head against the vanquisher.

But the inhabitants, though personally his friends, were opposed to his party, and refused to sustain him in his heroic resolution. As Cæsar entered the city, Cato, unable to arrest his steps, sought consolation on the occasion by tranquilly reading the admirable dialogue of Plato on the immortality of the soul, and finally saved himself from the pardon which Cæsar in his clemency would have cheerfully given, by opening up with his sword the immortality that was the theme of his contemplations and the dream of his life.

A curious tradition is still preserved in the country in regard to Cato, which I give as I received it, not vouching for its historic accuracy. Cato is known to have been more reverenced and honored after his death than in his life; and, when the same tyranny that precipitated his death had centuries afterwards desolated Utica, obliterating all traces of its material greatness as of its manly vigor and even of its name, Cato was remembered, and the spot where he gave up his life rather than assent to his own and his country's servitude, was designated as *Bou Shahter*, i. e., Wise Man or Father of Wisdom. The rude natives still call the site of Utica *Bou Shahter*. We presume, however, that they have about as little idea of Cato's wisdom or greatness, as they have of the meaning of the Christian cross, which is sometimes found marked upon the foreheads of Arabs residing in the interior of the country.

All the other enemies of Cæsar miserably perished. Sittius conquered Saburra, and made prisoners of Afranius and Faustus Sylla, at a moment when they were attempting to escape with a body of troops. Scipio reached the sea and killed himself upon his vessel in the roadstead at Hippo, where St. Augustine breathed his last at the approach of the Vandals, 475 years afterwards. Juba and Petreius yet lived, but in disgrace and despair.

Nearly all Numidia had revolted. Juba came and tried to enter Zama Regia, his capital. The inhabitants, unmoved alike by his menaces and by his entreaties, closed against him their gates. They remembered the declarations of Juba on the eve of his departure against Cæsar. He had resolved, in case of defeat, to celebrate his voluntary death by ceremonies horribly pompous and cruel. An immense funeral pile, erected in the public square, had been prepared for the occasion. He was to have the inhabitants on whom he would wreak his vengeance first cast upon the burning pile; then himself with his family and treasure were to perish together. Seeing himself repulsed, he asked for his wife and children. These were refused. He then withdrew into a country house with Petreius and a few soldiers. Cæsar had in the meantime quit Utica, and was marching towards Zama. The Numidian king and the Roman general understood that the hour of death was at hand. After a sumptuous banquet, they rushed upon each other, sword in hand, to effect a mutual death. But the Numidian, the more vigorous of the two, killed the Roman and then attempted to plunge the bloody weapon into his own breast. Not succeeding, he called upon a slave to have compassion on him by putting an end to his miserable existence.

Thus perished that ostentatious and cruel barbarian who cherished for a time the thought of ruling Africa by employing the partisans of Pompey to overthrow Cæsar, and, then of destroying them as soon as they had ceased to promote the objects of his ambition.

Cæsar entered Zama and proclaimed Numidia a Roman province. He gave the government of it to Sallust with the title of pro-consul. The extortions and injustice which Sallust perpetrated during his administration, and the accusations which his subjects brought against him at Rome, are a matter of history. Though acquitted through the influence of Cæsar, he was never afterwards honored with any public charge. It was with the fruit of his robberies and extortions that the celebrated historian built at Rome the palace and magnificent gardens still designated by his name.

In less than six months, Cæsar annihilated the party of Pompey in Africa. It remained for him to exterminate that party in Spain, and then return to Rome to receive the perpetual dictatorship, which he exercised for a while with all the haughtiness of his genius, and then in his turn fell down and died, pierced by twenty-three daggers at the very foot of the statue of his great rival and victim at Pharsalia.

CHRISTIANITY IN AFRICA.

Christianity was nowhere more flourishing than in North Africa for several centuries after its propagation. From Egypt to Tangiers, from the desert to the coast, arose innumerable churches, and, throughout this territory where to-day the Koran reigns, the gospel prevailed till the sixth century.

In spite of the decay of the empire, the destructive invasions of the barbarians, and especially of the Arabs, who came last, there remain enough documents of this African church, the second in the west, to enable us to understand its history and admire the courage of its many martyrs, the number and activity of its bishops, and the science, zeal and eloquence of its learned men.

We are unable to explain the origin of Christianity in Africa. It is supposed that about the end of the first century, some missionaries, leaving Asia or Europe, came into Africa to proclaim the glad tidings, and that Carthage was the first Episcopal see. Christianity spread, as everywhere else, with surprising rapidity, from the slaves to the first citizens. According to St. Cyprian, at the end of the first century, there were in Africa Proper a great number of bishops. Aggrippinus was at that time bishop at Carthage. There are not on record the names of any bishops before his time.

Alarmed by the success of Christianity, the Roman emperors wished to extirpate it in this province, as they tried to do wherever their jurisdiction extended. Under Septimius Severus, occurred the first martyrdoms for the cause of Christ in Africa. Twelve inhabitants of Scillium, now called Casreen, cheerfully gave up their lives rather than disown their Saviour; and their example was followed in every direction with an enthusiasm that greatly extended the influence of the church. Then* appeared to protest against this sanguinary violence and to show its folly, the rude and impetuous Tertullian, and his vehement *Apologetica* is at the same time a justification and an exposition of the gospel. But the persecution continued, and among the generous victims who perished in the amphitheatre at Carthage, we cannot recall without emotion, the names of Felicita and Perpetua, two young women equally sublime and heroic in their sufferings and in their death. The first was a slave, the second a patrician; but they became sisters in faith, hope and charity, suffering the cross to win the crown. The persecution of Christians extended into all northern Africa, which did not breathe freely again until the reign of Alexander Severus. At this period, was held the council

---

* Latter part of the second century.

of Lambessa against the heretic Privatus. Ninety bishops sat on that occasion.

Cyprian, who was appointed bishop at Carthage in the year 248, and who had already become celebrated as a divine, assembled in that city in 251, a council of seventy bishops, and then another of forty-two bishops, to combat schismatics who had set up against him a competitor on the ground that he was too lenient towards apostates. He wrote and preached against his opponents; and, after having been the light of his church, became in the time of danger its magnanimous champion. In 257, under Valerian, he was exiled. Returning to Carthage in 258, and brought before the pro-consul, he replied with firmness; then, in the presence of an immense throng of people variously affected by the serenity of the martyr, twenty-five pieces of gold were counted out for his executioners, and Cyprian was beheaded. Theogenes, the bishop of Hippo, shared the same fate. At Utica, 200 Christians were cast into a heated furnace. At Carthage, Cirta and Lambessa were numerous martyrs, whose blood became the fruitful seed of the church.

The edict of Nicomedia, by which Diocletian, instigated by the ferocious Galerius, vainly ordered the destruction of Christianity then flourishing in the empire, was speedily executed in Africa and at Cirta, where the persecution began. The clergy showed themselves by turns bold and feeble. Influenced by force or fear, they delivered up the consecrated vases, sacred urns, church ornaments and the contributions in money and clothing destined for the poor.

But the bishop of Tibur (Tibursicensium civitas, Teboursuk) acted in a manner worthy of his office. Menaces, chains and the sword, could not move him. To the first interrogatory he replied with firmness under the sword of the executioner: "I have all the things which you demand: but I ought not to give them up; I will not give them up."

Though at Carthage there was less violence than in some other places, noble examples of resistance were not wanting. The bishop, Mensurius, courageous and at the same time sensible and prudent, forbade excesses of zeal to avoid unnecessarily irritating persecutors, but he knew how to give an example of true greatness of soul. He had concealed in his house one of his deacons, whom they wished to put to death because he had written against persecution. Mensurius refused to give him up and was summoned before the imperial court to render account of his conduct and be punished. He appeared before the Cæsars at Rome, and, by his eloquent and firm language, succeeded in justifying himself; then departing for Carthage, he died on the way there.

It was during this persecution that Arnobius, an illustrious writer and orator of Sicca (Kef), wrote to defend the Christians whose faith he had embraced; and it was shortly after the death of Mensurius, that began the famous schism of the Donatists, enlisting passions that desolated Christian Africa for centuries, and hastened its decline and ruin. On the occasion of the election of the new bishop at Carthage, a violent party opposed the choice of deacon Cecilianus. This opposition, whose chief was the Numidian bishop

Secundus, and whose real soul was the priest Donatus, of Casæ Nigræ (Black House),* pretended that Cecilianus should be set aside because he had been consecrated by treacherous prelates. They designated thus (traditores) those who had so far yielded to persecution as to give up the property of the church to officers of the civil government. Seeing the firm bearing and imposing manner of Cecilianus, seventy bishops of the opposition assembled at Carthage and elected in his place Majorinus, a simple reader, who was protected by the powerful influence of the patrician, Lucilla. They did not take possession of the basilica which contained the episcopal chair, but held their sessions in another church, and appointed Majorinus after a lively recrimination against Cecilianus, on which occasion one prelate named Purpurinus, descended to personal menaces. The church of Carthage was then divided by this schism of the Donatists, which drew its name from Donatus, of Casæ Nigræ, and another Donatus, who was the successor of bishop Majorinus.

The emperor Constantine, informed of this great scandal by the pro-consul of Africa, gave instructions to his officers to thoroughly suppress the disorder. But the dissenters drew up a long memorial; and Constantine then ordered that Cecilianus and ten clergymen who favored his views, and Majorinus and ten clergymen of his choice, should proceed to Rome to be judged by a council. This council, composed

* Casæ Nigræ was a city in ancient Numidia, (actual Tunisia), which Dr. Davis believes to be identical with Hydra, and Mr. Guerin, with Ammedera.

of three Gallic and fifteen Italian bishops and presided over by pope Melchiades, sat during three days, and after having heard the contradictory statements of the two parties, condemned the Donatists in the year 313 A.D. Donatus of Casæ Nigræ and Cecilianus engaged, for the sake of facilitating a reconciliation, not to return into Africa, and commissioners were sent there to exert their influence for peace. But the dissenters soon protested and appealed to a second council which took place at Arles in Gaul. This council met in the year 314 and, besides numerous bishops from Africa, Numidia, Mauritania and Tripoli, it included sixteen Gallic bishops and two from Britain (York and London). It confirmed the sentence of Rome. The Donatists then appealed to the emperor who ratified the preceding sentences and ordered them to be executed under severe penalties (315 A. D.).

The most deplorable violence afflicted the African church. Ecclesiastical councils and pontifical and imperial edicts seemed to produce only discord, strife and defiance, aggravating the difficulties and intensifying the bitterness and animosity of both orthodox and heterodox Christians. In proportion as efforts were put forth to secure uniformity and conformity, an opposite result was reached. The ordinary prescriptions for the erratic tendencies of the day proved worse than useless. The Donatists successfully resisted the combined authorities of church and state. Organizing their forces, they took possession of Constantine. Taking into their ranks discontented and revengeful servants and slaves, they at length com-

mitted frightful depredations. These *circumcellions**
remind us of some fanatics of the middle age who,
assuming different names, wandered over several
countries of Europe. These mystic bands, formed to
resist the tyranny of the dominant church, called for
the reign of equality, and, while pillaging and plundering in their course, assumed the title of saints
and professed to be invested with a divine mission
that required their entire devotion. Some carried
their madness so far as to demand that those whom
they met upon the highway should kill them; and if
they refused, they assailed them by way of punishment. Debauchery and all kinds of excesses broke
out in the midst of this multitude, as sensual and
gross as it was fanatic and savage; and some of the
Donatist leaders themselves had in the end to claim
the protection of the imperial officers against their
own forces. An army was sent against these bands
and succeeded in dispersing them only after a long
warfare.

"The *circumcellions*," says the eminent Saint Mark
Girradin, "represent in Donatism the manners of
Berber Africa; but there is in Donatism something
which characterizes Africa in general; it is the spirit
of independence in regard to emperors; it is the
hatred of unity, whether of the temporal unity of
the empire or of the religious unity of the church.
The Donatism of the fourth and fifth centuries is an
expressive evidence of original traits of character
which Africa has maintained under all rules and at

---

* Circumcellions was the name given to Donatist vagrants, who wandered about from house to house, accomplishing their chosen mission.

all times,—of a character which is almost a schism in religion and a revolt in politics." These observations appear to us just and pertinent. The Arabs, as well as the Vandals, found here supporters and partisans of the Donatists, or inheritors of their opinions and hatred. Donatism in name and form continued but a few centuries; but its cause, being somewhat climatic and very human in its nature, has not been and cannot be overcome by the combined or separate influence of emperors, popes and sultans. There is always a protest against uniformity even among Mussulmans.

After numerous struggles, pacifications and troubles of various kinds, two hundred and seventy Donatist bishops held a council at Carthage and agreed on conciliatory measures, which served to secure tranquility for several years; but, by-and-by, the struggle was renewed with intense violence in consequence of a harsh measure of the emperor Constans, who showed schismatics no mercy. At the same time the Catholic bishops of Africa held a council at Carthage, to examine again the eternal question.

Under the emperor Julian, in 361, the troubles broke out anew. Carthage, Numidia and Mauritania were desolated by party violence. It was worse than a civil war. The most fiendish passions were aroused, and were indulged in the name of religion. Under Valentinian, the country enjoyed a moment of tranquillity. Then suddenly the controversy, which had been open nearly a century, was renewed on a grand scale, giving occasion for animosity and violence. After St. Optatus, bishop of Mileum, there appeared on the arena the priest, Aurelius Augustinus, since known as St. Augustine. His is the most striking figure in Christian Africa, and must for a moment engage our attention.

He was born in 354, at Tagaste, among the mountains of Numidia, near the Algerine frontier. His father, Patricius, was a magistrate of his city, and his mother was a Christian. He studied first at Madaurus upon the Bagrada, near Tagaste; then at Carthage, the literary metropolis of Africa, where he was incited to renewed efforts by reading the works of Cicero. He then returned to Tagaste, where he taught grammar and rhetoric. But his native village not satisfying his intellectual ambition, he returned to Carthage and taught and pursued his favorite studies for a considerable time. He then went to Rome, and from there to Milan, where he was a professor of rhetoric.

At Milan, the current of his life was turned into a new channel. Until then he was a Manichean philosopher, worldly-minded and of irregular habits. But he became suddenly serious by reading the works of Plato, so justly styled *the preface of the gospel*, and also the tears and prayers of his mother made a profound impression on his heart. The eloquent counsels of St. Ambrose, archbishop of Milan, and the reading of the epistles of St. Paul, determined his conversion, which took place when he was thirty-three years old. St. Ambrose baptized him at the same time with his son Adeodatus, and his friend Alypius.

Becoming a fervent Christian, he had soon to mourn

the sudden death of his mother at Ostia. Then after passing a year at Rome, he returned to Africa, burning with zeal to devote to the cause of truth his vast attainments, and his eloquence purified and ennobled by his new faith. At first he lived a retired life, and began that long series of works which hold so large a place in Christian and general literature. He took orders in the Catholic church, and, as a simple priest, became the counsel of the bishops. Valerius, bishop of Hippo, advised him to leave his monastery and preach the gospel, and he followed his counsel. His words were keen and pointed and rarely failed to effect their object. He exerted a masterly influence over his auditors, and, by means of a single discourse at Cæsarea, secured the abolition of a barbarous custom, which neither the authority of the bishops, nor that of the councils had been able to destroy. He took strong ground against the Donatists, always numerous in Africa, and also against the Manicheans whose* doctrine was at that time favorably regarded. The assistant and then the successor of bishop Valerius, he regulated for thirty-five years the bishopric of Hippo, and morally ruled the Catholic church in Africa for that entire period. It can be said that St. Augustine personifies Christian Africa, not alone in his time, but during its entire existence. Donatism lost ground through the efforts of its illustrious opponent. But he occupied himself also in destroying the remains of polytheism, then found among the descendants of the Phœnicians and Carthaginians.

* Belief in the existence of two equal and antagonistic principles of good and evil.

These tenacious pagans had preserved at Carthage, in the year 391, the ancient temple of Astarte, transformed into that of celestial Juno. This temple was closed by order of Theodosius, and dedicated to the Redeemer; but the pagans entering it by force, the authorities had it destroyed to prevent a collision. Notwithstanding these checks and the recent edicts of Honorius, a strong party of the natives remained faithful to the ancient worship, which found even at this period able defenders like Symmachus and Lybanius. These polytheists reproached Christianity with being the cause of the decay and ruin of the empire, whose greatness had declined only after the abandonment of their gods. Paul Orosius by his *History*, and St. Augustine, by his *City of God*, defended Christianity, presenting elevated considerations upon the vicissitudes of empires and the action of Providence in history.

A new council took place at Carthage in 411; and afterwards several public conferences, in which St. Augustine took the leading part. An indefatigable opponent of Donatism, he combated it with extreme ardor and perseverence, sometimes with that excess of passion which does harm to the best of causes. But, we must acknowledge that in general, St. Augustine was moderate, tolerant, just and charitable. We shall cite, in confirmation of this remark, only a part of his memorable letter to judge Marcellinus, in which he prays that he would graciously spare the lives of the Donatists who had assassinated several priests of his church. "In the name of the mercy of Jesus Christ, I conjure you," wrote he, "not to make them suffer for that which they have done. We would not have the sufferings of the servants of God avenged according to the law of retaliation. We earnestly desire that these men, without losing their lives and without becoming useless, be watched and restrained by the laws, and thus led from their fatal wanderings and evil deeds to the calm of good sense. Let them have some useful employment. Leaving them no more opportunity for crime, permit them the remedy of repentance. Christian judge, perform the duties of a tender father. In your anger against crime, remember to act in favor of humanity; and in punishing the capital offences of sinners, exercise not yourself the passion of revenge."

After the lapse of fifteen centuries, these words could be appropriately engraved on the frontispiece of every tribunal on the face of the globe, as the eternal ideal for the administration and economy of social justice. Notwithstanding our boasted civilization, they are not yet realized to the letter anywhere on either hemisphere. This extract may serve to give some idea of the noble spirit of St. Augustine, but to set forth his various distinguishing merits would require volumes instead of this brief paragraph. After having written much to counteract Pelagianism, a new heresy* of British origin, and seeing his opinions adopted by two successive councils in 416, St. Augustine devoted himself to theological and philosophical speculations and to acts of charity and benevolence. When Count Boniface, the traitorous governor of

---

* This doctrine rejected the divine grace which accompanies, according to the orthodox faith, the exercise of free will in man.

Africa, had invited there the Vandals, the bishop of Hippo, uttered patriotically his protest and wrote to the count: "If the empire has done you good, you must not render evil for good; if it has done you evil, you have no right to render evil for evil." Boniface repented and wished to correct his error; but it was too late. Soon the clamors of the barbarians reached the ears of St. Augustine at Hippo. The evils that befell the empire and the church, inflicted the last blow upon that body already worn down by fatigue and hardships, and his grief hastened his death. He descended to his tomb, bearing with him Christian Africa.

Soon, under the reign of the Vandal Arians, there remained in fact only the three episcopal sees of Carthage, Cirta and Hippo; persecution desolated all Africa. Transportation, exile, imprisonment and capital punishment were successively employed to destroy this vast and illustrious church, which, from Tangiers to Egypt, included more than four hundred episcopal sees. Carthage, the metropolis *par excellence*, contained twenty important churches.

At the fall of the Vandal kingdom, (534), this church attempted to rise from its ruins, and two hundred and seventeen[*] bishops united for this object at Carthage, and put themselves in relation with the other churches of the Christian world. But in the midst of the revolts which disturbed at each instant civil authority and were excited by religious

---

[*] It is presumed that in spite of the suppression of most of the episcopal sees under the Vandals, the church continued to name bishops, and that the titular bishops after the fall of the Vandals, assembled at Carthage to become bishops *de facto*.

animosity, the African episcopacy was paralyzed in its work of restoration.

The Arabs then came to make the ruin more complete. Yet not every trace of Christianity disappeared; for in 1054 we see still Thomas, archbishop of Carthage, complaining to Leo IX that the other prelates contested his supremacy. There were then five bishops. In 1076, there were only the two of Carthage and Hippo. It has been remarked that the ancient religious glory of Africa was so far forgotten that the Roman chancellor, not knowing where the ancient church of St. Augustine was situated, located it in Mauritania Sitifensis, in the bull sent to bishop Servandus.

At the same period, Syriachus, archbishop of Carthage, accused before the Saracens by some of his own flock, had to suffer the most cruel outrages. We find little in history about Christian Africa during the middle ages. It is remarked that some intrepid monks, among others the famous Raymond Lulle, came to preach upon this land once illuminated with Christian light. Several churches continued till the time of St. Louis, in 1270, when it was stipulated in the treaty of peace then made, that Christians and their priests should enjoy full liberty of worship.

*A singular persistence of tradition and symbolism

---

* Tertullian at the beginning of the third century, speaks thus of the universal use of the sign of the cross:

"Whenever we move, whenever we enter and go out; in dressing; in washing; at table; when we retire to rest; during conversation, we impress on our foreheads the sign of the cross. Should you ask for the scriptural authority for this and such like practices, I answer there is none. But there is tradition that authorizes it; custom that confirms it, and submission that observes it."

may here be noted. Far away from European centres, among the mountains and even in the desert, you often find tattooed on the foreheads of the natives of the Libyan race, that cross of whose meaning they have no conception, and from which they do not shrink with horror like the Shemitic Arabs on the coast. I have seen, generally the Greek, but occasionally the Latin, cross thus marked on many persons, and am assured that the Kabyles and several other powerful Libyan tribes of the interior, keep up this custom. At Tebourba, an ancient city fifteen miles from Tunis, is a mosque called from time immemorial *the Mosque of Jesus,* and the Mussulmans there have the tradition that it stands on the site of an ancient Christian church. At Baja, ancient Vacca, is a mosque called *the mosque of Christ,* and one of the dignitaries of the place recently told a friend of mine that Christ used to live on that spot, and hence the mosque took his name. I conclude that if the spirit of Christianity were as well exhibited by its professed followers as are its symbols and souvenirs by its professed enemies, we might hope yet to see this sad land once more illuminated and gladdened with heavenly light and truth. But, alas! though Christian truth is dealt out in formularies and heard from the lips of preachers, its transforming power is not sufficiently exhibited in the conversation and lives of its professed followers to win over Mussulmans and Jews. It is a melancholy observation that more Christians are converted to Moslemism than Mussulmans to Christianity, and the few examples of converted Jews we find are wanting, with rare exceptions, the requisite Christian vigor and manhood to constitute them even worthy hirelings.

SECTION V.

THE VANDALS AND BYZANTINES IN AFRICA.—FIRST ARAB INVASION.

We come now to the period of the Vandals. These barbarians, finding themselves in difficulty in the south of Spain, coveting the riches of Africa and hoping to make Carthage the centre of a powerful empire, yielded to the invitation of Count Boniface, the rebellious governor of the Roman province of Africa, and arrived at Carthage by the strait of Gibraltar to the number of about 50,000 soldiers and 30,000 or 40,000 aged men, women and children. Cordially received by the urban and rural population whom the imperial tax-gatherers had ruined, favored by the Donatist sect, which sought an occasion to triumph over their oppressors of the Roman church, and especially encouraged by the persistent remains of the Punic race; the Vandals were in the year 429 scattered over Mauritania, the two Numidias and Africa Proper. They arrived in the year 430 under the walls of Hippo Regia, of which they took possession after a siege of fourteen months. During that siege, St. Augustine, the illustrious father of the Latin church, who resided in that city thirty-five years, passed away from the scene of his labors.

Count Boniface, returning to his allegiance, and aided in his efforts for the restoration of imperial power by general Asper, who was sent thither from Constantinople, was beaten in two successive battles, and the court of Ravenna treated for the first time with the Vandals in 432 A. D. In 435, a new treaty was made, and the Vandals continued their ambitious projects until 439, when, seeing the empire in a desperate condition, Genseric, their king, threw himself suddenly upon Carthage, taking possession of it and marking his entrance with such deeds of cruelty as then characterized Christian warfare. He then subjected to himself the whole pro-consulate of Africa and Africa Proper, leaving to the eastern empire only Tripoli. He attacked at a later period Sicily and Italy, and obtained from the disheartened emperor, Theodosius III, a treaty which guaranteed to him his possessions in Africa.

In 455, after the senator Petronius Maximus had usurped the crown and while he was trying to constrain the empress Eudoxia, widow of Valentinian III, to marry him, this princess invited to her aid against the usurper Petronius, Genseric, the leader of the Vandals, who speedily arrived in Italy. Genseric, filled with hatred against the Roman power and hierarchy, gave up Rome to pillage and plunder during sixteen days, and sent to Carthage as trophies the chief dignitaries and the richest spoils of the city, including works of art that were taken from Carthage six centuries before. The successors of Genseric were: Huneric in 477; Gontamond in 486, and Ebrasamond in 497; all of them Arians and persecutors of Latin Christians, as the Latin Christians were persecutors of them. Under all these princes, the African episcopacy was severely tried, and its members were dispersed and decimated. Hilderic, son of Huneric, ascending the throne in the year 524, displayed a toleration which shocked the Vandals as much as it pleased the Romanists, and by which Gelimer, a descendant of Genseric, profited to establish his right to the throne and to actually get possession of it in 531.

It was the toleration of this prince that caused the fall of the Vandal monarchy. The emperor Justinian, under pretext of reëstablishing Hilderic upon the throne, though with the distinct object of raising the African church from its ruins, sent Belisarius with an army which defeated, by land and by sea, the Vandals under their king. After the decisive battle of Tricameron, Belisarius took king Gelimer prisoner at Mount Papua in Numidia; effected a speedy re-conquest of the country; reëstablished the Roman church in comparative splendor, and finally returned to Constantinople, where, in the year 534 A. D., he received by order of the emperor Justinian the honors of a triumph, after the custom of the ancient Roman conquerors, and a medal, which is still extant, was struck off in his honor, inscribed: "Belisarius gloria Romanorum."

After the departure of Belisarius, his lieutenant, Saloman, was obliged to suppress a revolt of the Moors who came to invade Numidia and Byzacium. The war lasted five years with various turns of fortune, and ended in 539, A. D., in the submission of eastern Mauritania. In the year 543, A. D., occurred another insurrection which extended to Tripoli, and in which Salomon was killed. During three years, the country was a prey to anarchy. John Troglitæ, a general who had distinguished himself in the war against the Persians, was then sent into Africa (546 A. D.). He had to encounter an extensive confederation of natives, including even many nomads of the desert. After suffering several defeats, he was completely successful, and from 550 to 564, this country enjoyed peace and profound tranquillity. But Mauritania became by degrees independent under native chieftains, and Byzantine jurisdiction was forced back towards the east. From 564 to 597, revolts, begun on the frontier of Numidia, succeeded each other without cessation, in spite of energetic efforts for their suppression. The natives found a chief named Gesmul, who, having become powerful by his victories, organized his forces in the most approved manner and brought them under efficient discipline. He even attempted an incursion into Gaul, but failed. At the end of this period, we have no record of the scenes that transpired in Africa, until we come to the reign of the emperor Heraclius, who, as is known, was a son of the exarch viceroy of Africa, and was sent by him against Phocas, whom he dethroned and replaced in the year 610 A. D.

History has recorded the vicissitudes of this reign of thirty-one years, during which a brilliant succession of victories over the Persians came between two series of reverses. Conquerors of the Byzantines in Syria, the soldiers of Chosroes invaded Egypt and

Cyrenaica; took and sacked Carthage and Tunis; but soon driven back by the Byzantine patrician, they turned again towards the east and abandoned to him the conquered provinces.

We approach now the Mussulman conquest. Under Abubeker, the first calif, general Khaled, who was styled *the Sword of God*, entering into Syria, broke at Aiznadin the legions of Heraclius and took Damascus; and, under Omar, the second calif, he achieved by the battle of Yermuk, in 636, the conquest of Syria, Palestine and Mesopotamia, while Amrou, another lieutenant of Omar, reduced Egypt to his jurisdiction. It is this Amrou who is generally represented to have destroyed the famous Alexandrine library. A word may serve to correct this statement.

The famous Serapion library, once composed of 700,000 volumes, had been already nearly destroyed in 390, under Theodosius; from which it appears that the vandalism of Amrou was not so disastrous as it is commonly represented to be, and the story of the baths of Alexandria being heated six months with those volumes must be rejected as fabulous, especially if we consider that parchment or papyrus is not good for producing and maintaining heat. Historians of the time, even Mussulmans, singularly sacrificed truth to their taste for the marvellous, and succeeding historians have generally failed to duly rectify their statements. That library was rather a prey to sectarian animosity among professed Christians, than to Moslem fanaticism or vandalism.

After organizing his government in Egypt, Amrou passed into Nubia; recruited there his little army with large and ferocious blacks; returned towards the sea; invaded and took Barca and western Tripoli; then at the death of the calif Omar, he returned to Egypt, and, in spite, or rather on account, of his successes, was deprived of office by the third calif, Othman. Amrou was subsequently restored to his command by Abdallah ben Sayd, a foster brother of Othman, who undertook to continue towards western Africa the conquests of his predecessor.

He left Tripoli for Gabes at the head of 25,000 Mussulmans, defeated in many engagements the Byzantine troops, and, at Akouba, near Sufetula (Sbeitla), encountered the patrician Gregory, the governor, or rather the sovereign of the country, who, with his 120,000 men, had an engagement of several days duration, and was finally overpowered and killed. An immense tribute procured the retreat of the conqueror, who left as his lieutenant a certain Jenahr (John?), and returned to Egypt, taking in his train as spoils of war immense numbers of Christian slaves and treasures of various kinds gathered in his victorious march through the country (648 A. D.).

CHAPTER III.

History of the Middle Age from the Seventh to the Sixteenth Century.

SECTION I.

THE ARAB CONQUEST AND THE COUNTRY UNDER THE LIEUTENANTS OF THE ORIENTAL CALIFS AND UNDER ITS FIRST INDEPENDENT PRINCES.

IN the year 662, after the foundation of the dynasty of the Ommyades, Okbah ben Nafy invaded Byzacium; and in 666, Moavia invaded it again. After the latter had defeated near Tripoli the troops sent by Constans II from Byzantium, the cities of Susa and Bizerta and the island of Gerba fell one after the other into his hands. Having extended the terror of Mussulman arms from Egypt to Tunisia, Okbah wished to have a point of support for Islamism, and, for this purpose, founded in the year 670, in a fertile and flourishing plain in the centre of Byzacium, the famous city of Cairwan, which became henceforth the holy city of Africa and the capital of the Mussulman possessions in the Maghreb (west).

Appointed for the second time governor of this province, to succeed in office Moavia and Dinar,

Okbah extended the Arab conquest to the extreme west, stopping only at the Atlantic, whose waters he entered on horseback, calling on the God of Mohammed[*] to witness that he stopped in his victorious march only where land failed him.

In 694, Hassan ben Noman took and destroyed Carthage and Tunis. The Berbers arose in arms and resisted his sway at first under Koussila, who took possession of Cairwan. Afterwards, under the heroine Damia, surnamed Kahenna, they inflicted upon the Arabs severe losses and drove them back as far as Gabes. But soon Hassan defeated Damia in a general engagement, and employed the subjected Berbers to combat the independent tribes at a distance.

Master of Sfax and of Constantine, Hassan organized the government of the country and returned to the east, where he exhibited the spoils of the Maghreb to encourage recruits for the conquering army.

Musa ben Nosair succeeded him in Africa. It was he that conquered Corsica and Sardinia and sent his lieutenant Tarik to take possession of Spain through the treachery of count Julian (707–711) under the calif Walid. After that period until the establishment of the dynasty of the Abbasides in the east and from the foundation of the califate Ommyades in Spain, the unity of Moslem rule in Africa began to give way, and many rival principalities sprang up, combating by turns each other and the inhabitants of the country.

---

[*] According to Mussulman scholars and usage, their prophet's name is *Mohammed*. The French, however, employ the epithet *Mahomet*, which is adopted by some of our best writers doubtless for the sake of euphony, regardless of strict historical accuracy.

In the year 800 A. D. (184 H.), Ibrahim ben Aghelib, appointed emir by Haroun-ar-Rashid, founded in Africa the independent dynasty of the Aghlabites, which had eleven princes, and with Cairwan for its capital, extended its rule from Tlencen to Tripoli. It was under the reign of its third prince, Abou Mohammed, that the conquest of Sicily took place in 827. The last Aghlabite was driven away by insurgents who were led on by Abou-Abd-Allah.

The dynasty of the Edrissites, contemporary with the Aghlabites, reigned over Morocco with Fez for their capital. North Africa was found then divided into eastern Africa, with Cairwan for its capital under the Aghlabite califate, extending from Tlencen to Tripoli; and western Africa, with its capital at Fez, and its territory extending from Tlencen to the ocean.

The Fatimite califs, who claim to be the descendants of Fatima, a daughter of Mohammed, began to establish their power at Segelmessa in Morocco, and, by the aid of the natives, extended their sway rapidly towards the east. They soon reached Egypt, where they founded Cairo, which became the second city of the east and the seat of one of the two vast califates, which undertook the control of the Mussulman world, treating each other as usurpers. Segelmessa, Tahart, Cairwan, Media and Cairo, were successively the capitals of the Fatimite califate in Africa. When the Fatimites established their headquarters at Cairo, their lieutenant in the Barbary provinces, Yousef (Joseph) ben Zeiri became by degrees independent and founded the new dynasty of the Zeirites, which prevailed until 1148 (543 H.), under eight different princes.

But in 1007, Hammad, of the second branch of the Zeirites, founded the Hammadite order of sovereigns at Bougie and Constantine; and in 1055, arose in the Maghreb the Almorabides, who professed to be the special friends of religion. The last of the Zeirites, Hassan Ben Aly, (1121–1148), reigned and fell in the midst of disasters and disorders of various kinds. The Normands of Sicily had conquered Gerba, and king Roger of Sicily, profiting by the wretched state to which famine had reduced the country, took possession of Tripoli, Media, Sfax, Susa and Tunis, while Hassan fled to the east.

Then Abd-el-Moumen, founder of the dynasty of the Almohades in Morocco, left that country, in 1159 A. D., (554 H.), with 100,000 men. He took Tunis, Sfax, Gabes and Tripoli, and established governors in each important city and a supreme lieutenant at Media. According to the Arab historian, Ibn-Khaldoun, the Almohades had thirteen princes, under whom occurred many insurrections, and several emigrations were made into Sicily and Spain.

In 1195, the Beni Merin, a Berber tribe, driving off the Almohades, took possession of Fez and Morocco. In 1266, (665 H.), the last Almohade, Aboul Ali, was conquered and killed by the Merinites, who inherited his dynasty. There were twenty-five Merinite princes who had their capitals at Fez, Segelmessa and at Morok. They reigned until the end of the fifteenth century, when they were supplanted by the actual dynasty of the scherifs* of Morocco. But in the thirteenth century, the territory of the Merinites corresponded nearly to the present empire of Morocco; for the Beni Zian established themselves at that time at Tlencen, and ruled over most of the actual province of Algeria, and over *Ifrikia*, which constituted the present department of Constantine together with Tunisia and Tripoli. The Beni Zian founded the new dynasty of the Hafsites or of the Beni Hafs in 1228 (626 H.).

SECTION II.

THE DYNASTY OF THE HAFSITES.—EXPEDITION OF ST. LOUIS, 1270 A. D.

The last of the native dynasties which prevailed, one after the other in Tunisia, was that of the Hafsites. This family governed Tunis from 1205, and reigned definitely from 1228 to 1535. Profiting by the distance of the capital of the Almohade empire and by the intestine wars which rent it, the first chief of this family of Berber origin, or as some claim, of negro origin, Abd-El-Ouahid, after having obtained from prince Nassereddine the government of Tunisia, established himself there so effectually that his successors boldly adopted the title of kings, and extended their rule over surrounding countries, and, among others, over Bougie in Algeria. Abou Fares,

* This word implies nobility. The scherifs claim to be lineal descendants of Mohammed, through his daughter, Fatima.

his immediate successor, had scarcely mounted the throne when he was driven off by his brother Yahia, surnamed Abou Zakariah (1222–1249). It was during the reign of Abou Zakariah, that the first treaty of commerce between the Mussulmans of Africa and Europeans was signed in the year 1230 A. D., (627 H.) The republic of Pisa was the first to make a treaty with the sultan of Egypt, and the first to interest European merchants in the Maghreb. Its example was followed by the emperor, Frederic II, king of Sicily, and by Genoa, Marseilles, Catalonia and Venice.

All these treaties regulated commercial transactions and guarantied the liberty and safety of merchants together with the free exercise of their worship and the right to have churches, baths, cemeteries and even to possess real estate. The consuls were made judges of their subjects, while they were not responsible for the crimes committed by them, and had the right to appear before the prince, wherever he might be, once a year. Abou Zakariah observed faithfully the treaties and exercised impartial justice towards foreigners. Near the end of his reign, suddenly yielding to religious scruples and fear, he gave up his claims to independence, submitted to the Almohades and died in 1249 A. D. (647 H.).

His son Abou-Abd-Allah Mohammed Mostancer Billahi did not imitate his example. He regarded himself as the actual sovereign of Tunisia. And in 1254 (652), the Merinites recognized his sovereignty, and in 1259 (657), the scherif of Mecca sent his submission to him, as to the most powerful orthodox prince of that period. His reign was, however, disturbed by revolts and other troubles, and the Jews established in Tunis were subjected to great trials and sufferings.

Mostancer Billahi opposed the progress of the Christian kings of Spain, who had taken the Balearic islands from the Almohades in 1229, and had at a later period rejected Tunisian aid sent them by Abou Zakariah; yet he made no hostile movements against other Christian powers, and he even signed with the king of Aragon, Don Jaeme, a treaty of peace and commerce, on the 14th of February, 1270, which was but a few months before the expedition of St. Louis.

In the eighteenth year of the reign of the Hafsite sultan Abou-Abd-Allah Mohammed Mostancer Billahi, in the year 1270 of the Christian era, and 669 of the hegira, on the 17th day of July, some Tunisian galleys descried to the north-northwest an immense fleet covered with sails, and forthwith turned back in great haste to the Goletta. It was the naval force of St. Louis, king of France.

The object of this fleet was to effect the fulfilment of treaty stipulations in favor of a French prince, and also to secure upon this land important commercial advantages for France and the Christian world.

While the German emperors were kings of Sicily, they imposed on the Tunisian princes an annual tribute, and Charles of Anjou, who succeeded to their rights, in vain pressed his claims during five years on El Mostancer for the payment of this tribute.

Too feeble to repress the arrogance of the Hafsite king and reduce him to the necessity of discharging his obligation, Charles of Anjou turned for aid to his brother Louis IX, whose courage and ambition were unaffected by the disasters of his recent crusade. Charles explained his griefs and by clever representations made the king appreciate the importance of Tunis in a military and commercial point of view.

Besides, in taking possession of Tunis, they would cut in two that "great serpent of Islamism," whose head they had in vain attempted to crush at Cairo three years before. Religious zeal and political ambition decided St. Louis.

On the one hand, to plant the cross upon the ruins of a powerful Mussulman kingdom, and to restore to Christ a country where his light had shone; on the other hand, to secure to the arms and the already flourishing commerce of France and of Christendom, a region which would with Sicily complete a kind of central bar of the Mediterranean, involving the control of it: such was the double object, glorious and comprehensive, of St. Louis.

He left then the government of his kingdom to Matthew, abbot of St. Denis and to count Simon of Nesle, and embarking at Aigues Mortes with a fleet of 1,500 vessels of every size mounted by 60,000 men, took with him his brother Alphonse, count of Toulouse, his three sons, Philip (afterwards Philip III), John Tristan, count of Nevers, Peter, count of Alençon; his nephew, Robert, count of Artois; John, count of Flanders; John, eldest son of the duke of Burgundy, and Thibaut, king of Navarre. Prince

Edward of England and Charles of Anjou, king of Sicily and Naples, were to join the fleet on the voyage.

Embarked from Aigues Mortes on the 1st of July, 1270, the expedition was beaten about and dispersed by a violent storm, and was with difficulty rallied at Cagliari, where the squadrons from Naples and Genoa came to join it. It appeared on the 17th of July before cape Carthage, and disembarked the same day. "Friday," wrote St. Louis to the abbot of St. Denis, "we landed. We advanced as far as the ancient city of Carthage and encamped."

In the midst of the ruins of the famous city, some new constructions had just arisen and some fortifications still unfinished defended this important strategetic point. In these, the Mussulmans reposed confidence, and, rushing upon the shore near by with cries of *djehed* (holy war), put forth earnest efforts to drive the Franks back to the sea. The latter, guided and urged forward by their king, who, as at Damietta, was the first to leap on shore, struck down the defenders and took Carthage and the neighboring village of the Marsa. They then encamped and fortified their position, waiting for power to march upon Tunis, which movement the whole army earnestly demanded.

Meanwhile the Tunisians were solidly organized for defence in their capital, and were scouring the country around with fleet cavalry. They came to weary the Christians by incessant attacks, and constantly refused a regular battle. These partial combats, multiplying without cessation, had soon reduced to extremities an army covered with iron armor, under a burning sun reflected by the sand, and already vanquished by this torrid climate with its brackish water and fiery tornadoes.

The courage of the bravest flagged. Consternation reigned throughout the camp. Diseases broke out. The living saw with fright the increase of mortality. They soon became unable to bury their dead. The plague speedily filled the trenches of the encampment with heaps of dead bodies, and the ancient city became a vast putrid cemetery.

Philip of France was sick; John, his brother, almost dead, was borne upon his bed to a vessel in the harbor; the counts of Vendôme, of Marche, of Montmorency; and a multitude of barons and knights had given up the ghost. The implacable and devouring breath of summer and the incursions of the Saracens continued their work,—but Charles of Anjou did not arrive.

St. Louis, always active, redoubled his efforts to animate the discouraged, to relieve and heal the sick, to console the dying and to superintend the burial of the dead. He was attacked in his turn. He withstood the attack at first and struggling against the disease, devoted himself to his usual duties a whole week. But his body, enfeebled by age and by the fatigues of government and war, finally broke down, and when the death of his unfortunate son, John Tristan, was announced to him, he submitted to the blow, and put himself upon his bed to rise no more.

He ceased not, nevertheless, to maintain his self-possession to his last hour, occupying himself almost incessantly with the sufferings of others without complaining of his own; turning his thoughts where his presence was wanting and dictating with a singular serenity the most noble instructions for his son and successor.

While he was dying, on the 24th of August, two embassadors from Michael Palæologus, emperor of Constantinople, arrived at the camp. They came to implore the good offices and influence of St. Louis with Charles of Anjou, whose ambition was disquieting Byzantium. As they were refused admission to the presence of the dying sovereign, he heard the conversation, ordered them to be introduced, received them with cordiality and promised to speak to his brother, if he should live to see him again.

On the following day (August 25th), at three o'clock P. M., lying upon a bed covered with ashes, uttering his last words to his sons and his barons who were sobbing around him, giving his last thought to his dear kingdom ("doulx royaume"), and his last look to the heavens above, Saint Louis crossed his hands over his breast, closed his eyes and died.

At that very moment, Charles of Anjou was entering into the gulf. He disembarked, and, crossing the camp in gloomy silence, ran to the tent of his brother; confused and groaning aloud, he cast himself despairingly upon the dead body and there prayed for a long time.

He then assembled the chiefs of the army and showed himself to the soldiers, encouraging all by cheerful words and by the distribution of the succors which he had brought. A gleam of hope and confidence seemed to pass over this vast camp in grief and mourning. They gained courage and fought still during two other months.

The Moors, broken in various encounters and especially in a great battle between the Goletta and Tunis, for whose siege the crusaders prepared, were expecting to see their capital invested and carried by assault. El Mostancer, anxious in his turn, decided to obtain a truce and the departure of his enemies on any terms, and he accordingly made to the crusaders a proposition for an accommodation.

Most of the princes and Christian barons were favorably disposed to it; but it was the cherished purpose of Philip, the Bold, proclaimed king, to achieve the chosen work of his father, whose ideas he hoped victoriously to realize. It seemed to him easy to take Tunis and to raze it to the ground, and thus not be obliged to leave there a garrison. But he yielded to the reflection that his presence was needed in France, and to the counsels of the kings of Navarre and of Sicily. He consented to the peace in a memorable treaty, which was signed the 20th of November, 1270, of which the following are the principal clauses:

1. A truce of fifteen years between the belligerents.
2. To secure to their subjects reciprocal immunities and privileges.
3. The liberty of reciprocal commerce.
4. Free exercise of worship accorded to the Christians and to their priests; the building of churches upon grounds given by the king of Tunis.
5. The payment by the king of Tunis to the king

of France and to his allies, the expenses of the war estimated at 210,000 ounces of gold; one-half of which should be paid immediately and the other half in two equal payments respectively at the end of the next two solar years; the king of Tunis to furnish securities for the Christian merchants established in his states.

6. The king of Tunis, "calif and prince of believers," should pay immediately to Charles of Anjou, king of Sicily, the arrears of the tribute to which Tunis had been for a long time subjected, and he should pay in the future the double of the previous tribute.

This treaty was declared common to all Christian governments and lords that took part in the war; that is to France, to almost all Italy and to England. It was honorable and advantageous to France and to Christendom; but did not satisfy the soldiers who could profit but little by the indemnities given, and were disappointed at being deprived of the privilege of taking and pillaging the rich and flourishing city of Tunis, as a compensation for their many sufferings.

Philip III ordered the camp to be broken up and the anchors to be raised, and, while the prince of England, recently arrived, was sailing towards Palestine, the son of St. Louis, with his shattered fleet and the remnant of his army, was on his way to his kingdom, where he speedily assumed the reins of the government.

CHAPTER IV.

Modern History from the Sixteenth to the Middle of the Nineteenth Century.

SECTION I.

FALL OF THE HAFSITES.—EXPEDITION OF CHARLES V AND THE SPANISH DOMINATION.

FROM the expedition of St. Louis to that of Charles V, the dynasty of the Beni Hafs had the intelligence and tact to maintain its hereditary and governmental system and, in spite of many struggles with competitors and the revolts of several provinces, it succeeded in elevating Tunisia to the rank of one of the most flourishing Mussulman states of the middle age. In 1533 (940 H.), Muley Hassañ, son of Muley Mohammed, ascended the throne, though he was the youngest of all his brothers. He owed his promotion primarily to the influence of his mother. To establish himself upon the throne, he had all his elder brothers put to death with the exception of Rashid, who took refuge at Algiers under Khayreddine, the celebrated Barbarossa, whose protection he implored and obtained.

Two brothers, or at least supposed to be such, both famous pirates, are designated by historians of that time under the name of Barbarossa. The common explanation is that they received this epithet on account of the color of their beard; but it is more probable that *Barbarossa* is a corruption of *Baba-aroudj*, meaning *the eldest*. According to most historians, they were born on the island of Mitylene, and their father was a renegade Sicilian; but, according to Brantome, these two adventurers were only French knights, who, after having formed part of a maritime expedition, sent to the east by king Louis XII to aid the Venetians against the Turks, embraced Islamism and became pirates to gratify their desire to play a great part in the world.

However this may be, they became corsairs at the end of the fifteenth century, and, after having demonstrated their power and spread terror in all the Mediterranean, they succeeded in taking possession of Algiers, which they presented to the grand sultan, in order that his sovereignty might be a shield to them in their predatory career. Khayreddine, becoming king of Algeria, obtained from the sultan the title of captain Bashaw or grand admiral of the Turkish empire.

Khayreddine received Rashid with an eagerness and benevolence so much the more marked, as the presence of the unhappy prince seemed to furnish him an excellent opportunity to realize his project for the annexation of Tunisia to Algeria. He escorted him then to Constantinople, and urged Soliman I to serve his own interest in the name of Rashid; in other words, to conquer Tunisia and take possession of it under the pretext of protecting the unfortunate prince. This plan was approved, and an imposing fleet, commanded by Khayreddine, appeared before Tunis with the distinct object boldly set forth of placing Rashid upon the throne. But, before raising anchor, the prince was cast into a prison where he died.

On the arrival of the fleet at Bizerta, the inhabitants offered their coöperation for the execution of a plan so much the more popular, as Muley Hassan was detested. Barbarossa then sailed for the Goletta. The Tunisians received him with joy, and, believing that he came to drive Muley Hassan from the throne, they took up arms and themselves drove the detested tyrant out of the city; and then invited Barbarossa to intervene for the restoration of their legitimate prince, Rashid.

The way was thus open for Barbarossa. He landed with about 10,000 men; marched up to Tunis; fortified himself in the Kasbah (fortress); turned its cannon upon the city, and replied with shot and ball to the summons of the people tumultuously assembled and already suspecting his treachery. The entire city rose in arms at the sound of his cannon. Three thousand six hundred Tunisians fell under the fire or by the sword of the Turks, who, entrenched at the Kasbah, readily overcame all opposition. Barbarossa, after this demonstration of his force, proclaimed the fall of the Hafsite dynasty, and assumed the government in the name of the Sublime Porte. He then accorded a general amnesty, scattered gold about in profusion, and sent emissaries to gain by presents the most warlike tribes in the interior, and a garrison to occupy Cairwan.

Muley Hassan, wandering a long time in the environs of Tunis and in the interior of the kingdom, vainly attempted to unite his partisans to continue the struggle. He then fled to Constantine; and there, under the advice of a Spanish renegade named Ximea or Jimea, decided to ask the aid of Charles V, engaging on his part to second the intervention of the emperor with a numerous body of native troops.

Already dissatisfied with the conquest of Tunis by Barbarossa, which in his opinion endangered Christendom, Charles V resolved to strike a terrible blow for the overthrow of the Mussulman power, newly established at Tunis. The pope, the king of Portugal and the order of Malta concerted with him, and immense preparations were made in the arsenals of Spain and Italy.

Khayreddine, alarmed at this news, claimed the aid of the Sultan Soliman, who induced him to rely solely on his own forces. He then put forth his efforts for the most effectual resistance. He fortified the Goletta; protected it on the northeast by a wall, which was incompletely built for the want of time; but which was rendered useful by means of piles and bags of sand; the wall was pierced with embrasures for cannon; the canal was enlarged to protect ships which were not in action, and twelve were brought there for safety; 7,000 Turkish and Tunisian troops were put under the command of the renegade Jew,

Sinan, and of another renegade, Ali, familiarly styled in Italian, *Caccia Diavolo*, Devil Chase. Most of this work was performed by Christian slaves, kept in awe by the clubs of their Mussulman masters. In all Tunisia, the proclamation went forth: "*El djehed fy sebillilahi*, — *The holy war in the path of God.*"

Charles V left Barcelona the 31st of March, 1535, with the forces belonging to Spain, Flanders, Portugal and Genoa. He was met at Cagliari by some galleys from Malta and Italy. In all, there were 400 sail, and from 27,000 to 33,000 troops.*

The combined expedition arrived off Point Carthage, and a landing was effected on the site of the ancient city in the latter part of June. The troops were speedily employed in opening trenches and in other offensive operations before the Goletta. Sinan defended that place with a vigor equal to that of the attack. The army of Charles had much to endure from the incursions of the Arab horsemen, and especially from the excessive heat, which overpowered the soldiers under arms in the midst of interminable combats.

Muley Hassan arrived at the imperial camp, affecting the greatest respect for the emperor and filled with confusion at bringing with him, instead of the numerous troops which he had promised, only a hundred horsemen. Charles received him with the haughty politeness of a sovereign.

On the 14th of July a decisive attack was made by land and by sea. The Goletta fell. The powerful

---

* For further details, see Robertson's Charles V, and Rousseau's Annales Tunisiennes.

cannon of Charles broke the ramparts, making a great breach, by which Charles, the Infanta don Louis and Muley Hassan entered together. The Turkish garrison bravely defended itself, and then withdrew towards Tunis, covering the borders of the intervening lake with its dead and wounded. More than 80 galleys, with about 300 cannon, fell into the hands of the conquerors.

On the 17th, or, according to others, on the 20th, of July, 1535, the army began its march against Tunis along the right shore of the lake. Khayreddine, at the head of 10,000 veterans, encountered the emperor near what is at present called Rowena (the *half-way house*), between the Goletta and Tunis, where beasts find water, and men coffee and nauseous drugs at their pleasure. The Christian army, whose discipline it was almost impossible to maintain, under a torrid sun which produced a parching thirst, promptly came to order in presence of the enemy. After a fierce onset, Khayreddine fell back, defeated, upon Tunis.

There were then about 30,000[*] Christian slaves in the prisons of Tunis. During the last battle they revolted; broke their chains; killed their jailers; armed themselves as best they could, and took possession of the kasbah (citadel) under the orders of the commander of Malta, Simeoni, who planned and directed this glorious *coup de main* for their deliverance from thraldom.

Khayreddine, discouraged, withdrew, accompanied by some troops, into the interior, and, finally abandon-

[*] Some authors say 70,000, but this seems to be an exaggeration.

ing the kasbah, his treasures and his women, he directed his course towards Algiers. Tunis capitulated, and Charles V was received under the walls of the city by a deputation which came to offer him the keys and to implore his mercy.

He entered Tunis as a conqueror, covered with a magnificent armor, which is still preserved in the museum at Madrid. Terror-stricken, the Mussulmans shrank from view; Christian slaves, delirious with joy, rent the air with their huzzas, to which were added in strange contrast the ferocious yells of the soldiers, who, in spite of the positive orders of Charles, already scented the prey of every sort which this great city offered them. The pillage lasted three days, and, without speaking of the other cruel excesses committed by a soldiery whose sufferings had aroused their fiercest passions, it is sufficient to say that 70,000 persons were massacred. We involuntarily recall the not less horrible entrance into Jerusalem of Godrey of Bouillon, in 1099, when the victorious crusaders literally inundated the streets of the city with *blood ankle deep*, says a historian of that time.

Muley Hassan, reëstablished upon his throne, began by a memorable treaty which recognized his entire dependence on the emperor. The following are the principal clauses of this treaty signed on the 6th of August, 1535:

1. The unconditional liberation of all Christian slaves.

2. The right of Europeans to unrestricted trade at Tunis, to live there and build churches.

3. The engagement of the kings of Tunis to give no countenance whatever to corsairs.

4. The abandonment of the Goletta to Spain, and the payment of an annual tribute of 12,000 gold crowns for the maintenance of the Spanish garrison of this city.

5. A perpetual concession to Spain of the coral fishery upon all the Tunisian coast.

6. The recognition of the perpetual sovereignty of Spain, shown by an annual present of twelve horses and twelve falcons.

7. In return for all these engagements, Spain promised to protect Tunis against all other powers.

At his departure, Charles V left at the kasbah 200 picked men to be under the orders of Muley Hassan, until the entire pacification of the country. He assembled all the cavalry at Rades, and ordered them and the materials of war to be put on board the ships. He then returned to his headquarters at Carthage, and, before sailing, directed the construction of a strong fortress at the Goletta, and 1,000 men were left under the orders of Mendoza, and twelve galleys under Antony Doria.

Charles V reached Trapani in Sicily, and from there sent an expedition of 5,000 men against Media. A storm prevented the success of his plans, but the Spanish fleet occupied the cities of Bizerta and Bona, where it left garrisons.

Soon, however, the restored power of Muley Hassan was shaken by insurrectionary movements among his subjects. The natives could not bear to see their prince appear as the vassal of an infidel monarch.

Susa and Cairwan revolted. In the latter city, a scherif named Arfa, laid pretentions to the throne, and found numerous partisans.

Muley Hassan asked anew the aid of Charles. The viceroy of Sicily sent ships and troops against Susa; but the Spaniards were defeated there, and suffered a severe loss. It was only two years afterwards that the illustrious admiral Andrew Doria avenged this loss and placed Susa under Muley Hassan. He also took possession of Kalibia, Sfax and Monastir, and left a Spanish garrison in the last-named place. It was by the aid of this garrison that Muley Hassan attempted to re-take Cairwan. Abandoned by his Mussulman soldiers at the moment of the combat, he had to retreat under the efficient protection of the Spaniards.

When, subsequently, the garrison of Monastir was withdrawn by Spain, that city, as well as Kalibia, Susa and Sfax revolted again and called to their aid the famous Turkish corsair, Dragut. But Doria returned to reduce Monastir; and Susa of its own accord came again under the jurisdiction of Muley Hassan.

The latter, to put an end to the rebellions always breaking out, once more solicited in person the aid of Charles. He departed in 1542, leaving the government to his son, Muley Hamida. Profiting by the absence of his father, Hamida had himself proclaimed king of Tunis, despite the protest of the garrison at the Goletta, which, however, was too feeble to resist him.

On receiving this news, Muley Hassan hastened

from Sicily with 500 Mussulman soldiers and 2,000 ill-assorted Christian recruits. Contrary to the wise counsels of Don Francisco de Tabar, the Spanish governor at the Goletta, he insisted upon giving battle before Tunis. He was defeated and taken prisoner. His son Hamida had his eyes put out and then let him depart for Sicily and Italy, where he died in 1545.

The garrison at the Goletta, reïnforced by 1,500 men sent from Naples, drove off Muley Hamida and put in his place his uncle Muley Abd-el-Malek, a respectable prince who lived to enjoy his throne but thirty-six days, and was succeeded by his son Muley Mohammed.

Muley Hamida, drawing back to the interior of the country, and fomenting everywhere civil war, took possession of Monastir. He then marched boldly upon Tunis and drove off his cousin, who fled to the Goletta and lost permanently his throne. The corsair Dragut profited by these events to make Media the base of his operations in Tunisia, and take possession of Gerba.

In 1551, Don Juan de Vega, viceroy of Sicily, came and besieged Media. The corsair arrived too late to defend it. The city capitulated, and Don Alvar de Vega, the son of Don Juan, maintained himself there some time, but was finally overcome by a revolt of the garrison, which took for its chief a certain *Aponti*, and lived by pillaging the country around. Charles V decided at length to abandon this place. The fortifications were destroyed and the garrison was recalled in 1553.

In 1560, king Philip II resolved to destroy at Tripoli the power of Dragut. Don Juan de la Cerda, duke of Medina-Cœli, came with 113 ships and 14,000 men to take possession of Gerba, where he was detained many weeks by bad weather. This delay saved Tripoli. For the Turkish admiral, Piali Bashaw,* hastening with an imposing fleet at the call of Dragut, surprised, while anchored in the roadstead of Gerba, the Spanish ships which had not time to escape. Nineteen galleys and fourteen transports were taken, and 5,000 Spaniards were reduced to slavery.

Don Alvar de Sande remained upon the island with his brave band. After many weeks of cruel privations, they resolved to force their way to the shore through the enemy and embark in the first vessel. The little band marched out of the entrenchments full of courage and fought with heroic tenacity, but was speedily outnumbered and overpowered. Its commander, one of the last survivors, leaped upon a ship sunk in the harbor, and there encountered single-handed a multitude of assailants. His heroism excited the admiration of the barbarians that surrounded him. They saved his life and conducted him to the bashaw, to whom alone he would consent to deliver up his sword. The latter showed him the most marked tokens of respect.

The unfortunate companions of Sande were massacred to a man. Their skulls were then collected and arranged in the form of a pyramid, and consti-

---

* This title is variously spelled and pronounced; *pashaw* is Persian and Turkish; *bashaw* Arabic and Moorish.

tuted for nearly three centuries a mournful trophy of which Mussulman fanaticism boasted, and which, standing out in bold relief upon the shore, appeared to every Christian traveller a monument of shame and humiliation. In 1846, the Catholic bishop of Tunis obtained, through the mediation of the consul general of France, permission to have this monument destroyed. The sad and glorious materials of which the *tower of skulls* was constructed were carefully collected and interred; and, on my visit to Gerba in 1866, as I surveyed the scenes of these events, it was a satisfaction to know that the fraternal grave finally and forever protects from the inclement elements and human passions the remains of those brave men nobly confounded in heroism and in death.

Muley Hamida, constantly involved in difficulty with the tribes of the interior and with the garrison at the Goletta, had soon before him an enemy much more formidable. To rule Tunisia had been the constant dream of the masters of Algiers, and this dream had already been for a moment realized by Khayreddine Barbarossa. Ali Bashaw wished to continue and satisfy that traditionary ambition. He invaded the Tunisian territory, encountered and completely routed Hamida near Beja. The defeated king sought and received protection among the Spaniards at the Goletta, while Ali took possession of the kasbah and assumed to˙ be the supreme ruler of the country. He then returned to Algiers (1570), leaving for his lieutenant the Kaid Ramdan, with about 2,000 men as a garrison.

Philip II, alarmed at this manifestation of the power

of Algiers, hesitated not to yield to the entreaties of Muley Hamida, and sent against Tunis a fleet with a complement of 20,000 men, under the orders of Don John, of Austria, natural son of Charles V. Philip, believing that the African establishments were not of sufficient advantage to Spain to justify the great expense incurred for their maintenance, thought it the part of wisdom to give them up, to destroy all the cities in his possession, and finally to abandon the Goletta itself.

But Don John planned for the formation of a Tunisian kingdom for his own interest and for the advantage of the Christian world; and the court of Rome and the tendencies of the time encouraged him in that idea. He entered then Tunis as it was abandoned by the Turks; placed there a garrison of 4,000 men; put upon the throne Muley Mohammed, a brother of Muley Hamida, who refused to accept the power on the conditions proposed to him; he strengthened the fortifications at the Goletta, and built the new fort Borge Gedid, between the city and the lake, in order better to command the city.

He appointed count Cerballon governor of Tunis, and Porto Carrero commander at the Goletta. He also left a Spanish garrison at Bizerta. Then Don John returned into Spain, where he hoped that Philip II would sanction his plans for the government of Tunis; but soon events justified the anticipations of the king.

Spanish rule could not be of long duration at Tunis. To maintain it, would require an organization altogether more powerful than for the conquest of the country, and Spain had neither the means nor the disposition to make great sacrifices for this object. The religious sentiments of the Tunisians were shocked; their habits and customs were disturbed, and their pride wounded by the infidel rulers. Everywhere and at each instant, they encountered in their streets, and sometimes even in their houses and their mosques, the insolence and presumption of their masters. They were compelled to see, arrogantly seated by the side of their prince, the Spanish governor of Tunis, who they knew controlled their affairs and imposed his opinions and decisions on their country. The display of the Catholic worship was to them little less shocking and offensive than idolatry itself, and their ears were ever pained by the incessant peals of bells, whose hated sound seemed to pursue them without mercy. Thus agonized, the Tunisians waited and prayed for an occasion to take their revenge.

SECTION II.

Turkish Domination, 1574-1650.—The Deys, 1590-1702.

On learning of the establishment of the Spaniards at Tunis, the Turkish sultan Selim resolved to drive them off. In the spring of 1574, he sent against them a considerable fleet under the orders of Sinan Bashaw, a famous admiral and conqueror, who was, according to several historians, only a Milanese renegade of the illustrious family of the Visconti. The former Dey of Algiers, the same person whose rule at Tunis Spain had broken up, had the title of captain-bashaw and lieutenant-commander. The fleet made a murderous but ineffective assault upon the Spanish fortification at Tabarca, and then appeared before the Goletta. A vast encampment, powerfully entrenched, was immediately established, and the attack was begun with vigor.

While the garrison at the Goletta, slightly protected by its ramparts against the formidable artillery of Sinan, made up for its inferiority of numbers and means by an admirable courage and activity, the Spanish garrison at Tunis, despairing of its ability to maintain itself in the vast and dilapidated fortifications of that great city, withdrew to fort Borge Gedid, constructed, by order of Don John, just out of the city on the right of the Marine, and there maintained itself for a long time with great energy against the attacks of the lieutenants of Sinan.

But at length the Goletta was carried by general assault. Sinan Bashaw had all the garrison and the inhabitants of the place put to the edge of the sword, sparing only the Spanish governor, Porto Carrero. Then the fort at Tunis was taken in its turn; but the garrison made a bold sally and, passing successfully through the hostile ranks, took up a menacing position upon the borders of the lake. A terrible combat ensued. Almost the entire army of Sinan, composed of the best Mussulman troops, fell upon these brave Spaniards, who were finally hemmed in and overpowered. All were massacred except two hundred artillerymen, who were made slaves.

Cerballon, the Spanish governor at Tunis, Porto Carrero, of the Goletta, and Mohammed-el-Hafsy, the last Hafsite, were the only persons spared by Sinan. The first was claimed by Spain and the pope, and was exchanged for many Mussulmans of high rank detained in Europe. The other two were sent to the sultan, and died at Constantinople.

Before leaving Tunis, Sinan sought to organize and establish Turkish rule. He left 4,000 men divided into forty companies, each of which was under the orders of a chief, bearing the title of *dey*. The supreme government was entrusted to a bashaw-bey, assisted by a council of the regency called *the divan*. All the details of the military and civil administration were carefully defined. The military government of Tunis belonged to the bashaw. *Agas* were delegated to govern the cities or to exercise by proxy the military authority of *the deys*. Prayers were to be henceforth offered in the mosques in the name of the reigning Turkish sultan, and his name was also to be struck upon the coins of the country.

But this organization did not long continue. The military rose against the civil authorities; overturned the divan; massacred almost all the members of it; instituted a new divan, and declared that the president of it should be the military chief and supreme commander under the title of *dey*.

The ottoman porte, whose representative *(the bashaw-bey,)* was driven off several times, had succeeded in reëstablishing another delegate of its authority on the following conditions: The offices of bashaw and of bey should henceforth be separated; the bashaw should be changed every three years, and should take no direct part in the administration; a bey, independent of the bashaw, should have the control of the finances, and should collect the imports under the authority of the dey, the chief of the divan and of the troops.

"But the beys," says Mr. J. Marcel, "did not long remain in that state of dependence and inferiority. By degrees their influence increased, either by means of the considerable sums of money which passed into their hands, or by their habitual relations with the troops, which accompanied them in their fiscal expeditions, or by bonds of friendship and alliance which they had the opportunity to form with the most powerful chiefs of the tribes in the interior of the regency; soon all the power passed into their hands, and they left but little influence for the divan and the dey."

During nearly a century the history of Tunis offers only a monotonous spectacle of conflicts for power, complicated with all the intrigues and bloody catastrophies which are their natural consequence. Without troubling ourselves with a confused mass of uninteresting details, it will suffice to notice several remarkable events which distinguished the domination of the deys until 1705, which is the date of the definite establishment of the beys.

It was under Otman Dey (1593–1610), that a great number of Moors, driven from Spain by Philip III, came to establish themselves in Tunisia. Depositories of the industrial and agricultural traditions of the flourishing Saracenic kingdoms of the middle age, they induced considerable activity at Tunis in favor of the cultivation of olive and mulberry trees, and of the manufacture of wool and silk, and formed important settlements and centres of business at Zaughan, Testour, Medgezel Bab and Soliman.

In 1605, the plague desolated Tunis for the first time, and the little island of Zimbra, situated near cape Bou, gained some notoriety for a veritable siege which the crew of five Maltese galleys, stranded there, sustained against the Tunisians. A merchant ship succeeded in saving most of the sailors. The rest were made slaves. During this same year, Count Savary de Breves, embassador from France to Constantinople, arrived in Tunis in company with a Turkish envoy, Mustapha-aga, to claim the execution in Tunisia of a treaty concluded between king Henry IV and the sultan.

The object of this mission could be accomplished only by encountering innumerable difficulties and dangers, which Count Savary met with admirable tact and firmness. While Count Savary was at Tunis, 1,400 men coming in three Maltese and seven Sicilian galleys, landed at Hammamet, a city on the eastern coast; after taking possession of that place, they were soon overpowered and massacred to a man, and many of their heads were afterwards exposed on the walls of the kasbah at Tunis, and savagely drawn through the streets.

It was in 1607, under Otman Bey, that St. Vincent de Paul, an honored name in Christian history, after serving two years as a slave, succeeded in escaping in a small vessel and reached France, where he became the magnanimous benefactor of foundlings and of the sick and unfortunate of every kind. Putting forth earnest appeals, he organized an association of devoted Christian women, whom he drew into the service of humanity. The members of that association were called *sisters of charity*, and their usefulness I have had an opportunity to observe in several oriental cities. At Tunis, these devoted females are known only to be honored for their deeds of mercy and beneficence done without regard to religious or national distinctions.

Yousef Dey (1610–1637), successor of Otman, administered vigorously the government of Tunis, which prospered during his reign. The bridge at Tebourba and the mosque which bears his name, are monuments of his time. Under Yousef Dey, the power of the beys greatly increased, owing to the intelligence, energy and popularity of Morad Bey, a Corsican renegade, who, in consequence of eminent services rendered at Tunis, and of victories over the Algerines, solicited and obtained from Constantinople the title of bashaw. His son Hamouda continued his work, and became so influential and respected that the Arabs of the interior had no idea of any other government at Tunis than his.

It was under Yousef Dey, that the city of Marseilles sent against Tunis seven ships, armed at its expense and commanded by a knight of Malta, to obtain compensation for damage done to its commerce by Tunisian corsairs. The compensation sought was accorded. In 1619, the island of Gerba, before belonging to Tripoli, was annexed to Tunis.

In 1624, the capucin fathers were first established at Tunis under the name of *procurers of slaves*. They devoted themselves to solacing and consoling unfortunate Christians, detained in the baths or condemned to ruder labors. It was finally under Yousef Dey that the states general of Holland concluded their first treaty with Tunis. We must add that it was Morad Dey who founded the present city of Porto Farina, peopling it with Moors from Andalusia.

In 1662, under Hadj Mustapha, England signed her first treaty with Tunis, and Holland her second treaty; but it appears that the conditions of these treaties were not promptly observed, for in 1665, admiral Robert Black bombarded Porto Farina to secure the liberation of all the English and Dutch slaves. From 1662, England and Holland began to have consuls at Tunis: which statement is corroborated by an article in a treaty signed about the same time by the duke of Beaufort, a French admiral, authorizing the consul of France to represent all commercial nations in Tunis except England and Holland.

Under the government of the dey Shaban, subsequently deposed by the influence of Morad Bey, the French admiral, who was the marquis of Martel, came to secure the fulfilment of the stipulations made with the duke of Beaufort. At this time, the two brothers, Mohammed Bey and Morad Bey, irritated by the resistance of the divan which had just named as dey against their wishes Hadj Ali-el-Las, left Tunis and went to Zaughan to establish a camp, at the head of which they marched against the army commanded by El Las and by his creature Mohammed Aga, just elected bey. The two victorious brothers imposed their wishes on the divan and had Hadj Mami Gemral appointed dey.

Another French squadron arrived in 1675, under the orders of the marquis of Rully, to make a demonstration before the Goletta in favor of the Christians, who were subjected to great sufferings in the midst of these domestic troubles. Morad Bey left at his death three sons, Mohammed, Ali and Ramadan.

After numerous struggles without historic interest, each of these brothers came successively into power. Ramadan Bey was dethroned and killed by his nephew, Morad, son of Ali. Ibrahim-el-Scherif assassinated him and took his place. The last was driven off by the Algerines, who renewed their ambitious efforts to reduce Tunisia and bring it under their jurisdiction.

To his place, the divan and the army elected Houssein Ben Ali, son of Ali, a renegade Greek according to some, and a Corsican according to others, from whom sprang the dynasty of the reigning family at Tunis.

SECTION III.

THE BEYS OF TUNIS, 1705–1869.

Houssein Ben Ali, founder of the actual dynasty called from his name Houssenite, contrived to get rid of his competitor for the throne, Ibrahim-el-Scherif. He enticed him into the regency with the promise that he would abrogate in his favor, and then put him to death. His reign was, however, peaceful and prosperous. He selected for his treasurer and confident a Christian slave, to whom he showed the strongest tokens of friendship. Treaty stipulations with the principal European powers, including one with France in 1720, greatly extended the commerce of Tunis.

He had named for his successor his nephew Ali Bey, when unexpectedly he had a direct heir by a late marriage with a Genoese slave. But, by means of gold distributed among the members of the divan, and rich presents sent to Constantinople, he succeeded in having this child, which was named Mohammed Bey, recognized at Tunis and at the Porte as the legitimate heir to the throne. He afterwards had two other children, Mohammed and Ali.

Meanwhile his nephew Ali Bey, whom he at first designated as his successor, pretended to be resigned to his fate, and accepted with expressions of gratitude to his uncle the title of bashaw, and then withdrew among the mountains of the interior and raised up a rebellion in 1728. He was beaten in the first battle by his uncle. Then going to Algiers and returning with large reinforcements, he defeated his uncle, who fled first to Cairwan, then to Susa, and finally sought refuge upon Algerine territory. But the unfortunate Houssein was assassinated upon his way to Algiers by Younas Bey, the son of his nephew and rival Ali.

Ali Bey-Bashaw was planning to enjoy his usurped throne, when the same ambition, which had urged him to deeds of violence, armed his two sons Younas and

Mohammed against each other. Younas was to be arrested at the instigation of Mohammed. He entrenched himself in the kasbah at Tunis, where he was besieged by the soldiers of his father, from whom he escaped and fled to Algiers. Mohammed, then putting a younger brother into prison to prevent any competition from him, was recognized as the heir presumptive to the Tunisian throne.

Meanwhile, Baba-Ali-Aga, the newly elected dey of Algiers, having once been insulted while on an embassy at Tunis, by Younas Bey, and seeing that prince then a fugitive in Algeria, sought revenge for that affront by inducing the bey of Constantine to place upon the throne of Tunis the legitimate heir of Houssein-Bey-Ali. Ali-Bashaw was defeated and strangled, and Mohammed, the eldest son of Houssein, was crowned bey of Tunis in 1756. Mohammed was fitted to elevate the country, half-ruined by internal dissensions, but he reigned only two years and left at his death in 1759, two young children, Mahmoud and Ismail.

The brother of Mohammed, Ali-Bey, second son of Houssein-Ben-Ali, mounted upon the throne with the express condition of restoring it to his eldest nephew when the latter should come of age. But he studiously kept his nephew in the shade and brought before the public his own son Hamouda, for whom he obtained the title of bashaw and commander of the troops. Hamouda managed so shrewdly that at the death of his father, his cousins, who were the legitimate heirs, were the first to recognize and salute him as bey in 1782. Ali-Bey reigned twenty-three years. The tranquillity of his reign was disturbed only by difficulties with France, begun in 1770.

Corsica had just been annexed to France. Before this event, that island formed a part of the republic of Genoa, and was in open hostility to Tunis. After it became a part of France, it was natural to suppose that its ships would enjoy the same privileges as French ships. But the Tunisian privateers, in disregard of this principle, captured many of them and imprisoned the crews. The cabinet of Versailles protested and demanded satisfaction. Ali Bey gave a haughty and unsatisfactory reply. Other circumstances served to disturb the relations between the two countries. French ships were captured while engaged in the fisheries at Calle, and the captain of a French mercantile ship was insulted by a Tunisian corsair named Souleyman-el-Gerba.

Three ships of the line speedily appeared in the waters of the Goletta. They took on board the French consul, and put all the French ships that were at anchor in the roadstead in order of battle. During twenty-five days, they kept the Goletta in a state of blockade, and were joined on the 21st of June, 1770, by a squadron of sixteen ships under the orders of the count de Breves. The admiral made the following demands: First, the recognition of Corsica as a part of France; 2d, the restitution of all ships and slaves, even those taken before the annexation of Corsica to France; 3d, the continuation of the privilege of the coral fishery in favor of France at Calle and Tabarca; 4th, the punishment of Souley-

and the bey, and American commerce suffered greatly from Tunisian corsairs. The preliminaries of a treaty of peace were arranged in 1797 by Mr. Famin, a French merchant, and a definite treaty was signed by authorized American agents in the beginning of 1799. Much of the correspondence relative to this stipulation, preserved in the American consulate, is exceedingly interesting and instructive. The treaty cost the American government about $100,000, and one of its articles, since annulled, was, that the Tunisian government should receive a present of as many barrels of powder as it fired guns in saluting American men-of-war. The presents made and expenses incurred at the raising of the first American flag over the consulate, where it has since continued to wave, amounted to about $20,000.*

Hamouda Bashaw, on becoming firmly seated upon his throne, began to encounter and by degrees destroy the influence which the Turkish troops, styled janissaries, had maintained at Tunis, especially from the reign of Ali Bey. Some of their chiefs, under the title of prætorians, exercised a controlling and tyrannical influence. He gradually appointed for their chiefs, and to fill important offices about his person, devoted men, selected principally from among Geor-

* The correspondence about the treaty with the dey of Algiers, found in the first volume of the American archives at Tunis, is exceedingly interesting. The dey first demanded presents amounting to 2,561,000 Mexican dollars, and finally accepted $702,500. The account is signed thus: "Richard O'Brien, late master of the ship Dauphine, of Philadelphia, but was captured the 30th of July, 1785, fifty leagues to the westward of Lisbon, by an Algerine corsair of 34 guns and 450 men, and remained in captivity until the 11th of September, 1795. Redeemed in consequence of the peace made by the United States with Algiers."

gian and Circassian mamelukes (slaves) and European renegades; seizing every occasion to repress the abuses of this troublesome class of soldiers.

The Turks finally revolted on the 30th of August, 1811 (10th Shahban, 1225 H.), with the object of dethroning Hamouda and putting in his place a Turkish bey of their own choice, as at Algiers. A band of the conspirators was to assassinate Hamouda and all his court at the moment of their leaving the mosque. This plan failed because Hamouda did not leave his palace that day as usual. The Turks then believing that their plot was discovered, and not wishing to give time for effective measures to be taken against them, rose in rebellion the same day, and entrenched themselves in the kasbah to the number of about 3,000 men. They then elected a new bey and announced the event to the other garrisons within hearing by the firing of cannon, which was the concerted signal to be repeated from fortress to fortress throughout the regency.

But on receiving this news, the governor of Porto Farina, then minister of the navy, marched upon the Goletta with an army of Arabs and Zouaves, and the first minister of the bey entered Tunis with all the soldiers he could collect.

The Turks raised the Ottoman standard and declared their resolution to reëstablish the sovereignty of the porte. All the cannon of the city were pointed upon the kasbah, which valiantly sustained the fire. A cannonade of six hours was without result, when, at the suggestion of the French consul, some European artillerymen, then at Tunis, took charge of the cannon of the bey and speedily silenced the batteries of the kasbah. About 1,700 Turks left the citadel. The Tunisian troops had orders not to disturb them in their retreat. The Arabs, who hated the Turks, were charged to exterminate them in the country. They did not fail to do their work. The Turks defended themselves with signal valor among the mountains, but were soon overcome. The newly elected bey, the members of his government and his principal accomplices were detained until they had made all the confessions useful to Hamouda, and were then strangled. The Arabs received as their recompense all the rich spoils of their victims. The Turkish troops were thus annihilated by Hamouda Bashaw the same year as the mamelukes in Egypt by Mohammed Ali.

The reign of Hamouda Bashaw, which lasted thirty-three years, is the longest in Tunisian history, and is regarded, in spite of its stains of blood, as the most prosperous reign and the best administration of the Housseinite dynasty. Greedy of gain and given to excesses, but possessed of discrimination and firmness, Hamouda demonstrated superior tact and skill in administering the government of Tunisia. Respected at home and abroad, he occupied himself in developing the resources of the country. True, he favored piracy; but that was a branch of the administration at that period, and a convenient means of raising a revenue; in short, though a semi-barbarian, he inflicted as little evil in pursuing his policy and executing his plans, as was perhaps possible. Hamouda Bashaw died of poison on the last day of the great feast of Ramadan (September 15, 1814), and was succeeded by Otman Bey who, in his turn, was murdered on the 20th of December following.*

Sidi Mahmoud, who succeeded Otman Bey on the 21st of December, 1814, was the son of Mohammed Bey and the elder of the two princes whom the usurpation of their uncle, Ali Bey, had excluded from the throne. With Otman and his two sons perished the collateral branch descended from Ali Bey, and the power was restored to the elder and legitimate branch of the Housseinites.

An infant child of Otman, however, survived him, which was at once thrust into a subterranean dungeon at the Bardo, and under the care of his black nurse remained there forty-one years. On the ascension to the throne of Mohammed Bey in 1855, this child with a man's frame was removed, and is believed to be still living with his black nurse in a state of incurable idiocy.

Mahmoud reigned without éclat nine years. It was under his rule, in the month of April, 1816, that Lord Exmouth, coming from Algiers and proceeding to Tripoli, made at Tunis an imposing display of the sentiments of the Christian world shortly before explained at the Congress of Vienna. No European demonstration, unless we except that of the conquest of Algeria, which occurred many years afterwards, ever so humiliated Barbary insolence. In view of

---

* To enable our readers to form a clearer idea of the state of affairs in this regency in the year 1814, we give in Appendix A, some pertinent extracts from a valuable journal, preserved among the archives of the American consulate at Tunis. The entire journal, with explanatory notes, would constitute an excellent history of that period.

the cannon of a magnificent fleet, and the haughty demands of the British admiral, who had just humbled the dey of Algiers, a part of the Christian slaves were given up without ransom; others were purchased at a moderate price, and the bey made a written promise, which he did not keep, to abolish forever Christian slavery within his dominions.

In 1818, two English and French squadrons, under the orders of admirals Freemantle and Jurien, came in the name of all the European states with a formal and imposing summons for the bey to abolish immediately and forever piracy. Formal promises satisfied the admirals.

Houssein Bey ascended the throne in 1824. In 1825, he sent an embassador extraordinary to sit with the diplomatic corps at the coronation of Charles X, king of France. In 1826, a Dutch squadron appeared and obtained redress for certain grievances which had delayed the appointment and reception of Cæsar Nyssen as the consul from the Netherlands. In 1827, an old dispute was revived, and a rupture occurred between Tunis and Spain in regard to a Bremen ship conducted to Barcelona and sold there by a Tunisian corsair. This question remained open for an indefinite period, until the ideas of the beys of Tunis were modified and Spain was swept into another channel by the current of passing events.

It was in 1827, also, that the blockade of Algiers by the French fleet was denounced at Tunis. The bey and people, though humiliated as Mussulmans, were inwardly satisfied with the lesson thus given to their insolent neighbors and persistent enemies. The battle of Navarino, where the bey lost almost his entire navy, produced a profound sensation at Tunis. The people and court with enforced resignation became very respectful and courteous towards Europeans.

Finally Algiers was taken and Barbary piracy effectually and forever stopped. Houssein Bey sent a distinguished personage to compliment general Bourmonte in the citadel of Algiers. Besides a very natural sentiment of fear, he was probably influenced by political ambition to take that step which was a cause of reproach among all good Mussulmans. The union of Algeria and of Tunisia, under the Housseinite government, was always a cherished plan of the bey. Also, at a later period, he adopted with zeal the proposition of Marshal Clausel, offering the beylics of Constantine and of Oran to two Tunisian princes, on condition that they should become vassals and tributaries of France. Mustapha Bey, a brother of Houssein, would have become bey of Constantine, and Ahmed, a son of Mustapha Bey, of Oran. The convention was rejected by the French government, and the Tunisian troops which had already occupied provisionally Oran, returned to their country near the end of 1830 and the beginning of 1831.

Towards the middle of the reign of Houssein Bey (1829), occurred the fall of the prime minister Mustapha Bash Mameluke, who was in fact the virtual sovereign of the country. The extortion and waste, the pillage and lavish expenditure of the public treasure, had exhausted the finances of the country.

The expenses exceeded the receipts, and the crops failed. The prime minister made loans. But this was only a palliative. He then pledged and sold the future crops and received their value in advance. This system of imposing on the future the burdens and difficulties which belong to the present is unfortunately still in vogue in Tunisia. Its immediate results are commercial and financial crises, and bankruptcies more or less disguised, and its final consequence must be the ruin of the state.

There was then a financial crisis. Payments were to be made, and the bash-mameluke, seeing no means of making them, declared to the bey the government to be in a state of bankruptcy. Houssein until then had been careless, ostentatious and prodigal, supposing the riches of the country to be inexhaustible. He was amazed and astounded at the truth thus brought to his knowledge, and, seeing no remedy, wept like a child. It was at such a moment that a Circassian mameluke named Shekir, already keeper of the seal, but lost to view, like all the other dignitaries, in the dazzling presence of Mustapha, arose before his sovereign and, with a daring superior to that of the greatest military chieftain, offered to take upon himself the charge and responsibility of saving and relieving the state, on the condition of being invested with the necessary authority. Houssein removed from office the bash-mameluke and put in his place the intelligent and intrepid Circassian.

Shekir showed unusual tact and skill in fulfiling his engagement. By voluntary offers which he obtained by his own example and influence among the leading men of the state, he promptly sustained the credit of the government. Then regulating the payments and indemnities claimed by European merchants, he resolved on reforms that were indispensable to prevent the recurrence of similar catastrophes. He abolished the ancient costly and vicious military system, and organized regular troops. He inspected and controlled the expenses of the court, even those of the bey, which he brought under a sort of civil list. He regulated the imposts; made excursions through the interior of the country to encourage agriculture, and, in fine, labored heartily and intelligently for the prosperity and future of Tunisia; and he would probably have secured his objects for a considerable time, if his career of usefulness had not been cruelly interrupted. Shekir was destined to furnish a memorable example of the fate of men superior to their age, especially in Mussulman countries. When the decay of a country becomes irresistible by a tide of abuses and by a general deterioration of character, he who plans and labors to arrest it and resist the course of events, may at first excite astonishment and pass for a public benefactor; but soon he excites the jealousy and hatred of those on whom his firmness and decision are imposed. In time, these men become exasperated with their benefactor, and are like travellers fatally lured to their final sleep in the midst of mountain snows. If they lie down for repose in the mountain drifts, they are sure to die; and yet they madly beat off the compassionate hand that seeks to raise them up and urge them on. They end the struggle by getting rid of him who disturbs them and hinders them from taking their ease in the torpidity of death.

In 1831, Tunisia narrowly escaped a war with Sardinia, in consequence of an insult offered to the flag of a smuggler. A Sardinian squadron was anchored before Carthage, and the city of Tunis was profoundly agitated with the cry, "The holy war in the path of God." Through the intervention of Sir Thomas Reade, the British consul-general, and the prudent counsels of the kaid Ben-Ayad, Houssein Bey consented to give the satisfaction demanded, and a peace was concluded.

Houssein Bey was succeeded in 1835 by his brother Mustapha. His reign of two years is remarkable for nothing but for the disgrace and execution of Shekir. This minister was too patriotic and intelligent for the new bey and his short-sighted counsellors. He had effectually resisted and checked the retrograde movement of his country, and had inaugurated a progressive policy; but he had not so moulded the character of his countrymen as to secure the permanence and final success of his measures. The cause of his fall was the jealousy and defiance of Ahmed, who was a son of Mustapha, and also the bey of the camp and the presumptive heir to the throne. The pretext was, that the all-powerful prime minister was suspected of having plotted at Constantinople to overthrow the Housseinitès and reëstablish Turkish rule.

He was called to the Bardo, accused in haste, and condemned without being heard, by a sort of private council presided over by Ahmed. He was then given over to slaves and strangled; and forthwith the regency of Tunis resumed its old policy, which it still pursues to the very borders of death.

Ahmed Bey succeeded his father on the throne in October, 1837. This prince, praised in his life-time with much exaggeration, had some good points in his character. He was generous, though vain; and impulsive, rather than energetic. But he was not in our opinion a great statesman. He lacked the intelligence to understand the needs of his country. He did not manifest the spirit of integrity, nor a dignified and circumspect bearing in the exercise of power. He had not the habits of economy and watchfulness which alone can prevent a ruinous waste and an exhausted treasury. A great man or *an African Napoleon*, as some flatterers called him, comes not from a mania to play the soldier by fastening to the lacerated sides of an afflicted country, in addition to official vampires, the cupping glasses of an army, too large for the population and resources of the state, together with incessant bleeding from the follies, and especially from the shameful prodigality of the sovereign. Ahmed showed this weakness. He counteracted the reformatory measures adopted by Shekir, and thus hastened the decline and fall of his country.

I am aware that Ahmed Bey abolished slavery in his dominions, for which act he was called by a celebrated French poet, *the Friend of Humanity*. But in estimating the credit due him, we must not forget the influence of the civilized world, exerted especially through the French and English consuls, who were his political preceptors and powerful monitors. In making a demand for the surrender of a family of slaves that had taken refuge in the enclosure at Carthage, Ahmed was advised by the French diplomatist to escape from the difficulty, and astonish and gratify the civilized world by the abolition of slavery. Teachable and vain, Ahmed caught the idea, and improved the occasion to immortalize his name.

Our expressions may seem harsh. For to Ahmed Bey belongs the honor of having planned and executed the emancipation act, which had to encounter the prejudices, habits and individual interests of his country. Whatever may have been his weaknesses, he demonstrated in this reform a generosity and courage which demand expressions of gratitude and an honorable notice.

Born of a Christian mother, Ahmed showed himself friendly towards Europeans. A neighbor and friend of France, he favored the French and maintained intimate relations with the family of Louis Philippe. The dukes of Montpensier and Aumale, and the Prince de Joinville visited successively Tunis (1845), and had splendid receptions. Ahmed resolved to go himself into France. He embarked on the 5th of November, 1846, and returned to the Goletta the 30th of December following. Received as a veritable sovereign, he was distinguished for brilliant wit and pertinent repartees. He gave presents to the poor, and diamond decorations to his admirers. He expressed astonishment at what he saw, and a great desire to emulate it. He was the first Mussulman sovereign to visit Europe, and Europe ought to give him credit for this. As to the Mussulmans, they will never pardon him for not having made, on the contrary, a pilgrimage to Mecca.

France on her side seized every occasion to encourage and patronize Ahmed. In 1838, admiral de Lalande prevented, by the presence of his fleet, an attempt to land by the Turkish admiral Tahir Bashaw, who consoled himself by proceeding to occupy Tripoli in the name of the sultan. At the Tuilleries, Ahmed was received as a king, in spite of the protestations of the Ottoman embassador, and in exchanging decorations with him, the French government also implicitly recognized his sovereignty. Though France probably followed this course from a regard to her political views and interests, she has to sustain her the records of history. All the powers of Europe have since the eighteenth century treated directly with the beys, sending them embassies or receiving from them embassadors. The sovereignty of the Porte, purely nominal and religious, has never been political and effective except during the Turkish domination, which lasted only from 1574 to 1650.

Ahmed Bey reigned until 1855. His reign was more costly than useful. He had an army of 35,000 men, organized in European style and instructed by a French military mission, and directed by several colonels and by one brigadier-general. Large and commodious barracks were constructed; an extensive manufactory for woolen cloth was built at Tebourba, on the Majerda, and light-houses were erected at the entrance of the gulf, upon the islet of Cani and at Sidi-Bou-Said. Near by this village, the ancient hill of the Byrsa was ceded to France, which erected thereon the chapel of St. Louis. It is just to recall the solicitude and generosity of Ahmed at the breaking out of the cholera in 1849 and 1850; he hastened to supply the wants of the needy without regard to race, nation or religion. It was under Ahmed's reign, that a French missionary, the worthy and lamented abbot Bourgade, provided, by the sacrifice of his modest patrimony and by charitable contributions, the means of education and assistance for European residents in Tunis, by endowing the college of St. Louis, and furnishing a school and an infirmary under the care of the *Sisters of St. Joseph*. These humble germs of civilization have not been as yet greatly developed; but this does not diminish the honor of having provided them in the name of the civilized world, which will sooner or later reap their fruit.

In 1853, Ahmed, broken down by excesses of every kind, had an apoplectic shock, and two years later he died, leaving the throne and the ever-increasing responsibility of the Tunisian government to his cousin Mohammed Bey. The latter, benevolent, unpretending and practical, endeavored to revive agriculture, neglected by his predecessor, and might perhaps have succeeded in the course of time. In 1857, he granted to Tunisia *a sort of preface to a constitution, made in thirty-six hours*, under the influence of a French squadron hurriedly sent there to make a demonstration on account of the *judicial assassination* of an unfortunate Jew, accused of blaspheming Islamism, to whom the bey had promised pardon. Mohammed was, in January, 1858, rewarded for his liberal promises by the *grand cordon*, with the insignia of the Legion of Honor in diamonds; but he died the following year (1859), and his brother, Mohammed Essadak, succeeded him.

Essadak Bey developed and promulgated in 1861 the promised constitution, which was, however, very badly applied. Without studying here this interesting subject which intimately relates to the present state of the country, we will simply say in passing that, in the eyes of every sensible man, the kingdom of Tunis, governed by a constitution awkwardly copied from the constitutions of Europe and still more awkwardly applied, resembled very much an unfortunate bedouin forced to adopt a European costume and gaining nothing by it except a constraint in his gait and movement, as painful as ridiculous to look at. In 1864, the bedouin in question protested against this torture by an extensive insurrection which had for its effect the removal of the constitution, that is of the odious costume; but, as was not fully foreseen, the government, in relieving its beloved people of the disguise that exasperated it, left it nothing in exchange; and in truth, as in the metaphor, the bedouin has now only to take up with his old cast off garments in utter rags.

The actual bey has, since coming to the throne, taken special pains to cultivate intimate relations with most of the European courts. He has sent envoys to several of the great capitals, and has exchanged decorations with some of the sovereigns. He sent an embassy to the United States in 1865, together with his full-sized portrait and letters[*] of condolence for the death of president Lincoln. In

[*] For copies of the letters sent to Washington, see Appendix B.

return, the portrait of Washington was sent to him in 1866, and is now suspended with the portraits of Tunisian beys and European sovereigns in the Hall of the Throne at the Bardo.

During Essadak Bey's reign, the country has been seriously afflicted. To suppress the insurrection of 1864,* required all the energies of the government, and caused a pitiful waste of property in addition to much suffering among the deluded victims. The cholera, which raged in the summer of 1867, caused a general stagnation of business, and greatly diminished the population. The crops proved a failure for two successive years; and the famine and typhus fever, that set in at the close of 1867 and beginning of 1868, continued the work of death and ruin carried on by the cholera. And in addition to these ills, the public treasury has been exhausted, financial credit ruined, and a crushing foreign debt left hanging threateningly over an impoverished people.†

SECTION IV.

RELATIONS OF BARBARY IN GENERAL AND OF TUNIS IN PARTICULAR, WITH DIFFERENT CHRISTIAN NATIONS UNTIL 1830.— CORSAIRS AND SLAVERY.

It would require volumes to fully explain the relations of Barbary with the Christian powers, from the establishment of the Mussulman kingdoms in Africa to the conquest of Algiers. Algiers, Tunis, and

---

* For account of the leader of this rebellion, see Appendix C.
† For chronological list of the deys and beys of Tunis, see Appendix D.

Tripoli, influenced by fanaticism and the desire for gain, assumed for centuries to exercise a kind of maritime supremacy over the Mediterranean, and imposed burdens upon all the Christian powers whose vengeance they did not immediately fear. And not only the ships of nations that refused to pay tribute were pursued and captured, but frequent descents were made upon their coasts and the inhabitants were carried off and compelled to serve as slaves and subjected to cruel hardships and indignities.

The European powers, without harmonious action and jealous of each other's influence, tolerated for a long time this shame, and instead of uniting to suppress it by one decisive blow, limited their efforts respectively to compromises by which they gained some commercial advantages, overcame some of the evils of piracy and improved the condition of the unfortunate captives, who were from time to time ransomed and liberated at enormous prices and at humiliating sacrifices.

It was a matter of comparative indifference to the Barbary governments whether they were at peace or at war with Christian states. Piracy was a very lucrative business, and its profits were greatly increased by the very panic which prevailed among Christians, and facilitated predatory operations. The knights of Malta, though brave and doing good service with their galleys, were utterly insufficient to guard the Mediterranean, infested by thousands of freebooters, who claimed this as their domain, and made their cruises with an assurance and composure, like that which our whalemen show in roaming for their prey over the Pacific and Northern seas.

France was the first nation and England the second to command comparative respect among the Barbary powers after the close of the sixteenth century and the decline of the Spanish monarchy, which had for a time restrained and chastised the arrogance of these barbarians. Naples, Sardinia and the states of the church were the most exposed and ill-treated, and it was only by becoming open tributaries that they obtained repeated concessions. Holland and Sweden took upon themselves burdensome obligations, furnishing the arsenals of the African buccaneers with most of their munitions of war. America, young and proud, on making her first treaties, resigned herself to an exercise of extraordinary liberality, and England and France did not shrink on many occasions from doing the same thing under the pretext of observing the usages of the country, that is, of making magnificent presents.

The most celebrated feat of the Tunisian corsairs was the capture and removal in 1799, of nearly all the inhabitants of the island of San Pietro, situated southwest of Sardinia. This was effected during the night with wonderful audacity and dispatch. Twelve ships were loaded at San Pietro, and arrived in port with full cargoes. Mr. Ambrose Allegro, who was at that time employed as the secretary and interpreter in the American consulate, under the famous general William Eaton, witnessed the landing at the Goletta, and has assured me that he never beheld so pitiful a sight as was there presented. When the poor creatures were brought upon land, they wept, warmly embracing each other, and the women and children then clung to their cats and dogs, as their last solace in exile and slavery. One young man, brought into the regency at that time and thenceforth called Ali Ben Abdallah or Baba Ali, will form the subject of a special notice.* Thrown into the slave prisons of Tunis, where Christians of every rank and nation were subjected to all the humiliations and hardships of captivity and servitude, these unfortunate beings suffered for years and died in large numbers. At length, the king of Sardinia offered half a million of francs to redeem them; but this proposition was without result. At a later period, a humane association formed at Cagliari, enlisted in their behalf the efforts of the French consul, Mr. de Voize, who occupied himself actively with negociations, and, after great difficulties, succeeded in emancipating and sending off a numerous party in which were 120 captives who had in vain claimed the protection of the French flag long before their capture at San Pietro.

The war, which the United States began against Tripoli in 1801, and successfully terminated in 1805, accomplished much for the cause of civilization and good government. The youthful republic showed the spirit and vigor of manhood, striking a blow that made piratic rulers tremble on their thrones, and gave hope and courage to European rulers and people.† The bey of Tunis, before and during that war, apparently sought an occasion for a conflict of arms; but

---

* See Appendix E.

† During the war with Tripoli, in which Decatur and Eaton were especially distinguished, the Americans were called, on account of their deeds of daring, *wild men*, which epithet was afterwards significantly employed at other places along the Barbary coast.

on seeing the victorious ships enter his waters, suddenly changed his tone, and sent a special commissioner to Washington to effect an amicable settlement of the difficulties then pending. The appearance of an American squadron, commanded by Decatur, in the waters of Algiers early in the summer of 1815, and the prompt capture of the dey's largest frigate, caused that ruler to give ample satisfaction for his insults and injuries to the American flag and commerce. In 1816, a British squadron, under Lord Exmouth, improved upon the lesson given by the Americans. Speaking and acting in the name of the great powers of Europe, this fleet destroyed the fortifications of the dey of Algiers, and set at liberty 1,500 Christian captives. After securing promises of good conduct, Lord Exmouth passed on and appeared in the harbor of Tunis, where he promptly demanded the abolition of piracy, and the unconditional surrender of Sardinian and Neapolitan subjects in that regency. Three hundred Sardinians were delivered up without ransom, and five hundred Neapolitans at a stipulated price. "In one day," says an eye witness, "3,000 Christian captives of various nations were set free, many of them giving on the occasion delirious demonstrations of their joy." The visit of admirals Jurien and Freemantle, two years later, was also made with a view of securing more effectually the humane object sought by Lord Exmouth.

But all these demonstrations were really but half-measures, so long as the Barbary navy existed. The only way to effectually accomplish the object in view was to annihilate the means of attaining that object.

Piracy and Christian slavery could be fully suppressed only by the destruction of the piratical navies and of their headquarters for rapine and plunder. The battle of Navarino was the first great step for the attainment of that object, and the conquest of Algiers consummated it. For it was not until after 1830, that the emancipation not alone of Christian slaves, but of the civilized world, could be considered an accomplished fact.

We will next briefly notice the slavery of Europeans at Tunis. When a Tunisian corsair entered the port of the Goletta, the extent of the prize was signalled by means of cannon. The prisoners were soon landed, and, after being drawn out in single file under the baton of soldiers, they were marched trembling and with bare heads before the bey, in order that he might make his choice and decide the fate of those he did not want for his immediate service.

Commanders of captured ships, priests, doctors, and all the prisoners of any distinction, received some indulgence in the hope of large sums for their ransom. All the laborers and tradesmen were employed on the public works, under the whip of a Mussulman guard. To speak only of Tunis, where Christian as well as negro slavery was much milder than in the other Barbary states, there is to be found to-day scarcely an important edifice on which Christian slaves were not employed as masons or hod carriers, and, in passing through the great courts of the palaces of the bey or former dignitaries, we may still find, rudely carved upon marble columns and walls, numerous names of unfortunate captives who were doomed to aid in the construction of those walls, or pass their lives there in servitude.

Most of the slaves belonged to the state; for after the bey and his ministers had selected their servants from a slave gang brought in by some corsair, a few were sold to traders and scattered over the country, and there usually remained a multitude of unfortunate beings who were cast into slave prisons and subjected to painful labors. Each slave received for his support a little bread made of refuse flour or meal, and some pieces of copper money, which pittance, however, he had to share with his overseers, or be subjected to their hatred and cruelty.

Unhealthy and insufficient food on the one hand; excessive labors on the other; enduring a burning sun or half clad breathing the close air of damp cells; bastinadoes, confinement, bad usage, fatigues and divers grievances; all these could only add homesickness to despair, enfeebling the health and breaking down the constitution of the captives. They died in large numbers, and those who survived owed their lives to their extraordinary power of endurance or to exceptional circumstances which ameliorated their condition. When far from the reach of some charitable European, they were attacked by disease, the poor sufferers received no aid or pity. They were beasts of burden that could no longer serve and were abandoned to their sad lot. Though their masters regretted the loss of their servants, as Mussulmans they rejoiced to see the number of infidels diminished.

At the end of the eighteenth century, this state of things was a little modified, and the slaves had a hospital, which is the Catholic church and monastery of to-day. A religious Spaniard of the order of the Trinity, having been enslaved, was moved by compassion for the sufferings of his companions in captivity, and being very wealthy ordered from Europe large sums of money which he employed for the relief of his brethren without thinking of his own ransom, which he refused to effect in order that he might accomplish the greater good among his fellow-captives. Anticipating a speedy death and indifferent whether that should occur in Africa or in Spain, he devoted his life and possessions to a work of charity, founding at Tunis, Algiers and Tripoli hospitals for sick and suffering slaves. The funds of these pious establishments were increased by the offerings of other benefactors, and it is easier to imagine, than to explain the advantages and benefits which resulted to Christian slaves until the period of their final emancipation by the suppression of Barbary piracy and emancipation of Christian captives.

It is not uninteresting to notice the conditions on which captives were purchased and exchanged. Consuls were generally charged with this business, and with the necessary communications with Europe. The price for the ransom of a man was ordinarily about seventy dollars, and that of a woman about double this amount. When the captives to be redeemed belonged to opulent families or had occupied a certain rank in their country, the bey fixed arbitrarily the ransom and often made exorbitant demands.

As to the exchange of prisoners, whatever were the condition of the Mussulmans liberated, the bey gave in return only Christian slaves of the lowest class and in the worst state. By an analogous procedure, if the question were in regard to the ransom of a Mussulman, his value was put much below that of a Christian, and it was generally understood that to redeem five Mussulmans, it was sufficient to pay a sum equivalent to that required to redeem two Europeans. This arrangement, which seems at first inconsistent with Islamitish arrogance, is, on the contrary, in perfect accord with it, securing very important advantages for the Mussulmans.

All Europe sanctioned such a system as established the humiliating inferiority of its children, and thus implicitly recognized a sort of natural right to the revolting tyranny of the African pirates. One fact will serve to confirm this representation, and show how Europe bowed her head before insolent injustice and effrontery. The French coral fishery company at Calle had a stipulation that if a Mussulman killed a Christian, he should pay 500 piastres; but if, on the contrary, a Christian killed a Mussulman, he should pay 800 piastres. Now, when we consider that France had played an important rôle in the east for centuries, and was regarded by the Mussulmans of Tunis as perhaps the greatest Christian nation in the world, this fact speaks volumes. This boasted nation gives an official recognition that the blood of a Mussulman is worth almost twice as much as the blood of a Christian. Nay, worse; this strange stipulation established a relation between any Mussulman whatsoever and a particular Christian,—a Frenchman. The blood of the Mussulman being absolute, and that of the Christian relative to the power of his country, it results from it that in the eyes of the Africans, it was a privilege, a favor and an honor conceded to France to fix 500 piastres as the price of one of her sons, and does not at all serve as a precedent for other powers less feared and esteemed. Nothing would have hindered the bey from offering a few piastres or nothing at all for the first Christian that a Mussulman might choose to assassinate. Sardinians and Neapolitans were massacred with impunity or executed in defiance of law at Tunis: *Experimentum in anima vili!* Every civilized man must blush with shame and be stirred with indignation at the recital of such deeds!

The condition of the negroes until the time of their emancipation[*] in 1845 would form the subject of a most interesting chapter. An immense annual caravan furnished the bazars of Tunis with this human merchandise, bought or seized and brought by force from the frontiers of Soudan. Mussulmans alone had the right to purchase negroes; for most of these negroes were Mussulmans, over whom Christians could exercise no authority.

The inhabitants of Tunis had the habit of promptly pronouncing judgment on the worth of negroes by certain personal marks and peculiarities. Their judgment was favorable when the slave had beautiful, well-opened and very clear eyes, with the pupil of a light color and distinctly delineated; the gums and tongue of a vermillion hue without any brown or darkish spots; the palm of the hands and the sole

---
[*] For interesting documents on this subject, see Appendix F.

of the feet of flesh color, and the nails clear and regular; such slaves readily found purchasers. But, on the contrary, negroes who had the white of the eye of a brownish or reddish hue or furrowed with little reddish veins, and the gums and tongue of a brownish tinge, were judged to be obdurate and incorrigible. Such slaves were sold cheap or sent to other markets. The different characteristics and qualities of negroes were noted with the same interest and attention as are wont to be shown by amateurs and traders in regard to different breeds of cattle and horses, or as were shown by Mussulman lords in the days of the corsairs in selecting servants from among Christian captives.

The slaves were sold at auction to the highest bidder. Women and young girls, adults and infants were exposed for sale, often entirely naked, and were carefully examined from head to foot by purchasers. Besides the sale on the market place, cargoes of negroes were sent to the Levant. It was a very lucrative trade. The price of men varied according to their constitution and characteristics; children were of small account, while pretty females were in great demand.

Though slaves, the negroes at Tunis were in comparatively easy circumstances; for they were classed as merchandise, and received attention to prevent their deterioration. There they lived better than in their own country, having less privations and dangers to encounter. And it is due to say that Mussulmans were forbidden by their religion to maltreat their Mussulman slaves; nay, they were enjoined to exercise kindness towards them, and it was a meritorious act to emancipate them; and in general they were not cruel masters.

We must state some of the principal causes of negro slavery. The continual wars which desolated, and still desolate that vast tropical region called Nigritia or Soudan, converted prisoners of war into slaves, and slaves into merchandise. Barbary and Egypt early profited by this state of things, and organized the slave trade. This was profitable, since large numbers of human beings were received in return for pieces of glass ware, bad utensils, and coarse cloth, which the poor negroes in a half savage state needed. Besides the wholesale commerce in open market, there was also the retail or contraband trade. That which the tribes practiced upon each other in the name of law, was speedily imitated and justified by individuals, until personal security ceased to exist. By force or by stratagem, beings formed in the image of their Maker, were stolen and sold for gain. A sort of *man-hunt* was regularly organized. It was a ferocious association of the strong against the weak, which was developed and maintained by the very facility and importance of the results.

The slaves had to traverse the great desert. Imagine them once arrived at the end of their journey; they regarded themselves in a land comparatively happy, and their joy which was often manifested at the bazar, even under the whip of their owners, before and after their sale, arose less from their stupidity and brutishness, than from their hope and belief that they should no more have to encounter the dangers and torments of their previous existence, and especially of their journeyings from their native land.

If we but reflect on the condition, for centuries unhappy and brutifying, of this great black race, which occupies the interior of the African continent, and is scattered over a part of America and of Oceanica, we can better account for their comparative inferiority, and their defects of character will astonish us less and awaken rather our compassion than our indignation.

Whatever be their defects and their inferiority, we are not disposed to despair of the future of the blacks. For however low they are fallen in the scale of humanity, they are of the human family, and with their place in the sunlight, they can claim, and we have faith to believe they will yet claim, their part of that immense patrimony of liberty and progress, which surely does not belong by right of primogeniture exclusively and inalienably to the white race.

The duties of nations and races, as of individuals, become enlarged with the fortunes and importance which they acquire, and which depend as much on fortuitous circumstances and the mysterious laws of universal existence, as on their merits and activity. The will of man is a necessary and essential condition of his improvement and greatness; but let not pride and success lead us into the belief that it is the sole condition, and that left to ourselves we could create anew our destiny. It is less the will and the activity which are wanting to unfortunate negroes, than the conditions and the means. A fatal chain of degrading causes has disfigured in them the divine image; but it has not so blotted out the divine mipress as to authorize the whites, who are not themselves without blemish, to deny their commonness of origin, nature and destiny.

To secure the future of the blacks, is the duty of the whites, and it will be their honor to render that future possible and certain. It depends on them to hasten it, as well as to establish it, first by liberty and equality of rights and duties, and then by fraternal relations. If the sentiment put forth by the blind bard of Greece be correct, that, in taking from man his liberty, we rob him of half his virtues, we restore to negroes half their virtues by restoring to them unconditional and unrestricted liberty. For it is important first of all to make citizens of them: by equality of rights and responsibilities, they will march under our ægis, following our example in the discharge of duty; and will thus develop a nobler manhood; for they will feel, as a consequence of emancipation and of civil and political equality, the great need of that emulation which is the soul of the activity and progress of man, and the want of which has hitherto been a great defect in their character.

In spite then of the difficulties and dangers even to be encountered in the accomplishment of an act so profoundly just and humane, as the general emancipation of the blacks upon the entire surface of the globe, we must have the courage to accomplish it; for we have no right to put off this act; we cannot procrastinate and temporize without ourselves incurring in the light of history and before God, that monstrous iniquity which has been committed for an ignoble end, consigning to fearful shame and misery a notable part of the human family.

To efface in the memory of men the trace of so many tears and so much blood, we must promptly stop the source of the evil by boldly repudiating the past, and, with all our heart and strength, making amends for it by a future, in which our former victims shall march by our side, under the shield of liberty regulated by law, and in the light and pride of a civilization truly Christian.

Part Second.

ACTUAL STATE OF THE COUNTRY.

Coat of Arms of the Bey of Tunis.

CHAPTER I.

Natural Divisions, Extent and General Aspect of the Country.

WE have already said elsewhere that Tunisia is the geological continuation of Algeria. This last country is naturally divided into three zones: the Sahel, the Tell and the Sahara; and Tunisia is only a prolongation of these three zones.

The coast of North Africa generally runs parallel to the equator and is comparatively little indented; but in Tunisia it is much indented and suddenly changes its general direction at cape Bon, taking a meridional course nearly as far as the borders of Tripoli and sloping and winding around a part of the great oriental basin of the Mediterranean. Also the two chains of the Atlas, which traverse Algeria parallel to the sea, run nearly at right angles to the sea in Tunisia. The northern chain ends at Sidi Ali Mekki and at cape Bon, and the southern at Gebel Akerit, near the Gulf of Gabes. The space between the two chains is only the flattening of the Algerine plateaus of the Tell, which plateaus are sustained by very irregular mountainous chains, which diminish in height from the Algerine frontier to the sea.

"The regency of Tunis," says "Pelissier, "lies between 37° 20', and 33° north latitude, and between 7° 40' and 11° 40' east from the meridian of Greenwich, and can be divided into four regions: 1st, the region of the north, comprising all that territory which lies at the north of the first Atlas chain, and consequently the Tunisian valley of the Majerda;* 2d, the region of the west, extending between the two Atlas chains, from the Algerine frontier to the most eastern of the chains; 3d, the region of the east, which lies between the second division and the sea; 4th, the region of the south, comprising all that territory which lies to the south of the second Atlas chain, and extends to the frontiers of Tripoli. The most important and populous places of these divisions are: in the northern region, Tunis, Beja and Bizerta; in the western region, Kef; in the eastern region, Cairwan, Susa, Monastir, Media and Sfax; and in the southern region, Gafsa, Tozer, Nefta and Gabes." It is in accordance with this simple and rational plan, that we proceed to give a summary description of Tunisia.

The northern region comprises the lower basin of the Majerda. This river is the largest of Barbary, though it is not navigable. The valley through which it runs is broad, fertile and magnificent. Unfortunately the banks of the Majerda are so steep and elevated as to render it difficult to employ the

---

* The Majerda, ancient Bagrada, rises in the Algerine Tell, a province of Constantine; a part of its valley is then beyond the Tunisian frontier.

water for irrigating the country, as is done along the banks of the Nile in Egypt. This difficulty was overcome in the seventeenth century at Tebourba, by the construction of a bridge and dam provided with a system of sluices, which served to shut off the water or let it on and distribute it over the country around. But the gates of the sluices have long since disappeared. This part of Tunisia, so fertile in spite of the want of culture, would become exceedingly productive if agriculture were revived and some plan devised for utilizing the waters of this river, now not only useless, but often effecting much damage by overflowing the banks and heaping up sand upon arable ground and cultivated fields. In advancing towards the sea, we come first to Beja; a great depot for grain; then to Mater in the midst of a superb country; then, at the end of two united lakes, to the unique little city of Bizerta, situated near the entrance of the channel which joins the two lakes to the sea at the side of a semi-circular basin or gulf, whose extremities are capes Blanc and Zebib.

In passing along the coast to the south of cape Zebib, we find, upon the right bank of a little lake, Porto Farina, and a little lower down, the present mouth of the Majerda;* then some alluvial lands

---

* The mouth of the Majerda was formerly much further south than at present. Mr. Daux, the able commissioner of Napoleon, has recently traced the former channel of the river, which ran in an easterly direction from Tebourba, and emptied into the sea within six or eight miles of Tunis; whereas, at present, it runs in a northeasterly direction and reaches the sea twenty-five miles from Tunis. This change is readily explained. In the course of centuries, the bed of the river became filled up with alluvium, which finally served as a dam. The waters, thus pent up, struck out a new channel, running as described above, and reaching the sea near the site of

somewhat marshy, and below them lake Soukra; then cape Cammart and the peninsula of Carthage, with the two hills of Sidi-Bou-Said and St. Louis; then upon the tongue of the land which extends from the north to the south, the port of the Goletta at the entrance of the great lake of Bahira, commonly called by foreigners the lake of Tunis. At the western extremity of this lake, is found the city of Tunis, the capital of the regency. To the east of the gulf and roadstead of Tunis, stretches out from southwest to northeast the peninsula of cape Bon, to the south of which is the eastern region, commonly called the Sahel. Between Tunis and the peninsula of cape Bon, the Oued Meliana, which is one of the most considerable streams of the country, runs in a northerly direction and empties into the sea. This northern part of Tunisia, besides the fertility of the soil, the agreeableness of the landscapes and the beauty of its gardens, is rich in minerals of iron and lead, of which one mine only is worked at this time; it has magnificent forests and quarries of marble, which, though once a source of opulence and prosperity, are now scarcely known.

Behind the northern division, and serving as its support, widens out along the Algerine frontier the western region, whose principal city and capital is Kef. This mountainous and volcanic country has the physical aspect of other parts of the globe of

Utica, which city was situated in the period of her glory, upon the sea shore. But the sea has receded several miles from the site of Utica, and the constant accumulation of sand and soil, brought down by the waters of the Majerda, doubtless causes the sea to recede century by century. The area around the former mouth of the Majerda, is now the salt lake of Soukra, and around the present mouth is formed an extensive marsh.

similar origin. It has elevated peaks; deep gorges; stratified rocks; perpendicular cliffs, and walls of limestone and calcareous marble; it has mineral springs, and volcanoes that are extinct or still smoking. The mountain upon which Kef is built is an extinct volcano, as is also Gebel Zerissa, forty miles southwest of Kef. To the north of Kef, in the territory of the Konir, is Gebel Betounæ, which, after a long sleep, began to smoke in 1838. A ramification of this robust frame-work of mountains, belonging to the western region, sustains the peninsula of cape Bon, and it is not unprofitable to notice, upon the western side of this peninsula on the eastern side of the roadstead of Tunis, the mountains evidently volcanic and the abundant mineral and hot springs of Hammam-el-Lif and Hammam-Corbus. Now, if the line of direction of the Atlas chain which terminates at cape Bon be prolonged upon the chart, it will soon join the line of the Sicilian mountains, and meet the volcanoes of Etna, Stromboli and Vesuvius. This is a geological fact which is neither without interest nor importance. Mountains being only a violent uprising of the surface of the earth, caused by a current of heated matter or by inflamed gas, they must naturally form net-works, whose large lines sometimes interrupted on the surface of the globe by the ocean, are easily recognized; because the subterranean gallery, which is formed in the entrails of the earth and over which the mountains are elevated, continues immense distances and depths until rejoined to the interior system of burning rivers, whose only result is the exterior system of mountains. Also, earthquakes and volcanic eruptions, in countries situated in the same geological regions, are observed to occur simultaneously or in rapid succession. The vibrations of the soil in North Africa have almost always preceded or followed the formidable explosions of Ætna, Vesuvius and Stromboli.

The eastern region is the richest portion of Tunisia. From cape Bon to the gulf of Gabes, are produced large quantities of oil and wool, which are exported to Europe. The centre of the Sahel (territory of Susa) is an immense forest of olive trees. Nabel, Hammamet, Susa and Msaken, are comparatively flourishing towns. In this region, are numerous large lakes, beginning at Hammamet, and the most important streams are Oued Gilma and Oued Fekka. In a westerly direction from Susa and almost in the same latitude, is the *Holy City* of Cairwan.

Beyond the preceding region, in a southerly direction, the country becomes arid and desolate; and yet it could not have always been thus, if we judge by the numerous ruins that cover it. Gafsa (Capsa, the ancient capital of Jugurtha) is situated at the entrance of a valley which opens into the Tunisian Gereed, the most beautiful part of the Sahara. The magnificence of its horizons corresponds with the freshness and beauty of its numerous oases, among which we must specially notice Tozer and Nefta. The sun and the living waters so fertilize and enrich these admirable isles of verdure, as to transform them into immense gardens, where the various vegetables of the world thrive and grow with little care. Many springs, somewhat warm, form rivers abounding with fish, and flow through the oases. Forests of palm trees produce an immense quantity of dates. Not far from Nefta is the great salt lake of the Gereed, or marsh of Pharoon (ancient lake Triton). This is the most considerable of that system of sebkas, or salt lakes, which commence at the gulf of Gabes and advance a little obliquely towards the Atlantic. The study of this vast region, which appears scarcely emerged from the waters, would confirm the hypothesis that the sea once overflowed it in a manner to form a great island of Morocco, Algeria and Tunis. The raised ground of this basin is the desert, and the great island which is to-day a part of the continent was, according to the just inferences of learned men, only the famous Atlantide of Plato.

At a little distance from Teref-el-Ma, upon the gulf of Gabes, are mountain links which enclose between the Gereed and the sea the charming country called *El Arad*. Orchards, gardens, abundant waters, a light and fertile soil, smiling landscapes, all conspire to give this province an agricultural and commercial importance which it is far from having at the present time.

We shall return now from the south to the north along the coast, to pass in review the Tunisian islands. In front and to the east of Gabes, is the island of Gerba, the ancient Lotophagitis or Meninx, which Homer makes his hero, Ulysses, to have visited, eating with the natives the fruit of the lotus. It has a comparatively numerous industrial population and enjoys a limited prosperity.

Opposite Sfax is the group of the Kerkenna, whose largest island is rendered illustrious by the visit of

Hannibal and Marius, both fugitives. This archipelago has scarcely any agricultural or commercial importance. It serves as a place of exile for Tunisian criminals, and the sponge fishery is carried on to a limited extent along the shore. Off Monastir, are Kuriat and other small islands without value. On beyond cape Bon, at the entrance of the gulf of Tunis, are the two Zimbras, the ancient *altars of Ægimurus*, which are at this time uninhabited, though the larger island serves as a lazaretto.* Opposite to cape Sidi Ali Mekki, are Plane and Pillau. In passing along the northern coast line towards the Algerine frontier, we observe the rocky islands of the Fratelli. Afar in the deep, is Galita, and near the line of Algeria is the woody island of Tabarca.

No country of North Africa has such coasts and islands as Tunisia. It is a land predestined by its position and conformation to enjoy a commercial prosperity, whose most important element was for centuries, and could be again, agricultural prosperity. The character of the soil has been singularly misrepresented. Its former fertility is supposed to be exhausted. But wherever the ground is tilled, it justifies its ancient renown and encourages the brightest hopes for the future. The celebrated German chemist, Liebig, is then, in my opinion, wrong in ranking Tunisia among the countries which were once ex-

---

* Virgil, in the first book of the Æneid, 109th line, thus speaks of these islands: "Saxa vocant Itali mediis que in fluctibus aras." The Italians call these rocks in the midst of the sea altars. Pliny, in speaking of them, says: "At contra Carthaginis sinum duæ Ægimuri aræ, scopuli verius quam insulæ." But opposite to the gulf of Carthage are the two altars of Ægimurus, which are more truly cliffs than islands.

ceedingly fruitful, and have lost their fertility and productiveness by their very excess of production. What is wanting for this marvellous land, always fertile and inexhaustible, is the labor of man, of which there is certainly a lamentable exhaustion. Agriculture is neglected, and the consequence is a general aspect of desolation and death. But upon whatever points the hand of industry is exerted, the rich vegetation and abundant crops prove that it is not the strength and productiveness of the soil that are wanting, but the will and energy of the inhabitants; these are gone, perhaps irrecoverably gone. Destitution sweeps over the plains, once fertile and covered with verdure, only where tyranny and injustice have produced their legitimate result, blinding, degrading, shrinking up and dispelling the population.

It is an old saying that "as is the land, so is the man;" but in the name of liberty and of history, we will affirm also as a truth, that "as is the man, so is the land." Worth begets worth, but the blight and decay of manhood are the effectual cause of general devastation and ruin. History clearly shows that we are not to expect perpetual prosperity from beautiful domains, rich soil, genial climate, proud forests and inexhaustible mines of wealth. Without an intelligent, energetic and manly people, all these will serve no good. Behold the land of Hannibal! still rich in natural resources, but, in fact, poor and wretched! We will not, however, despair of the future. A soil that has been trodden by those possessed of the dignity of a true manhood may be so trodden again. Many agricultural and mechanical experiments, that have failed on account of the prevalence of ignorance and fanaticism, may succeed through the diffusion of light and knowledge. The mines, that enriched the Carthaginians and Romans, may be opened and become centres of industry, supplying again other countries with the precious metals. With the dissemination of liberal ideas and the establishment of just and humane institutions, we believe ruined cities may be rebuilt, desolate fields made once more to bloom and flourish and this pitiful country transformed into a thriving and prosperous state.

CHAPTER II.

Population.--Races.--Religious Creed, Rites and Ceremonies.--Pilgrimages to Mecca.--Manners, Customs and Superstitions.

THE population of the regency of Tunis must be stated as a conjecture, or, at best, as a rough estimate, rather than as a well ascertained fact; since the taking of the census is there forbidden by a religious tradition, which dates back probably to the famous act of David, that was rebuked by the appearance of the plague in his kingdom. Pellissier estimates the population at 800,000; while one of the bey's ministers estimates it at 3,000,000; and it is variously stated by different authors at 2,500,000, at 2,000,000, and at 1,500,000. The late Mr. Charles Cubisol, long vice consul of France at the Goletta, who gave much attention to this subject, was quite decided in the opinion that the population was 2,000,000, confirming this statement by carefully prepared estimates of the population of every village, city, district and tribe in the regency.* We are inclined

---

* Mr. Cubisol thus gives the population according to religious distinctions: Mussulmans, 1,929,000; Catholics, 25,570; Protestants, 20;

to the opinion that the population is not less than 1,500,000 and is not more than 2,000,000. This is a small number of people to be scattered over a territory of 60,000 or 70,000 square miles; and we are more impressed with this truth when we recall the fact that on the same soil subsisted in the flourishing period of the Roman domination 15,000,000 souls. In the first centuries of the middle age, the population was greatly reduced. Now the population is not only reduced, as we have stated, but it becomes sensibly smaller from time to time as the condition of the country becomes worse. Of late pestilence and famine have combined with other ills to diminish the population and reduce the territory to the condition of a desert.

What are the races that inhabit Tunisia and how are they distributed over the territory? In the actual state of the country where Islamism has been for centuries passing its rude level over all the diverse elements of the Tunisian people, thus singularly mingling and confounding them together, it is impossible for us to answer this question with precision. Yet we can, I think, adopt the following classification to indicate the great divisions of the population.

1. Upon the coast and in the maritime cities is a mixture of the ancient peoples: Libyans, Phœnicians, Carthaginians, Romans, Vandals and Byzantines, amalgamated with Arabs, Turks, Spaniards and other mod-

Greeks, 410; Jews, 45,000; total, 2,000,000. We think his estimate of the Jews and Protestants too low, and that of the Mussulmans too high. He puts down the number of Moorish inhabitants of cities and villages at 717,500, and the number belonging to nomad tribes at 1,211,500.

ern Europeans. This mixture constitutes the population usually called "Moors," which term we shall explain further on. 2. The Berber element, which exists pure or nearly so among the mountains of the interior and of the south; it is sometimes found in fixed abodes, and sometimes moving from point to point. 3. The Arabo-Berber element, resulting from the mixture and fusion of Arab tribes with the Berber tribes that existed in the country at the period of the Mussulman conquest and so similar to the tribes of the invaders as to be partially fused with them. 4. The pure Arab element, which is found only in a very few tribes. 5. The Turkish element, in itself feeble, including the Turko-Moorish element, which is of some importance and constitutes the "Koulouglis," the descendants of Turkish fathers and Tunisian mothers of whatever race. The Koulouglis generally live in the cities. 6. The native Jewish element, embracing the Jews who have been regarded as the natives of the country and subjects of the bey for a long time, of whom we shall particularly speak in Chapter VIII. They are to be found in the cities along the coast and at some points in the interior; they even constitute slight fractions of Arab tribes, and a few of them lead a nomadic life and are styled the "Jewish bedouins." 7. The Negro element, including the sub-elements resulting from the inter-marriage of Negroes with other races, found with various admixtures of blood and shades of color throughout the regency.

We see and affirm that, notwithstanding the opinion set forth by Mr. Pellissier and some other writers, the Arab element is far from being dominant in Tunisia and throughout North Africa. In Algeria, it was lately shown by a series of investigations, that more than half the population belong to the Kabyle (aboriginal) race, and we are convinced that the same is true in Tunisia. The Arab race succeeded by means of violence in mixing up with the people of North Africa, and imposing upon them its religion and language, its nationality and even its name; but could neither destroy, absorb nor transform them. That which seems to authorize Europeans to attribute to the Arabs an importance which they do not possess, and to confound under that vague denomination all the races of Barbary, is the common and false idea that the *tribe* being characteristic of the Arab race, all the tribes came originally from Arabia. Now, *a priori*, it is probable that, as the analogy of the soil involves that of manners and customs, there must have been, from the early period of the world, African as well as Arabian tribes, and all historians are agreed on this point. It is besides a very important historic fact that a deputation of these tribes to the calif Omar was the immediate cause of the Arab invasion. These tribes have been perpetuated by the side of those of the conquerors, with whom they have become somewhat mixed in certain quarters; always continuing, however, to be the very heart of the population, that ancient and powerful Libyan race (Berber and Kabyle) that has resisted twenty conquests, and is indestructible, like that Atlas, whose declivities and hills it peoples, and which is for it as for the soil, the source of its strength and the means of its resistance.*

This ancient race is distinguished from the Arabs by its features and manners. The Kabyle is in general tall, well built, with broad, high shoulders and a short neck. His features are strongly marked; his complexion dark and his forehead straight and square. The Arab is ordinarily of medium stature; his complexion pale; his face long, and his forehead slightly tapering. His firm features and long neck contrast with those of the Kabyle. In his person he bears indications of melancholy and indolence, which also contrast with the rudeness and roughness of the Kabyle. The Arab is in general a shepherd; the Kabyle a farmer or mechanic; and he consequently has a fixed habitation. We think that if North Africa is to be regenerated, it must be accomplished mainly by the development of the Kabyle element. This should receive more attention than has hitherto been accorded it. To this the future may belong, we mean, with the concurrence of the civilized world; for though less degenerated than the other inhabitants of the soil, the Kabyles are still so weak as to render it difficult for them to rise unaided and bring back to their country the grandeur and renown that belonged to it in better times.

* Mr. G. L. Ditson, writing from the Kabyle country among the Atlas mountains, says: "The Kabyles have looked down from their inaccessible heights and seen the Carthaginians, Romans, Vandals, Saracens, Spaniards, Turks, come in their pride and strength and pass away, while they remain untrammelled and unchanged; — have seen successive tides of humanity roll in and fret themselves awhile around their rocky barriers, then recede and leave them in their untamed fierceness and independence."

Tunisia is, like Algeria, divided from east to west into two distinct parts; the country of the coast and of the Atlas mountains on the one hand, and the country of the Sahara or of the plains on the other. The Tell with its valleys, mountains and streams, is peopled by Arabs and Berbers, leading nearly the same life, but often distinct in race and in manners. They are divided in a general way, as people of the thatched cottage, people of the farm, and people of the tent, according as they are villagers, farmers or shepherds. In these divisions, are not included the inhabitants of the important cities, who, though fundamentally belonging to the Berber and Arab races, have acquired by a long residence in the cities special habits and characteristic features. The inhabitants of the cities and towns are designated in all North Africa by the name of *Hadars*, fixed residents. The Sahara, comprehending the Gereed with its plains, oases, magnificent horizons and vast pasturage is mainly occupied by the Rahala Arabs, a people properly called nomads, who lead a migratory life, moving their tents and flocks from point to point. We need not say that these two great divisions of the country have only one general character, and that there are nomads in the Tell, as there are Arabs with fixed residences on the plains of the Sahara; since there is no clearly defined line of demarcation between these two portions of the soil; and the two divisions, though quite distinct in some respects, have a strong family resemblance.

We propose to study the characteristic features of the inhabitants of the cities, called Hadars by natives, and Moors by Europeans; the Arabs of the tent, and the Kabyles or Berbers, without occupying ourselves with the varieties of these three great divisions of a population, on which Islamism has stamped a remarkable uniformity of ideas and sentiments. The Jews, constituting a peculiar race, will receive special attention in another place. Before engaging in the study of manners and customs, we think it due to pass in review the diverse tribes of the country.

In the valley of the Majerda, we find the following tribes: The *Trabelsia* or Tripolitans, originating in Tripoli, as their name indicates, and embracing the three tribes of Troud, Sylyn and Tahouane, which are devoted to agriculture, and a fourth tribe, that of the Ferjane, leading a pastoral life.

The Oulad-Bou-Salem is a very populous tribe which occupies the territory called the *Dakhela*, whose valuable products are renowned in all Tunisia. This tribe holds a great fair for grain and cattle every Thursday. Between the Dakhela and Testour are the less important tribes Kouka, Zwaka and Oulad-Merah. Below the Oulad-Bou-Salem and still in the valley of the Majerda, is found the tribe of Jendouba. In the valley of the river Mellagua, a tributary of the Majerda, is the tribe of the Hakim, and further on, the tribe of the Oulad Sdira, which dwells along the frontiers.

Between Mater and Tabarca, the country, designated under the general name of the Mogody, is inhabited by many small tribes placed under the kaid of Mater; among others, the Jeniat, the Oulad Saidan and the Malia. To the west of Beja and Tabarca, upon the very frontier of Algeria, is the mountain tribe of the Komir, who are a warlike and almost independent people; the Amedouane and the Oulad Sidi Abid; and to the south of the Komir are the Shaia, the Grezwane, the Gresara, the Oushetlata and the Warka. All these tribes are turbulent subjects and disciplined warriors. They are placed under the sole command of the kaid of Kef, who each year makes a tour into their country to levy contributions which are not habitually received without the exchange of some shots and the loss of some lives.

The district of Tunis, together with the province of cape Bon, dotted over with towns and villages that are inhabited by Moors, contains but few tents and tribes. In the east, at the end of the system of Zaughan, we find, not far from the gulf of Hammamet, the Oulad Said, a tribe which was once very powerful and struggled for centuries against the Turkish domination, but is now very much reduced in numbers and strength. It is divided into six parts: the Oulad Daoud, the Oulad Aoun, the Oulad Amer, the Oulad Menaoud, Abdallah and the Oulad Tiba.

In a southerly direction, the district of Cairwan is occupied by the great tribe of Jelas, subdivided into many parts such as the Jelas Oulad Tdir, the Jelas Sendassine and the Jelas Kwab. In the centre of the territory, is Gebel Oussela, once occupied by the warlike mountaineers, whose descendants constitute the zouaves, a body of irregular troops belonging to the army of the bey. The Jelas are a large tribe; they are sometimes governed by one kaid, but have at the present time three kaids. They can readily put 3,000 horsemen under arms.

To the southwest of the Jelas, is extended over a vast territory the tribe of the Majer, divided into three fractions, but governed by one kaid. It can furnish 2,000 cavalry. To the west of the Majer, upon a still larger territory, are the Frashish, having 1,000 horsemen. The Hamema encamp south of the Majer, and the Frashish and their territory extend to the Gereed. Their kaid holds habitually his "smala" (court) under the walls of Gafsa. They can put 4,000 horsemen in line of battle. They are divided into four fractions, which are often at war with each other. The Hamema have a well established reputation for their turbulence and rapacity. Between the Hamema and the sea are the Swassi, divided into many parts, and reckoning 10,000 horsemen. They are known for their habitual resistance to tax-gatherers.

South of the Swassi are the Metelith, whose territory extends south and west of the district of Sfax. Their soil is excellent and produces abundant crops of grain and olives, but as they are easily reached by way of Monastir, Susa and Sfax, they are more especially exposed to the exactions of beyal tax-gatherers, who show them little mercy, scarcely allowing them to enjoy the ease which with a wise administration would become general. Though they live in tents and have no fixed villages, they are much more laborious and partake less of the character of vagabonds than most nomads. With their industrious habits and a fertile territory, they would constitute, under an intelligent and protective government, excellent farmers. They can furnish about 3,000 horsemen.

Between the Metelith and the Hamema, are the Mahedeba and the Taifa, which are parts of the same tribe, separated by the Nafat, a more important tribe, scattered over a light and sandy soil, which is nevertheless very productive during the rains of winter, and which they leave during the parching heat and drought of summer. The Nafat have about 800 horsemen.

In the Gereed, where the people live in the oases, we find the Nafzawa and the little tribe of the Shawia. The latter governs itself, paying annually to the bey of the camp a tax agreed upon from time immemorial, in order to be left free in the management of its affairs. There is also the little wandering, pillaging tribe of the Nemensha. The inhabitants of the Gereed are divided for administrative purposes into five districts, which are governed by kaids residing respectively at Gafsa, Nefzawa, Nefta, Tozer and Oudian.

In El-Arad are the inhabitants of the oases and the Nomads, who live on the intermediate plains. These are the Beni Zid in the north; the Allaya and the Hamerna in the south. Mixed up with this last tribe are very many Negroes, enjoying precisely the same rights, wearing the same costume and living the same life as the whites, in the midst of whom they have been established for centuries.

In the southeast of El-Arad is the tribe of the Ourguema, established upon the plains and upon the mountain slopes of the Tuniso-Tripolitan chain. In the fruit season, they take up their abodes in numerous villages surrounded with gardens; the rest of the year they go upon the plains, living in tents or in light portable huts covered with mats, so that in truth they lead both an agricultural and a pastoral life.

The Ourguema often have contests with the Oulad Näil, a pilfering tribe of Tripoli, whose territory is in a southeasterly direction. On the east, are the possessions of the Akara, who inhabit the shore from Zerzize to Biban, the extreme point of Tunisia. Mr. Pelissier visited Zerzize in 1844, and made the following interesting statement: "At this time a female is the chief magistrate of Zerzize. Her name is Ralia. In the full bloom of youth and of a beauty still remarkable, this woman played an important part in the troubles with Tripoli. Brave as a man could be, she often showed herself in the midst of combats, giving proofs of the greatest courage; but immoral as an oriental woman who throws off her veil, she had numerous lovers, whose rich presents secured for her a fortune which she has known how to manage. Retiring to Zerzize, she married a peaceable man, who is no longer known except as the husband of Ralia, a very common kind of distinction for all those who marry celebrated women. She has done me the honors of her village, where she wields the influence which a comprehensive and resolute spirit, regardless of sex, always exerts over the Arabs. Her manners are polished and agreeable; her conversation engaging, and her good sense remarkable."

In the north of the mountainous part of the country of the Ourguema, is the tribe of the Matmala, who are mostly villagers with dwellings dug out of the calcareous sandstone, of which numerous hills are formed. The streets of these singular villages are upon the roofs of the houses. South of the Ourguema are the Ouderna, on the very frontiers of the regency. Their sheik is in fact independent of the bey of Tunis, who even furnishes him with a little detachment that he may protect well the Tunisian frontier.

The tribes of El-Arad are constantly in a quarrel. The Ourguema and the Beni Zid are at the head of the two principal factions that occupy the country. It is a curious fact that the term "Arad" signifies in the Arabic language *discord,—dissension*. The Berber population of Gerba is distinguished from the Arab populations by its origin, language and religious rites.

To complete this brief notice of the diverse tribes and populations of Tunisia, we have but to turn to the west and centre of the regency. Beginning at the Algerine frontier, below the tribe of Sharan, we find the Oulad Bou Ganem. Below them are the Zeralma, and then the Frashish. To the east of the Bou Ganem, are the Wartan, the Doufan and the Tlmansa. The Wartan are of Kabyle origin and live in habitations of stone.

We come now upon the territory of El Kef, called *the Rakba*. The lieutenantcy of Kef has been exercised more than forty years by a chief who is now about ninety years old, known throughout the regency under the name of "Sheetan-el-Kaïlah," the demon of the south, on account of his energy, courage and masterly activity. He is much beloved in all the western part of the regency, where he rules directly or through members of his family. Through his firmness and the justice of his administration, the tribes under his orders are seldom oppressed and rarely rise in rebellion, notwithstanding their warlike character.

It is in the plain of El Sers, which extends to the east of Kef, that the sheik of the great tribe of the Drid ordinarily holds his court. The Drid, who are numerously found in the province of Constantine, have no other fixed territory. They are scattered through the north and west of the regency, where they are shepherds or farmers, on lands that are private property or belong to the state. They are a tribe of the Maksen. In the spring time, they accompany the bey of the camp to the Gereed, where they carry grain and bring back dates, which transaction proves a source of profit, since they take a portion of dates as their right. The Drid, notwithstanding their dispersion, are all subject to the same kaid, who rallies them in great numbers at the period of the expedition to the Gereed. This chief can then count about him more than 1,500 tents; and his "smala," formed by the principal tents around his own, has never less than 300 tents.

"It is," says Pelissier, "the most magnificent Arab village that I have ever seen, as well on account of the aspect of riches which it presents and the neatness and order which reign there, as for the vigorous beauty of the men and women. We find there a large number of Jews living exactly the same life as the

Arabs, armed and clothed like them, taking the part of horsemen and warriors as occasions occur. These Jews are so intermingled with the rest of the population, that it is impossible to distinguish them. They have lost that nasal accent which almost everywhere characterizes this race."

Above the plain of El Sers is the plain of Gorfa, inhabited by the Melita, and to the south, is the considerable tribe of Yacoub, inhabiting a large and fertile plain. The Oulad Ayar, a tribe of 4,000 souls, occupy the slopes and valleys of Gebel Hameda to the south of the Oulad Yacoub. To the northeast are the Oulad Aoun, with 2,000 horsemen and 12,000 inhabitants.

Upon the territory of the Sfin, who are a part of the tribe of the Oulad Aoun, is found, a few miles from Teboursuk, the famous Zawia (chapel) of Sidi Ibrahim Riah. This establishment is due to a famous mufti of Tunis, to whom the bey made, a third of a century ago, important concessions of land in that district. The mufti asked and obtained complete exemption from taxation for all the Arabs who should reside upon his property. He then built the Zawia which bears his name, and soon a village was formed about it, for those who cultivate lands have no demands made upon them except for a tenth of all their products devoted to the service of the Zawia.

Southeast of Oulad Aoun is the small and peaceable tribe of the Oulad Yahia; and to the south is the famous Gebel Kissera, an oval mountain, upon which are two plateaus crowned with rocks almost perpendicular on every side. At the entrance to the first plateau and along the slopes which lead there, is a group of houses built in the midst of ravines, torrents and cascades. In the cool season, one might about as well, so far as personal comfort is concerned, take up an abode among glaciers; but during the scorching heat of summer, a residence there is rendered very agreeable by the freshness of the air and the shade of the trees which are found upon these heights.

To the east of Gebel Kissera, is the territory of the Konab and the Kwassin, which tribes are under the same kaid. Gebel Oussela extends between their territory and the plain of Cairwan. It appears bristling with pointed rocks, and is all cut up with gorges and ravines. It was the last place of resistance which the native race held, after having for centuries heroically contended against their foreign invaders. Up to the middle of the eighteenth century, these mountains constituted the retreat and citadel of a Berber population, which held in check the Turkish beys. After a heroic struggle, the Ousselatians were overpowered and obliged to disperse, abandoning their country, which has since become a mere wilderness.

If we observe the central situation of Gebel Oussela in Tunisia, and compare it with diverse points elsewhere which have had an analogous importance, we shall arrive I think at the idea that there is, in inhabited regions as in the human body, a central point where energy and resistance concentrate at the moment of danger, taking refuge and holding out long after even all hope is lost. These places become the centres of life and the scenes of the last heart-beatings of the nations that succumb under victorious foreign invaders.

The inhabitants of cities are, as before stated, designated by the name of Moors. This term, which antiquity has bequeathed us and which we have vaguely extended to all the inhabitants of North Africa, we believe to be derived primarily not from Mauritani, the inhabitants of Mauritania, but from the Hebrew word Mahaurim which signifies simply *occidentals* (western people) in contra-distinction from *orientals*; for in all time, the Semitic peoples have distinguished nations according to their position relative to the sun, and now also North Africa is for the Arabs "the Magreb," the west, and its inhabitants are designated by them under the name of Magrebeen, the western people in opposition to the Sharakeen, the inhabitants of the Shark or orient. At this point, we will make, in passing, two remarks which have their importance. In the middle age, the terms Saracens and Moors were in constant use, and continue to be used in all the books relative to that period. Now, this term Saracens is simply a corruption of the word *Sharakeen*, which signifies orientals; and, as to the epithet *Moors* applied to the Mussulmans of Spain, it thus indicates its true meaning (western people), since whether of the African race or not, they came from North Africa.

The Moors have a mixed origin. They are the descendants of all the races that have established themselves and succeeded each other in the cities and villages and which have by the force of time and circumstances become *fused* together, from the Phœnicians down to the European slaves turned Mussulmans. A certain number of Arab origin or descendants of the Moors of Spain fled back into North Africa, especially after the fall of Granada.

The men are generally above the medium size and height. Their beard is almost always black; their complexion slightly brown or sallow; their nose aquiline or straight, never flat; their eyes black with that penetrating look peculiar to all orientals; their movement measured and their aspect grave. Such are their general characteristics. The turban is wound about their sheshia and comes down over their ears; a long tunic extends half way down their legs, covering a standing waistcoat, a broad girdle and bagging pantaloons; the shoes are red with a round point, or yellow with the point turned over; or are made almost in the European style, but however made, are worn as slippers; and a great bernouse is thrown over their shoulders. Such is their habitual costume, modified as to color, material and fitness according to the conditions and tastes of the persons. We must remark that the tunic is specially worn by people in easy circumstances and the upper classes. The more common classes, including workmen, wear only a waistcoat. The Moors who are well off wear white stockings; the others go with their legs bare.

The women are lively and pretty looking, but soon acquire *embonpoint*, which is much prized by the Moors. Their indoor costume consists of a *coufia*, a sort of silk cap, from which is suspended a veil called *derraya* which comes around the face and hangs over the shoulders with tresses more or less ornamented with ribbons. A silk tunic descends to the knees; the arms are almost uncovered in the light and floating sleeves of the chemise; silk pantalets wrought with gold or silver and quite tight, though clumsy looking on account of the thickness of the material, descend to the ankles; a profusion of jewelry, including bracelets and great rings of gold or silver about the ankles, complete the costume. We shall speak elsewhere of the *koheul* and henna, and give other details of the life of Moorish women. They scarcely ever go out except when they become old and lean or have the bath in view. Their costume then is not in the least attractive. They are enveloped in white linen and light mantles, which cover them from head to foot, and are protected besides by a thick silk veil, whose extremities they hold with the arm extended in front in order to see their way. They appear to us more like walking bundles of linen, than like charming and beautiful ladies.

The Moors are shopkeepers, merchants and artisans. But as shopkeepers and merchants, they are surpassed and outwitted by the Jews; and as artisans, though still very numerous, they have less work from year to year, partly because they fail to keep themselves supplied even with their defective tools and partly on account of the active and successful competition of European workmen.

Shaw, in his valuable work written nearly a century and a half ago, represents the Tunisians as milder and less turbulent than the inhabitants of any other Barbary power. His remarks probably hold good at the present time. These Tunisian Moors are nevertheless proud-spirited, though courteous and often servile in their manner. Keen witted, intellectual and possessing a versatile talent for eloquence and action, intercourse with them is in general agreeable for those who know how to guard against a bad faith which seems indigenous to the soil, and is in their eyes all right when they have dealings with infidels.

The influence of their climate and sedentary habits and the insensible torpor which creeps over the inhabitants of a country in full decay, contribute to render the Moors lazy, indolent and apathetic, and to take from them that elastic force which belongs to the people of the west and especially of the north, where they are often stirred into such feverish activity as amounts to a tyranny of the mind over the body. It is precisely the opposite kind of tyranny that prevails from natural causes among all the orientals in general, and the Tunisian Moors in particular. They spend most of their day, dozily resting with legs crossed and head and shoulders bent forward, upon the carpets or mats of cafés or upon the benches of their shops; and in their houses their almost constant place is upon a lounge, where they incline at their ease, leaning for hours upon their elbows.

They taste with extraordinary moderation a little cup of black coffee, which from their manner one would suppose inexhaustible, and which is nevertheless succeeded at intervals by other cups, which are sipped in the same style, usually accompanied by the pipe, which is smoked with even more languor than is diplayed over the coffee. The very workmen contrive to lounge half the day, drinking their coffee and smoking their pipes, at periods fixed in advance. The shops which are seldom opened before eight o'clock in the morning in the summer months, are regularly closed with rare exceptions at about three o'clock in the afternoon, and at this hour repose and silence creep gradually over the Mussulman city. In return for this, the cafés become animated and often crowded until eight or nine o'clock, which is the ordinary limit of evening occupation or amusement. At ten o'clock in the evening, the streets are quiet and gloomy, being lighted only by an occasional passing lantern, except perhaps the piazza of the Europeans, where some lamps may glimmer to render the general darkness more striking.

The Moors affect for the nomad population a contempt which is often well repaid by the latter. They seize every occasion to reproach the Arabs with their want of intellectual culture, civilization and neatness, and with their neglect of religious duty and their frequent bloody quarrels. The Arab in his turn commiserates the Moor for having to breathe the impure air of cities; rebukes his cowardice and want of hospitality and ridicules him as a mere shop-keeper. When the Arab has need of the Moor, the latter, taking advantage of his necessities, uses, abuses, and jeers him without pity. In return for this, when the tribes rise in rebellion and the victorious Arab can pass his squad of horsemen within the city walls, he falls upon the humiliated Moor, robbing and plundering him without mercy.

At this time, it is true there are few occasions for

this antagonism to be strongly manifested; for the wretchedness of the country is such that there is comparatively little commerce between the tribes and the cities, and, moreover, the incursions of the Arabs into the cities are almost forgotten. The insurrections regularly fail, like everything else with a people that is failing to sustain its hold on life.

Meanwhile the government keeps a clear account with the tribes, while it concerns itself little with the Moors. No kind of oppression drives the latter to desperation; while the former, though naturally patient, always end in being exasperated by tyranny, and at length trying the virtue of powder and steel in open revolt. The Moors strongly resemble in features and habits the "Koulouglis," who are descended from former Turkish soldiers married to Tunisian women. The Koulouglis, however, are not very numerous.

Genuine Turks, who preserve their peculiar habits and are easily recognized by their odd martial bearing, singular costume and foreign accent, are reduced at this time to about one hundred persons, venerable but perishing relics of the soldiery that once played in Tunisia as in Algeria a part analagous to that of the prætorians of Rome during the decay of the empire.

There remain, as special types, the Negroes, the Warglias and the Mzabias. The Negroes, who are the offspring of former slaves from Soudan, amount probably to 25,000 in the regency, of which number 2,000 reside in the capital. They are found in large numbers occupying the position of servants, especially the women, many of whom are white-washers, bakers of bread, and pedlers of flour. It is amusing to observe how fond these Negroes are of bright, clear colors, as if their object were to set off their native complexion. Most of them are clad in white, always showing a preference for the most brilliant and striking colors. They have distinctive manners and customs, and some of them also a peculiar language. At certain seasons of the year, they hold great meetings for rejoicing or sorcery. These are held during the night by the light of lanterns, and are accompanied with savage music and inarticulate cries, while the multitude are making frantic gestures and dancing as if impelled by some demoniacal influence. This scene usually ends with the utter prostration by fatigue of many of the fanatical and infuriated multitude. Converted to Islamism, whose worship and prescriptions they observe with marked scrupulousness, the Negroes have nevertheless preserved some of the idolatrous or fetish superstition of their race, and, among other practices, that of sacrificing cocks, the burning of incense, the use of amulets and magic or diabolical operations, all particularly national.

The Warglias, who come from the oasis of Warglia in the Sahara, are an intermediate tribe between the Negroes and the Berbers. They are not black, but of a tawny color, with features slightly analagous to those of the Negroes, whom, however, they do not much resemble either in tongue, habits, features or color. They are mostly servants, and a few of them reside in Tunis. They have among themselves a kind of corporation with its officers and regulations like those of the tribe.

The Mzabia or Beni Mzab come from the Algerine tribe of that name, situated also in the Sahara. They are Berbers, come to Tunis to make a little money. Probably prompted by selfishness, they maintain very proudly their character as French subjects, though they constitute a sort of corporation, whose chiefs protect and govern them. They speak Arab with a particular accent and are found numerously peddling charcoal and taking care of baths.

Having completed our sketch of the Moors residing in the cities, we propose now to direct our attention to the people in the country, far otherwise important, who, whether dwelling in tents or under thatched or tiled roofs, constitute the great body of the Tunisian population. We are to speak of the Arabs and Kabyles. We often meet with their types in the cities. They come there to sell the products of their country and to purchase cotton and other goods, or to exercise temporarily certain trades.

The Arab wears two sheshias; the white one is next to his head and the red one is put outside as an emblem of his religion. When he has important papers, he puts them between these two sheshias. Upon the red sheshia he wears the haik, which is a long piece of light cloth, fastened with a cord made of goat's or camel's hair, which is wound around the sheshia like the turban, but is less voluminous and more regular than that of the Moor.

A long woolen tunic (the *gandaura*) covers his shirt, if he has one, and comes down to the calf of his legs.

Scarcely any but wealthy persons and magistrates wear breeches and girdles. The costume is completed by the bernouse or great-hooded mantle, from which the Arab is rarely ever separated, and by shoes without heels, which are always worn like slippers. Arab chiefs wear two bernouses and, ordinarily, richly ornamented boots. Horsemen also wear bootees to which are fastened long iron spurs. A long gun, two pistols resembling blunderbusses, and a long flat sword, constitute their arms.

The Kabyle wears for a head-dress the red cap, sometimes surrounded among the upper classes, with the haik; a woolen shirt which is much shorter than the Arab tunic and is drawn tight around his loins and fastened with a girdle; clumsy sandals; a leathern apron when he is a workman, and finally the inevitable bernouse. The arms are about the same as those of the Arab, but are of Kabyle manufacture, while the Arabs are neither gunsmiths nor mechanics of any kind. The Arab is a laborer or shepherd, serving in either of these capacities according to circumstances and occasions. The Berber or Kabyle is everywhere an artisan and gardener. The Arab is a traveller, shepherd and laborer, and is indolent, contemplative and fond of revery and of poetic forms. He has a finer intellect than the Kabyle and a more social nature. The Kabyle is mason, blacksmith, gunsmith and farmer, and is positive, practical, headstrong and parsimonious, yet intelligent without having the versatility of talent and agreeable manners of the Arab.

Though these two races have become mixed and

confounded in some places, forming an intermediate population, they still exist very distinct in regions where each of them has been concentrated, generally the Kabyles in the mountains, and the Arabs in the plains. A word about the manners and customs of these two races.

THE ARABS. The aggregate element which forms the basis of their social law is the tribe. It is the union of families which are believed to be *ab antiquo* of common origin. It was the spirit of communion and union that formed the tribe, and it is that which still maintains and perpetuates it.

The tribe is then only the extension of the family and the union of individuals of the same stock. Its form of government is also derived from the authority of the head of the family; it is aristocratic or rather patriarchal, represented by the sheik or elder, who is elected by the tribe itself or by the kaid who is delegated by the central power. For in proportion as the tribes were constrained to submit to a central power, the latter governed them by means of kaids and their delegates chosen in the tribe; but in modifying things at the top, it could not change them at the base. The organization of the tribe remained substantially the same. The tribe has always formed a little state in the state, preserving in general the right to govern itself by means of men chosen by itself or drawn from its bosom, and the right to enjoy exclusively the territory where it lives.

Thus the tribe is the political and administrative element. The dowar or ring of tents is the family element in the tribe. Every head of a family and proprietor of land forms the dowar, whose chief is the sheik or elder of the dowar chosen on the ground.

Several dowars form the *farca* or division of the tribe when it is large; for in general the ordinary tribes are constituted by the union of dowars. The farca has a sheik appointed by the united dowars. The tribe is a collective body, embracing from 500 to 40,000 souls. It has control over a large extent of territory, but a small part of which is improved or needed for its support.

The kaid, delegated by the central power as the chief of the tribe, is always selected from families in high standing. His authority and jurisdiction are complete in his district. He presides over the markets, administers justice, divides off lands and levies taxes. He has for his assistant, the *khalifa*, for his police, the *shaoush*, and for his troops, the regular cavalry of the tribe.

The other functionaries of the tribe are the cadi, who is the judge in all civil and criminal cases among Mussulmans, and is *par excellence* a public notary to receive and legalize acts; he never officiates unless assisted by two *adels* or secretaries; the *mudair* or schoolmaster, who teaches reading and writing, however well or ill, and to commit and recite passages from the koran with the desired intonations; the muezzin, who calls to prayer five times a day with his face turned towards Mecca, his thumbs resting on his ears, and his open hands parallel with his face.

All Arab property is classified as being either private property; the property of the Beylic or state; the property of the tribe, or as religious property consecrated by its donors to some special object on certain conditions. Large amounts of property are put into the last form in Mussulman countries to prevent its being confiscated by the state, especially in cities and their environs.

The cultivated land of the tribe becomes during the period comprised between seed-time and harvest, the property of the "farca" of the tribe which cultivates it. Uncultivated land remains common property. The consequence of these irregular conditions of property is that one farca succeeding another on such and such portions of land, the Arab is little interested to improve the condition of a soil on which he is not sure to remain more than a year, or even than several months.

We have said that the tribe occupies in general more land than is needful for its subsistence; notwithstanding this, there are dowars which possess no territory of their own, and which are composed solely of farmers employed by the farcas charged with tillage.

The Arabs recognize three kinds of aristocracy:—

1. That of birth, embracing the *shorfa* or nobles, properly so called (in the singular *scherif.*) These are the descendants of Fatima, the daughter of Mohammed, and of Sidi Aly-ben Abi Taleb, uncle of the prophet. The koran recommends the *shorfa* to the respect of the faithful. They are much respected, but they have prerogatives rather moral than material. Haughty, insolent and altogether severe and grave in their bearing, they wear with dignity the green turban as a sign of their extrac-

tion. At Tunis, however, a multitude of the common people, such as butchers and the lowest class of laborers are *shorfa*. In other parts of the regency also, and throughout the Mussulman as well as Christian world, apocryphal nobles are numerous.

2. The military or temporal nobility, the *juads*, descendants of ancient illustrious families or of a celebrated tribe, especially that of the *Beni Koraish* or Korashites, to which Mohammed belonged. The juads are mostly descended from the Arab conquerors. They are the chiefs of the tribe who lead to the combat. Honored with the title of sheik or elder, they are fond of pomp and show, and sometimes tyrannical towards their dependents, but yet skilful in maintaining their influence by an affected generosity and by hospitality and protection spontaneously offered.

3. The religious nobility composed of *marabouts*, which word is an exact translation of the Latin word religati, signifying *bound back*. These are families devoted for a long time to the religious observance of the koran, and to the edification of the faithful. This nobility is like the preceding, hereditary. It is around *zawias*, or chapels consecrated to some celebrated marabout, that the marabout families are grouped and form their *dowar*, which is then called zawia, followed by a proper name; for example, *zawia Sidi Mahres*. The marabouts are very influential. They intervene as peace-makers and arbiters in discords; protect caravans and travellers with their pass which is always respected, at least by all the members of their tribe. They excite to

holy war against infidels, and are, as it were, the soul of their tribes. The Emir Abd-el-Kader owed his extraordinary influence in Algeria, as much to his triple character as marabout, juad and scherif, as to his natural abilities.

The marabouts live on contributions made by the public for their zawia. Splendid offerings of every kind, including lands, are made to them, and their neighbors often contribute a tenth part of their income. The zawias are governed by the most influential man of the religious dowar. The marabouts perform no manual labor, devoting themselves to giving instruction and exercising hospitality in the interior of zawias, which are at the same time seminaries of learning and pious inns. The tribes entrust to them a certain number of pupils, who become *tolba*, i. e., lettered. When they have passed through a very limited course of elementary study, acquiring some knowledge of the koranic dogmas, grammar, jurisprudence and Arab history, they are proclaimed skeiks, i. e., elders and men of science, and *kodja*, i. e., scribes, and have the right to perform the marriage ceremony pronounce divorces and legalize contracts, all under the authority of the cadi. As they advance in years, they can aspire to becoming themselves cadis, muftis or imans in the mosque.

Corresponding to the zawias, are the *medersa* or high schools, attached to the mosques. The *tolbas* who are distinguished, are proclaimed *aoulamas*, i. e., learned men or doctors. When age, favor and intrigue fail to elevate them to religious dignities, they often become charlatans, enchanters, fortune-tellers, exorcists, makers of amulets and casters of lots. The tolbas are the most worthy representatives of Mussulman fanaticism, which must naturally be in direct proportion to their science, since they try to give the highest idea of Islamism, and the most deplorable opinion of infidels. The *hadji* or Mecca pilgrims, form also a kind of nobility, but it is of a personal character. They have the right to wear the green turban, which they rarely fail to do.

The Arab sheiks, like the Roman patricians and the lords of the middle age, have a multitude of dependents crowding into their great tent in the centre of their "smala," which is the name of the headquarters of the sheik and is composed of his tents and those of his lieutenants, judges, counsellors and protectors. These sheiks receive and hear everybody, giving orders to some, advice to others, and the light of their countenance to all. With the sword always drawn and the hand always open, there is certainly ostentation in the courage and liberality in the action of the Arab sheik; but his liberality or his courage is ever at the disposition of every one that desires it enough to pay for it. The marabouts and juads are not always agreeably situated; but in the most infamous transactions, they maintain the prestige of their class, no one presuming to purchase their favor.

The lower classes present less variety among the Arab shepherds than among the agricultural population. Among the latter, there are the proprietors of the soil, farmers, workmen and servants; among the shepherds, on the contrary, there are scarcely any except the owners of the flocks and herds with their dependents; and their principal property consists in camels and various kinds of stock. Living under tents, there are no professional traders. The transportation of merchandise would encounter too great difficulties and risks. There are, however, blacksmiths who make plows, horse-shoes, large stirrups and long spurs, and repair or injure arms; also, saddlers and shoemakers. The women wash and card wool; make yarn and weave cloth, which, whether coarse or fine, is always strong. They also make bernouses, haiks, hair cloth and tents. Small transactions generally take place between neighbors by exchanges or by paying ready money. The needful articles which the Arab of the tent cannot produce, such as cotton goods and spices, are ordinarily obtained of Jewish pedlers, found in various settlements. The principal commerce in grain, cattle and the different products and manufactures of the tribes is carried on at fairs which are held on fixed occasions, where a great multitude of buyers and sellers come together under the authority and supervision of their skeiks or of their deputies.

Let us attempt, in conclusion, a sketch of the Arab and of his desert life. It is important at the outset not to confound the epithets, *nomad* and *wandering*, which, though often employed as synonymes, are primarily different in their meaning. The nomad tribes all lead a pastoral life, removing according to the seasons, but yielding to a regular oscillating movement, which, at the same period, brings them back again to the same point. Whereas some wandering tribes lead an adventurous life, hunting, trading, pillaging or depending on successful warfare for support.

The Arab of the Sahara, full of pity for the Arab of the village, is in general nervous, ardent and passionate. He is courageous, hardy and temperate, but on occasions shows a ferocious appetite. His white teeth, unharmed by the condiments of civilized life, shine in the middle of his face, that is pale or simply browned by the sun; his features are nobly marked; his eye is expressive; his black beard, that has never known a razor, is fine and glossy, and his expression haughty and pensive. He has always for a companion and friend the well-beloved horse, which surely is not a mere animal, since Baroc, the mysterious companion of Mohammed, in his nocturnal voyage, is in paradise in the midst of the houris and the elect,—the horse, the object of his care, kindness, devotion and enthusiasm; with his fleetness in the race, his intrepidity in the combat; his participation in the fatigue, valor and victory of his master, who proclaims that the happiness of this world and the paradise of earth are attached to the flowing manes of noble steeds. Also, horses, in combats, love and religion, are one of the inspirations of the poets of the tent. Taking part in all the vicissitudes of Arab life and the events of Arab history from the time of Mohammed, they have a place of honor in the annals of his people, like Baroc, in paradise.

The Arab woman has preserved a little of the influence which she enjoyed before Islamism, a period when in her native liberty she was the glowing and poetic soul of the tribes. She still excites to combat and to deeds of honor and valor. But the almost annihilation of her legal existence and her ever-increasing ignorance have robbed her of her royalty of other days. However, in the wars between one tribe and another, women still assist in the combat; from the tops of their palanquins borne by dromedaries, they animate the combatants, bestowing the most marked compliments on some, and uttering curses and withering reproaches against others; while the chiefs in splendid garments, the cavalry turning their steeds and the infantry closing up their ranks for the onset, all press forward, saying in their hearts: *to-day we will die for the women of our tribes.*

The swift-footed dromedary is the attendant of the nimble steed. His patience, sobriety, intrepidity and impassibility; his slender form and dizzy speed, all contribute to render him precious and dear to those who know not how to live without him.

But the Arab without a dromedary or horse to run for him makes a virtue of necessity and becomes himself an indefatigable walker. With his legs enveloped in brodekins or his naked feet in the sand, he passes over immense distances. A courier extraordinary, he reposes only two hours at night, and as he takes his sleep lights a piece of cord whose flame awakens him on reaching his body at the end of the time fixed for its burning, which he calculates with remarkable accuracy. The merchants, residing at the important points along the shore, employ as mail carriers both on account of certainty and expedition, Arabs that are dependent on their legs.

Under the tent of the chief, the labors are entrusted to servants, mostly negroes and negresses, who yet hardly know of the emancipation proclamation by Ahmed Bey in 1845. To milk sheep and camels, make butter, grind grain, weave cloth, make tents, bags, clothing, curtains, thread, hemp or palm-leaf ropes; to prepare leather, and leathern bottles, and great jars for water; to bake bread and make couscousou;—such is the vast field for their unfailing activity.

Hunting is one of the greatest and most stirring occupations of the desert. The antelope, gazelle, wild sheep, and ostrich are pursued and taken without danger and without combat. The hyena is reached and overpowered in his den; but the lion resists the empire that audacious man pretends to impose upon his haughty nature in that desert which is his domain also, and by his thundering roar he proclaims, according to the Arabs, the destiny that puts him in the face of man: "Ana-an-ben-el-mra," he says growlingly, I and the son of woman.

The lion appears there with the calm of his restrained force and fury; lightning in his eye; his teeth and claws impatient for exercise; his jaws dry with thirst and vengeance are ready open to be thrust upon bloody muscles. But it is said the intrepidity of man imposes upon him; the lion retreats sometimes; and, whether from admiration or disdain, slowly draws back before the menaces and cries of women. Meanwhile, men, mounted on war horses and instinctively shivering with terror, challenge him. The noble and terrible animal accepts the challenge; throws himself with a bound through balls which hiss around him, and his blood runs mixed with that of his torn adversaries, the sight of which revives him until at length, under the weight of numbers and the agony caused by his wounds, which are cruelly multiplied under a tempest of shots, he falls and dies, rather annihilated than vanquished.

Besides numerous other careers open among the Arabs to warlike activity, there are long voyages for curiosity or commerce facilitated by caravans. In the regency of Tunis, there are caravans established between the principal cities, which perform a service analagous to that of diligences in Europe and of mail stages in remote parts of America. But veritable caravans resembling a city on the march, are those of the desert. Every traveller adopts his own style; takes his beasts of burden and store of provisions, or is provided by the director of the caravan, or he goes afoot and lives like the multitude. In general, everybody has arms. Camels alone are ordinarily employed in their character as "ships of the desert." When the route is suitable, however, horses and donkies are used.

The conductor of the caravan is made responsible for accidents. He pays awards for all damages occurring to travellers, when it is proved to be his fault or that of his subordinates. But it is well understood that though the right is undeniable, no reclamation is ever made on the way; for the safety of the traveller might be endangered by the disappearance of the conductor. The man who fulfils these difficult and perilous functions, is ordinarily very experienced, firm and courageous, having been tried in these respects on previous occasions. He is the organizer and recognized head of the party. He has, as assistants, guides, whose duty it is to point out the routes; guards to maintain order or organize, in case of need, defence against assailants; a scribe to record and legalize important acts, and a muezzin to proclaim the hours of prayer.

Caravans are exposed, even in provinces near great cities, to attacks by pillaging tribes or isolated bands of brigands. On the routes through the Sahara to Soudan, they often encounter the Touaregs. These are nomad Berbers, scattered here and there between the southern part of North Africa and the country of the negroes, and are divided into two principal groups, the Occidental and the Oriental. With a slender frame and a very white skin; veiled with one end of their turban, which they draw down over their faces in such a manner as to leave only their eyes uncovered; enveloped in a flowing robe which is more full than that of the Arabs, and with ampler folds in their bagging pantaloons; bare-footed or wearing light sandals; always mounted on fleet horses, or dromedaries that even surpass horses in speed; armed with a long lance and with a broad buckler made of the hide of an elephant, the Touaregs are the terror of their neighbors and of caravans which venture into their country. They are Mussulmans, but being monogamists, are accused of heresy and disliked by the orthodox sects. They are nevertheless very hospitable and temperate. They show much deference to their women, whose faces they leave unveiled, and in their manners are comparatively simple and honest aside from their pillaging habits. They live in villages, in oases or under tents, according to their territory; and their riches consist especially in immense herds of dromedaries. They are, besides, intrepid and industrious hunters, and, pillaging being in a line with their interest, is pursued as if it were an honorable trade rather than with the spirit of brigandage. What confirms this view of their character is that they are often satisfied with levying taxes on caravans, which they could readily rob with impunity. When resistance is offered, they become ferocious and merciless.

THE BERBERS OR KABYLES. The word *Kabyle* is variously explained by etymologists. By some it is supposed to be derived from the Arab verb *kebala*, meaning *accepted* or adopted, because the Kabyles adopted Islamism; according to others, it comes from *kebel*, meaning *before*, because it is applied to a population which preceded or came before the Arabs; and still others derive it from *kebila*, meaning *tribe*, and *kebail*, *tribes*, asserting that the conquering Arabs designated all the native tribes by this vague and general appellation in contra-distinction from all their own tribes which were called by their proper names.

According to very confused historic traditions, which we have elsewhere noticed, the Berbers or Kabyles were gradually formed out of the following elements:

1. Of the first occupants of North Africa, who were, according to the Bible account, confirmed by

oriental and African traditions, the grand-sons of Shem. The historian Ibn Khaldoun, names *Masigh* among the ancestors of the Berbers, and it is worthy of remark that a great part of the race have retained till the present time the name of *Amazigh*. 2. Of Canaanites, who emigrated from Palestine in the time of Joshua. 3. Of Phœnician colonists. 4. Of Arab colonists, who came from Yemen long before the Arab conquerors of the seventh century. Such are ordinarily regarded as the sources from which sprang the Berber race; but we are disposed to take account also of the Germanic or Vandal element introduced at a later period, traces of which though not recognized by most authors, remain to the present time, since we not unfrequently meet Kabyles with blond or reddish hair, and eyes blue or of a greyish green tinge.

The Kabyle, as before stated, is distinguished from the Arab by his features and by his character. He has also a distinct language. This language, whose alphabet is unfortunately lost, is written with Arab characters. It is not spoken by all the Kabyles. Those who have mingled with Arabs or have had for centuries intimate relations with them, have become *Arabized* Kabyles, that is, speaking Arab, while others have continued to speak their native (Berber) tongue, which is the Numidian more or less modified. The Arab neither knows nor tries to learn Berber, while the Kabyle is forced to learn and speak Arab by the very exercise of his religion.

At all the invasions, the Kabyles fell back upon the mountains. The conquerors of the country stopped before those formidable citadels of nature defended by an indefatigable valor. France did not definitely subdue them until 1858, and even now the old Kabyle spirit of independence is often manifested in fight.

Other distinctive traits of the Kabyle are: attachment to the soil; not nomad but living in tents, active and industrious as a mason, gunsmith, blacksmith, manufacturer of tools and household utensils, soap, powder and balls; he cards wool, spins and weaves, cultivates the soil, and has swarms of bees constantly supplying him with honey. The Arab neglects his arms; the Kabyle polishes his with care. The Arab is restive and lazy; the Kabyle stirring and impetuous; the former is vain, but servile when he cannot be arrogant; the latter is invariably inflexible and haughty; the Arab serves his ends with falsehood; the Kabyle detests such a resort; the Arab is satisfied with taking the price of blood as a punishment for murder according to the law of the koran; the Kabyle is satisfied only with the death of the assassin. In war, the Arab likes to cut off the head of his fallen foe; the Kabyle never. The Arab is generally a robber and, purely avaricious, hides his money in the ground; the Kabyle robs only his enemy; he is more selfish than the Arab or more intelligent in his avarice, letting his money, contrary to the koranic law, at enormous interest. The Kabyle, who is almost always a monogamist, literally buys his wife, but he respects and consults her much more than the Arab. When a son is born, he makes a general feast; for a daughter, none. At funerals, all the village take part, and sometimes several neighboring villages. Among the Arabs, at the birth of a son, there is a special season of rejoicing, but only in the family; at the birth of a daughter, the feast which takes place is solely for the women, and funerals are attended only by the relatives or special friends of the deceased.

The Kabyle woman is more free than the Arab woman. The latter never appears out among men unless her face be closely veiled. The former goes out with undisguised face, visiting the markets and the public assemblies at her pleasure. There is one sign altogether peculiar to the Kabyle woman; it is a cross tattooed on her forehead between her eyes. This cross, which is an evident trace of the primitive Christianity of the race, is never found among the Arabs, and a circumstance that well confirms its signification is, that no devout personage ever marries a Kabyle woman until he has by means of a solution slightly corrosive obliterated that hated emblem of the Christian faith.

The tribe is the political and administrative element among the Kabyles as among the Arabs. The chief kaid, khalifa, sheik and aga are chosen among distinguished religious or military families corresponding to the different nobilities. Each part of a tribe is governed by an *amin*, charged with maintaining order and the usages of the tribe. There are also amins-in-chief, appointed at the general assembly of the tribe.

Among the Mussulman peoples, the Kabyles are the only ones that have, besides their code taken from the koran, a particular national code which is always in vigor. It is a remarkable fact that in this code, the death penalty prescribed by the koran is laid aside and exile is put in its place; but the way is nevertheless open for private vengeance, which comes almost always in its time. The bastinado, so common among the Arabs, is unknown among the Kabyles.

More still than the Arabs, they have a profound veneration for their marabouts, who are supported at the expense of the tribes, and are in truth the overseers, counsellors, directors, and, morally speaking, the sovereigns of the nation. Besides, the Kabyle, it must be acknowledged, makes rather a pitiful show as a Mussulman disciple, often violating the prophet's injunctions, and causing scandal among the saints by dining on the wild boar that his unerring bullet has reached among the mountains.

The Arabs pay their contributions directly to their sovereigns; the Kabyles, almost republican in their character, deposit theirs only in the mosques. They do not recognize any taxes imposed upon them, except for their mosques and cemeteries, while, on the other hand, the Arabs often labor for their chiefs. The zawia, with the Kabyles as with the Arabs, is, at the same time, a religious seminary and a pious and gratuitous hotel. The three grades of instruction before named are given in the important zawias, but the Berber language is nowhere taught.

Among the customs peculiar to the Kabyles, we must at least mention the following before concluding this sketch. About the time for the fruits to ripen, the chiefs publish an order that within so many days no fruit must be gathered. At the expiration of this time, the proprietors repair to the mosques to testify upon oath that they have observed the order, or to pay the penalty if they have been remiss in their duty. They then count the poor, and each one feeds them in his turn. They proceed in the same way with the vegetables, especially with the beans, which are cultivated on a large scale.

The safe conduct or pass given by a Kabyle marabout or by a private person, is called *anaya*, and the union or national spirit is so strong among this people, that this pass is never violated. Among the Arabs, a safe conduct or pass is of little value beyond the tribe, but among the Kabyles it is available wherever it is met. In according a pass, some writing is given that is easily recognized and at the same time serves as a protection against imposition. The Kabyles belong to several leagues or confederations, which are proclaimed in the general meeting of the chiefs. The leagues are special or general, according to interest and circumstances. In time of foreign war, all the Kabyle tribes form one immense confederation.

We will conclude in the forcible language of general Dumas, a French officer, who has studied well Mussulman institutions and character, and who, during a long service in Algeria, devoted special attention to this aboriginal population. "We recognize," says he, "the Kabyles as the representatives of the aborigines of the country. The blood which flows in their veins is doubtless mixed, but the people are, for the most part, of kindred origin with the primitive stock as the basis. All were once Christians, and have never become completely transformed by their new religion. Under the blow of the scimetar, they accepted the koran, but they have never embraced it. They put on the dogmas of Islamism like bernouses; but they have ever preserved underneath their dogmas their previous social form. Though they have long since lost the spirit and significance of the Christian religion, they preserve its emblem tattooed on their foreheads, and this is not their only way of unwittingly demonstrating the symbol of the cross."

POINTS OF ETIQUETTE AND SALUTATIONS. The Arabs and Mussulmans in general (all being Arabized), are, in their attention to common civilities and courtesies, as advanced as any people that can be named, not excepting even the French. They make nice distinctions and have delicate shades of expression, which we will try briefly to explain. The Arab gives the title *Sidna* to the bey alone as the highest expression of respect, and the title *Sidi*, my Lord, to important functionaries and personages. *Si*, meaning *Sir*, and corresponding nearly with our Mr., is a more common title. But even this is withheld from Christians and Jews, and the term *arfi* is employed, which means *master*, not as an epithet of a gentleman, but as used by pupils and apprentices. This injurious distinction, probably suggested centuries ago by fanaticism, is tolerated to the present time by Europeans, sometimes doubtless because it is not fully understood, but generally, we believe, because it is regarded as too small a matter to quarrel about. Those who are conscious of their power and influence as lords and gentlemen, are rarely inclined to stickle about words which cannot affect their real standing and honor.

In regard to salutations, a similar invidious distinction is often made. When Mussulmans meet each other, they salute thus: "Your health and your health." But when they meet Christians or Jews, uttering no cordial wish for their health, they simply say: "How do you do?" When an infidel, whoever he may be, is found in a Mussulman assembly, and another Mussulman enters, the latter, instead of saluting collectively the assembly, will say: "Health to all who walk in the right way;" thus virtually withholding any expression of good wishes and an act of courtesy from the infidel. This conduct, arising from a species of bigotry, excites the indignation of some Christians and Jews, who, standing as squarely on their dogmas as the Mussulman on his, pay him back in his own coin. However, this kind of weakness, which unfortunately is not confined exclusively to Mussulmans, is generally regarded with pity rather than with indignation.

In the presence of old men or superiors, one must always assume an air of gravity, avoiding not only light expressions, but all allusions to indelicate subjects. Trifling or jesting is an offence against good manners, and, in general, ladies or women are never to be spoken of in direct terms. To ask about the ladies, one must employ a paraphrase, as, "How are your family?" or, "How are they at your house?"

The religious spirit predominates in the salutations as in everything among the Mussulmans, and the name of God is perhaps the word most frequently pronounced. "May God bless you," is said as an affirmative answer to a request. "May God prolong your days; protect you; save you; revive your spirit; show mercy to those who brought you into the world;" such are some of the utterances expressive of prayer and thanksgiving constantly dropping from the lips of devout Mussulmans. But they make a marked distinction between infidels and believers, never requesting for the former blessings which the koran accords only to the latter. Thus they carefully avoid asking God to have mercy upon the unbelieving dead who are by law eternally lost. When a believer dies, the prayer goes up on every hand: "May God have mercy upon him." But when a Christian or Jew dies, the prayer is thus changed: "May God have no mercy upon the dog;" or, "May the eternal fire begin for the dog." Though you receive from a Mussulman the most manifest proof of friendship, be not sure that when your life draws to a close he will show respect for your cold remains. You sink at your death, according to his creed, into perdition, and the earth is rid of an infidel. The most enlightened and civilized Mussulmans are sometimes unable to overcome the effect of their teaching in this respect. Their best instincts too often yield to the dogmas of the koran. Some scenes have been enacted in connection with funeral processions at Tunis which fully illustrate what I have here stated.

A person salutes his superior by kissing his hand if he be on foot, and his knee if he be on horseback. It is the rule to kiss the hand of ecclesiastical and civil dignitaries and of old men. Two equals kiss upon the cheek or simply touch each other's hands. At a little distance from each other their salutation consists in passing the hand first to the heart and then to the forehead, or in touching the head and then moving the hand from the heart to the lips and forehead.

All acts of politeness require a grave and dignified manner. Mussulmans ridicule our gay and jovial way of meeting each other. At most, a pensive smile may brighten the face of a friend at meeting. It is allowable to withdraw from a party without formally taking leave, but in cities the usage is otherwise. In society, it is the mark of a gentleman to seize every occasion to demonstrate his religious faith and his regard for the proprieties of life. If the name of the prophet be pronounced, he must exclaim: "Prayer and salvation be unto him." If he speak of another Mussulman deceased, he must offer up some prayer in connection with his name, as, "May God have mercy upon him." If he speak of a Christian or a Jew, his prayer must conform to the spirit of his religion. If his host sneeze, he must offer some prayer, as, "May God protect you," and a grateful reply is at once made. If his host commit a breach of propriety, it is noted, and the prayer goes up: "May God pardon that which has happened." To wish you a pleasant journey, he will say: "May God take you and return you in health and peace." To recall a person who has taken leave of you, is to bring upon him misfortune. To thank you, he will say: "May God increase your heritage, or your riches; may God fill your house with joy, etc." Also, Mussulmans temper all sorts of expressions with "an shallah," *God willing, or if it please God.* They employ this phrase so much the more, as it gives, in case of need, a certain elasticity to their promises. It is a Mussulman tradition that their prophet passed eight days without being able to reply to an argument against his revelations, because, in promising to reply, he omitted to say, *an shallah, if it please God.* It is also a saying that the lion that can carry upon his back a horse, ox or camel, is obliged to draw upon the ground a sheep, in comparison very small, because the first lion created said on beginning his terrible career: "An shallah, I shall take away such and such an animal;" in thinking of the sheep, the thing seemed to him so easy, that he neglected to say *an shallah*, and so was punished for his remissness and impiety.

In offering consolation, the ordinary expressions are: "God is great; it was written; it is decreed; it is a divine order," or "We are from God, and return to him; God alone is eternal! Praise to God!" A form of felicitation very expressive and laconic, is, "Mahbrook!" As much as to say: *Good!* or *good luck* to you! We should not stop here if we wished to pass in review all the forms of Arab civility; but what we have cited may serve to give some idea of these multifarious forms.

We have seen that infidels are not in general very politely treated. They are sometimes, however, despite deep-seated prejudices and the dark teachings of the koran, the objects of most marked attention and kindness.

The Mussulman is taught to seek the humiliation of infidels, and, to effect this object, he sometimes employs in his intercourse with his co-religionists, words which have a double meaning, winks and intonations that change a compliment into derision and insult. In his writing, this is effected in another way. By the simple change of a letter or of a vowel point which the Christian sees only too late, the pious Moslem cruelly loads him with abuse and maledictions, or indulges at his expense in the most bitter sarcasm and cutting irony. He will write, for example, instead of "iselmec allah," meaning, may God save you! "isémec allah," meaning, may God curse you! The two expressions hastily written present almost the same appearance.

Bad faith is an inherent quality of Moslemism, belonging to its spirit and characterizing its national traditions; and the triumphs of Europe have only irritated and envenomed the animosity of the Mussulmans. Here is presented one of the problems of the age. How are these people to be treated? I say, decidedly, not as their religion enjoins upon them to treat us. We need not resort to tricks and chicanery. Such a course has already injured us in their estimation. We can deal justly with them, and can command their respect and esteem only by showing ourselves worthy of them. Our interest and duty lie in this direction. We have already overcome them with the sword, but to acquire a moral ascendancy over them is far more difficult, requiring an intelligence, energy, and nobleness of character in striking contrast with the Christian (?) and Jewish examples generally set in Mussulman countries.

To affirm or attest the truth, there are curious forms in the Arabic language. "By the head; by the prophet; by the head of the prophet; by God;" or by way of imprecation: "May my religion be cursed!" "May God make me wear a hat or a cap!" "May God make me an infidel!" "May God make me a Jew!" The imprecation above relative to the cap or the hat is significant. The head-dress of Europeans is regarded as an emblem of their infidelity. Never can a Mussulman thus profane his august head, crowned with the turban and the sheshia.* It is for this reason that the Turks, Egyptians and Tunisians, while adopting the European costume, cling to their red cap. Mussulmans ridicule and reproach us for wearing the abominable hat, which they regard as a striking impiety and a gross infraction of the fidelity which we should maintain in regard to the costume of Jesus Christ, which was in no respect like ours, while, according to Mussulmans and in fact, it approached much nearer the Arab costume, the true costume of Mohammed, of Father Abraham himself, and of a veritable man worthy of eternal life.

THE HOSPITALITY OF THE ARABS is proverbial. It is a traditional saying of Mohammed, "Be generous to your guests; for in entering your house, he brings a benediction, and in leaving it, he carries away your

---

* Mussulmans scarcely ever uncover their heads. While we take off our hats as a mark of respect on entering consecrated places, they take off their shoes, leaving them at the door.

sins." The Arab of the tent is hospitable with simplicity and magnanimity. He salutes with a hearty welcome the guest whom God sends him. He then installs him in the most comfortable manner possible under his tent, and honors him with a sumptuous feast, selecting for him the best pieces.

This is perhaps the place to say a word about Arab and Mussulman dinners in general; for all Islamitish people are alike in their essential traits and usages. They never go to the table without washing their hands. As they take their seats, they make this short prayer: "In the name of God, bless, O my God, that which thou givest me to eat, and when this is consumed reproduce it!" A Mussulman must help himself to food only with his right hand; for Mohammed said: "The devil eats and drinks with his left hand." The left hand is traditionally impure, and Mussulmans never extend it to their co-religionists, but often present it as a sly expression of contempt to infidels, who in their simplicity sometimes accept it with joy. They must abstain from breathing on their food and in general from using knives or forks. Fingers take the place of knives and forks; for the pieces are cut small in a common platter, which remains in the middle of the table, where each guest puts his hand and with a singular skill helps himself without at all soiling anything around him. For some preparations they employ wooden spoons, which are particularly serviceable in eating couscousou, the national dish. They drink in general only once during the repast either water, curdled milk or palm wine, which is the sap of palm trees. Wine, properly so called, is rigorously forbidden; it is a sign of infidelity almost as bad as that of wearing a hat. But it is certain that this prescription of the koran is now openly violated or eluded by most Mussulman functionaries, who have adopted, among other European usages, the order of our meals, our table furniture, and our articles of food and beverage, including fine wines and liquors. However, not to bring scandal on their Mussulman guests, they remember sometimes to leave their bottles out of sight, often sending a special servant to fill with their contents a silver or gilt glass, which is reputed to contain a medicine.

They must not appear to notice guests at the table, but, leaving them to eat in their own way, must try to create an appetite by numerous dishes. At a special dinner once given on the island of Gerba, in honor of the American consul, sixty-three different well-prepared dishes were brought upon the table, and the plates were changed twenty-eight times, to say nothing of coffee, pipes, wines and liquors.

Eructation is permitted. Care must however be taken while relieving the stomach with all possible liberty, to cry: "Praise to God; I am satiated!" The host and the other guests immediately reply: "God bless you," or "God give you strength!" After dinner they wash their hands and mouth with great care. They are then served with coffee in a little cup resting in a peculiar kind of saucer, used to obviate the danger of being burned. They taste the coffee with the utmost moderation. Under the tent of the Arab and in Mussulman houses, faithful to oriental usages, the guests sit cross-legged upon carpets, mats or divans, about a low round table; but, in the principal houses of the city, they sit and eat like Europeans, having only a peculiar ceremonial for certain dishes.

A word about couscousou, the national dish of the Tunisians and of the Arabs in general. Couscousou is a sort of semolino, which, after being kneaded with a very small quantity of water, is put into a steamer over a boiler, and, seasoned with spices and mixed with butter, meat, vegetables and eggs, is kept steaming for hours, and, when taken out upon a broad platter, the meat, vegetables and eggs are arranged for display outside the semolino. Of the different kinds of meat employed, chickens and lamb are most in favor; under the tent the meat of young camels is frequently employed. The couscousou is arranged in a pyramidal form upon a broad platter, which some attack with a wooden spoon; but the bravest and most adroit with the right hand. The feast is usually interrupted once to partake of a cup of freshly curdled milk. Couscousou is a very palatable and nourishing food, and is, at the same time, light and easily digested. There is also another kind of couscousou called *masfouf*, which is sweet, without meat, and is seasoned with dates, pistachios and raisins.

The Arab kitchen is one of the richest and most varied in the world. We shall attempt to give no idea of it, except by saying that for various ways of preparing ragouts, pastries and delicacies, the cooks of rich Mussulmans could give some valuable lessons to our own, and that in a trial of skill to gratify the taste of even European judges, they might win the prize. Nothing can surpass the delicacy of taste as well as the juiciness of certain kinds of cake, of which butter and honey are important ingredients; we certainly have nothing to place in comparison with them. Everybody knows what was in the middle age, the splendor of the Islamitish civilization. Gastronomy is, perhaps, that which remains most brilliant to-day of that civilization, disappeared or on the point of being lost to view.

But these digressions have drawn us away from Arab hospitality, which engaged our attention. We shall only add some of its characteristics to complete this account. "The beard of the guest is in the hand of the master of the tent." This maxim is the practical companion of the precept of Mohammed, and well expresses the inseparable confidence and sincerity of the Arab at the reception of a guest. Once received into a tent or into a house, not only you have nothing to fear, even were you an enemy; but you need have no care. All your wants will be supplied, and you will greatly offend the host by obtruding your views in regard to your place, luggage and servants. All this concerns alone the master of the house, and you may be sure he will attend to it better than you can.

In each Arab dowar, by the side of the *kima* or collection of tents raised symmetrically around an open space called the *merah*, are several tents a little outside. These present a rich appearance and are destined for guests without distinction of person, position, or even race, except of course the modes of reception inseparable from believers and infidels. Each rich sheik charges himself in his turn with the expenses of these entertainments; though when the expenses are considerable, they are borne in common.

When a dowar has no special tents, the traveller is conducted to some central point, where he is formally welcomed and becomes the object of the most assiduous attentions. The remains of hospitable feasts which are, in general, of enormous proportions,—as after the feeding of the five thousand in the desert place, when twelve baskets full of fragments were taken up,—are always distributed among the servants and the poor, who eat in honor of the guests. I have repeatedly known seventy-five persons thus treated in honor of the American consul, and on the island of Gerba several hundred were thus feasted. Avarice or meanness in a matter of hospitality is detested and despised.

We cannot better terminate these remarks upon Arab hospitality, than by relating an incident illustrating this well-known trait of character, and giving an idea of the responsibility which the host feels to protect his guest from any saddening occurrence. The chief of a tribe received under his tent many travellers of distinction. While he was doing them the honors of his house, his only son, a promising young man and the hope of his family, suddenly died. The unhappy father, subduing his grief, had the energy and courage to maintain the utmost calmness in his tent, and to remain himself unmoved in appearance until the next morning, and it was only at the moment when his guests were departing that he announced to them the sad news, asking them in tears to be present at the funeral ceremonies of his son, and share his grief in return for that hospitality for which he had made such a sacrifice.

RELIGIOUS CREED AND USAGES. The population of Tunisia is of the orthodox Mussulman persuasion. It belongs to that Islamitish religion which has in the world more than one hundred and twenty million followers, and which, after having given birth to an empire greater than the Roman and to a brilliant civilization in the middle age, has become pitifully paralyzed and enfeebled, exhibiting no power to elevate the spirit of its degenerate disciples, who now appear scarcely more in the universe than a great embarrassment to modern civilization.

The true name of the Mussulman religion is the Islam, which means giving up or complete and absolute resignation (to the will of God). It claims to be the veritable, eternal religion; for the prophet was charged only with its definite promulgation. Whoever received the true faith in God before Mohammed's time was a Mussulman in principle. Thus Abraham, Isaac, Jacob and the apostles were Mussulmans* according to the common theory.

The creed of Islamism is very simple: "God alone is God, and Mohammed is his prophet." The authority of this creed resides in the koran, a sacred

---

* This term denotes primarily persons resigned to the will of God. We generally employ the word Mussulmans to indicate the followers of Mohammed, because it is the name which they take to themselves. They profess to be resigned to God, as he is revealed to them by their prophet, and some even claim to be Mussulmans, like the prophets and apostles, regardless of Mohammed's teachings.

book, claiming to be transmitted from heaven chapter by chapter to Mohammed by the angel Gabriel, who was a delegate of God in the revelation of Islamism. All orthodox Mussulmans believe in the oral traditions of Mohammed, and are hence called Sunnites. They are divided in regard to their rites into four sects; the Malekites, Hanefites, Shafaites and Hambalites, names derived from the founders of these sects, who were learned expounders of the Mussulman law. The inhabitants of North Africa are, a majority of them, Malekites.

Besides these four orthodox sects, there is a sect in Tunisia represented only by the inhabitants of Gerba and by the Saharian population of the Mzab or the Mozabites. They are dissenters, distinguished by certain odd practices and peculiar dogmas, which we shall explain further on. There are also some disciples of the Wahabite El Medani. The members of this sect formerly rejected the proposition that "Mohammed is the prophet of God," but now admit it only after saying ninety-nine times, "God alone is God," while the genuine orthodox never utter one of these propositions without the other. Outside of orthodoxy are also found the Shiites, who reject the traditions, and also recognize only Ali as the legitimate representative of the prophet, to the exclusion of Abubekir, Omar and Othman, and who acknowledge, for imans or sovereign pontiffs, only the descendants of Ali. The Wahabites of Arabia profess a sort of deism and admit only in form the mission of Mohammed, the founders of the sect having wished even to destroy his tomb.

The Mussulman religion reposes on an absolute *unitism* or unitarianism, stated in four forms: 1, The one God alone adorable in the universe; 2, the prophet sent from God without companion, who is the seal of the prophets of all ages, and whose mission will henceforth be attested; 3, the caliph or vicar of the prophet or royal pontiff, and his sole legitimate representative of authority upon earth; 4, the husband and master in the family.

The God of Mohammed is doubtless gracious and merciful, as at each instant the koran and all Mussulman books represent him; but he is not the God of New Testament Christianity, loving humanity with infinite tenderness and permitting it to love him and pray to him with assured confidence and affection. He is perhaps a generous God, but shows his generosity by a sort of haughty commiseration, holding all his power menacingly suspended over the heads of his creatures and demonstrating a sort of pity for them on seeing their nothingness. He is really little more or less than a formidable despot whose will must be adored everywhere and always, and under whose blows we must bow simply because they are inevitable and because murmuring is impiety. This God, more tyrannic and cruel even than that of the Jews, draws upon the forehead of every creature who comes to the light his ineluctable destiny; and however it be, Mussulman resignation finds at the same time its motive and its expression in this word: *mactoub!* it is written. Consequently, it is a fatality, to which one is subjected, and foreördination and predestination are fully recognized. They say it is the good pleasure of God that governs the world and each man and creature in it. We have only to submit and be silent without seeking to discuss or understand this subject. We must do good not for goodness' sake, nor to acquire merit, but because God so orders it, when even (that which is not impossible), he judged fit to take no account of it and wrote from all eternity, that in spite of all, we should be lost.

I am aware that some expounders of the law and most Mussulmans in practice would maintain the liberty of man and his free will in order that he may be responsible for his actions, and as a consequence have the merit or blame naturally attached to them. But, in reality, this free agency is contrary to the principle that all power, all direct influence and all regulations of every kind are preëstablished; in a word, it is contrary to the dogma of the "mactoub," that which is written, and of the "mashay-lillahi," that which pleases God. Man is neither saved nor lost, whatever he may wish or do, except God has so written it in his eternal decrees.

But Mussulmans, in as far as they are Mussulman, are predestined in principle to eternal salvation. If some among them go to hell, it will be only for a time. Whence it follows that in fact it is immaterial whether their conduct is good or bad; since in the end eternal happiness awaits all who are registered for paradise without distinction of person. As to infidels, since they profess another religion than Islamism, they will be among the outcasts in another world, despite all the good they can do.*

* Koran, ch. III., verse 79.

There are verses in the koran which apparently contradict this doctrine; this, however, should astonish no one; since the koran is filled with contradictions; but we must compare all the verses with each other, and, after having weighed them *pro* and *con*, we arrive inevitably at this conclusion: "Whoever is an unbeliever in God and his prophet is doomed to wretchedness."

Christians and Jews, especially the former, are the objects of some kindness and indulgence on the part of the prophet. "These are," says he, "the people with a book," i. e., people furnished with a book of revelations, "and we must engage in no discussions with them except in the most becoming manner." But we must remember: 1, That all the chapters of the koran were not written at the same period; 2, that there are verses which annul other verses, and that most of the verses annulled are those which are in their nature very moderate if not reasonable; 3, that, judging from the experience of twelve centuries, the following precepts contain the veritable programme of Islamism:—

"Make war upon those who do not believe in God; upon those who regard not as forbidden that which God has forbidden through his apostle; upon those scriptural men (Christians and Jews) who do not profess faith in the truth.* Make war upon them till they all pay the tribute and are humiliated;† combat in the way of God;‡ kill them wherever you shall find them. Fight them until you have no

* Koran, ch. IX., v. 29. † Ibid. ‡ Koran, II., verse 186, 187 and 189.

temptation to fear, and all worship be that of the one God."

While it is unnecessary to give further extracts, it is only just for us to remember that notwithstanding their terrible and bloody march across the Christian world, prompted by the inspirations of the koran, the Arab conquerors showed themselves in their victories more humane and merciful than the Christian warriors who were their contemporaries. For as the spirit of Islam was to diffuse worship by the sword, Mohammed recommended moderation towards religious people, old men, women and children, regardless of their religion and nationality. It is just also to remark by way of correction and in explanation of the law of conversion by the sword, that according to usage the lives of refractory persons were spared, provided they consented to pay the tribute.

But we must have no misconception here; it remains always well understood that Islam is the sole religion *of right* and *by law*, and that consequently the rule of the world is promised to Mussulmans alone. Whence it results that the rest of the human family must choose between death, conversion and the tribute.

It may be remarked that the word *koffer*, ordinarily translated *infidel*, means rather an ungrateful wretch who conceals the truth. Thus Mussulmans see in us not only infidelity, but ingratitude and bad faith. We resist, wittingly taking sides against the ascendancy of the truth. Ours is not merely an error of opinion; it is a malicious and open rebellion, and an insolent and abominable impiety.

And this opinion must not astonish us. Jews, we

are believed to have falsified the bible; Christians, we have disfigured the gospel. For, according to Mussulmans, in these books and especially in the gospels which the koran calls the book of light, the mission of Mohammed was prophesied and it was bad faith alone that took out these significant passages. The koran undertakes to prove in its peculiar way these pretended falsifications. It gives also biblical or evangelical histories, completely distorting the truth; and Mussulmans in general, having no knowledge of historical criticism or of the value of written testimony, are misled.

The koran, however mixed, strange and confused, contains great and beautiful maxims, and just observations and prescriptions wisely adapted to the spirit and manners of the Arabs. But we must not forget that it is tributary to the bible and the gospel, drawing thence its highest inspirations and noblest sentiments; for Mohammed wrote it or rather dictated it only after long conferences with a Jewish rabbi and a Nestorian priest, who gave him an approximative idea of the old and new testaments. Mohammed, ignorant but of quick perceptions and of lively imagination, reproduced and modified in a manner to suit the needs of his cause these incomplete details of the two revealed religions that existed long before his time.

Whatever may be said of his personal character, this Mahommed is one of the most singular and extraordinary men of history. Obscure, unlettered, a simple conductor of caravans, though of a noble family and of a renowned tribe, he conceived and realized the project of disciplining and uniting together all the Arab tribes then hostile or indifferent to each other, and sending them forth for conquest over the *debris* of empires and religions which then covered the face of the earth.

After twenty years of meditation, reverie, hallucination and forsooth of inspiration (for why may we not admit that such a reformer was of good faith and that profoundly religious, he thought himself obeying an impulsion from on high?), Mohammed applied himself to his work; prescribed the new religion or rather the restored worship of his first ancestor, the religion of Abraham. He successfully encountered all obstacles and perils; strengthened and extended his cause and his party by victories; became the soul of a new nation suddenly formed under the impulsion of his genius and activity, a nation *improvised* by the intimate association and union of twenty different tribes, strongly bound together by unity of language and unity of faith; a double unity, which finds its monument, symbol and palladium in that koran which he boldly placed on one side of the scales, when the Bible, the gospel and all the diverse religions were on the other side to counterbalance it.

Simple, modest, humane, charitable, of agreeable manners, though much given to pleasure, the prophet of the Arabs was in his private life the counsellor, example, pride and object of veneration of his disciples, occupying himself with manual labor, sober, religious without affectation, redressing grievances even for infidels, doing all the good and discharging all the duties which he urged in his preaching, constituting himself without haughtiness and pageant the type of the veritable believer, he continued by the influence of his personal character the work which his preaching and the sword began. It is interesting to observe how philosophical, serene and almost saint-like was his death. Perceiving his end approaching, he spoke to those assembled around him and, after asking their sympathy and prayers, requested them not to let him die without helping him to make some amends for what evil he had done in life. An old woman then stepped forward and asked for the payment of a small debt which had been for a long time forgotten. Mohammed had the debt paid, thanking the woman for having thus relieved his conscience at his last hour. He then resumed in a few simple and penetrating words the instructions of his life, and apparently without fear or regret pronounced with his parting breath this Mussulman or rather Jewish and Christian formula: "We came from God and to God we shall return."

We have said that according to the koran the gospel is "the book of light." According to the koran also Jesus Christ is the Messiah, born miraculously of a virgin; Spirit of God made man so superior to the rest of the human race and of the prophets that God, having divided off all possible merits into ten parts, gave nine of them to Jesus and one alone to the entire human family. He was not put to death as Christians and even Jews say, but taken up to heaven, while God put in his place a phantom to deceive the hatred of his enemies, who, in effect, wished to crucify him. He will come again upon the earth at the end of time. He will break down the cross as an instrument of idolatry and will annihilate the hog, the unclean animal. He will exterminate the anti-Christ, his enemy, and will establish peace and harmony upon the earth, even among the animals most opposed to each other. He will practice Islamism and will make a pilgrimage to Mecca at the head of 70,000 pilgrims. He will restore the marvellous city built for Solomon by the genii, the walls of which were of alternate gold and silver brick. This city, buried by divine order in the sand of the desert at the death of the Jewish king, will be given to Mussulmans that they may have on earth a foretaste of celestial joys. After having restored also the ark of the covenant which will be found at the bottom of lake Tiberias and married a young and charming daughter of the Arab tribe of the Beni Rassan, he will extend Islam over all the earth and will ascend again to heaven before the day of judgment.

In a practical point of view, Islamism recognizes the six following bases: 1, Circumcision; 2, prayer; 3, alms-giving; 4, fasting; 5, pilgrimages to Mecca, and 6, the profession of faith. We propose to say a few words successively on each of these topics.

1. CIRCUMCISION. This Jewish practice was adopted by Islam with this difference, that the Jews perform this ceremony on the eighth day after the birth of the child, while the Mussulmans defer it until the eighth *year*. Several days before the ceremony, there is a great feast in the family. During the operation they try to divert the attention of the

boy, and almost stun him with noisy prayers and the sound of numerous instruments. Then they console him by representing the advantages he has just obtained in being counted henceforth in the number of Mussulmans, the sole elect of all the human family. Notwithstanding the importance attached to circumcision, it is sometimes dispensed with when an infidel embraces Islam beyond a certain period in life.

2. PRAYER must be offered five times every twenty-four hours. From the minarets of all the mosques, *muezzins* remind believers of the canonical hours, proclaiming aloud: "God alone is great; God alone is God, and Mohammed is the apostle of God. Come to prayer. Come to salvation," etc.

There is something profoundly pensive and touching in this mournful air, issuing from above the housetops and floating through all parts of the city, in the silence of the night. It is then the thought, faith and hope of man, watchful amidst the majestic slumbers of the world, and mounting slowly to God in solemn modulations. The five canonical hours of prayer, are: at dawn of day; at noon; at three o'clock, P. M.; at twilight, and later in the evening.

Their prayer consists in repeating some verses from the koran, which they select themselves, taking special care never to omit the *fetha* or first chapter, which is the prayer par excellence, and such pious exclamations as "*Allahou Akbar*," which they utter with groans and sighs, pressing their foreheads upon the ground, and "*Selame, Selume*," which they pronounce, bending to the right and left as if moved by angels. Their attitude varies. They begin in a standing posture, with their unsandaled feet upon a little rug or something analogous, as a mat or sheep-skin; for they would hardly know how to pray upon the bare earth; some moments afterwards, they bend simultaneously their knees; they then lean forward, pressing their forehead upon the ground; then they alternate between the upright position, in reverence bending their bodies without kneeling, and again press their foreheads upon the ground. They must articulate distinctly their prayers. The Malekites, who are most numerous at Tunis, chant them in a low key and with canonical intonations. The Hanefites also pronounce them with a low and solemn voice. The prayers must be repeated audibly or they amount to nothing.

Before every prayer, they must purify themselves by ablutions. Ablutions are of two kinds; *the small ablution*, which is ordinarily practiced five times a day; and *the great ablution*, by which they attempt to rid themselves of all the impurities of the flesh. It may not be uninteresting to indicate the method which they have rigorously to follow in this religious rite.

In the ordinary ablution, they strip their arms and legs; then pour water into the right hand, then into the left, and, proceeding to wash, they say: "In the name of God, compassionate and merciful, I offer this prayer." They must take the rings from their fingers or clean them, turning them round. It is rulable to gargle the mouth and throat three times, and also drawing water into their nostrils to snuff three times, saying: "Make me breathe, Lord, the perfume of paradise." Then taking water into the hollow of the right hand, they wash successively with care the face, ears and beard. They then wash their arms as high as the elbow, always beginning with the right arm. Then bringing their hands together, they put them in water, fingers first; then separating their hands, they move them to their chin and wash their neck; finally, they wash their feet, always beginning with the right one, and not neglecting their toes in the same order. When they are away from home at the hour of prayer and have no water, they can go through with their ablutions with fine sand, and in case they have no sand, they select a clean stone or neat spot, take off their rings from their fingers, their sandals from their feet, spread their bernouse, make the passes as if engaged in washing, and say their prayers perhaps with as much favor as under ordinary circumstances. Mussulmans do not regard the gaze of men; wherever they are at the time of prayer, they seek a favorable corner and offer their prayer without false shame or affectation.

The great ablution must be performed in a bath or in a flowing stream, and the following formalities are repeated three times. They sprinkle the middle of the body; then wash their hands, saying: "My God, I would be totally cleansed from all my impurities; wilt thou cause that they disappear." Then they proceed as in the ordinary ablutions, always washing their right side and right limbs first. After the great ablution, they feel themselves justified and in a state of angelic purity.

3. ALMS-GIVING is much recommended and exten-

sively practiced in Islamitish countries, not in favor of people regardless of religion, but for the faithful. It is unusual for a Mussulman to be so moved by the wretchedness and distress of an infidel, as to provide succor and relief. This would defraud the poor Mussulman brother, who, in principle, is alone entitled to the generosity of his co-religionist.

The holy law of the prophet teaches that almsgiving closes seventy doors to evil, appeases the wrath of God, and enables him who practices it during his life, to triumphantly pass, at the final judgment, over the bridge "Siraté," which is narrow and slender like the blade of a razor, and extends from earth to heaven over the abysses of hell, into which condemned mortals miserably fall while attempting to pass. Mussulman alms-giving is performed with fervor and zeal, but hardly corresponds to ideal charity, which is the development and consecration by religious thought of the natural instinct for commiseration. Mussulmans conform to the precept that enjoins alms-giving because it is a precept. Having, however, but a faint idea of the fatherhood of God, it is not strange that they but feebly appreciate the brotherhood of man.

4. FASTING. The sacred month of Ramadan is the ninth of the Mussulman year of twelve lunar months and is devoted to fasting, because during that month the koran descended from heaven.

Fasting is one of the bases of Islamism, as already stated. It is very rigorous and consists in abstaining not only from every article of food and beverage, but from every perfume, pleasure and idle word, from the dawn of day to twilight; originally Mussulmans had also to maintain absolute silence.

The Ramadan begins when, after the month of Shahban, certain persons appointed to watch the heavens declare on oath that they have seen the new moon. The fasting must continue until it is announced through the same formality that the moon of the succeeding month has been seen.

At Tunis and in all cities where Islamism prevails, including even Algiers where the French have had the complaisance to keep up this usage, a discharge of artillery announces to believers the commencement of Ramadan, and during the entire month two discharges of cannon a day, one at dawn and the other at evening twilight, announce the beginning and the close of the fast. At Tunis, they fire a cannon simultaneously at the casbah and at the bardo, the residence of the bey.

Every Mussulman youth at an age to exercise his reason and not having the legitimate motive to right action, is constrained to observe the fast through fear of committing the great crime of infidelity which can be legally atoned for only by a charitable contribution, a subsequent fasting of two entire months or putting a slave at liberty. If one is sick or on a journey or there be any other reason for dispensing with the fast, he can do so with the advice of a good counsellor on condition of compensating for this omission, as soon as possible, according to the letter of the law.

The first days of the fast are hard to endure, especially when they occur in summer; for Ramadan makes the tour of the year, since the Mussulman year is a lunar year, and is always eleven or twelve days shorter than our year. But these people become by degrees habituated to their new order of existence. They forget their hunger with pious reading and conversation, and towards evening take rides and walks. But rich people so well reward themselves at night for the privations of the day, that they lose none of their physical proportions during the Ramadan. The daily fast serves but to give them an appetite for their nightly feast. The poor laborers, however, who are obliged to work in the heat of the sun without the right of even moistening their lips and assuaging their thirst, suffer frightfully when they have to fast fifteen consecutive hours. In general, during three-quarters of the day, Mussulman cities are plunged into a profound calm, where all appear to be swooning from exhaustion. Most of the shops are closed, and none are frequented.

During Ramadan few Mussulmans are in the streets, and many are sober, anxious, in bad humor and more than ever disposed to seek quarrels with infidels. They were formerly accustomed to assume an air of superiority, especially towards Jews. Woe to him whom they saw eating or smoking! It was in their eyes at the same time a profanation and a provocation, and often resulted in regrettible scenes. Now, the pious fasters are much more moderate in their demands. They understand that the time is past for them to revenge their penance by tyrannizing over those who do not and cannot share it. But much more! They bear with resignation the jesting and teazing, sometimes quite unreasonable, which Christians and Jews do not fear to indulge, eating or smoking with cruel avidity in their presence; and this last act is so much the more grave, as the smoke of tobacco breathed even by chance immediately breaks the fast for the day, and consequently obliges them to fast in compensation another whole day after the Ramadan is ended. Notwithstanding this, quarrels are rare; the faster is more forbearing than he would like to be; he restrains his anger, and, not to breathe the smoke floating around him, he removes it with his hand or covers his mouth and nostrils with his handkerchief.

As the evening draws nigh, the city shows signs of life, and by degrees becomes animated and noisy. Distinguished personages and rich Tunisian merchants ride out in their carriages or upon richly caparisoned mules, and ordinary persons go forth on foot. All, however, withdraw from the promenades so as to be at their homes at the sound of the cannon. Meanwhile, at all the corners of the streets are met poor people; some of them in an exhausted condition, with a loaf of bread in one hand and a little jar of water in the other, anxiously awaiting the sound of the cannon. All at once the joyful summons rings through the city. A merry shout goes up, followed by a long murmur rising in every direction, and neither bread nor water are lost between the hand and the mouth of those who were awaiting the signal. All the minarets are illuminated; the solemn and drawling voice of the *muezzin*

calls believers to the evening prayer. They break
the fast with this short invocation: "My God, I
have fasted to obey thee! I break the fast, feeding
myself with thy food! Pardon me all my sins;"
and forthwith they eat some light cake and fruits,
and soon proceed to make their first repast. To
defer it would be so much the more out of character,
as it is the custom of the Jews to wait a long time
after the period fixed for the end of their fast.

Though Tunis is gloomy and sad during the days
of Ramadan, it is animated and lively during the
nights. The illumination of the mosques throws
over the city, sunk in darkness, a gay and fantastic
air; the bazars and shops are lighted up and visited
for trade and curiosity. Multitudes of believers
and infidels throng the Mussulman quarter, which
becomes the centre of veritable nocturnal festivals.
In the cafés, story-tellers prattle with unusual vivacity; dancers exhibit their agility and skill, and rhapsodists chant in nasal tones love songs and mournful
ditties, while the auditors sip their coffee and smoke
their pipes in apparent delight. Jugglers, mountebanks and exhibitors of serpents and reptiles dispute
with each other elsewhere to gain public notice. But
we regret to refer to one significant feature of public
morals. He succeeds best and wins most money and
applause, whose exhibitions are the most indecent.
For example, *Chinese ghosts*, which are nothing but
the most disgusting and obscene pictures, magnified
and turned around to gratify the taste of depraved
persons, constitute a special attraction during the
evening hours. This disgraceful exhibition, which

would not be tolerated in a civilized community, is witnessed by both sexes, including youth and even children of tender age. Reflections here are superfluous.

The reader will perceive that this sacred month of Ramadan constitutes a very rude lent during the day, and a very free carnival during the night. The one seems a compensation for the other. *Utile dulci!* The mosques are open all night and grave and pious people go there at least once in company with their friends, with whom it is customary to pass the larger half of the night which they give to feasting, prayer and conversation, leaving but little time for sleep which they take during the following day. From the setting sun to the dawn of the following day, they can eat, drink and amuse themselves to satiety. The rich do not fail to avail themselves of their privileges, and coffee, refreshments and sumptuous banquets succeed each other. Yet the rule is to make only two substantial meals, one soon after sunset and the other at three or four o'clock in the morning, allowing, of course, intermediate refreshments. But in general the tables are about as well supplied at the collations as at the two stated meals. The poor man tries to imitate afar off this sumptuousness by spending his pitiful earnings, or by supplying himself by begging from door to door. But in general, he is limited to one meal, which he renders as abundant as possible, and, instead of collations, he is satisfied with some sweet-meats or pastry, such as *haloua* or *zlebia*.* At the dawn of day, the

---

* *Haloua,* literally meaning sweetness, is ordinarily composed of sugar or

fast begins with the sound of the cannon, and ceases at evening twilight; and thus it occurs for twenty-nine or thirty consecutive days, which is the greatest length of Ramadan.

The night of the 26th is devoted to the commemoration of the descent of the koran upon the earth. God is thanked not only for this favor, but for the sovereign act, which, at the same time, fixed forever the destiny of each of his creatures. It is for this two-fold reason that this night is called "Leilet-el-Kader," the night of power, and the bey and his court, who are habitually at the Bardo, always come to sleep in the palace at Tunis. The animation and joy of the city become then very marked. The multitude come out in their best attire, and illuminations are on every hand. The mosques are still more frequented, and his highness, the bey, goes to offer his prayers at the principal mosque, passing through streets thronged with people, who repeat the formula of respect and devotion as faithful Tunisians: "May God protect our sovereign."

The day, which succeeds the Ramadan is called the Little Bairam, in distinction from the Great Bairam, which comes later. This fête is celebrated at Tunis with great pomp and merits special notice. At the commencement of the evening watch, the discharge of a cannon announces to believers the ceremonies of the next day. All the notable personages of the country and foreign consuls pay an official visit to the bey, on which occasion the ceremony of kissing

honey, ginger, almonds, etc., and is sold by special traders called *halouani*. Zlebia is a pastry fried in honey, and is much used during Ramadan.

the bey's hand is still observed by all Tunisian subjects. At six o'clock in the morning, there reign in the palace of the Bardo great animation and a joyous air of festivity. The first court is occupied by a battalion under arms. The second court is filled with Arab chiefs of a subaltern order. The steps to the white marble lions, which are an ordinary work of art, and to the peristyle with elegant columns of black and white marble, with arcades covered with arabesques and wooden corridors in gaudy colors, are also crowded by a multitude still more select, composed of *kaids*, sheiks and superior officers. The third and last court with elegant columns and a white marble fountain, is occupied on one side by a line of superior officers, generals and dignitaries, and, on the other side, by a battalion of troops with their standards and bands of music. They are waiting for the bey, who soon appears followed by the heir presumptive to the throne, the princes of the blood, his ministers, aides-de-camp, and officers of ordnance. As he advances, giving salutations with his hand and receiving them from all the personages present, the latter fall back behind him and form a magnificent cortege, which finally takes in the whole multitude then assembled in the palace, and moves towards the mosque with the discordant sounds of a native band, composed of three base drums, three great cymbals and of many bagpipes. These instruments of torture for delicate ears are manœuvred by native virtuosos. This procession is led by twelve armed heralds, who march a little in advance of the bey. They are clad in red or scarlet, and carry staves resembling base-drum sticks ornamented with small copper chains, and they are commanded by their chief, who is ordinarily a man of formidable stature and embonpoint, and who bawls out rather than pronounces the following words in the Turkish tongue: "Salvation to all the people! May your life be long under the providence of God, and the authority of the sultan, our august master! May his life be long and happy! May he live a thousand years!"

This is one of the remains of the ancient Turkish ceremonial which the beys of Tunis like to preserve with the view of showing their profound respect for the sublime porte, however only in a purely religious point of view. For Mussulman people are in general contented and prepared to yield almost unlimited authority provided appearances are kept up in favor of their religion. It is in the midst of the most touching demonstrations of humility, veneration and almost worship that the vassals of his highness come each from his side to paralyze their sovereignty of long standing and escaping from all authority emanating therefrom, to put in its place only a purely nominal and religious sovereignty.

But let us return from Constantinople to the bardo to rejoin the bey at the mosque. Being infidels, we cannot cross the threshold, but we soon know that the prince has entered the sanctuary and that the the bash mufti begins the customary prayers; for lo, the signal. A salute of twenty-one cannon makes the old walls of the Bardo tremble, and immediately over the great entrance gate rises and floats majestically in the air the *bagal*, the flag which is at the same time national and religious, having in bold relief the double-bladed sword of Islamism, and in the background green, red and yellow stripes interspersed with crescents and stars.

The native music begins more noisy than ever; the drums beat on the plains and the copper instruments of enlisted musicians in a red uniform produce sounds almost European. The bey returns to the palace with the same ceremonial and by the same way and proceeds to the hall of the throne. Formerly he sat in the third court under the portico formed by the columns and in an armed-chair once belonging to Hamouda Bashaw, which was made of the bones of a whale that was stranded and taken in shallow waters near the island of Gerba at the close of the last century. Now it is in a veritable hall of the throne built in European style, where the bey has his grand receptions. In a splendid uniform, he sits upon a throne which is an exact imitation of that of Louis XIV, seen in the palace at Versailles,—risum teneatis, amici?—and in an imposing attitude he awaits the homage which is promptly paid him. The ceremony of kissing the hand begins. The bey of the camp and the princes, the ministers, the officers, the employés of the court of all ranks succeed each other according to the law of the hierarchy and of etiquette; then come the sheik-el-Medina, the prefect of police and the president of the municipality with all their personnel; then the kaids of the principal tribes of the interior, and the kaid of the isle of Gerba. The governor and notable personages of this isle are, with those of Tunis, the only ones who enjoy the privilege of representing their fellow-subjects on this occasion. The other cities of the regency have no deputation.

After this first part of the ceremony, which lasts about two hours, the bey passes into another hall where he waits on a divan for the visit of all the princes too young to take part in the preceding ceremony.

Soon *the bash mufti* of the Malekite sect, who is the head of religion and of justice, arrives, followed by all the learned men who compose his tribunal. This group of dignitaries is truly imposing. They are clad in the long native tunic and draped in a double white bernouse and wearing on their high turban a double white veil, except the bash mufti who wears the green. They wear as another distinctive sign morocco shoes entirely unlike each other; for one foot they have a pump with light sole, and for the other a slipper sharply pointed and turned over. Their general aspect is picturesque and unique, and their bearing dignified.

On their approach, the bey goes to meet them. He kisses them upon the right shoulder, and they kiss him upon the breast; then, while the bey sits, all raising their hands to heaven, recite together the first chapter of the koran:

"Praise be to God, Lord of the worlds!

"The compassionate, the merciful!

"Thee only do we worship, and to Thee do we cry for help!

"Guide Thou us in the straight path!

"In the path of those (Mussulmans) to whom Thou hast been gracious!

"Not of those with whom Thou art angry! (Jews).
"Nor of those who go astray." (Christians).

After this prayer, each puts his right hand upon his beard, and a conversation takes place between the bey and the bash mufti; coffee and cake are served; they then sprinkle the hands of all present with rose water, and envelop the company in a cloud of smoke made by burning perfumes. The bey and his visitors recite anew the prayer; then the cortege withdraws and the bey followed by his dignitaries returns to his apartment.

The ceremony of kissing the hand of the bey is continued for those who were not admitted on the first day. On the second day of the festival the consuls are received, as explained in Chapter IX. The sights presented at the Bardo during these great ceremonies are picturesque and varied. All the civil and military uniforms are advantageously seen, from those of ministers and major-generals to those of secretaries and private soldiers. Some officers have for decorations broad ribbons with brilliant colors; others plates of gold set with veritable brilliants, while the *chevaliers of the order of Nishan* wear plates of pewter or some other base metal sprinkled with pieces of white glass. The uniforms of the zouaves are gaily embroidered. In gazing, we involuntarily contrast the flowing and imposing costume of the Arab chiefs, consisting of turbans made of camel's hair, white veils, silk robes, red embroidered boots and magnificent bernouses, with the pinched and quixotic habiliments of the surviving Turkish troops. We see thus brought before us at the Bardo all the employés and notable personages of Tunisia in the midst of a multitude, in which are pressed and mingled together curious persons of many races and countries, having each his type and special dress, and all busily enjoying a sight, of which they constitute a part.

On the tenth of the twelfth and last month of the Mussulman year, takes place the fête called *the Great Bairam*. The first day, which is the most important, the fête lasting four days, is called the day of the sacrifice. It is so called because all Mussulmans who can, kill on that day some animal, as a sheep, ox, or camel, and consume a part of its flesh and distribute the rest by way of alms-giving. This bloody passover is celebrated with great pomp at Mecca, where pilgrims from all parts of the world flock together on that day.

In regard to the Great and the Little Bairam, it is to be remarked that the four orthodox sects of Islamism do not designate them in a uniform manner. Thus for the Hanefites and the Shafaites (oriental sects), the Great Bairam is that which follows the Ramadan; while it is the feast of sacrifice for the Malekites and Hambalites (western sects), who constitute the majority of the people of Barbary.

The feast of the Great Bairam is solemnized in North Africa with less splendor than that of the Little Bairam; yet official receptions take place at the Bardo as on the day after the Ramadan.

Another feast remarkable for the religious zeal to which it gives place is the birthday of Mohammed, the Mussulman Christmas. But, as there are no official receptions, its celebration is limited to religious ceremonies, public amusements and alms-giving.

5. PILGRIMAGES TO MECCA. Every Mussulman ought once in his life make the pilgrimage to Mecca. It is a precept instituted by Mohammed, and is one of the six bases of Islamism. Those who accomplish it acquire the title of *hadji* (pilgrims), and the privilege of wearing the red turban. In the early period of Islamism, the califs and subordinate Mussulman princes went in great pomp to Mecca, having a host of attendants and making magnificent presents on the way. Now, as for centuries past, such examples are unknown. But most Mussulmans have, nevertheless, an earnest desire to make this religious journey, and while awaiting an opportunity, they communicate with those who accomplish it, and charge them with bringing back souvenirs from the holy places which they propose to visit later in life.

Each year numerous caravans depart from Morocco, Algeria, Tunisia, Egypt, Syria and the extreme orient, at a time so as to be able, at the same period of the year, to meet each other at Mecca. The itinerary for each of them has been fixed for centuries, together with a list of the provisions required and of the resting places at the various points on the way. Every pilgrim caravan receives marks of respect from the population along the way; but the zeal manifested for its reception comes not alone from the religious spirit. Pilgrims to Mecca are not strangers to commercial speculations, and the numerous classes of the Mussulman world which they meet, are also occupied in promoting their material interests. Most of these people go and return with small quantities of merchandise, which they dispose of on the way, and whose profits cover their expenses and compensate them for the fatigues of the journey. The day when the caravans pass any given point is known in advance, and traders come from afar to meet them, bringing provisions and taking in exchange the merchandise of the pilgrims. When the pilgrims encamp in the desert, the exchanges are made with each other. The caravan is under the authority of a sheik or elder, assisted by a cadi, who maintains order and decides all differences between pilgrims.

Pious travellers, flocking from so many countries, arrive in Arabia in three principal groups; first, those from the west (North Africa); second, those from the orient, and, third, those from Bagdad and the neighboring regions. These three groups go on the very day of their arrival at Mecca to Mount Arafat, from whose consecrated summit an iman offers with a loud voice a prayer to which the pilgrims listen with bare heads and feet. According to a tradition, the number of believers present at this solemnity must be on each occasion 80,000. If it were more, God would reduce it by a scourge; if less, the angels would complete it. Then they go to worship (before) the black stone of the holy *kaaba*, which is the temple built or at least founded by Abraham. The black stone, which was from time immemorial the object of an idolatrous worship on the part of the ante-Islamitish Arabs, descended from heaven, according to Mussulman tradition, perfectly white during the innocence of Adam, and became black only at his fall. Upon this stone Abraham rested while superintending the construction of the kaaba, in which labor the angels took part.

The sanctuary of the kaaba is erected in the middle of the vestibule of the great mosque at Mecca. It is of a square form, and surrounded with a black veil raised in festoons from point to point. Pilgrims make the tour around the kaaba seven times with naked feet, and with special tunic when they have had the good fortune to perform their ablutions at the sacred fountain of Zemzem. This is the same fountain near which the angel found Hagar, shortly before the birth of Ishmael. Every believer must throw into it a pebble, and religiously partake of its water. In short, pilgrims at Mecca spend fifteen days going through with numerous religious ceremonies, and then set off for Medina to complete their pilgrimage by visiting the tomb of the prophet.

The mosque at Mecca is called *the dwelling of God*, and that of Medina which contains the tomb of Mohammed, *the house of the prophet*. The two cities are inseparable in the veneration of believers, and are frequently called the two Meccas. As the pilgrimage to Mecca is the only sign of the collective life of Mussulmans, great importance is attached to it by persons of every shade of belief; and, with a view of affording facilities for making this long journey, the French have annually sent steamers from Algeria, touching at Tunis, since 1842, and there is now competition among Mediterranean steamship companies in securing the patronage of pilgrims. Great numbers take this more expeditious and less painful way by sea; but still a majority, who have not the means of paying their passage, take the land route, which, though particularly tedious and fatiguing, is regarded as more meritorious.

Many Mussulmans make the pilgrimage to Mecca a second time; and there are those who repeat it many times, and their renown for holiness becomes so much the greater, with some exceptions, which have given place to a malicious Arab proverb of ancient date: "If your neighbor has made the pilgrimage to Mecca once, suspect him; if twice, be on your guard, and if three times, move away from him."

6. PROFESSION OF FAITH. Mussulmans are bound on every occasion to make their profession of faith, thus: "I bear witness that God is God, and Mohammed is his prophet." It is not enough to adopt this creed; every Islamite is bound to impose it on infidels, who must also adopt it or suffer the prescribed penalties. This has been the prevailing rule for the extension of Islamism. This armed proselytism is called *the holy war*. "Fight," says the koran, "until all worship be that of the one God," evidently meaning until Islamism is everywhere established. Proclaimed by the iman, the holy war becomes obligatory on all. Riches and life must be ready as a sacrifice for the cause of God. It is in this sense that Mussulmans repeat the saying, that "paradise lies in the shadow of swords." Yet, before beginning the attack, they must summon them to be converted to Islamism. If infidels reject the summons, they may be punished by death or by the

infliction of a special tribute. Once all infidels in Mussulman countries were subjected to this ordeal. The prophet declared that the holy war should last until the day of judgment; there might be a truce, but never a peace. Thus the world is considered as divided into two great hostile factions, believers on one side and infidels on the other. These last, who are the perpetual objects of the holy war, until they are converted or submit to the tribute, have no right to govern themselves or even to live. Government belongs by right to Islamism, which tolerates the independence and even the existence of infidels, only while awaiting the favorable occasion to impose upon them the alternative of the tribute or death. Such is the scope of Islamism, as taught by the koran, though practically it is now very tolerant.

SLAVERY, though long since abolished by the laws of Tunisia, is sanctioned by the koran, on certain humane and paternal conditions. The slave is a servant who belongs to the family, and who can demand to be sold to another master, if he is not satisfied with the one he has. After years of service, the slave ordinarily gains his freedom. He becomes then, as it were, a dependent on the family, in which he passes his declining years. A female slave who becomes a mother by her master, acquires the same rights as a wife, and her sons become citizens of the tribe with all the rights and privileges possessed by their father. These conditions, relatively mild, are an amelioration which Islamism introduced into the manners of the ante-Islamitish Arabs, among whom slavery was much more rigorous; the son of a slave could become free only by the will of his master, and never by right of his origin. Among Mussulmans, slavery results from this religious programme: Fight infidels; take possession of them, and convert and regenerate them by restoring them to freedom.

DERVISHES. The respect which Mussulmans manifest for that which touches or seems to touch the province of religion, is cultivated by a multitude of gross, if not corrupt, idlers and vagabonds, who, making a profession of poverty and devotion, are called dervishes. These men are noted in most Islamitish cities for their squallidness and pious pride. There are many kinds of dervishes. Some are pious and exemplary in their way; they wear the red or green turban; have continually upon their lips the name of God and of the prophet, or select verses from the koran and avail themselves of every occasion to talk against infidels; and, in return, are the objects of great veneration on the part of believers, who emulate each other in providing for all their wants. Others are stupid or idiotic creatures, covered with disgusting rags or nearly naked, given to drink, uttering inarticulate cries, practising ventriloquism, muttering in barbarous tones sacred words and not satisfied with exorbitant liberties, take shameful and revolting license. No restraint is imposed upon them. Their folly itself, if observed, becomes in the eyes of Mussulmans a sign of predestination; for orientals have for insane and idiotic people in general a sort of superstitious deference; and with good reason when these wretched creatures become dervishes, who are in some respects the *mendicant monks* of Islamism.

RELIGIOUS FRATERNITIES. There are found throughout the Mussulman world and especially in North Africa religious fraternities, which have a great number of mosques and zawias. They are restricted to certain practices, and their conditions and rules resemble certain secret societies of the Christian world. Naturally only Mussulmans are admitted into them, as they are established mainly to promote Islamism.

We shall mention, as the most singular of these fraternities, that of the Aicawias, founded by Sidi Mohammed-Ben Aica. The entire city of Maknas in Morocco belongs to this order. There are some of the members of this fraternity in Algeria, but more in Tunisia where, about the time of the anniversary of the birth of Mohammed, they make solemn processions to their quarters and, at the conclusion of their devotions, give themselves up to certain inexplicable and repulsive practices. Arranging themselves in a circle under the direction of their chief, they chant in their peculiar style grave prayers in honor of their founder. Then accompanied with cymbals and drums, and becoming gradually animated by the music, they raise their voices and quicken their time and are thus wrought up by the precipitate rythm of their strange concert to such a pitch of excitement that they appear like maniacs. At length, their songs become little more than savage cries, accompanied with wild gestures and convulsive contortions. Then some of the brethren, breaking from the ranks and dancing upon the same line, draw from the pit of their stomach in hollow and rough tones the sacred name of "Allah" (God), pronouncing it each time with an intonation more savage. Soon the sound augments and becomes a tumult. Playing and dancing cease. The sheshias and turbans fall from their shaven heads; the sashes around their loins are loosened and drop to the ground; they cease to dance, becoming hampered and entangled on every hand; disorder is complete. The most furious of the company fall upon their hands and knees, pale and crazed, with haggard eyes and contracted mouth, and imitate, each according to his ability, the movements and cries of ferocious animals with a frightful and deplorable naturalness.

When the excitement has become fearfully spasmodic and convulsive, the Aicawias, covered with perspiration, exhausted, panting and shaking with sudden nervous chills, prepare to begin the juggleries for which they have become renowned through the entire Mussulman world. They call with loud cries on their chief for food. He responds to their request, giving them pieces of glass, which they break between their teeth, and thistles, thorns and nails, which they swallow or appear to swallow. Some of them take into their hands and lick with their tongues red-hot irons, without appearing to perceive the heat. Others wound themselves with knives, and, joining their feet together, leap upon the blades of swords extended before them; put their hands into bags, drawing out serpents, lizards and venomous scorpions, and torturing them while full of life between their beautiful teeth. Sometimes, they pounce like wolves upon a living ram, beat the creature to death, and, tearing his limbs apart with their shrivelled hands, hideously devour his raw and palpitating flesh; break his bones and horns, and, covered with blood, the filth of entrails and bits of flesh and wool, utter forth beastly howls, and leap, gnashing their teeth.

Mussulmans attribute all these practices, in which the Aicawias indulge with impunity, to a supernatural cause. Europeans do not offer any satisfactory explanation; for the marvel does not consist in appearances alone; since more than once physicians have testified that these persons receive dangerous wounds while practising their juggleries, without however experiencing serious consequences, such as would result to other men.

FUNERAL OBSEQUIES. At the death of men and women of every condition, the servants of the house as well as the relatives and friends of the family rend their clothes and disfigure their faces, uttering piercing cries. When the head of the family dies, his widow dresses in black and puts a rope around her head and body; then, with dishevelled hair and bruised and bloody face, she enters the room of the dead, where his relatives and friends are assembled, and where they form at her arrival a concert of groans and howls, to which are added the deafening noise of funeral drums. This tumult is interrupted only to hear a eulogy upon the deceased, pronounced extemporaneously by some one or more of the attendants, though frequently varied by other noisy manifestations of grief. This lasts some time, during which relatives, friends and appropriate officers cease not to recite prayers around the dead body, placed unveiled upon a low table. Then they carefully stop with cotton all the openings of the body, and the corpse is then washed with water aromatized with camphor and perfumes. Rich and poor must be sewed in a shroud of new linen. Then they proceed to the cemetery, bearing the body extended upon a bier, with a pall more or less costly according to the condition of the parties. The bier is borne upon the shoulders of four men who are relieved on the way by others. The procession is led by religious persons, who recite with saddened animation passages from the koran. Multitudes continue to join the funeral party till they reach the grave. There, after new prayers, the dead man in his winding sheet is placed at the bottom of an arched grave, built for him according to his rank and wealth, and covered with brick well white-washed, or with a polished marble slab with pious inscriptions. The graves of men are distinguished by a little column surrounded by a turban; and those of women by a little pillar of a square form though round at the top. At certain fixed periods, the relatives of the dead visit the grave; the women are also authorized to go there to mourn, provided they go alone.

When a person who has a reputation for sanctity is buried, everybody is eager to assist as one of the bearers, or at least to touch his shroud. At the departure from the house of the dead and at every halt of the procession for changing bearers, a pious competition, sometimes involving blows, is manifested by those who would render assistance, and the force of the blows is naturally in direct proportion to the reputation of the dead. Holy personages in whose behalf these warlike posthumous demonstrations are made ordinarily obtain the honor of having a place of prayer built over their grave, which becomes a scene for miracles.

THE MOSQUES have high walls, provided only with small windows, that are inserted nearer to the roofs than to the floors of the buildings. Within, are porticos which lead to the sanctuary, composed of one or of several naves divided by colonnades. The mosques have no images or pictures; for the Islamite is an iconoclast. The walls are naked or simply ornamented with verses from the koran in relief. Chandeliers and lamps hang midway between the roof and the ground. The floor is covered with mats; for worshippers leave their shoes at the door. Nothing is more simple than their ceremonies. They pray with a loud voice and listen to a kind of sermon, which is pronounced from a pulpit situated always at the left near a niche whose base is the floor of the mosque. This niche is more or less ornamented and indicates the point towards which worshippers must turn in order that their prayers may be effectual. The preacher in the pulpit has always his right hand resting on a staff or a wooden sword, which is an emblem of authority and of the holy war.

On Friday, which is the Mussulman Sabbath, the mosques are crowded at the noon-day hour for prayer, when special petitions are offered in behalf of the Grand Sultan, who holds the same relation to most of the faithful that the Pope of Rome holds to the body of Catholic Christians. The Mussulmans of Algeria, it is said, offer a prayer for the Emperor of the French. It is doubtless a prayer with some cunningly devised words and a mental reservation to save them from committing such a terrible impiety as a genuine expression of good-will would imply. The mosques are visited almost exclusively by the men. Women are not positively prohibited from going there; but if they go, they must go alone, unless they are old and ugly looking. The men, fearing that their attention might be diverted by the presence of females, undertake to display zeal and devotion enough for all.

The mosques are ordinarily surmounted with white or green cupolas tapering like pyramids, and the minaret overlooks the whole building. It is a square, round or hexagonal tower, rising to a great height with a look of nakedness, and bearing, into the azure on the summit of the pyramid which crowns it and above the gilt ball of bronze, the glorious crescent of Islamism. It is much oftener the contrast of the colors and materials, than the labor of the chisel that animates the coldness of the minarets and mosques, all of which seem to reflect in their outlines the sadness of fatalism and the gravity of the koran.

SUPERSTITIONS. Besides the existence of angels and demons, Mussulmans in general admit that of different kinds of spirits, some of which are good and some evil. The *genouns* are genii of both sexes appointed to guard underground treasures. They can exercise extraordinary power at their pleasure. They are ordinarily propitiated and their good offices secured by means of talismans, cabalistic words and magic operations. These genii show themselves in general as formidable giants, uttering frightful cries, which men cannot understand without being overcome. When they are of the female sex, they lend superior charms and attractions to their votaries. These are the fairies, peris and *undines* of the legends of most European people in the middle age.

The formidable *ogres* with the mongrel features of men and beasts, haunting the saddest ruins and solitudes, and holding in their deformed and hideous claws pieces of human flesh or entire dead bodies, wander solitary in the track of belated travelers, fascinate and devour them, and as guests in cemeteries, profane the tombs. The *silahs*, a species of the *ogre* family, inhabit ponds and deep waters. When they take human beings, they sport and play with them as cats do with mice. An astonishing fact is that, by the permission of God, wolves are the bitter enemies of *silahs*, and can devour them if they reach them.

The *amlóucs* partake of the nature of men and of *silahs*, whose habits they have. The *delhaths*, which have a human form, inhabit distant isles and deserts and look after ships in distress to make a prey of all on board. The *hirriths* are the genii of deserts, tormenting travelers with heat and thirst. The *mazhabs* are demons which delight in placing lights before travelers and rendering them various services with the object of effecting their ruin. The *raddars* or hobgoblins call with loud cries persons, who if they unfortunately reply, find a sharp and crooked cudgel suddenly thrust through their bodies. The *shicks* and the *nasnas* have only half the length of the human body, presenting on one side all our features and on the other a simple *silhouette;* they have only one eye, one arm and one leg, but nevertheless they can make prodigious leaps and run with astonishing rapidity. They attack everywhere lost and belated travelers.

All these strange beings can enter into communication with us, aside from their sudden attacks. They can take possession of individuals of one or the other sex according as they themselves are masculine or feminine. The persons ordinarily beset by them are subject to incurable maladies, such as epilepsy and convulsions. The obsession or possession is manifested at first by nervous attacks or simply by hypochrondia. To solace the afflicted, or rather disconcert and disarm the demon, special musical or rather noisy concerts are given with tabors and various stringed instruments. Under the influence of music, the afflicted, who are almost all females, begin to dance, and as the music becomes lively the dance becomes rapid and more frantic until the dancers fall exhausted upon the floor. It is then that in the midst of languishing groans the malignant spirit constrains them to manifest that which it demands to be appeased. Often it is a particular dress with brilliant colors; for these genii, or rather the women which they afflict, foolishly adore pretty dresses; it may be some odd and expensive food, a change of residence to some other house or place, and if these desires are gratified, the spirit shows itself appeased and reasonable.

But these diseases can be radically cured only by exorcising the malignant spirit by means of certain religious and cabalistic formulas. In all Mussulman countries, there are some pretended exorcists who are much consulted and who gravely maintain the honor of their calling. But their services are said to be attended with danger; for these genii are vindictive. I have known an old *taleb*, who pretended to expel malignant spirits without fail; his reputation was in all the country around. He was wont to give amusing accounts of the tricks which these spirits played on him. They put his furniture out of order, burned his books and papers, suddenly inflicted upon him sharp pains, shook his house, deafened him with formidable noises, frightened him with horrid images; in fine, disturbed his sleep, inflicting upon him frightful dreams, and literally tormenting his life. But there was a limit to their malicious power. As to this life of ours, God protects it as with an impenetrable buckler by means of a passage from the koran, with which the *taleb* was always armed and which he repeated with a loud voice and with perfect success, unless perchance he was caught off his guard. But the spirits nevertheless returned to the charge more spiteful than ever at each failure of their efforts against their adversary, whose destruction they had sworn; but he always met them with a strong resolution never to become their victim, though always subject to their assaults.

Strange stories circulate in all Tunisia, as throughout the orient, about nocturnal scenes of which certain houses are the theatre. There are, in fact, dwellings which the *genouns* and *sheetans* (demoniacal spirits) specially delight to occupy. These are generally those where clandestine murders have been committed or treasures are buried; and the burial of important treasures is usually connected with the murder of some black servant. These houses are filled, especially during the gloomy nights of the rainy season, with groans, shrill cries and clear bursts of laughter, succeeded by strange apparitions or by the movement and agitation of a multitude, who shake and overturn everything without appearing in visible form. Who would enter great deserted suites of rooms, or risk, in solitary corridors, dying of fright or receiving formidable thumps or becoming mad by the things he might suddenly see or the diabolical noises that would rend his ears? Numerous examples are cited of these victims of imprudence or destiny.

Even in ordinary houses, it is necessary to guard against malignant spirits by being circumspect in act and word; for there are persons who strangely offend them and excite their wrath. It is a protection to have at every occurrence the name of God on the lips and invoke at the very moment of danger His protecting aid by means of the following formula: "We invoke the protection of God against Satan accursed." For all malignant spirits depend on Satan, and in weakening his empire in general by invoking the name of God, they disconcert all his satellites from one end of his hierarchy to the other.

They also have recourse to amulets and talismans, formed generally with verses or words from the koran, but which have their full effect only by a special arrangement which is understood exclusively by men of the profession, such as magicians, necromancers, exorcists and enchanters. By means of these talismans, which they sell at a very moderate price, considering their value, these men exercise not only a repressive power upon malignant spirits, but heal some diseases reputed to be incurable, alleviate others, inspire with love whoever has a right to it, and in general bring luck and fortune to all their patrons.

There are, besides, persons whose special vocation is to discover hidden treasures, find out unknown robbers, unveil the future, and call up images of the dead and of the living, holding positions similar, we presume, to that held by the witch of Endor in the time of Saul of Tarsus. In short, in Tunisia and throughout the Mussulman world, ancient superstition reigns and governs with all its force in the midst of moral blindness and material wretchedness.

Among the superstitions in vigor in Mussulman countries, is that of the evil eye. These people believe that by expressing astonishment, disgust or admiration in reference to some quality of a person in his presence occasions misfortune, and that the turn of an eye may also effect mischief. To prevent this bad effect, it is recommended never to offer a compliment without adding, "*tabarek Allah!*" may God bless! This pious invocation shields him who makes the compliment from harm. As to him who is the object of it, certain amulets having the form of a hand and of a fish are employed with the same result. In conspicuous places in all houses, baths, cafés and public buildings, especially in those which are newly built, are painted in lively colors mysterious hands and fishes, and many ladies imitate in their dresses these two forms. The teeth of fish, the horns of certain animals, branches of corals, crescents, including horse shoes and all objects which present several points of view are employed as preventives to the evil eye.

The bad influence of the stars is also very much dreaded. Eclipses of the sun and moon give occasion to manifestations of general terror and to processes of conjuration to prevent disastrous influences. These processes consist in uttering prolonged cries and stoutly beating musical or rather discordant instruments, including all the metalic utensils of the kitchen. The impression seems to prevail that this unearthly clatter must reach the celestial spheres, appeasing the wrath of the Most High and bringing back light from the averted face of the sun and moon; and as they witness the gradual disappearance of the frightful phenomena and the restoration of the heavenly order, they are confirmed in their views.

With these superstitions is connected the practice of astrology, whose adepts are found among learned Mussulmans who still occupy themselves, as did the astrologers of olden time. They gravely draw horoscopes and ransack for years the folios consecrated to this pretended science, whose infallibility appears to them certain. This opinion is confirmed by numerous examples of coincidence between the horoscopes and the events predicted. They cite among others the verification of astrological prophecies about several of the Beys of Tunis, the duration of whose reign and even the order of succession was predicted many years in advance of the event.

CHAPTER III.

The Mussulman Woman* and the Mussulman Problem.

WOMEN among the Arabs played a great part previous to the time of Islamism. Regarded as elevated creatures, almost super-human, keen-witted, intelligent, poets by inspiration and by traditional education acquired without letters, the women excited to combat and to deeds of valor and vengeance, or became magnanimous mediators between hostile tribes. Conscious of their power and importance, like the Roman matrons, they hesitated not to resort to bold measures and extraordinary expedients to promote the interest and glory of their tribes, to which they sometimes left their names.

Islamism put a stop to their intervention in public affairs, and seriously injured them by contracting their sphere of activity as moral and intellectual beings; but on the other hand it regulated their

---

* The koran speaks of women in the following chapters: 2, 3, 4, 5, 9, 16, 17, 23, 24, 30, 31, 33, 36, 46, 60, 65, 66, 70.

THE PROPHET'S MATRIMONIAL TROUBLES.

position in the family by constituting the husband the sole ruler of the household.

Before the time of Mohammed, the Arabs took as many wives as they could maintain, and an unlimited number of concubines and slaves. Mohammed limited the number of wives to four, and left undetermined the number of concubines or slaves. But divorce gives the husband liberty to take successively ten, twenty, forty lawful wives. With the anti-Islamitish Arabs, female captives were at the mercy of the conqueror. At the present time, this rule holds if they are Mussulman, but they must be respected. In regard to women, as to property of other kinds, Mohammed naturally enjoyed, in his character as prophet, extraordinary privileges. Thus every Mussulman had to divorce his wife in order to pass her over to the prophet, if the latter wished it; but no one had the right to marry a woman who had once belonged to Mohammed. At his death, he left nine wives who always remained widows. It was lawful for him to marry a woman without her consent or that of her parents, and even without a wedding present, which was essential for ordinary persons; he was also privileged to take any woman he might choose for his concubine.

He was the husband at one time of seventeen instead of four wives, and had withal a touch of connubial infelicity. Jealousy sprang up among his wives on the following occasion. He had received as a present from the governor of Egypt two beautiful slaves, one of whom he chose for his concubine, Maria the Copt, who became his favorite and had a son Ibrahim (Abraham) who died in his boyhood; but Maria was enfranchised before the death of the child. The partiality of the prophet for Maria, however, caused discord in the family. Mohammed divorced Hafsa, the principal malcontent, and summoned his other wives to behave with discretion and propriety. He deprived them for a whole month of his presence, devoting himself exclusively to Maria. He consented then to take back the repentant Hafsa. The sixty-sixth chapter of the koran is mostly devoted to these domestic details. According to the koran, God intervened to establish order and peace. He admonished the refractory women, declaring Himself for Mohmamed and giving him the right to divorce at his pleasure all his wives; He also notified the latter that He (the Most High) would enable the prophet to make an advantageous exchange.

It can be said in a general way that Mohammed had a great and delicate tenderness for women. He tasted with a relish the pleasures of the family. He loved and loaded with caresses his daughter Fatima. To him is attributed that beautiful and profound saying, that *man attains paradise at the feet of his mother*. He was, towards all Mussulman females, gentle and benignant, giving them words of encouragement, consolation and hope. He extolled marriage, and, it can be added, confirmed his precept by his example.

When he began his mission, human sacrifices were common and women were everywhere victims. He abolished these sacrifices. Also, girls were often buried alive soon after their birth or abandoned in the desert because the father wished for a son, or being poor, refused to support a useless child and risk dishonor at a later day. These usages were particularly in vogue among the Korishites, the tribe of Mohammed. Zaid-Ben-Amer, an Arab chief who became later in life a Mussulman, had combated these cruel usages before the prophet's time and, purchasing the victims, had acquired a glorious renown among his people, by whom he was called "the man that raiseth from the dead." Mohammed persevered and achieved this reform, inserting in the koran energetic protests against these odious practices: " Do not kill your children through fear of want and wretchedness; to them and you we (God) will give all things needful."

Islamism regulated the material and social position of woman; it accorded her some rights but it cut off her intellectual enjoyments and weakened her moral influence by limiting her sphere of action and her range of thought. To secure fidelity, it built up the harem, that veritable prison, where emasculate beings guard and often torture unfortunate women, henceforth prisoners and captives according to the very expression of Mohammed, who recommends them with this title to the kind care of the husband. According to the koran, woman is under the protection of temporary or conditional marriage; but every contract of marriage which does not attribute some value to the woman, by naming the marriage dower or wedding present, is null and void. According to the Mussulman law, marriage is virtually a sale, and woman is the article passed over to the purchaser;

the husband must always buy—not win—his wife. The minimum price is fixed at about forty cents, while the maximum price is unlimited, but no woman would consent to be married for the minimum price. The marriage dower is then in the Mussulman world a very important consideration.

The respect which Islamism recommends for woman is only to prevent any harm befalling her husband or any man related to her; it is not for the woman herself; for the most serious Arab books are filled with severe maxims against her, and pretend that ancient wisdom sustains the conclusion that woman is nothing but deceit and incarnate perfidy.

This explains the kind of life to which woman is condemned, and which is sanctioned and forcibly established by the severity of the law that gives over the adultress to be stoned to death or drowned as a public malefactor. But the end proposed is probably less generally attained than is imagined. The harem is not the place where spotless purity is to be found; the inevitable consequence of imprisonment and hard treatment on the mere hypothesis that she is capable of perfidy and deceit is to drive woman into the most pitiful excesses. Suspected of criminal intentions and subjected to hardships on that account, she seeks and too readily finds means to justify the common opinion in regard to her character.

Before Mohammed's time and in the first period of Islamism, the forms of family relations had still their primitive character. Woman preserved a kind of dignity, and regarded herself, and was regarded, as endowed with attributes and rights which entitled her to rank with her husband. Among the celebrated women of this class, we shall name only seven who were illustrious in the Arab traditions previous to the time of Mohammed. In the early period of Islamism, was the famous Zobaida, who acted the same part for Calif Haroon-er-Rashid as the nymph Egeria performed for Numa at Rome. These seven women are the four wise women of ancient Arabia: Sohr, Anna, Jouma, and Tlind, celebrated for their poetic talents, the nobleness of their characters, and their influence over their tribes; and the three happy mothers: Cabya, Mawia and Fatima-ben-Koni-Shoub, celebrated, like the mother of the Gracchi, for the superior education they gave their sons, who became men of mark.

Now, the husband is the master and despotic sovereign over his wife. Not only she has no deliberative voice, but, created for the pleasure and material advantage of man, and reduced to serve as living furniture more or less precious, she must never forget her position; for besides the legal right of removing her from his presence and shutting her up, the husband can exercise also that of beating her with the full authority of the koran itself, or can delegate to hideous eunuchs that coercive power.

There were once among the Arabs marriages which took place in consequence of the sympathy, affection and inclination of the parties immediately concerned. Now there are scarcely any inquiries made, and no information is given except in regard to the physical condition and docility of the woman in question.

There is not one woman in a hundred thousand who receives any instruction properly so called. From infancy she is prepared for marriage, but materially, by employing every means to give her embonpoint, vanity, and taste for dress. The betrothal of a young girl is sometimes made while she is in the cradle. Ayesha was engaged to Mohammed when she was five years old and was married when she had hardly reached her ninth year.

The man never sees the female to whom he is engaged till the ceremony is concluded, unless she be of the lower class. She remains impenetrably veiled if, contrary to usage, he be permitted to approach her for conversation. Communication between them is ordinarily carried on through a female mediator, who goes from house to house, or from tent to tent, or else, when it takes place directly, a curtain, mat or carpet is used like a partition to separate the two lovers.

Once, on the contrary, the Arab woman enjoyed the liberty of her person and asserted her right to employ her arts in deciding who should be her husband. She sought a husband or waited to be sought as a wife at her option. She could test his intelligence and learn his character by means of skilful questions and artful devices. Often she consulted with her mother or sisters and other friends. To-day she is disposed of like an article of furniture, without even being notified of her sale until it is effected.

Marriages are contracted by an arrangement between parents or by means of old women who are by profession marriage brokers. But it is always the fathers or relatives who decide on the terms for the wife. When the terms are arranged, they are reported to the Cadi, who reduces them to writing, stating just what the dowry shall be, and what money and other presents shall be given the bride. This contract is put on record. The first chapter of the koran is repeated and the day fixed for the marriage. When that day arrives, the bride is as richly apparelled as her circumstances will permit; her eyes are powdered with *koheul;* her fingers are colored with henna, her person saturated with perfumes, and she is gravely seated upon a sofa and awaits the setting sun, the moment when her relatives and those of her betrothed and his intimate female friends who have aided her in her morning toilet, come to conduct her to her husband. Two old men take her by the hand and the procession commences, frequently joined by throngs of people with torch lights and music. In the house of the bridegroom a room is prepared, ornamented and lighted. The bride and the women of her suite feast there and remain till midnight, while the men remain in another room, where they partake of a sumptuous banquet. It is a curious fact that the bridegroom takes his refreshment alone in a separate room, doubtless with a view of avoiding the temptation to commit excesses at the table and of being able, by means of abstinence, to present himself in the most favorable light to his bride. The bridegroom and bride come together at midnight, the sacramental hour when the mosques are reöpened; the friends, after the usual display of compliments, tility to him, shall come out of her grave in the day of judgment with her tongue lengthened out to resemble a dull flesh-colored light, seventy cubits long; which fearful member shall wind around her neck like a hideous collar. Every woman who, fixing discontented looks upon her husband, shall speak shameful words, God will twist her eyes, deform her body, and transform her person into a mere loathsome and repulsive mass of flesh. Every woman who seeks by her dress and coquettish airs to attract the gaze of other men takes the road to perdition.

"Ayesha, every woman of gentle speech, rich in works of benevolence, interested for her husband, fond of her children, and well disposed towards every creature of God, shall enter into paradise with the messiahs and prophets of the Lord. Ayesha, the Angel Gabriel has told me that woman was formed of a rib; now, how can we put a rib in its place again without breaking it? Enlighten other women with your counsels! Recommend without cessation all women to practise virtue and do good! If the days of woman have their trials, they have also their recompense. The woman who has brought a child to her husband has all the merits of fasting in the time of abstinence, of praying during the watches of the night, and of the believer who in the midst of dangers combats the enemies of the faith. On the day of child-birth, angels hover around her; at each affectionate approach, an unhappy mortal is delivered from the torments of hell and the sins of the mother are pardoned, even though they be as numerous as the leaves of the trees. At the moment when the child comes to the light of day, the angels say: 'Happy mother! God protect thee with His compassion!' And if the wife succumbs to her sufferings, God gives her an abode with the elect."

And after speaking once more of the chastisements which await the woman who speaks injurious words against her husband, the prophet thus concludes his remarks: "And then, also, my dear Ayesha, the husband, who with caressing words cheers and encourages his wife, shall receive ten favors from God; the husband, who with benevolent arms shall press his wife to his heart, shall receive twenty favors from God; and the husband who tenderly kisses his wife shall receive for each kiss thirty favors from God!"

The enumeration here ends; and, without entering into further details, Mohammed resumes his remarks about matrimonial life, and concludes them as follows: "Yes, the lawful caresses of husbands are recompensed with the favors of the Lord."

We see that the wife must not only be pure and loyal; she must subject herself without restriction or reserve to her husband; if she fail to do this, she loses her chances of happiness in another world. Nay, more: according to time-honored tradition, if she incur even the displeasure of her husband without receiving his pardon before her death, fearful consequences will befall her in the other life. Her mission is limited to conjugal pleasures, patience and obedience, which, considered aside from a higher principle, are only the virtues of slaves. As to her part in the education of her children, in the development of society and in elevating the spirit and heart of her husband, no question is raised.

And where and what are the duties of the husband? They appear to consist alone in caresses and purely material kindnesses, which have some importance if shown to the wife as well as to the mother; but the true mission of the wife and mother, her part in the formation, government and happiness of the family, not a word of Mohammed indicates it or authorizes its admission.

To this woman, effaced, annihilated in respect to her most legitimate and highest prerogatives, and reduced to her natural instincts, which often, thanks to God, correct the injustice of the law; to this Mussulman woman, so inferior, I do not say alone to the Christian woman, but perhaps even to the savage woman, in many points of view; to this woman, what is promised as a recompense for the complete discharge of her duties? Mere sensual and material happiness in this world and the next. And in this relation, how great also the disproportion! The husband that is even the most loved by his wife has the right to bring rivals into his house, while she, poor victim! is not permitted the pitiable satisfaction of even complaining, or attracting the admiring gaze of other men, and in paradise this will be even worse still; for in this world the husband can, if he will, content himself with one wife; but in the celestial kingdom, where it might be pleasant for him to find again and continue his happy household with his one beloved wife as the central attraction and the highest object after God of his affections, he must of necessity join to her at least sixty-nine women; for it is written, every one of the elect shall have the eternal enjoyment of seventy women of unfading youth and beauty.*

The law of the koran has anticipated the cases, necessarily very numerous, resulting from the established system of marriage where the married parties cannot continue to live together without each violating his reciprocal obligations and being reduced to a deplorable existence. By divorce, it seeks to obviate this inconvenience and sunder unions that are acknowledged, no matter with what motive, to be incompatible, and even to favor others to which one or the other party can be an obstacle.

In this respect the Mussulman law is so accommodating and complaisant that in certain foreseen cases, a woman can be regularly married three successive times in a single month. But repudiated or divorced women, as well as widows, must wait a specified time before being married, provided any suspicions of dishonesty are excited.

The husband has naturally other privileges, when there is question in regard to his wife's breaking off the marriage contract. He can if he will promptly put her away, but the wife has not the same liberty in regard to him. She must clearly establish the

---

* The theological doctors of the Mussulman world have gravely debated the question, to which husband a woman would belong in paradise who had been married many times. Some have thought that she would belong to her first husband; others to her last, and still others have maintained with more reason that she would belong to her best husband. But I do not conceive it to be so easy to settle the difficulties which the Mussulman system of divorce introduces for the celestial reëstablishment of the family here below when the woman has been divorced and re-married many times.

fact that she has been maltreated in order that the judge, who is not slow to act when the husband is the complainant, yield to her demands for redress. In fact, the wife has in all matrimonial disputes not only the law against her, but has to appear before a tribunal that is in advance a party against her sex. Before Islamism, the wife could by a very simple formality repudiate her husband; she had only to open or obstruct, according as it was movable or not, the passage way to her quarters. The husband understood that to be preliminary to a separation which speedily followed.

If the parties divorced have children, the boys can remain with their mother till they are seven years old, when their father can take them, if he chooses; girls ordinarily remain with their mother unless there be formal opposition from the father, in whose favor the law inclines. Thus men and women can be married many times. We need not believe, however, that in these family changes, the children of different mothers necessarily become embarrassments in their relations with each other in respect to divisions of estates and the laws of property. The koran anticipates every imaginable case, regulating the rights and obligations of parents and children. Islamism having abrogated every other law, all nuptial ceremonies that are not conformed to Mussulman usage are of no effect. Mussulmans can take infidel wives with the hope of effecting their conversion, while Mussulman women are expressly forbidden taking infidel husbands, lest falling into their errors, they should be consigned to perdition.

Polygamy, being an integral part of the Islamitish system, will last as long as the system itself. But we must not believe that it is generally practised. It is easy to understand that it would be impossible; since in any country, the number of the women is almost the same as that of the men. At Tunis, it is not rare for the men before marriage to agree to have but one wife, especially if they are persons of distinction. They still have the right, however, of maintaining concubines. Though the husband is invested with discretionary authority over his wives, he commonly seeks to maintain harmony and peace by giving them respectively an apartment or a room for private use and the pleasure of his company. If this division is equably made and regularly observed, the women usually become satisfied with it; but if caprice is manifested, jealousy and discord break out, as in Mohammed's case, and are followed by storms of passion from the husband in the vain effort to produce quiet and contentment.

Distinguished personages have in their houses special apartments not only for their wives, but also for their children who have arrived at the age to leave their mother. Husbands, wives and children take their meals separately, never coming together at the same table. Children are excluded from the table of the father with a view to increase their respect for him. This respect is, it must be acknowledged, very marked among Mussulman people, and whatever be their age and position, children never fail to give public testimony of it on every possible occasion. It is not rare to see men whose locks are already hoary with age rise before their venerated father; kiss his hand in token of submission; remain silent till he speak; abstain in his presence from smoking, laughing and jesting, and in fine, avoid not only everything that savors of the exaggerated "sans-façon" of modern manners, but the familiarity that we regard as allowable and even inseparable from certain elevated sentiments. I have been painfully impressed with this lack of freedom and confidence; but I have also often felt that there is something elevated in this kind of grave and religious manifestation of filial sentiment and in this homage rendered to the authority of the head of the family as the foundation and type of all earthly authority. In presence of this authority, truly of divine origin, if respect cannot serve for more tender sentiments, it is certain that nothing can make up for the want of respect.

The Mussulman family being thus divided, each member of it can give invitations from her own quarter; but this mode of living is not found except in wealthy families. Evidently it is entirely impracticable with laborers and others who are crowded together in close quarters. Whatever be the position of the Mussulman woman, we can readily fancy the monotony of her existence in her prison more or less gaudily furnished and delightfully situated! Alas! Even a fairy palace, if one could not pass the threshold, would be nothing else than a prison! Rich women go, it is true, to their villas, but there also are hermetic trellises at the windows, and monastic enclosures limiting their view and shutting out splendid landscapes in the distance; in a word, in the midst of nature that spreads out her glories and blooms in her magnificence and liberty, there is a captivity more melancholy and galling than that of the convict in his narrow cell.

She needs, then, amusement and employment to allay the weariness of being enclosed long days, weeks and months within those sombre walls; but in her ignorance and indolence she knows not how to have needful diversion and employment. She cannot always be looking over her jewels and personal ornaments, repeating her exercises at the toilet, coloring her eyebrows and eyes with *koheul*,* reddening her fingers and toes with henna,† giving sweetness and color to her lips and mouth with *souek*,‡ swimming in numberless perfumes, and dressing and parading without end before mirrors. It is no longer possible for her to go to the public baths when she has marble ones at her home. As to the mosque, for her to go there would be an indelicate if not a disreputable act; besides, it would show a want of tact and good sense, unnecessarily giving the impression that she was an old woman free to go to such places without causing scandal. How then can she kill that time which hangs so heavily on her and passes so rapidly with us? She has recourse to female musicians, sing-

---

* *Koheul* is sulphur of antimony, with which oriental women color their eyes, eyebrows and eyelashes. It is regarded as favorable to the eyes, and gives them grotesqueness if not beauty.

† *Henna* is a shrub from whose leaves is extracted an orange-red color, which the fashionable ladies of the east delight to give to their fingers and toes.

‡ *Souek* is also an extract from a kind of walnut tree. It is of a yellowish-red color and an agreeable flavor, and is much employed on the gums and lips.

ers and dancers. The harmony is not very delicate; the voices are, however, rather agreeable despite some harshness and prolonged nasal tones; but the dance is only a series of hops more amusing than modest. But the poor recluse is gratified; her mind, at the same time infantile and reflective, is awakened to reveries without end in the midst of these concerts and sights which serve at least to divert and amuse her.

But we must mention one extraordinary means of seeing the heavens outside her home and enjoying comparative liberty; it is to go on a pilgrimage to some renowned marabout. The husband usually consents, for the spiritual good of his wife or wives, and often becomes the director of the pious caravan, which he leaves in peace at the holy place, where he will return in the evening or after several days, according to the nature of the vows and devotions proposed. It is well understood that the places where these pilgrims go are divided into two parts with a view of accommodating the two sexes. In general, the women make these devotional visits to marabouts either alone or in company with female friends. I state the fact without any attempt to verify the malicious suspicions which are almost always circulated on parallel occasions, especially when prayers for the birth of children are duly answered, through the intercession of pious marabouts.

But in spite of the inferiority, abasement and degradation of women in general, we must not believe that their influence in the family and in society is radically destroyed; for nature never loses entirely her rights, and there are examples of women of heart and head even among Mussulman women, such as the koranic law has made them. Yet this influence can be exercised only within circumscribed limits and in accordance with fixed habits of life; for the ignorance of woman and the barriers which separate her from the world are insurmountable obstacles to the legitimate extension of her moral empire. But we must state as an extenuating circumstance, if not a ground of hope, that Mussulman people, while holding woman as a minor or rather as a humiliated slave so far as they can, do not absolutely deny her the right and power to manifest qualities and virtues worthy of public esteem and veneration. The proof of this statement is in the great number of women to whom popular opinion accords celestial beatitudes and over whose earthly remains are erected in their honor places for prayer. Among those women who receive extraordinary homage are some who, like the famous Lalla Manoubia having a renowned sanctuary near Tunis, are the objects of public veneration and reverence on account of their chaste and pure lives; and this homage rendered to abstinence from sensual pleasures in countries so corrupt is, it seems, very remarkable, showing the persistency of that high philosophical and religious idea of the triumph of the will over passion, and of the spirit over matter. Another interesting fact is that female advocates are found at Tunis, whose distinct office is to manage the cases of female plaintiffs and defendants coming before the highest tribunal in the land, and also to plead the cause of condemned female criminals, who are subjected to unreasonable sufferings in their cells. There are at Tunis, three of these professional advocates, one of whom I heard make an effective appeal to the bey at a regular session of his court.

Yet it is too true that if this high ideal of woman's capacity and destiny exists among Mussulmans in a speculative point of view, it has little practical influence on their lives. Where unlimited polygamy is sustained by religion and law, the corruption of morals is fatal. Man has there only one object set before him — to enlarge the circle of his carnal pleasures by multiplying the number of his wives. But on the one hand, it is scarcely possible for him to satisfy all his wives, and yet in spite of all the rigors of their prison, the poor creatures sooner or later resign themselves to their allotments.* On the other hand, by the very fact that everybody has the right to polygamy as a principle, only a very small number can actually practise it, monopolizing the women to the detriment of the majority, some mem-

---

* Mussulman women have succeeded in establishing an opinion as ridiculous as it is unfavorable to morality, and whose consequences can render illusive and useless the system of seclusion to which they are condemned. This opinion, admitted by the doctors of the law themselves, is, that an infant, once conceived, can, according to the consecrated expression, *sleep* for years before its birth. In accordance with this notion, there are women who testify that their child has slept during five, six, and even eight years. Sometimes a woman several years after her divorce bears a child which she declares was conceived before her divorce; and her late husband hastens to take her back and recognize his long-delayed paternity; again, a wife perceiving a coldness on the part of her husband, seeks his favor by exciting the hope of offspring, and then amusing him with the plea of sleep. This theory is often very satisfactory to long absent husbands, who, returning, find their household enlarged. Distinguished personages gravely cite the example of a charming young widow of an aged mufti, who brought forth a child for him many years after his death.

bers of which must, of necessity, and not from choice as in christian countries, resign themselves to having no wife; for there would not be enough for every man even were each one to take but two. The fact that there are about the same number of individuals belonging to the two sexes is a material and evident proof that monogamy is a natural and divine law. The want of women for some men and the satiety of their company for others, lead to refinements of corruption and loathsome depravity; and in Africa as in the Orient are seen in the light of day monstrous vices which astonish only the simple European.

If polygamy had only this effect, it would be sufficiently condemned; but its most direct and disastrous, though least suspected, result is the rapid depopulation of countries where it prevails. With rare exceptions, the more wives a man has the less children, and those children are neither robust nor long-lived. Add to this, eunuchism and its very numerous victims, besides a large number of girls who grow old as servants in harems. To complete the view, we must consider the corruption of morals arising on the one hand from the separation of the sexes, and on the other from continuously keeping together many persons of the same sex. For harems are not, alas! exempt from the abominable depravity prevalent in the east; and it is easily understood why Mussulman people, especially those residing in cities, etiolate, diminish and disappear. It is the most formidable of the different organized diseases of Islamism; but it is not the only one. The most aggravated among others are fanaticism and fatalism, ignorance, hatred, bad faith towards other religionists, apathy, indolence and ever-increasing wretchedness, and, in a word, the debasement of the understanding and character with all its fearful consequences.

In short, Mussulmans have played their part and are quitting the stage of life. The system of Mohammed, which is only a human system, is hopelessly exhausted, and the people that it united in a momentary triumph and progress, bound together by the same creeds, traditions and tendencies cannot be separated in their decay and ruin. We have said that these nations, once highly flourishing and prosperous, are to-day little else than obstacles to civilization. They should then, we are told, be cleared away, or means should be devised for their regeneration. The execution of one of these measures appears about as difficult as the other. But, it is added, we could at least drive them back into their deserts or steppes or constrain them to accept the conditions demanded by the civilized world.

It is easy to talk of driving them back into the sands and steppes; but the measure is too radical to be practised upon 150,000,000 of men; for, it must be acknowledged, Mussulmans are not so desirous of our civilization as is generally supposed; for the adoption of a little material progress really proves nothing.

The reason is simple. Emulation is a desire for equality in the presence of a recognized superiority. Now, the least of the Mussulmans believes himself as much superior to the first among us as Islamism is superior to the other religions that are more or less stained, according to him, with idolatry and bad faith towards the prophet and his book. The sight of our civilization either excites his pity, confirming him in the thought that we are simply fitted for and devoted to the vain and perishable things of this world, while true believers occupy themselves with those of heaven; or it profoundly irritates him by the unfavorable contrast with his own country. Christian people make a sad mistake in believing and repeating that civilization, as they understand it, is making rapid progress among Mussulmans. The latter pretend to have to do only with our lessons, and in their eyes it is in principle an insolence on our part to offer them lessons, without speaking of the childishly free manner which we are wont to adopt towards them.

Immovable and haughty in the presence of our pretensions, they disdain our menaces, whose effects they are ready to experience, while bending before God who tries them, but who could if He would, and who perhaps will suddenly reëstablish upon our ruins the ancient power of Islam. If sometimes an account of our prosperity and material and scientific wonders seems to you to make an impression on them, be not deceived; they will hasten to say to themselves mentally, or to cry in a spirit of pride that is not without something of grandeur: "That which the infidels have not found and will not possess and the true believers alone have established, is to proclaim until the last day from the tops of all the minarets of the world that God alone is God and Mohammed is his prophet!"

What incurable fanaticism! exclaims one. Alas! It is a fanaticism spiced with vanity, that would irritate us less if it did not clash with our own. Let Mussulmans but attempt to speak to us of the necessity of adopting their civilization, and what would be our reply? Why, our very free-thinkers would lift their hands in holy horror and cry out with rage. And yet I have heard such a proposition gravely entertained by an accomplished Mussulman, and have listened to prolonged arguments in its support.

Yes, but our civilization is quite another thing, each one replies. And among Mussulmans are those who regard us as indifferent disciples of the Arabs of the middle age. It results that for the want of admitting an ideal common to all races and peoples, such as: *the glory of God and the good of man;* an ideal differently understood and pursued by different means, but identical at the base and which should be carefully kept in view, the parties are eternally and without profit bandying hard names and applying reproachful epithets, and in case of need confirming these amenities at the point of the sword and at the mouth of the cannon.

But is there then nothing to be done with Mussulmans? Yes, much. First, in our relation with them, as with every adversary with whom we have intercourse, we should give up all boasting about our proud or contemptuous superiority; leave to them in need this monopoly, as that of ceremonious and hypocritical advances; be simple, true and benevolent in our bearing and language; avoid wounding their convictions and disturbing their conscientious scruples (often feigned) by wanton remarks or a careless manner. When discussions come to be established, we should maintain them with candor, skilfully drawing them into the circle of opinions and beliefs that are common to us; it is upon this common ground, much broader than is generally supposed, that we can show and hold our advantages; the superiority of a religion or of a system is minutely manifested in a serious conversation. In a word, all consists in making ourselves acquainted with the work before us and in beginning it without unskilfully exciting needless prejudices. We can only hope that the work of reconciliation and regeneration once well begun will go gloriously on to its final consummation.

Moreover there are in the Mussulman world itself encouraging signs. A change is visible in favor of communion with us in thought and sentiment on the part of numerous individuals of Japhetic race who, Mussulmans in creed and Europeans in spirit, are much more accessible than the Shemites whose turn to approach us will come later, as the way shall be prepared. We could give some most encouraging facts illustrative of this statement. We know men in Tunis who are exerting their utmost energies to disseminate light and inaugurate a new era in their history. Not to speak of the progressive measures lately adopted in the Ottoman empire, we will merely name among the hopeful signs of the times a recent work by General Kheredine, entitled, "Reforms Necessary for Mussulman States," and several valuable essays by General Houssein. The late General Otman

Hashem exerted his influence to the last in favor of liberal institutions. And it is also a fact worthy of note, that pianos are introduced into the families of several distinguished personages, and a desire manifested to become acquainted with the French and Italian languages.

The harmony and fusion of races and creeds cannot be effected without time, nor accelerated by partisan strife. It is satisfactory to have evidence that a movement is incontestibly begun in this direction which it is our duty to vigorously aid and encourage. Mussulmans, however refractory they may be, cannot withstand a manifest tendency of the age. Their estrangement from the rest of the human family must yield to better influences. As Christianity becomes in fact, as its founder declares it to be, the way, the truth and the life, rather than a mere dogma or formulary, its power must be felt and acknowledged. As Mussulmans are more doggedly dogmatical than Christians can be, it is worse than useless, it is folly, to encounter them with other dogmas and formularies. Their strength as dogmatists produces their weakness and ruin as men, and hence if they break away, as they must in time, from their shackles, it will be only to breathe the pure and invigorating spirit of the gospel.

The way, then, must be opened and prepared through the diffusion of the spirit of the gospel in the lives of its professed followers, and the restoration and regeneration of the great Mussulman world will follow in the order of Providence to crown the life of humanity.

CHAPTER IV.

Climate.--Products of the Soil.--Manufactures.--Arts and Trades.

THE regency of Tunis, situated between 33° and 37°, 20' north latitude, enjoys for the most part a mild and healthy temperature. The seasons succeed each other so gradually as not to cause the sudden changes of the barometer and thermometer which occur in most European countries, and in different parts of America. There is scarcely ever frost, except among the highest mountains, and the heat of summer is very suffocating only during the prevalence of the desert wind called the sheely.

The year is divided into four seasons of unequal length, nearly as follows: spring scarcely lasts the two months of March and April, while summer continues the five months of May, June, July, August and September. Autumn embraces the three following months of October, November and December. January and February come with copious rains and a chilly, damp air to make up a winter. Though the number of the seasons is the same as in the temperate zone further north, the length and character of these seasons are essentially modified by the proximity of the country to the desert and the sea, as well as by its mountains and latitude, and on the same principle, different points have different climates. In Tunisia, as in those countries where the seasons correspond nearest to the terms employed to indicate them, no two years are alike; one season runs into another; a clear sky, a genial atmosphere and dust, instead of mud and rain, sometimes occur in winter; while in spring, or perchance in early summer, the showers come dashing down upon the thirsty earth. These occurrences are, however, the exceptions. Winter is in general cloudy, wet, muddy and chilly. Spring and autumn have alternate rain and sunshine, mud and dust; while in summer the sun bears full sway, and the dust often rises as if in honor of the prince of light.*

The winds are frequent and variable at Tunis. Those of the north, west and northwest bring on

---

* During my residence at Tunis, my observations with the Fahrenheit thermometer were so irregular as to be of little value. I never saw the mercury below 50° in winter, nor above 120° in summer. With my best efforts to keep my house cool in the warm season by having the doors and windows opened and the floors sponged early in the morning, and the doors and windows closed later in the morning, the mercury regularly ranged between 80° and 90° at mid-day. When the mercury stood at 84° in my room, on one occasion, it promptly rose to 120° on being put in the shade out doors. At Susa, which is 1° further south and on the sea, Mr. Pellissier, formerly vice consul of France, made observations from 1845 to 1848 inclusive, and drew up the following table as the average of each month in that locality: January, 57 1-5°; February, 59°; March, 62 3-5°; April, 66 1-5°; May, 68°; June, 93 1-5°; July, 102°; August, 104°; September, 91 2-5°; October, 74 3-5°; November, 64 2-5°; December, 62 3-5°; average, 75½°. I have seen a statement that the average range of the mercury in the regency for the year is 85°.

ordinarily fine weather in summer, and rain in winter; those of the east and south are almost always dry and hot. These last often succeed each other day after day, especially during the months of July and August, and then the heat becomes truly oppressive. In general from May till September, the winds of the northeast and of the east prevail, and during the rest of the year those of the northwest and of the east. At the period of the equinoxes, a violent wind from the southwest habitually sets in. This is the "Africus," producing hurricanes, which had a great notoriety at an earlier period of the world. The winds of the northeast and of the northwest are fresh and agreeable, and serve to moderate the intense heat of summer.

As we have said, it rarely rains in summer, and then the showers are of short duration and are succeeded by fine weather. On the contrary, in winter, we have seen the rains continue for successive weeks, deluging the country, and bringing on a damp and chilly atmosphere, much harder to endure than the dry, frosty bite of old Boreas among the Swiss mountains or the snow-clad hills of New England. When one of these very long storms comes on, its endurance is rendered much more difficult by the sad condition of the streets. The dirt and dust, that blind and choke us in summer, become soft mud in winter, through which, as we painfully wade, we are often reminded of the witty observation of an Arab poet:

"In summer, no shade, but a vast sea of dust;
In winter, all shade, and mud enough to engulph an ox."

We must promptly add that these disagreeable effects of winter storms have been greatly diminished within a few years by sanitary measures and improvements in the streets effected by the municipality. The first rains, after the parching heat of summer, usually fall in the month of September, though they are sometimes delayed till October. After the ground is well moistened and softened, it is ploughed and prepared to produce new crops. The grain, consisting mostly of wheat and barley, is sown, and the peas, beans and other like products are planted usually before the month of December.

If the rains are copious in winter and the last showers fall in the early days of April, abundant crops of grain are almost sure to follow, which are regularly gathered at the end of May or early in June.

Though the Tunisian soil is less productive to-day than it is represented to have been under Roman rule*, the average yield of wheat is, according to Pellissier, sixteen to one. Dr. Franke says that in certain districts it is not uncommon to see a single grain of wheat produce twelve or fifteen blades, and he was assured that forty and even eighty blades had been known to spring from a single grain; and he further adds that many blades have several heads. In regard to the accuracy of these representations, I am unable to testify from personal observation. I

---

* Pliny, the elder, in book xvii of his excellent natural history, cites in support of the extraordinary fruitfulness of the African province, and especially of Byzacium (actual province of Susa), a plant which had produced three hundred blades from a single grain, and says the ordinary yield of wheat is one hundred and fifty-fold.

have simply noticed thick clusters of blades, and two or three heads on the same blade, and that these were remarkably well filled out, while the blades were not of unusual size or height. The heads of the barley are also very large, while the blades are very short.*

In gathering the grain, the reapers make use of small instruments which would be called knives rather than sickles. When the harvest season begins, men, women and children are often seen in the fields together in large numbers; the women and children have very rudely formed knives which rather break than cut off the blades of wheat. The grain is not threshed, but is trodden out under the feet of horses or mules. This operation, in vogue in the early period of the world, and still practised in the south of Europe, is more expeditious than threshing, but it is not so neat or economical; for on the one hand the grain is mixed up with the powdered earth where it is trodden out; and on the other, the straw is so broken to pieces by the feet of the animals, and by the iron teeth of the heavy drag to which the beasts are attached, as to lose much of its value. The grain is winnowed by being thrown into the air against the wind, to effect which large shovels are used. After this operation, it is collected and put for safe keeping, throughout the whole of North Africa, into large subterranean magazines, called *matmouras*.

* Since writing the above, I have consulted several competent and trustworthy Tunisians, who fully confirm the statements of Pelissier and Dr. Franke. One witness testified that he once counted fifty blades of wheat sprung from one grain, and that most of the blades had two or three heads. And he added, putting his hands together, "I had more wheat from that one grain than I could hold in my hands thus."

Besides cereal products, flax, hemp, tobacco, indigo, saffron and cotton are cultivated, but textile plants are not raised in large quantities, for the want of a proper appreciation of their value, and especially for the want of the right kind of culture. Among tinctorial plants, we must mention henna and madder. Henna is a pretty little tree whose leaves give a reddish brown color with an orange tinge. This is much employed by all the females of the country, who make any pretentions to gentility, in coloring their nails and the ends of their fingers. This is considered an elegant embellishment, without which no Tunisian lady would be regarded as having completed her toilet, notwithstanding her gold embroidery and silk scarfs of variegated colors. The madder is also much cultivated and is employed for dyeing purposes, as in other countries.

Among vegetables and kitchen garden plants, aside from the kinds known in Europe and America, we will mention the *mlouhia*, whose leaves reduced to powder are much employed in the oriental kitchen and constitute a dish of a darkish green color, which, though its look is forbidding, has a palatable taste and an inviting aroma. It is sometimes served up alone, but generally with stewed meat. The *ganouia* is raised like peppers, and like them it may be used fresh or dried, without any sensible difference in its taste. It has a reddish grain, an agreeable taste, and is also used in connection with stewed meat or is fried in oil.

The principal fruit trees are the almond, which blooms in the month of January and produces ripe

FRUITS OF THE COUNTRY.

fruit in April and May; the apricot, with three or four varieties of fruit, all exquisite in taste and flavor, which are gathered in May. The plums and cherries are not so good as those found in Europe and America. Also, the apples and pears are decidedly inferior to our own. White and dark figs are collected in June, July and August. The peaches, though juicy, will not compare with those found further north. The pomegranates, which are of excellent quality, are ripe in August. We must not forget the orange trees, which are found in rows and thickets in all the important gardens, and the flavor of whose fruit is not surpassed by that of any other country. The lemon, quince, walnut and pistachio are also found on every hand. The finest flavored grapes abound in Tunisia. There is no doubt that with their juice might be made wines that would rival in excellence those of Greece, Spain and Italy; but to make wine, a special permission from the government is requisite, and it is rarely ever attempted, except by Europeans. The followers of the prophet scrupulously abstain from competing with Christians in this line of business; but when the wine is once made and placed before them, and the question is simply about *drinking* it, their scruples often give way. The great proportion of the grapes of the country is dried and converted into raisins, which constitute an important article of exportation. In fine, the climate and soil of Tunisia are suited to the production of most of the fruits of the temperate zone and of the sunny regions of the south, and it would require only the activity and energy of intelligent freemen to create throughout the regency orchards, the excellence, variety and abundance of whose fruits would gain a world-wide renown.

When gardens are not provided with running streams, which are rare, they are supplied with water from wells. The cheapest and most common contrivance for raising the water consists of a pulley and cylinder elevated over the well and connecting by means of cords with a large leathern bucket. This machinery is worked by some beast of burden, approaching and moving from the well. The other contrivance is the *naoora*, which is extensively used in Spain and Egypt. This consists of two cog-wheels, one horizontal and the other vertical, and numerous buckets or jars, usually earthen, fastened to a band which descends into the well and passes over one of the cog-wheels. This machinery is worked, like the old-fashioned cider mill, by some beast of burden, moving around the well. The water is conducted off over the garden by means of troughs and trenches.

Here we will offer a few remarks upon the culture of the olive and the date palm, the two most important trees of the country, both of which are stamped, in token of their importance, on most of the national coins, and the palm tree once constituted, as seen on our title page, a part of the symbol of Carthage. Much attention is given to the olive. The trees are trimmed and the ground loosened about their roots. Efforts are made to save all the water by means of little trenches which end at the trunk of the tree. But according to Pellissier, an excellent crop can be depended upon only once in four years. The gathering of the olives begins at the end of October, and continues several months. The olives are beaten from the trees with poles. They are then collected, together with sticks and leaves, and should be ground and pressed at once; but as the number of mills is very limited, they have to wait their turn; and to prevent their being injured by fermentation, they are cast into trenches and preserved by means of several layers of salt.

The mill is composed of a cylindrical crushing stone, whose horizontal axis joins a vertical beam, which is usually put in motion by some beast of burden, though there is one mill at Tunis propelled by steam, which has been in operation several years. The olives are first crushed, and acquire the consistency of paste or pulp. The best oil is that which is first extracted, and its quality is injured, as the olive *mash* undergoes experiments with water and pressure. The oil which oozes out of the mash or floats upon water applied to it is called *darb-el-may;* the mash is then subjected to pressure, and a thicker and inferior oil is produced, called *beldah;* the second operation of the press produces a third class oil, called *beldah-filoura;* a fourth and still inferior oil is produced from scrapings and watery matter, called *kourna;* this looks like greasy mud, and has a very disagreeable odor.

The olive *mash*, left after the first quality of oil has been extracted, is not always subjected to the press; it is often put into jars, and, after being mixed with barley meal, is made into unsavory bread, which is extensively used throughout the regency, and even this is not always to be had by the poor.

The olive mash, after all the oil has been extracted, is used for fuel in cooking and other operations, and when grass or shrubs cannot be found for the camels, this is mixed with a little barley and given them as food.

Tunisian oil is not held in very high esteem in Europe. European purchasers usually denounce it as fit only for making soap and oiling machinery. The best of it will not compare favorably with that of Provence, in France, and of Italy. Its inferiority arises, in the opinion of competent judges, from the fact that the trees are not grafted as they are in the countries before named. Yet it is stated that much of the oil of Tunis is exported to Genoa and Marseilles, and after being purified there, is sold for Italian and French oil, and no one can by any analysis detect the difference. The best oils of Tunisia are those of Gerba, Hergla and Susa. The olive tree lives many centuries, but does not continue to bear fruit to the end.

The date palm will vegetate in different localities; but to bear fruit, it must have a warm climate, a good supply of water and careful attention. The foot of each tree is surrounded by a bed of manure, which is covered over with earth. It must be watered at least every four or five days, and care must be taken to cut off every sprout from its trunk. This operation should be performed so skilfully as to allow no sap to escape, and the wound should be speedily dried and healed. It is the pruning operation which explains the peculiar form of this tree, its lofty height and joints resembling those of the bamboo and the cane. The date palm is generated from the stones of its fruit and the sprouts of its trunk. The latter means of generation is preferred; for if the sprouts or saplings receive careful attention, they bear fruit in six years; whereas the palms generated from the stones bear fruit only after fifteen years.

The sexuality of the date palm is universally recognized, and receives special attention in the production of fruit. The experiments in this regard appear to us very curious. Female trees bring forth only dry fruit, destitute of flavor, unless they have an opportunity in the appropriate season to communicate with the pollen of the male trees. This fecundation, which can be produced, as with most other trees, at considerable distance, by the transmission of the pollen through the air, takes place ordinarily in March or April. It is aided by those who have charge of the trees in the following manner: They place among the flowers of female trees flowers plucked from male trees. A male palm can thus fecundate a great number of female palms. Dr. Franke puts the number at 400 or 500, and Pellissier at 25; but this last figure appears to us too small when compared to the same mode of propagation occurring among other trees.

This process was understood by the ancients, and Pliny speaks of it under the name of *caprification*. The Arabs employ it also for other trees, especially for fig trees, whose male blossoms are suspended among female blossoms.

The date palm ordinarily lives about two centuries. Reaching its maturity in about thirty years, it bears fruit sixty or seventy years, and produces an average of fifteen or twenty clusters of dates, each cluster weighing from twelve to twenty pounds. The best dates of the Tunisian Gereed are unsurpassed in flavor and richness. This Gereed is composed of several oases, each of which is an immense forest of palm trees, watered by numerous limpid streams. The oasis of Tozer alone is believed to contain 360,000 date palms.

As to field or farm labor, the average price of ordinary hands per day is twelve cents, and in harvest time sixteen cents, the laborer boarding himself out of that. The rent of land is paid either in the produce of the land or in money, according to the contract made, and varies from five dollars to twenty dollars for twenty-five acres. When a piece of land is cultivated on shares, the cultivator receives one-fourth or one-fifth of the produce raised, and the proprietor of the ground furnishes the seed and the beasts of burden, including oxen, horses, mules and camels. The labor of a camel well trained for farm work has the same value as that of a yoke of oxen.

Fancying the implements of husbandry patterned after those of the patriarchal period, our readers will be enabled, by the details already given, to form a sufficiently accurate idea of the agricultural labors of the regency of Tunis. As we have before said, agriculture is not alone suffering; it is dying out piecemeal. The want of encouragement, and, what is worse, the injustice and extortion committed by appraisers and tax-gatherers, and the want of hands, since the men are withdrawn to acquire tact and skill in the use of deadly weapons, instead of being engaged in the productive employments;—all these causes conspire to prevent Tunisian laborers from putting forth any efforts except those necessary to ward off death by famine. This explains why Tunisia is obliged often to depend upon cargoes of wheat and barley from abroad to supply the wants of men and beasts; she receives as a subsidy from Algeria a part of her own crops, which her Bedouins, to escape injustice and extortion, sell each year for good money upon French territory. This grain comes back upon its native soil to be there sold as foreign merchandise, enhanced in price by the cost of transportation by land and by sea, and by large profits taken by speculators. The population, discouraged, emigrate, or, enfeebled, fade away and disappear upon the place of their origin. Also, the desert, not the natural desert with its magnificence, but the gloomy desert created by the abandonment and faults of man, the desert of countries that decline and decay from apathy and misery produced by tyranny and injustice, this desert is extending and bids fair to be extended over this whole territory, once so flourishing and to-day so forsaken and desolate, and yet so fruitful and inexhaustible in its resources.

If the land goes to waste, its beasts cannot prosper. The bovine race of Tunisia has become utterly degenerated and degraded, and native butchers sell, under the name of beef, caouchoucine muscles as hard for the jaws as the stomachs of the consumers. And this is readily accounted for by the fact that there are no grassy meadows and no hay. Some Maltese butchers meanwhile have succeeded in producing eatable meat by feeding their cattle somewhat as in Europe. Cows are rarely, if ever, kept for their milk; during more than five years' residence in Tunis I was not privileged for once even to taste of cow's milk.

The Tunisian sheep has not so degenerated and lost its original character as the ox. It belongs to the broad, fat-tailed race so numerous in Africa. Its meat, has, moreover, no very savory taste; for, to speak plainly, it is rams and not ewes that are hung in state. If any one recoil before the slightly hircine taste of ram's meat, the taste of fat peculiar to old sheep will be sure to transcend the powers of his stomach. But in general only lamb's meat is placed upon the table of families in comfortable circumstances at Tunis, unless in the cool season. Lamb's meat is, however, excellent and abundant.

Pork is scarcely raised except by Maltese, since Mussulmans and Jews regard it with horror. The wild boar is readily found in the forests, and the Bedouins come to sell its meat to Europeans in the principal markets of the regency. The goat is found in every direction, supplying the place of the cow for milk. The camel, however, is the only domestic animal which is really in a thriving condition; perhaps it is because it requires the least care, and, created to live in the midst of privations, it finds itself at Tunis in its element. The support of this singular animal costs its proprietor scarcely anything, since it eats and digests the thorny leaves of the cactus (Indian fig), which abounds in the country; also, when it drinks, it takes a supply for many days, in accordance with its character as the predestined ruminant of the desert.

Tunisian horses have in general nothing to justify their ancient renown, and with no effort to improve their stock, their character deteriorates from time to time. There is, however, a mountain breed of horses that may justify a passing word. They are of small stature, snugly built, of tough muscle, and remarkable for their fleetness. It is possible, perhaps probable, that their blood might be advantageously mingled with some breeds found in Europe and America. Horses are allowed to drink as much water as they want when they are hot, provided they are driven afterwards. Their principal food, when kept in the stable, is barley and straw. Grass is not cultivated at all in the regency. During winter and spring, it is usually abundant without cultivation. I never saw any hay at Tunis except such as was brought from Algeria, and it was not produced there till after the conquest by the French. Asses and mules have all the qualities peculiar to their kind and necessary for service. Mules especially are held in high esteem, and are alone used, in strict accordance with court etiquette, by the highest officers of the state, including the bey. The horse is, however, used in war and military parades, as in the early history of the country.*

Among the fowls, hens or rather chickens, are good, abundant and cheap, as are also geese and ducks. Ring and turtle doves and different species

* See Appendix G.

of pigeons are found in large numbers both in a domestic and a wild state. Game, properly so called, is abundant in spite of the absolute freedom of sportsmen. Partridges, quails, larks, bustards,* thrushes, pintados† and starlings are found in the Tunisian markets, as well as hares and rabbits.

Fish are abundant and cheap. The tunny fishery is carried on along the shore at the appropriate season, and is a source of revenue for the government. The tunny fish belongs to the family of the mackerel, but in point of size bears no resemblance to it, often weighing 1,000 pounds. Tunny cutlets are very palatable, being in general preferable to Tunisian beefsteaks or mutton chops. These fish, when fresh, are substantial luxuries, but when cut up and salted, serve about the same purpose for the inhabitants along the Mediterranean as codfish for Americans.

Inferior kinds of fish are taken in the lake of Tunis, which has been the receptacle of the filth of the city for more than 2,000 years. These are eaten only by the poor. Good fish are found in abundance in the roadstead of Tunis, but the markets are mainly supplied from Bizerta. Here there is a large fresh water lake, communicating directly with the sea through a channel a third of a mile long. The inhabitants

---

* The bustards are very large birds, weighing from twenty to thirty pounds; and are numerously found in the southeast part of the regency. In their general features and habits, they resemble ostriches, which belong to the desert of the Gereed. They also look like wild turkeys.

† The pintados are a species of the gallinaceous order. They live on marshy ground in flocks composed of many females and only one male. Constituting an exquisite dish, they are much sought by sportsmen. They are of a grey color, and are commonly called the hens of Carthage.

profit by the currents of water, which set sometimes towards the sea, and sometimes towards the lake, to imprison in the large enclosures, which they have made with canes and osiers midway between the sea and the lake, quantities of fish, which are daily taken in nets under municipal regulations, and carried to the Tunisian market forty miles distant. Besides furnishing cheap food for the inhabitants of Bizerta and the neighboring villages, they give important aid to the treasury of the government. These people manifest an unusual familiarity with the instincts and habits of fish. They live upon fish and watch and care for them so much, that they may almost be said to live *with* them. They thoroughly understand the time when several different kinds of fish prefer salt water and when fresh water; when they produce their young and should not be disturbed; and when they are in a healthy condition for food, and should be brought into the market. On this knowledge, together with the natural facilities of the place, they profess to be dependent for their success. They further state that this system of raising fish was first introduced there many centuries ago by a colony of Greeks. They have twelve enclosures, which they pretend contain twelve different kinds of fish, though my observations on the spot did not verify this representation. Each enclosure is undisturbed by the net for eleven lunar months in the year, and is subjected to the exhausting operation of the net every day during one entire lunar month. I saw for several days the nets thrown, the fish caught and brought on shore, assorted in the fish house, sold and sent off to market.

While I have never made the instincts and habits of fish a special study, and cannot satisfactorily explain the details of the system of production adopted at Bizerta, I can testify to the general success of the experiments there pursued. The business is a government monopoly, and individual enterprise is allowed no scope. I was told that the general good could be secured only in this way. Anglers must go upon the roadstead or upon the lake for their pastime. The fish enclosures are situated midway between the sea and the large lake, in a place where the channel widens out, presenting the appearance of a pond. Each time when I was present, at least a cart-load of fish was brought ashore, where many purchasers were in waiting, and almost every day in the year one or two camels came loaded with these fish to Tunis, where they constitute a cheap food for the poor, and a rich dish at a very moderate cost for the best supplied tables. The mullet is the most abundant, weighing from one to five pounds.

As regards wild animals, the lion, the panther and the leopard are encountered in the solitudes of the interior, as are also the jackal, the hyena, the wolf and the fox. There are many sorts of serpents, venomous or harmless, and among the arachnida are the scorpions, whose bite is dangerous at certain seasons of the year. Insects multiply and abound, as in all warm countries; and during the rage of the dog star, the mosquitoes charge themselves at night with continuing the work of exasperation which the flies keep up during the day. I will say nothing of the more disgusting species, whose company the natives seem almost to court, and which are ever ready to welcome Europeans who undertake excursions in the regency. I may, nevertheless, observe, that fleas and bed bugs, however detestable, are not to be treated with simple indifference and disdain.

To complete the enumeration of the products of the Tunisian soil, we will say a word about the minerals. There are in Tunisia two lead mines, slightly argentiferous, at Jeba and at Jeladja. Some beds of iron are at Gebel Zerissa and in several other mountains lying along the frontiers of Algeria. Most of the mines are situated in the northwest part of the regency. Marine salt is taken from several sebkas or shallow salt lakes, where it is embedded on the surface in large quantities. Gebel Hadifa contains a considerable mine of rock salt. Plaster and lime are extracted on a large scale in the central and southern provinces, and soda is furnished, especially by the district of Cairwan. But in general these sources of wealth are disregarded or but slightly developed. The mines repose in the bosom of the earth, though their treasures are greatly needed by the government; the salt lies on the ground and embedded like crystal among the hills, though its sale is a government monopoly; and the forests, abounding in timber of every sort actually needed to supply the wants of the country, rest undisturbed by the axe of the woodman.

As in agricultural and mining operations, so in the manufacturing business, including various branches of productive industry, we find all tends to decay and death. It is of course understood that we speak of the arts and trades, properly so called; for no one can imagine anything in Tunisia corresponding with the modern system of manufacturing, where, by the use of formidable machinery and ingenious contrivances, one man is enabled to perform the work of one hundred or of five hundred men. Such marvellous inventions, by which cities are built, nations enriched and human beings enlightened and transformed into men, capable of controlling the elements and governing themselves, are not yet understood in Barbary, and some time will yet be required to effect this change.

Among the branches of industry not utterly discarded, we must mention the manufacture of woolen and silk goods, especially bernouses, coverlids and scarfs. These beautiful fabrics, which are of various qualities and colors, come mostly from the Gereed and from the island of Gerba; and the way in which they are manufactured upon old, rickety looms, and the yarn made with the spindle and the distaff in hand, as in the patriarchal period, would of itself form an interesting chapter. Silk fabrics are made at Tunis, Susa and Gabes, and those of cotton at Sfax. But all these establishments, not supplying the wants of the population, the export trade is quite limited.

Most of the articles of luxury and ornament come from Europe, as do also the wrought metals, arms and tools of the artisans and tradesmen. The great manufactories of Lyons furnish Tunis, as well as all the east, with quantities of brocades and silks, whose precious embroidery and elegant colors delight the eye. It is not that the art of the embroiderer has disappeared at Tunis. On the contrary, clothes, shoes and saddles are exquisitely ornamented with gold, silver and silk, giving proof of the skill of the workmen; but still the number of embroiderers is gradually diminishing, and for the simple reason that they cannot compete with the Lyonese artisans, who have the advantage of machinery, good materials and superior artistic culture.

The masons are still very skilful in building almost without scaffolding plain arches and arched roofs; but they have lost their skill as architects. Some of them have scarcely any knowledge of those beautiful arabesques in stucco which are found in many of the houses and public buildings of the east. All are enslaved to professional prejudices, which prevent their making any progress in their art. Also, most of the important building enterprises are entrusted to European directors and workmen, whose number is increasing, and who are by degrees producing great changes in the part of the city not exclusively devoted to Mussulmans. Similar remarks are applicable to such mechanics as coöperate with masons in building, including carpenters, joiners and locksmiths. Many of the materials come from abroad. The timber and iron are furnished by different European countries, especially by Sweden and Illyria; soft stone by Malta; marble by the north of Italy, and enamelled tiles for floors and ceilings by the south of Italy. European workmen come to supply the great insufficiency or incapacity of their fellow tradesmen belonging to the country.

Tanning, currying, and shoemaking, which furnish

employment for many hands, are, nevertheless, in a backward state. In these branches of business, also, Europe comes more and more in aid of the country. The raw hides that are sent off, come back beautiful leather and ready made shoes, and for choice boots and shoes and clothing, European materials and workmen are preferred. In the manufacture of essences, for which Tunis is renowned, Europe comes in also for her share of the honor; the pretty little phials so exquisitely cut and colored, which travelers delight to buy at a large cost, as a souvenir of Tunisian skill, come directly from Trieste; the essence alone is Tunisian, and often the phial contains only the odor, which is soon evaporated.

The cloth factory at Tebourba, the oil press and bakery at Tunis, and also the Hafsian foundry for cannon, can hardly be called Tunisian; since all these establishments are entrusted to European directors, foremen and workmen, and the machines used in them are brought from Europe. There is hardly anything Tunisian about them but their locality, their name and some native laborers.

It is evident, from what has been said, that the imports of the country must be very considerable, while the exports are limited almost wholly to raw materials. The most important article of commerce is oil, which is exported to Marseilles, Genoa, Leghorn, Liverpool, Trieste and Odessa. This business is carried on principally at Susa. After oil, may be named wool, soap, sponges, woolen and silk fabrics, cereal products, dried fruits, living animals, bones and rags.

The best wool is that which comes from the country of the Frashish; the soap held in most esteem is that of Susa; the fabrics preferred are those of Gerba and of the Gereed, and the best sponges come from Sfax and the Kerkenna islands. Living animals cannot be legally exported without a special permit, which is readily obtained; but many Europeans do not scruple to evade this law with the connivance of some of the bey's officers. The fruits exported are dates, almonds and pistachios, all essential products of the eastern and southeastern portion of the regency.

The principal imports are dry goods, raw silk, groceries, drugs, iron ware, colonial provisions, wine, brandy and other liquors, arms, implements and tools. Cotton cloths and coarse goods generally come from England viâ Malta and Leghorn, and the fine fabrics from France, as do also the colonial provisions and choice wines, while the heavy wines are brought from Sicily and Italy. Pellissier estimated, twenty years ago, the proportion between the imports and exports to be as seven to five. But the disparity is probably greater at the present time. The average annual commerce of the regency is roughly put down at $3,000,000, but after carefully considering the reports of our consular agents and the statements of Tunisian merchants, we believe this figure to be below the truth.

All imports are taxed on their entrance three per cent. *ad valorem*, except wines and liquors, which pay ten per cent. with the exception of a certain number of casks, fixed each year, for the personal use of European families. On this limited quantity only three per cent. is paid. The duty on exports is usually large, and it is often changed. The tax on exported oil was in 1867 about eight cents a gallon; on wheat about eleven cents a bushel; on barley, five and one-half cents a bushel, and on sponges a cent a pound.*

For some years past, the monetary system of the country has experienced frequent disturbances, caused in part by sudden changes or revolutions in commercial circles, and doubtless enhanced by injudicious experiments with the currency. The interest habitually taken for money loaned at Tunis is one per cent. a month. Though this may seem large, it is only the mininum rate. Interest rises, according to the rapacity of the lender and the exigency of the borrower, to four, six, and even eight per cent. a month. While Mussulmans generally refrain under religious injunctions from receiving interest or usury, they know how to pay it. Christians and Jews have no scruples on this point, and, we must add, sometimes cruelly take advantage of necessities which they have been instrumental in creating. With some very honorable exceptions, it is not the merchants of Tunis who could in conscience protest against the hard saying of Napoleon I, that "commerce is only a well-organized brigandage." It, however, leaves much to be desired in regard to its organization at Tunis.

---

* For an account of the weights, measures and coins of the country, see Appendix H.

CHAPTER V.

Principal Cities.---Their Characteristics and Peculiarities.

TUNIS, the capital of Tunisia, is situated 36°, 50' north latitude and 10°, 16' east of the meridian of Greenwich, seven miles from the sea, twelve miles from the Majerda and about seven hundred yards from the borders of lake Bahira, which extends to the Goletta and is there connected with the sea. It is situated partly upon a plane and partly upon a gentle slope occupying the middle of the isthmus between lake Bahira and the small salt lake southwest of Tunis. Its situation is unfavorable for commerce on account of the inconvenience of communicating with the Goletta which is its main port of entrance; and it is also unfavorable to health on account of the miasma from the lake into which the sewers of the city have flowed for more than two thousand years. In these two points of view the site of ancient Carthage has decided advantages.

Tunis contains the city proper (El Medina), and two suburbs, one north of it and the other south.

On the highest point of the city is the kasbah, a fortress of immense dimensions, which was once strong, though now in a ruinous state and almost dismantled. A part of this vast construction is attributed to the Spaniards. Until within twelve or fifteen years, were always seen suspended under the vestibule of the great entrance halberds and pikes of the sixteenth century with coats of mail much more ancient. Though the origin of these objects was uncertain, the Tunisians showed them with pride as trophies taken from conquered Christians. The Arabs compare the city of Tunis to an extended bernouse, whose hood is the kasbah. From the kasbah to the sea gate it is eight hundred yards, and seventeen hundred yards from one suburb to the other. Each suburb is almost as large as the city proper. The city with its suburbs is surrounded, except on the side towards the lake, with an embattled wall, which is in a ruinous state and is about six miles long.

Out of the south gate near the border of the lake, stands upon a steep hill the zawia of the celebrated marabout Sidi Ali-Ben Hassen-Esh-Shadeli; and further on towards lake Sedjoumi, is that of the celebrated *Lalla Manoubia*. Between these two points, which are joined together by a wall, is fort Ahmed Rais. This line prolonged is almost perpendicular to lake Sedjoumi, whose borders are commanded on the west of the city by steep heights, crowned with two forts. Tunis, seen from a distance, presents a certain picturesque grandeur, which fades from view as we approach it. Passing within the walls, we find the distinctive marks of an oriental city. Some parts of it, however, show signs of improvement. The new streets are wider than the old ones, and are lined with European houses. Of late, the sewers have been covered over and most of the streets have been paved. But the most notable and useful improvement is the introduction and distribution of water, brought thirty miles distant, by means of a modern underground aqueduct, from Zaughan, where Roman Carthage received her supply by means of the expensive contrivance at that time in vogue. It is only a few years since, during the torrid heat of the summer, Tunis had scarcely water enough to quench the thirst of its inhabitants. Cisterns, belonging to the houses, of various dimensions, two basins of water almost stagnant situated at the gates of the city, and some brackish wells a little way out were the sole means of supplying the wants of men and beasts. While to-day, living water is found in abundance at the corners of most of the streets; and behind the kasbah is the principal reservoir. This is a monumental construction, which, standing on an elevated point, presents a picturesque appearance with its sheaves of water falling back into a beautiful vase in a garden enclosed by an elegant iron fence. This aqueduct is the work of French engineers and contractors, who are charged with having shamefully cheated the government, at the same time that they accomplished a great good for the country.

The streets of Tunis are in general narrow (some of them being in places only three or four feet wide), as in other oriental and southern countries, where the object is to avoid the heat and enjoy the shade as much as possible. Numerous arched roofs, running from one house to another over the street, contribute especially to this object. The houses are for the most part square, with a large open court in the centre, called by Europeans *the patio*. Sometimes they have only a ground floor, and rarely have but two stories, though in the European quarter are houses three, four and five stories high. All the houses have cemented terraces, serving as promenades in the cool hours of the day, and also to conduct the rain water into cisterns. The building materials are stone, brick, lime and cement; also granite and marble, which are less common on account of their expense, and wood is only used for doors and windows and to uphold cemented roofs. The houses of the rich are interiorly commodious, elegant and even sumptuous. They are distinguished especially by the profusion of marble and arabesque. Flowers are often cultivated within the patios. It is rare to find windows upon the streets, and where there are any, they are very small and well provided with bolts and screens for safety and for the privacy of the family. Thus the great walls, with few windows and those rendered impenetrable by lattice work, give a singularly gloomy and monotonous aspect to most of the streets of Tunis.

Each trade has its appropriate quarter or street. The most remarkable are: the street of the shoemakers, the street of the gunsmiths, the street of the locksmiths, and the street of the cap-makers. There are also special quarters for merchants, and vast markets called souks, which are arched over or covered with boards; such as the souk-el-bey and the souk-el-trok. The bazar for the sale of jewelry and diamonds is a great resort for the curious. This was once used for the sale of female slaves. Another great market called souk talkæ, is filled with groceries and stores for the sale of iron ware. These shops are generally kept by Jews, whose special quarter, called *the Hara*, is near by. Here are found dirty streets, miserable houses, and many synagogues with schools below the surface of the ground. The Israelites were formerly cloistered in this "Ghetto," whose gates were closed each night. Thus huddled together in this filthy district, it is easy to imagine their misery. But now they have forced the barriers which superstition and fanaticism imposed upon them, and have taken up their abodes beyond their original limits; still the Hara is the general quarter of the majority of the Jews, and is properly the Jewry of Tunis.

There are in Tunis fifty mosques. Nine of them have schools with professorial chairs, of which four belong to the Malekites and five to the Hanefites. The most beautiful mosque is called Djema Zeitoona, i. e., the Mosque of Olives. It is a vast edifice, having seven large doors reached by flights of steps leading from the streets, and is surrounded on three sides by a wall elevated to conceal the interior of the structure from profane eyes. For at Tunis, infidels are excluded from the mosques, and in passing them their near approach to the door is regarded with suspicion. Yet by means of furtive glances, conjectures and information, we can form a pretty accurate idea of the mosque in question. It has several open courts with porticos sustained by modern columns, and the sanctuary of retangular form contains rows of columns, most of which are antique, with arches ornamented with arabesque. Gigantic chandeliers are suspended from the dome and immense mats cover the marble floor. Like all mosques, it is devoid of interior decorations; for Mussulmans are noted image-breakers. A square minaret surmounted with an elegant cupola crowns this metropolitan mosque. The other notable mosques are the Djema Saheb-et-Taba, the Djema Sidi Mahres and the Djema Djedida, each of which has an interesting history and a peculiar style of architecture, with many fine columns and other monuments of art brought from Carthage and other ruined cities.

The palace of the bey (Dar-el-Bey), situated upon the piazza of the kasbah at the souk-el-bey, offers exteriorly only a front of large stones of a yellowish-grey color, and has the appearance rather of military barracks than of a royal residence. But it has within magnificent halls and incomparable arabesques wrought in beautiful white plaster. It was built by Hamouda Bashaw in the latter part of his reign. The bey comes there only during Ramadan and sleeps there only on the nights of the 26th and the 27th of that month of fasting. This palace is habitually reserved for personages of the highest rank who visit Tunis. Among these illustrious visitors, we may name queen Caroline, the wife of George the IV of England, and the sons of Louis Philippe — the duke of Montpensier, the prince de Joinville and the duke d'Aumale; and prince Napoleon and his wife the princess Clotilda: and more recently, during my sojourn at Tunis, the prince of Wales, the prince and princess of Prussia, and the prince of Italy were among the distinguished guests entertained in this palace.

The municipality of Tunis which has now its offices in the Dar-el-Bey, was at first established in the magnificent house called *Dar-el-Ashra*, the house of the Ten.* This is now the property and residence of General Heussein, one of the most intelligent personages of Tunisia. Dar-el-Ashra is generally regarded as the most beautiful private house in the city. It has two courts, one of which with its tall and graceful white marble columns presents a magnificent appearance. It has also a profusion of fine arabesque and marble ornaments.

The kasbah or citadel, situated on the highest point of the city and at the upper end of the street which begins at the Marine, is a vast castle of a rectangular form and is surrounded with high embattled walls. It presents a miserable appearance from without, and within the look is still worse, containing only ruins and establishments for the manufacture of powder and leather. It once contained a palace which was the residence of the deys; but this was long since destroyed. We observe in wandering over this mass of ruined buildings many iron doors half buried in the ground. These belong to immense underground passages and abodes, long since abandoned,

---

* So called because it served at the beginning of this century as the residence of ten high civil and political functionaries.

and about which popular imagination does not fail to be greatly exercised. Very considerable treasures are supposed to be concealed there, and popular belief has enough historic support to give it currency. This was once the stronghold of the regency, and on many occasions the treasures of the city and of the country around were here amassed and interred for security, and then followed fearful revolutions and butcheries, rendering it altogether probable that some of the concealed treasures sometimes escaped the observation and search of the chieftains that succeeded to power; but now that these subterranean passages have been filled by natural causes in the course of centuries, we doubt whether curiosity or the desire for gain would be gratified by any excavations and researches. The little mosque which towers above the kasbah and from whose summit are signalled by means of a white flag the canonical hours of prayer each day, was built according to tradition by Yahia-Abou-Zakaryah about the year 630 H., and 1232 A. D.

We shall complete this cursory notice of the remarkable buildings of Tunis by naming in the European quarter, which is the lower part of the city: 1. The Catholic church, mostly concealed from view by the convent of the Capucins. Notwithstanding its different restorations, this edifice has nothing remarkable in its style of architecture, and it is not large enough for the multitudes which frequent it, often occupying every available point in the building. 2. The Italian college, a construction of good proportions recently erected at the expense of the

Italian colony near the Italian and American consulates. 3. The British consulate with a singular front, situated on the piazza which is the centre of the European quarter; and 4, the French consulate, situated out of the walls of the city in the new quarter of the Marine; notwithstanding its enormous cost, this building presents only the appearance of an ordinary private house in a great European city.

The Mussulman cemeteries in the city and its environs are in no respect remarkable. Some of them are not even enclosed by a wall. The same is also true of the Jewish cemeteries, whose innumerable white marble slabs and masonry, made white by the frequent application of whitewash, present the appearance, from a distance, surrounded as they generally are by verdure, of little oriental villages whose terraces only are in sight.* The Catholic cemetery of St. Anthony, established in 1655, is situated by the side of the Greek cemetery, nearly opposite the French consulate, and has some fine monuments and memorials of distinguished personages. The name

---

* Mussulmans and Jews avoid, as far as possible, keeping the bodies of the dead in their houses for any length of time, and especially during the dark hours of the night; and thus it not unfrequently happens that persons are buried alive, especially during the prevalence of epidemics. One case where this terrible disaster was narrowly escaped occurred in June, 1867, the details of which I learned from an authentic source. A Jewish girl having witnessed several sudden deaths from the cholera, dropped upon the floor and was supposed to be dead, when, forthwith, according to the custom of the place, she was laid upon a bier and borne to the cemetery. But while the bearers were letting her body into the grave, she recovered her consciousness just in season to prevent being buried alive, and she was taken up from the grave and walked back to her home. Both the Mussulmans and the Jews are buried with their feet to the east and their heads elevated, ordinarily without coffins, and always in a linen shroud.

of Sir Edward Baynes is seen on the left as we approach the chapel. He was British agent and consul general from 1849 to 1855. The monuments over the remains of the family of the late count Joseph Raffo, long an honored minister of the bey, do credit to the artist and to the filial piety of the son, who is still in the service of the government.

The Protestant cemetery of St. George is much smaller, but it is in a good condition and contains older monuments, some of them belonging to the first half of the seventeenth century. Here also repose the remains of several consuls, among which we must name Sir Thomas Reade, and John Howard Payne, the author of SWEET HOME. Sir Thomas was British agent and consul general from 1824 to 1849. John Howard Payne was instrumental in making the American consulate a tasteful and agreeable residence. He encountered much opposition in his efforts for the honor of the American flag, and some persons who failed to appreciate his services in life did not scruple to speculate on his private papers after his death.*

Before the establishment of these cemeteries, Christians were generally buried privately and in out-of-the-way places, to avoid exciting the fanaticism of Mussulmans whose delight seemed to be to efface every trace of persons not identified with their religion. In speaking of cemeteries it would be natural to say a word about the *Torba*, the tomb of the family of the beys; but infidels cannot enter there, and they can only distinguish the dark grey

---

* See Appendix I.

walls and the cupola covered with green earthen tiles and rounded over in a manner to represent a bulbous plant. It is a melancholy pleasure, as we enter the city on the Goletta road, to observe in the cemetery on the right a commanding monument erected in honor of the last of the Moorish kings, Muley Hamida, who was also styled the last of the Abencerage. To enjoy his usurped throne, this cruel wretch plucked out the eyes of his own father and then sent him off to live and die an exile in Europe.

Though Tunis is not a manufacturing and industrial city, yet in its character as the capital, all the products of the regency are there brought together, and the importations from Europe are very considerable. Of the local manufactures, we must name, first, the sheshias or red caps, for the production of which this city has no rival; fine silk tissues are also woven on miserable hand-looms; costly embroidery is executed in fine taste, especially on saddles; and delicate morocco slippers, variously colored, may be found in abundance; but the most indispensable arts and trades, such as are exercised by locksmiths, blacksmiths, carpenters and cabinet-makers, are, with rare exceptions, in a state of pitiable inferiority. We shall not dwell further upon this subject, as it has already received our attention, while explaining in a general way the state of the arts and trades in the regency.

In the exercise of the mechanic arts, as well as in commercial enterprises, the Europeans have a marked preponderance which gradually becomes greater, and the financial operations are mainly regulated and controlled by Israelites. It is enough to say that the natives and sovereigns of the country take a secondary place, and consequently the future does not belong to them. *He who does not go forward goes backward.* This incontestible law for nations and races as well as for individuals, has a striking application in the situation of all Islamitish people irreparably fallen, because, the spring of their activity being once broken, their movement is arrested, and this dates back already several centuries, during which other races have made decided progress, while they have become degenerate and fallen back.

Tunis probably has a population of 125,000 souls, of which number 32,000 are Jews, 13,000 Christians, and the rest Mussulmans. Among Europeans, the Italians are the most numerous. Their number has greatly increased within a few years and now probably amounts to 6,000; there are also nearly 6,000 Maltese British subjects; 1,500 French, Spanish and German subjects, and 300 Greeks. The Europeans are not subject to the local jurisdiction. The same is true of the Jewish subjects of the different European powers. All the European states and the American Union have at Tunis consuls-general invested with a diplomatic character and with judicial and commercial functions.

The Mussulman administration at Tunis is divided as follows: 1. The government of the city and its suburbs is administered during the day by the doulatli, *the shadow of the bey*, as represented by Mr. Pellissier. He is a veritable prefect of police, especially since of late years, in addition to his fifty *hambas*

BRANCHES OF THE ADMINISTRATION. 397

(mounted guards) he has a body of *dabtyas* or policemen. 2. The *sheik-el-Medina* (Mayor) aided by two assistants, one for each suburb, has the direction of the police during the night, and exercises his power by means of a company of watchmen who constitute a city guard.* 3. The chief of the municipality superintends and directs the public works, the distribution of the waters, the imposition of taxes on real estate, and the administration of certain establishments for the public good. The municipality of Tunis was established in 1858 and has already effected important improvements. 4. Civil justice is administered by two Malekite and two Hanefite cadis. From 1861 to 1864, while the constitution was in force, their duties were discharged by tribunals organized in the European style. With the failure of the constitution and the abolition of the tribunals in 1864, the cadis were restored to power and invested with the usual powers and responsibilities of their office. 5. At the head of the system of religion are two *muftis* belonging to the two leading sects, who may with propriety be termed Mussulman bishops. The Malekite mufti has the title of *bash-mufti*, i. e., chief mufti or high priest and elder of Islamism. This religious chief is much reverenced by the public at large, as shown by the fact that the sovereign of the country rises at his approach and goes to meet him,

---

* It is but just to say that the means of repressing and punishing crime are altogether insufficient, since Tunisian policemen have no right to arrest subjects of other governments, and when they attempt this they often become involved in difficulty and are punished; whereas, by not exposing European robbers and murderers, they have a chance to share their plunder.

and all the great dignitaries must take his step and movement, even though he be a worthless man as, unfortunately, is sometimes the case.*

The amusements common at Tunis are such as might be expected in a place by no means remarkable for moral and intellectual culture. Houses with sleeping and eating apartments and reception rooms gaudily ornamented are numerous; but homes with ample provision for social and domestic enjoyment are not abundant. Hence the multitude go forth for pleasure, and cafés are well patronized and the market places are thronged with loafers. Moorish cafés are often enlivened with music, and professional storytellers are also employed to entertain those who resort there. Also two or three European cafés are provided with journals and illustrated papers. A fourth class theatre is sustained during a part of the year, though it is but little patronized by the Moors. The different Christian, Jewish and Mussulman festivals are observed with marked zeal, especially the carnivals. Among the Moors and Jews there are assemblies in which hired female dancers furnish the principal entertainment. Among the Europeans, dancing parties and balls, numerously attended, usually begin in December, and continue to take place according to the convenience and pleasure of the persons interested, until March or April. Some of these great balls are brilliant in their way, affording occasion for ladies to display at the same time grace in dancing, elegant silks and quantities of jewelry,

---

* For statistics and notices of the churches, schools and masonic lodges at Tunis, see Appendix J.

and make drafts on the gallantry of the gentlemen whom they have at command. Musical concerts are rare, and lectures on scientific and literary subjects unknown. Billiard tables are found at the European cafés and cards are a very common amusement, but the dance enlists the most enthusiasm and constitutes a part of every important entertainment in fashionable circles.

To duly characterize popular life at Tunis is no easy task. "The people there vegetate rather than live," says a recent writer. While we have great respect for the vegetable kingdom, admiring trees that cast their roots deep into the earth and throw their branches high towards heaven, we honor more men who, grasping great truths, rise to the dignity of their natures. The most common classification of society at Tunis is according to religious profession. Thus every body is styled either a Mussulman, Jew or Christian, except the consuls who are always designated by their official titles. The types of character indicated by these terms are very different, yet in certain respects they appear so much alike that it is difficult to distinguish the one from the other. These religionists differ greatly in their formularies, but are alike in the tenacity with which they cleave to those formularies and in their want of appreciation of each other's creeds. They differ more in their traditions and dogmas than in their morals and conduct. The Mussulmans are perhaps the most ignorant and fanatical; the Jews, the most bigoted adherents to their forms and ceremonies, and the Christians the most arrogant in their manners and unscrupulous in their conduct. We have seen a bash-mufti, a grand rabbi and a bishop; their manners were much alike, but their dresses very different, and as for their characters we should be loath to attempt a description. We can say, however, for the bishop that he is an accomplished man, and we know nothing personally against the grand rabbi and the bash-mufti.

The division of society according to occupation is also very marked. The porters of the city have their mosques and cafés; the cooks their places of resort, where they meet and talk over matters that specially concern them; the merchants, their casinos and piazza; the Jewish brokers, their places of resort; and the masons and other tradesmen, theirs. In this way, Tunis has no need of newspapers and professional reporters. Small bits of news or scandal are greedily caught up and circulated in a few hours throughout the city. Public notices and advertisements are, however, sometimes posted in the bazars for the benefit of the few who can read.

A distinction of greater importance is between the natives of the country on the one hand, and the Europeans, including their protegés on the other. The natives, though wanting in energy, are proverbially mild and courteous in their manners. The corruption which prevails among them has sprung in no small degree from contact with the rough side of civilization. It is the Europeans who introduce poisonous liquors and induce the habit of using them. It is they who imbibe the larger proportion of their infuriating drugs and, under their influence commit most of the deeds of violence. It is they who take extortionary interest, acting the part of Shylock without any just judge to condemn them.* They acquire the vices of the country quite as readily as its virtues. Dr. Franke says in his able work that "the Europeans at Tunis rarely fail by long residence there to acquire the vices and obliquities of the Moors and Jews in whose society they pass their lives." Most of the business of the country is now in their hands, and the manner in which it is done would constitute an interesting enquiry, aside from our present purpose.

To exert an influence with the native government and encounter the small craft and cunning of this motley population, some nations have apparently adopted the policy of appointing consuls of like instincts and proclivities. While this course may favor certain temporary objects, it cannot subserve the cause of Christian civilization, nor promote the honor of the nations thus represented. On the contrary, its decided effect is to degrade the name of diplomacy, and make great nations appear in the diminutive proportions of their accredited representatives. It is not the language and manners of the east that need most to be understood, but the character and manhood that constitute the strength and glory of the west. Hence, care should be taken to send to the east only men that are well grounded in the elements of civilization. Mr. Pellissier speaks

---

* Dr. Davis, on the 334th page of his "Ruined Cities in Africa," gives account of a sheik who paid forty-eight per cent. interest, and one case came to my knowledge where a Christian (?) took seventy-two per cent. from a Mussulman.

of the disgraceful practice of selling consular protections. This is but one of the abuses of consular power well understood at Tunis.

When such examples are set in official ranks and there is not enough moral power to overcome their influence in private life, deleterious consequences are sure to appear throughout society. We have, then, to assent against our wishes to the remark that the people at Tunis vegetate rather than live. Lacking the vigor of genuine manhood, they allow honesty to go begging, while knavery is exalted to places of honor. They fail to embrace such fundamental truths as alone can elevate and dignify their lives. It is common to blame the native government for most of the ills that prevail, but we believe more responsibility rests upon Europeans than they are wont to acknowledge. They have a controlling influence, but fail to exert it for the highest ends. While we rejoice that Mussulman freebooters are passing away, it becomes us to guard against an order of character alike injurious to the best interests of humanity and more criminal in the sight of heaven, because founded and maintained under the protection of civilization by those who profess to walk in its light and serve as its champions. The Europeans of Africa need civilizing as well as the Mussulmans, and the only effectual way to reach the latter is to improve the former; and, to effect this purpose, the great nations of the world should look well to the character of their representatives.

A mile and a half northwest of Tunis in a plain, where dust and mud alternately prevail, stands the residence of the bey styled by the natives the Bardo, the flourishing. Between the hills which obstruct the view of the horizon on the west and on the east extends a beautiful aqueduct, with arches appearing singularly narrow on account of their great elevation. This aqueduct is commonly said to be the work of the Spaniards; but after careful research, we are unable conclusively to explain its origin. There are good reasons, however, to believe that the Spaniards did not build it. It seems to us altogether more probable that this structure dates back to the period of the Hafsite princes (1228-1535), who built the bridge, canal, dam and sluices at Tebourba, the bridge at Majez-el-Bab and many other substantial works of permanent utility. However this question may be settled, this long range of graceful and elegant arcades, which appear on approaching them of almost Herculean proportions, with a system of mason work truly enormous;—this line of arches, standing upon lofty buttresses, gives the landscape, which has few natural attractions, a certain air of picturesque grandeur, and forms as it were a formidable balustrade to the Tunisian Versailles. But the Bardo has no resemblance to the former Versailles except its character as the royal residence near the gates of the capital of the kingdom. For we should look in vain there for the splendors of nature and of art. It is an assemblage of hovels, houses, palaces and forts enclosed by a wall with many angles and armed with cannon; but forts, walls, buildings and cannon are hardly able to withstand the force of time, much less could they resist the attack of an enemy. The palace of the bey, which is picturesque if not beautiful, belongs to no style of architecture laid down in the books. It has an immense façade painted red and blue to resemble stone, and is liberally supplied with large windows and bull's eyes. It has also elegant balconies painted in the most lively colors. This façade appears at the very gate of the Bardo, where is terminated a sort of rampart formerly supported by a moat. On the wall in front of the palace are polished bronze cannon turned as if to destroy the innocent soil of the level plain which extends out in front of the palace. There, too, may be seen the lazy patrol moping back and forth or resting in the guard house.

In plain view from the palace windows is a beautiful fountain which plays on festal occasions, and a little one side is a watering place from which flows off across the plains a puny stream producing vegetation in its course. In front of the Bardo and beyond it for a mile and a half in a northwesterly direction, are numerous gardens and villas which constitute the village of the Manouba. Some former beys resided there. The beautiful palace of Hamouda Bashaw was after his death converted into military barracks. Several of the villas belong to distinguished personages of the actual Tunisian court. We shall again revert to the palace of the bey in speaking of official receptions. Let us note in passing that the road from Tunis to the Bardo is the only well made macadamized road in the regency, though one is begun from the Bardo to the Manouba, and another from Tunis to the Goletta.

Tunis, as we have said, is separated from the sea

THE GOLETTA AND ITS HARBOR.

by the lake of Tunis which communicates with the gulf by means of a narrow canal called by the Arabs *Halk-el-Oued*, which signifies mouth of the river. It is under this name also that the natives designate the little city which serves for the port of Tunis and is called by Europeans the Goletta.

On each side of the canal is a tongue of land; that on the north reaches out and joins the hills of Carthage; that on the south stretches on in the direction of the mountains of Zoughan, and widens out near the village of Radis, famed for the victory of Regulus over the Carthaginians. On each side of this canal upon this double tongue of land is built the Goletta. It is then naturally divided into two parts, which communicate with each other by two drawbridges. The northern part is the Goletta proper, embracing the town, the castle, the battery and the royal bathing house; its beach is also during three months of the year lined with tents, and morning and evening enlivened by bathing parties. The southern part contains the palaces of the bey, the prison, the arsenal, and the old and new docks, eighty or ninety yards square, where more vessels are lost by decay than are built and repaired by workmen.

Merchant ships anchor in the roadstead at a distance from the canal varying according to their draught; for the harbor of the Goletta has generally but little depth. Vessels of war cast anchor two or three miles from the Goletta in front of cape Sidi-Bou-Said, formerly called cape Carthage.

The roadstead of Tunis is of great extent and pretty sure, though it is exposed to the northeast and northwest winds, the prevalence of which requires great watchfulness on the part of mariners. In bad weather, the anchors are sometimes dragged, and it is rendered difficult to land and embark passengers and merchandise, which service is performed by means of heavy sail boats, familiarly called *sandals*, which are also employed on the lake. We believe that with comparatively small expense the harbor of the Goletta could be enlarged and transformed into a superior military post. But who will undertake this, is more than can now be told.

The importance of the Goletta has much increased since the ascension of Sidi Sadek upon the throne. He regularly passes there five or six months of the year, and during his residence the population, which ordinarily amounts to only about 3,000, reaches the number of 10,000. For all the employés of the government, and families in easy circumstances, follow the example of the sovereign, and already a village is built up outside the wall towards Carthage. The system of defence at the Goletta is supported by a fortress of which we have already had occasion to speak in the historical part of this work. It consists of a rampart armed with cannon, on the side towards Carthage, and of a long battery looking towards the sea. Constituting a part of this battery, are some magnificent bronze pieces which were received as presents from European sovereigns or taken as trophies by Tunisian corsairs. The most beautiful of these, called the St. Paul, has been recently presented by the bey to the king of Italy.*

---

* The St. Paul is a veritable work of art. It was founded at Florence,

These old cannon became by degrees almost unfit for use, and within the last four years have been mostly replaced by others purchased at great expense, which are said to be scarcely an improvement on the old ones. But in spite of the battery, rampart, embattled walls and little Tunisian squadron, one modern ship of war could readily take possession of the Goletta.

Five miles north-northeast of the Goletta, on a commanding point of land jutting out into the sea, stands the populous and holy village of Sidi-Bou-Said. On its summit is a light-house from which may be enjoyed a magnificent panorama of the gulf of Tunis, which is one of the finest of the Mediterranean. Standing upon this hill and looking towards the Goletta, we see several less important hills and a circuitous line of sea-shore. The whole scene has an aspect of nakedness. Here once stood Carthage, the mistress of the sea and the greatest commercial power of the ancient world. We shall notice its ruins, almost annihilated, when we come to speak of the monuments and traces of the past. In the midst of these ruins, upon the highest of these hills, which are connected with the culminating point of Sidi-Bou-Said, stands the chapel erected in 1841 by Louis Philippe to the memory of St. Louis, on the presumed place of his death. It is imbowered with trees in the midst of a beautiful garden which is enclosed by an octagonal wall. By a special article in the treaty signed the 8th of August, 1830, between

in 1638, by Cosimo Cenni, who held the same rank as a founder, as Cellini held as a sculptor and carver. Its weight is 27,500 pounds.

France and the bey of Tunis, the latter ceded to king Charles X* the perpetual right to the ancient hill of the Byrsa, that he might erect thereon this commemorative monument. The chapel is small and is not remarkable for its architecture or finish, and the statue gives a very imperfect idea of St. Louis. In the garden and in the buildings around it, are collected numerous fragments of antique monuments.

The Goletta is by its situation the centre of foreign commerce and the most important of all the ports of the regency. Also, unlike every other city or village, the majority of its inhabitants are Europeans. Tunis is reached from the Goletta by land and by the lake. The distance by land is about twelve miles, while by the lake it is only about half as far. It would be easy and profitable to have a small steam tug on the lake, and a horse railroad on the land route, but sail boats and donkey teams are more in accordance with the spirit of the place.

North of the Goletta and west of Carthage are the gardens of the Marsa, which is the summer residence of many native and some European officials. Still further on in a northerly direction, on the extreme point of the ancient peninsular of Carthage, is the hill of Camart, where are also found some inviting villas, which the sand begins to invade. West of Camart are some gardens in a state of decay, and the salt lake of Soukra, separated from the sea by a narrow strip of land. Some miles southwest of

---

* It is an interesting fact that this treaty was signed at Tunis the 8th of August, 1830, just a week after the fall of Charles X.

ARIANA AND BIZERTA.

Soukra and north of Tunis are the gardens of Djarfar and Ariana, and to the west of these is a vast forest of olive trees covering hill and dale for miles around. Ariana is renowned for the mildness of its climate and for its roses, which are collected in large quantities and employed in manufacturing ottar of roses which constitutes a branch of trade at Tunis. Also the gardens of some distinguished Tunisian officials constitute a special attraction.

Among the cities more or less important in the northern part of Tunis is Porto Farina. It is a small city situated southwest of the promontory of Sidi Ali-el-Meki, upon the lake into which are now poured the waters of the Majerda. Porto Farina, once the important military post of the regency, is now only a poor town of a thousand inhabitants. The accumulation of sand in the lake renders access to it impossible for vessels of any importance. This was probably the principal reason for abandoning this military post, which served for centuries as a general rendezvous for the Barbary pirates. A few miles south of the mouth of the Majerda, on the left bank of this river, is the site of Utica, of which we shall speak further on. To the east of Porto Farina and Sidi Ali-el-Meki, is the isle of Plane, so called from its want of elevation; and beyond the cape, towards the west, is the pyramidal isle of Pillau.

In following the line of the northwest coast, we double cape Zebib, and soon enter the roadstead of Bizerta, which forms a vast crescent, whose extreme points are cape Zebib on the one side and cape Blanc on the other. The city of Bizerta is situated upon the lower slope of an elevated ground near the north extremity of a great lake called *Tinga Benzerte*, which communicates by means of a natural channel with a smaller interior lake called Garat Leckeul. The wall around the city has the form of a triangle, and the kasbah is elevated on the side toward the sea. The harbor is formed by the channel itself, which is very deep in the interior of the city, but has not sufficient depth towards the sea to receive vessels of much importance. Competent judges maintain that without great expense this inconvenience could be overcome, and the channel between the roadstead and the lake be widened and deepened so as to create one of the best maritime ports in the whole world.

The channel forms in the interior of the city a little island which constitutes the quarter of about 500 European residents. The natives are estimated at about 5,000. The bifurcation of the river, the nearness of the lake, and the general position of the city give it a picturesque look which is rendered more striking by the beauty of the surrounding landscape. This country, often compared to the environs of Bona in Algeria (ancient Hippo-Regia), was once under excellent cultivation and had an extensive commerce in cereal products. To-day, its fields are little better than an unbroken wilderness; its prosperity is gone, and Bizerta with all its natural resources has no importance except as a fishery. In this respect it deserves some consideration and is duly noticed in another place.

Thirty-five miles west-southwest of Susa and ninety

south of Tunis, in an open plain that has numerous marshes, is the holy city of Cairwan, the religious capital of the regency. It is a Mussulman city, as yet unpolluted by the residence of infidels. Considered as a sort of African Mecca, it is by its historic souvenirs and incorruptible character, the veritable centre of Islamism in the Magreb. It was founded, says an Arab historian, by Okba-ben-Nafy in the year 55 of the hegira (675 A. D.), in the midst of an impenetrable wood infested by ferocious animals and venomous serpents, which at the inspired voice of the conqueror departed with their young and retired towards the desert, while the forest which had sheltered them disappeared of itself. This miracle, which is reported to have led to the conversion of the Berbers *en masse*, will explain at least the actual desolation of the country. The city proper is according to Pellissier 2,600 yards in circumference; but it has also seven suburbs, two of which are quite extensive. The walls of the city as well as most of the houses are built mainly with brick on account of the scarcity of stones in that region. Along the top of the walls numerous cannon stare menacingly at the beholder, and at various points are round or square towers which, with the minarets of the mosques and places of prayer, give to Cairwan an imposing monumental aspect.

There are in Cairwan twenty-six mosques and fifty-five chapels dedicated to Mussulman saints. The most important mosque, founded by Okba and called the mosque of Olives, is celebrated throughout the Mussulman world. It is a vast quadrilateral structure, with numerous doors ornamented with superb antique columns. We are assured that within are very many similar columns, and that the splendor of the sanctuary is incomparable. But a Christian must rest satisfied with these *hearsays;* for the mosque of Cairwan is one of the last places in the world to be opened for the profane steps of the *koffer*. "God most high will protect this city and this mosque; His religion will there be firmly established, and until the end of time, infidels will be given over to humiliation." Such are the divine words which fell upon the ear of Okba, when he learned by revelation in his solitude the precise spot on which he should erect the seat of the iman of the new mosque. Let us add that according to a tradition accepted by the devotees and handed down from generation to generation, the mosque of which we speak was also built by miracle, the stones coming to their places themselves, one upon the other in perfect order.

In this temple as in the consecrated structures of Mecca and Medina, exclusiveness is a cardinal principle, whose legitimate fruits are quite manifest. The mosque of Okba has been repeatedly rebuilt and ornamented with marble and porphyry, taken from ancient monuments. It has two magnificent monoliths, of a red color, with yellow veins, taken, says the Arab geographer, el-Bekri, from a Christian church, and which a Byzantine emperor tried to purchase for their weight in gold. It has seventeen naves formed by four hundred and fourteen columns, and is reputed to be the most beautiful mosque of Africa. It is certainly regarded with profound veneration. When its lofty square towers, with three stories in retreat, one resting upon the other, break upon the view of Mussulman pilgrims, they glorify God and His prophet, pausing for worship and prayer. The various mosques and chapels have for Mussulmans an interest and reverence reminding us of Rome, though it is difficult to name two places more unlike than Cairwan and the seat of the Roman pontiff. They both have numerous saints, chapels and holy places. The finest chapel at Cairwan contains the tomb of Sidi Sahab, a reputed companion and barber of the prophet; but this popular tradition has been lately exploded by a learned Mussulman, showing that the prophet never shaved, and consequently never had a barber.

But if Sidi Sahab had not the honor of seeing that consecrated head *at the mercy of his hands*, which among orientals involves the idea of confidence, he had the honor, altogether of another kind, of a place in that court above which the angel Gabriel had *purified and rendered white as milk;* and consequently of being eternally associated with Mohammed under the title of friend as set forth in the famous Mussulman formula: "Blessings be upon our lord and master Mohammed, upon his family, his friends and his companions."

Cairwan is in general well built. Its souks are, like those of Tunis, divided according to the nature of the articles made and sold. They appear pretty well furnished and supplied with customers. The streets are clean and give fewer indications of decay than most Tunisian cities. The inhabitants live generally at their ease. Its most important articles of commerce are skins and leather, and the works of its shoemakers and saddlers which are renowned in all North Africa. It has a population of 15,000 or 20,000.

There are no fountains at Cairwan. The city was once provided with capacious reservoirs, but these have taken the course of nature and are no longer fit for use. Mr. Guérin remarks with force, that this scarcity of water would offer a hostile army a sure means of reducing Cairwan. But it is written that *infidels shall there be constantly humiliated.* The Cairwanians, then, do not trouble themselves with imaginary danger. If any city be well guarded by divine protection, it is understood it must be theirs.

No Christians or Jews reside at Cairwan. For Europeans to pass within the holy gates, they must have a special order from the bey, supported by the presence of an imposing escort, and then be occasionally subjected to sly insults and menaces from the inhabitants, who are only restrained from committing violence by military force. The children are brought up in horror of Christians and especially of Jews. Young Cairwanians, who have been brought to Tunis by their parents, have been known on meeting and recognizing infidels in the streets, to shed tears of rage, and in their fury commit violence on their own persons on perceiving their inability in the capital to follow a line of conduct in accordance with their fixed instincts and pious sentiments.

One fact is here to be noted which has not escaped the observation of Mr. Pellissier. *Cairwan is for a holy city very corrupt.* It has this in common with many other celebrated places in the world, and in our opinion the explanation is not difficult. It is that fanaticism there bears sway. And as fanaticism is the perversion of the religious sentiment, which, maintained in its purity, can alone check and overcome the insidious vices leading to degradation and ruin, we see here only a familiar illustration of the principal that *as ye sow, so shall ye reap.*

Mater is the capital of the Mogody, the region situated between the lake of Bizerta and Tabarca. It has a horse fair once a week, and about 1,000 inhabitants. Beja is situated in a fine agricultural country called Ifrikia. It has 9,000 inhabitants and is the centre of the most important grain trade in the regency. Twenty-five miles from Beja on a point of land opposite to the island of Tabarca, is fort Tabarca, which would acquire importance were the forests near by to be employed to supply the needs of the country. In passing this place, we will state an interesting historical fact. In the sixteenth century, Tabarca was ceded by Khayedine Barbarossa to a patrician family of Genoa named Lomellini as a ransom for his famous rival, the Turkish corsair Dragut. A Genoese colony was established and maintained there until the last half of the eighteenth century. At that period, the Lomellini wished to cede Tabarca to the French company of Calle to become the headquarters of the coral fishery in that region. But war breaking out between Tunis and France, the bey promptly took possession of this position, which he had for a long time watched. The Lomellini and other Genoese colonists were taken to Tunis, where they and their descendants have since been known as the *Tabarcans*, holding as a class an intermediate position between natives and Europeans. One Tabarcan lady married one of the beys of Tunis, and thus some of the sovereigns as well as ministers of the country have been of Genoese origin.

In the valley and near the mouth of the Majerda, is the Dowar of Bou-Shahter, built on the site of ancient Utica, and in a southwesterly direction, on the right bank of the same river, is Jedida, a village with delightful gardens and a fine stone bridge. A little further up the river is Tebourba, a town of 2,000 inhabitants, built on both sides of the river. El Bathan is an adjoining village, distinguished as the site of the only woolen manufactory whose machinery is moved by water power. This establshment was built by Ahmed Bey, but for the want of capital and enterprise, it does little for the country. Red caps are manufactured there, but they are of an inferior quality. Around Tebourba are fine gardens and groves of olive trees. There too was once a fine system of sluices for watering the country around, effected by means of the bridge, which is still standing. Further up the river is Mejez-el-Bab, a small town of 1,500 inhabitants, and still further on is Testour, with 3,000 inhabitants.

Ten miles south of Tunis, is the little abandoned city of Mohammedia, which was built up by Ahmed Bey, and became his favorite residence. The immense palace is without architectural beauty, and is one of those ruins made by the hand of man and destitute of the majesty and dignity of those which result from the action of time. Since the death of Ahmed Bey, this colossal dwelling, which cost fabulous sums of money, expended without discretion for marble columns, luxurious furniture and gilded ceilings, has presented a painful aspect. Its magnificent suites of rooms, now the abode of lizards, are regularly plundered of their rich ornaments. Its marble pavements and finely formed columns, once brought from Carthage and Oudena, are stolen away and sold. The rain trickles through its dilapidated roofs, and its walled ceilings, robbed of their enamelled tiles and gilt ornaments, are fissured and broken. Its beautiful marble steps are gradually carried off, and its once magnificent doors, which twenty years ago were covered with gilt copper, now scarcely serve to screen the pitiful ruins within. The elegant marble colonade, which forms the passage way to the palace, on the side of the square court where the soldiers and courtiers assembled, just below the balcony of the bey, has been brutally stripped of its marble pavement, and its walls, which were once covered with earthen tiles of variegated colors, now bear unmistakable marks of violence, prompted by hatred and the desire for gain. At the windows of the corridors are twisted bars of wrought iron and fragments of sash once supplied with glass, and on the broken balustrades are bits of massive copper fastenings, left by the pillagers of the palace. On the corners of the various halls are numerous nests of turtle doves and swallows, and through the roofs are openings which enable us to behold the azure heaven or the passing clouds, which we regard as fitting emblems of the generations of men and their works. The sight of this premature decay induces a feeling of sadness as we think how much gold was here expended with no other result than to gratify the vanity of a weak prince, and bring poverty and distress on his subjects. These ruins constitute, as it were, a monument of the disorder and folly of oriental governments in general, and of the Tunisian government in particular.

On beyond Mohammedia is a point in the chain of Zaughan, which extends in a southerly direction. This is the *Zeugitanus mons* of the ancients, and is the highest point in the regency. On the side of this mountain, thirty miles from Tunis, in the midst of a landscape incomparable in respect to the picturesqueness of its rocks, woody slopes, foaming cascades and azure summits, is displayed the little city of Zaughan, smiling with its sparkling minarets, tall palms and luxuriant gardens. This was colonized during the period of the Spanish expulsion, by Andalusian Moors. At present, it is an insignificant place, having scarcely any branch of industry but the manufacture of red caps. It is at Zaughan that is found, in the midst of a noted ruin, which is described in another chapter, one of the abundant sources which supply the aqueduct of Tunis.

Ten miles south of Zaughan, in the midst of mountains belonging to the same system, is Jougar, a small village, with fountains more abundant than those of Zaughan, and springing forth like the latter, from the midst of an imposing ruin, which probably once served as a bathing establishment. Mount Zaughan has two summits, one of which is 4,500 feet high, and the other, 4,360. The latter, called Sidi Bou Gabrin, is alone accessible.* The panorama which is enjoyed from this elevation is extensive and admirable. Tunis, Carthage, the gulf of Tunis and its capes are displayed in the horizon towards the north; in the northwest, the valley of the Majerda; in the south, the mountains of Jougar and Ousselat; in the southeast, beyond the heights of Jerad and Takoona, the cities of Hergla and Susa; in the east, Hammamet and its splendid gulf; and then in the northeast, between this gulf and that of Tunis, the peninsula of cape Bon juts out into the sea, with its hills scarcely discernable in the dim distance.

Near the entrance of cape Bon and the southern extremity of the gulf of Tunis, rises Gebel Cornein, the mountain with two horns, at the foot of which are the hot springs of Hammam-el-Lif. This mountain, whose general features resemble those of Vesuvius, belongs to the secondary system, of which Gebel Rasas (Lead Mountain), situated a little distance to the south, is the highest peak, and which is bound to the more important system of Zaughan, and by it to the other mountain ranges of the country. East of these mountain ranges is the beautiful plain of Soliman. Soliman, colonized by Andalusian Moors, is a place of 1,200 inhabitants, in a state of manifest decay. It was once the most important of all those colonies which the Spanish Moors, coming

* For an account of this ascent, see Appendix K.

into the country in the seventeenth century, founded as centres of industry and commerce.

Beyond Soliman, near the foot of volcanic mountains, whose sides appear almost perpendicular, are the hot waters of Corbus, whose medicinal qualities are more prized than those of Hammam-el-Lif. It is the opinion of skilful and competent men that if comfortable accommodations were provided at Corbus and Hammam-el-Lif, these waters would soon acquire a universal reputation. They are, besides, neither the only nor the most remarkable of the many mineral springs in the regency, but like most other natural sources of wealth, they are of no advantage to the government or people of the country.

Northeast of Corbus, are Sidi Daoud (David) and Aoonia. In a creek near Sidi Daoud, is an islet which serves as the centre of the tunny fishery, and near Aoonia, are the vast quarries which are the famous latomies described by Strabo. Some writers would have us think that Æneas and Dido took refuge in one of these caves from the storm that interrupted their hunting sport.

Doubling cape Bon and following the coast mostly in a southerly direction, we come first to Kalibia, a moorage at present of little importance; then to the delightful little village of Menzil Zemin, whose environs are noted for splendid harvests; then into the midst of fertile fields and gardens fragrant with roses, jessamines and oranges, the delightful Nebel. Though this city is now in a state of decay, it has still some reputation for its manufacture of earthenware and of woolen goods. It has from 4,000 to 5,000 inhabitants, and is a noted watering place, often visited by consumptive invalids on account of the mildness of its climate and the agreeableness of its situation. Its ancient name was Neapolis (new city). Nebel is often injured by freshets in the rainy season when the banks of the rivulets are swept by rushing waters which destroy in their course rich fields and luxuriant harvests. This system of devastation and ruin goes on century after century without any wisely directed efforts on the part of the natives to confine the waters to their appropriate channels. In this country wisdom takes no such practical turn. Human foresight and provision are disparaged, and that piety is alone honored that ascribes to God the sole care of all things. But, happily for the activity and well-being of the human family, God does not accept all the offices and responsibilities which the superstition and laziness of his creatures would impose upon him; and, in abandoning such presumptuous folly to disastrous consequences, he clothes labor with honor and encourages without cessation the activity and energy which form a part of his plan for the elevation of the human race. Mussulman people have always but partially understood, and now utterly ignore or forget, this truth, on which depend the greatness and the future of nations as well as of individuals.

Eight miles from Nebel, in front of the broad gulf of the same name, is the little city of Hammamet. It has a thousand inhabitants, and its fertile environs give it some agricultural importance. Below Hammamet, the coast winds a little towards the west and forms an arc whose extreme point is Monastir. It is very low until we reach the steep shore of this last-named city. During the rainy season much land is overflowed, and in these temporary marshes are often witnessed the curious effects of the mirage. In this plain are two salt lakes, one at Sidi Halifa and the other at Hergla. Continuing our tour along the coast, after passing several villages we arrive at Susa, the most important commercial point in the Sahel, the district which especially abounds in olive oil.

Susa, (ancient Hadrumetum) is built in the form of an amphitheatre, overlooked by a citadel. It contains twelve mosques, nine chapels, six schools, one of which is for superior instruction, a covered market, commodious barracks, and 10,000 inhabitants. It is well laid out and well built for an oriental city. Its advantageous position, numerous elegant minarets and tall palm trees, rising above the house tops and breaking the uniformity of its whitewashed edifices, give it an unusually picturesque aspect; but the agreeable impression made by an exterior view is speedily changed as we actually enter the city and leisurely survey its various streets. Susa was in the middle age a very important place; now it is only a great centre of commerce in oil and soap. It contains six hundred Europeans, most of whom are Maltese and Italians. Also vice consuls are maintained here by several European nations.

Southwest of Susa is the great town of Msaken, with ten thousand inhabitants, eleven mosques, and one superior school, which is celebrated throughout Tunisia. Msaken has a character for holiness which is specially demonstrated by the exclusion of Christians and Jews. Among other considerable places in the district of Susa, is Jemal, a town of 6,000 inhabitants. Passing from Susa, by Monastir, to cape Dimas (ancient Thapsus). the coast winds about mostly in an easterly direction; it then takes a southerly course as far as Ras Caboudia (Caput Vada); then it turns to the southwest, and beyond Sfax winds about to form the gulf of Gabes, and later takes a southeasterly direction. Monastir is twelve miles from Susa, and has 8,000 inhabitants. It is built on the site of ancient Ruspina, where Cæsar established his principal camp. Twenty-one miles in a southerly direction from Monastir, is Media (Mehedia, ancient Africa), with 6,000 inhabitants, founded three hundred years after the hegira, by the iman El-Mahedi, who gave it his own name.

In passing along the coast twenty-five miles from Media, we find the Ras Caboudia of the Arabs, the Caput Vada of the ancients, famous for having been the landing place of Belisarius in his successful campaign against the Vandals in 533-4. We also pass a great number of populous though unimportant places, whose wretchedness drew forth from Pellissier the remark that this country is placed under the ineffective protection of a great number of Mussulman saints whose influence is seen more in the erection of places for prayer, than in the elevation and well-being of the people. Sfax, which is situated on the extreme coast of the gulf of Gabes, is one of the largest cities in the regency. Like Susa, it is built in the form of an amphitheatre, with a picturesque and agreeable aspect, and is overlooked by its fortifications. It is surrounded with numerous gardens, and, seen from a distance, produces an agreeable impression, which, however, is speedily effaced as we pass within the walls. This is a fertile district, producing in abundance olives, almonds, pistachios and most of the fruits of Europe. On my two visits at Sfax, I was entertained at the Dar-el-Bey, where an extensive and delightful view of the harbor and the surrounding country was enjoyed, and my sojourn was rendered especially agreeable by the courtesies of the kaid and of the consular agents of the place. Under the walls of Sfax are numerous covered cisterns, built and kept in order by the pious legacies of benevolent Mussulmans. The exports of this city are mostly sent to Malta, and consist in olive oil, wool, sponges, woolen fabrics and dried fruits. Much trade is carried on by means of caravans between this port and the Gereed. Sfax stands on the site of ancient Taphnura. The river Shershar, which is the Tanais mentioned by Sallust, empties into the sea a few miles southwest of it. In the war against Jugurtha, before marching upon Capsa, Marius took his supply of water and provisions from this point.

Opposite to Sfax are the Kerkenna islands where, in addition to various other branches of industry, fish and sponges are exported. In catching fish, the inhabitants profit by the tide, which, though inconsiderable in the Mediterranean generally, becomes very apparent from cape Caboudia as far as the frontiers of Tripoli. The tide rises more than three feet at Sfax, and much higher at Gerba and Gabes. The Kerkenna islands are memorable for several historic events. Hannibal spent there some days before going into exile. Marius landed there on his way to Carthage, after being driven from Italy. During the war of Cæsar, in Africa, Sallust, the historian, then prætor, was sent to these islands to take possession of quantities of wheat stored there by the Pompeian party. Pliny speaks of a bridge which once united the two islands, the remains of which are still visible.

South of Sfax and the Kerkenna islands, is the gulf of Gabes (ancient Syrtis Minor), which maintains its early reputation for inconstancy and fickleness. The sea there swells and becomes furious at slight breezes. The *feluccas* which sail over these waters, are often greatly exposed to the violence of the waves, having few places for safe anchorage. The southwest coast of this gulf belongs to the province of El Arad, of which we have already spoken. The city of Gabes (ancient Tacape) is simply a group of villages surrounded by luxuriant gardens. It contains the tomb of one of the companions of the prophet, and several thousand inhabitants. Opposite to Gabes is the island of Gerba, the ancient Menynx and Lotophagitis, separated from the continent on the south by a narrow strait. With a smooth or undulating surface, its soil is fertile and tolerably well cultivated. It produces grain and fruits of all sorts, and manufactures oil jars, and a fine woolen cloth employed for ladies' burnouses; this last named article is renowned for its fineness and superior finish. It also produces soda and lime in considerable quantities.

The island of Gerba contains no walled cities and

no considerable villages, its population being scattered over the territory to an unusual extent. Its shores are nominally defended by six small forts, which, however, rather serve to keep the population in awe than to protect them from foreign foes. The inhabitants of Gerba are mostly of the Berber race, and resemble in their traditions, origin, language and religion the Sahara tribe of Beni Mzab. They have peculiar rites and are quite distinct from the orthodox sects, in whose eyes they are obstinate heretics. One article that gives offence in their creed is that faith alone is not sufficient for salvation. They are reputed, however, to be quite as moral and upright in their conduct as the orthodox Mussulmans, religiously observing the precept to abstain from wine and strong drink. But on the other hand, they eat the flesh of dogs and donkeys. In offering up their prayers, they prefer very elevated places, and seek to lay off the article of apparel that is most exposed to personal impurity. In entering their mosques, they leave their stockings, if they have any, at the doors, while the genuine orthodox wear theirs even into the sanctuary, only laying off their shoes.

In the Tunisian Gereed are Gafsa, Tozer, Hamma, Nefta, Nefzawa and El Mansour, each made up, like Gabes, of several villages, and having a numerous population, sustained by some special branches of industry. The great salt lake or marsh of Pharoon (ancient Triton), is seventy-five miles long and twelve miles wide. The Tunisian Gereed communicates with Central Africa by Gadame, which is ten days journey into the desert.

The most important point of the western region bordering on Algeria, is El Kef, the Sicca Veneria of the ancients, built upon a mountain slope and surrounded by a bastioned wall. It stands in a volcanic region, and the ancient crater of the mountain is still readily recognized. This city, now fallen into decay and stricken with poverty, contains a population of 6,000 Mussulmans, 600 Jews, and a few Christians. It has scarcely any importance except as a military post, in which light it was held in high esteem under Carthaginian rule. Mr. Guérin observed a curious fact on his visit at El Kef. Most of the grave stones in the actual Jewish cemetery have on them various Latin inscriptions, which, though partially concealed by the effects of age and coats of whitewash, conclusively show that these monuments once served the same purpose for a generation under the Roman domination, as they now serve for Tunisian Jews.

CHAPTER VI.

Archeological Sketch of the Country and Traces of the Past.—Carthage, Thysdrus, Utica, etc.

PROBABLY no country in the world, unless we except the Italian peninsula, is more sprinkled with illustrious ashes, and more remarkable for its memorable events than Tunisia. The seat of the empire of Carthage; the important province of the Roman world; the brilliant diocese of the Christian church; the Arab kingdom and also the califate; the Turkish province; the independent state; this country has preserved traces of all its long and eventful history; and for the man of science and learning, who should have the courage and perseverance to devote sufficient time to explorations and researches, it would not be impossible, in our opinion, to write out this history by means of its monuments, or rather by means of their ruins and *debris*.

But no domination has left such an ineffaceable impress as the Roman. While there remain of Punic Carthage only a few inscriptions of little importance, and aside from the cisterns, only traces of constructions without precise character; while the remembrance of Christianity is perpetuated aside from its written history only on epitaphs buried for centuries; by traditionary symbols observed but not understood by the natives, and by churches ruined and converted into mosques; while vandalism has left scarcely a vestige of its existence, and Byzantine supremacy is indicated only by its coins and silver table service occasionally found in tombs and elegant columns appropriated to mosques, and while few or no monuments have come down to us from the Arab middle age, the Roman period of Tunisian history has numerous imposing monuments and ruins.

We propose then to give a rapid archeological sketch of Tunisia, calling the attention of our readers only to the most celebrated traces of the past; for to describe all the antiquities that have been fully or partially explored in this country, would require one of those huge folios of the middle age which were then written, read and handled without difficulty, but which to-day weary our arms as well as our minds, when we are compelled to consult them, and which we have neither the time nor the disposition to undertake.

As the name of Carthage stands foremost in the country, her ruins* will naturally receive our first attention. They begin at ten miles northeast from

---

* For an extended discussion of the topography and antiquities of Carthage, we refer our readers to the learned work of Mr. Dureau de la Malle. Also the works of Messrs. Falbe, Beulé and Géurin may be advantageously consulted.

Tunis, near the little village of Malga, where some miserable Bedouin families have taken up their abode. There are to be seen distinct traces of an amphitheatre which was especially famous in the touching annals of the Christian church. Some masses of masonry embedded in the soil and scattered along a great eliptical depression are all that now remain of it. We have noticed elsewhere some historical events that occurred upon this spot. They come up afresh as we enter upon this arena. The solitude and desolation that now reign seem but to color our thoughts and intensify our impressions. We recall the image of Felicita and Perpetua, two admirable females, one a patrician and the other a slave, who, while undergoing martyrdom in this enclosure, calmly exhorted each other to persevere in the faith. We are reminded that near here where a Christian church was afterward erected, the most celebrated of the bishops of Carthage, St. Cyprian, calmly counted out some gold for his executioner, and, arranging his neck upon the block, bid him do his work. St. Augustine studied and taught, and at a later period preached in this city. We are reminded of the oath of Hannibal, of the insurrection and crucifixion of Bomilcar, of the fierce factions of Hanno and Barca, of Genseric, Belisarius and St. Louis; but we must proceed with our work of observation and exploration. It would appear from the Arab historians El Bekri and Edrisi, that this amphitheatre was in a good state of preservation in the eleventh century. "Actually," says Mr. Guérin, "the form of the amphitheatre alone remains to us; for the arcades have been demolished, and with them the buttresses and steps have been carried off piece by piece."

Half a mile south of the amphitheatre we find the outlines and entrances of a circus, which was, according to Mr. Falbe, 1,600 feet long, and 330 feet wide. It is situated near the hamlet of Dowar - Eshat (hamlet of the shore), so called from its nearness to the sea. A little to the north of the amphitheatre, on rising ground, is the village of Malga, of which we have spoken. In its centre are immense arched cisterns in a ruinous state. These used to receive the waters at the end of the great aqueduct of Carthage. In consequence of the complete or partial destruction of many of these cisterns, or of their being buried under the rubbish of centuries, it is difficult to ascertain with precision their dimensions. We can distinguish thirteen of them running parallel to each other, and one running at right angles to the others. According to Mr. Dureau de la Malle, these cisterns originated with the Phœnicians, and were afterwards converted into a reservoir for the aqueduct of Hadrian. Mr. Guérin infers, also, that they are of Punic origin and essentially Roman by construction. This opinion, established with much clearness and reason, seems to us acceptable; for it is certain that Carthage, like all ancient cities of Africa and the orient, must have had pools or public cisterns, and further that these pools were, in general, vast open basins like the *feskias* of Tunis or the pools of Jerusalem. It is natural then to suppose that, under the Romans, these pools were transformed into arched reservoirs for the waters of the great aqueduct.

This aqueduct, generally believed to have been built during the reign of the emperor Hadrian, conducted to Carthage the beautiful living waters of Zaughan and of Jougar by means of a channel sometimes under ground and sometimes on superb arcades supported upon towering buttresses. Remains of this aqueduct are to be seen extending from the cisterns of Malga across the plains as far as Ariana, and again in a less ruinous state beyond the Manouba and near Mohammedia.

Six hundred yards nearly southeast of Malga rises the famous hill of the Byrsa, the cradle and citadel of Carthage. Its identity, many times called in question, seems to us to have been definitely established in 1859 and 1860 by the researches and excavations of Mr. Beulé, member of the Institute of France. This hill, where the city of Dido and of Hannibal was begun more than 800 years before Christ, has a form almost quadrangular and rises seventy yards above the level of the sea.

With a steep ascent on the east and southeast, and difficult to be reached on the north and on the west, it naturally presented itself to the founders of Carthage as an excellent site for their acropolis, and fortified, the Byrsa became in fact the bulwark of the city. "These fortifications," says Mr. Beulé, "were on a gigantic scale, and authors give a minute description of them. On the side of the lake of Tunis, the wall served to fortify the city. Let us imagine two circles, the smaller enclosed in the larger, and the two touching each other at a common point. These walls were built of hewn stone. They were about sixty feet high and thirty-three feet thick, according to Diodorus. They were hollow and covered. Some stories had admirable conveniences within. On the ground were stables for three hundred elephants, with necessary provision for their support. Above them were placed 4,000 horses, with barley and straw for a long seige. In fine, 20,000 footmen and 4,000 horsemen lodged in these magnificent walls, which the consul Censorinus compared to an encampment.

No ruins were apparent upon this celebrated hill when Mr. Beulé began some excavations which resulted in finding deeply buried in the earth some walls which he regards as remains of Phœnician fortifications and vestiges of a Roman palace. These discoveries were made near the chapel of St. Louis, at the eastern extremity of the enclosure. This chapel, built by Louis Philippe in 1841, upon ground ceded to France by Ahmed Bey, is erected upon a platform in the midst of an octagonal garden, and has nothing remarkable about it except its look of nakedness and desolation.

The garden of St. Louis is ornamented with various antique ruins, shafts of columns, bas-reliefs, inscriptions, pieces of marble raised on pedestals or fastened upon the walls under the porticoes of the apartments designed for the consul of France and the chaplain. The most remarkable object there is a beautiful marble torso, of large size, found at El Gem (Thysdrus); it is erected upon a pedestal, accompanied by a long inscription found in the same place.

The chapel of St. Louis is built upon the site of the ancient temple of Heshmoun, the Phœnician god, corresponding to the Esculapius of the Greeks and Romans. Some fortunate excavations of Mr. Beulé brought to light a part of the peribolos or first court of that edifice. Like most of the ancient monuments of that period, erected by a people of like origin, or possessing analagous traditions (Egyptian, Syrian and Grecian), the temple of Heshmoun had to be protected. It was the place for the deliberations of the Punic senate. In case of a foreign invasion, it became the last asylum of the religion and independence of the country. We know that when Carthage was taken by Scipio Æmilianus, this temple was the last place to hold out against him, and was carried only after the Roman deserters, commanded and forsaken by Hasdrubal, had devoted themselves to the flames to avoid the terrible vengeance which Scipio sought to inflict on them as deserters and traitors.

But it was not to escape the vengeance, but the probable generosity of the conqueror, and that she might not avail herself of the baseness of her husband who, through the love of life, had "lost with his honor the right to live," that the wife of Hasdrubal, after uttering scorching reproaches, precipitated herself with her children into the flames. How much less poetic and grand is the Dido immortalized by Virgil who died the same death from another motive! Dido had not the courage to live. No profound sentiment braced her for the struggle of life. But the wife of Hasdrubal, honored as a wife and mother, wished not to survive her country with a dishonored husband. Dido was the victim of passion and wounded vanity, that is, of selfishness; the wife of Hasdrubal was the martyr of honor and patriotism, that is, of self-denial. The temple that was the theatre of this devotion was then destroyed and was at a later period rebuilt, at the same time as the rest of the city, with white marble in the Corinthian style, as proved by the excavations of Mr. Jourdan, the architect of the chapel of St. Louis in 1840, and by those of Mr. Beulé in 1859 and 1860. The palace of the Roman pro-consuls was twelve or fifteen yards from the temple of Esculapius and Mr. Beulé has found seven parallel arched halls terminating at the very base of the chapel of St. Louis.

In front and to the north of the Byrsa, is a hill of about the same dimensions having numerous cisterns and covered with rubbish of every sort. Upon this hill was once erected the temple of Tanit or of Astarte, whose worship and oracles were greatly respected at Carthage and continued till the fifth century of the Christian era, when the emperor Constans, to put and end to complicated rites of prostitution, ordered the temple to be destroyed, and its enclosure was converted into a cemetery. Of this temple, as well as that of Baal, (the Apollo of the Greeks and Romans); of the temple of Molock (Saturn), famous for its human sacrifices and for its colossal statue, made with open mouth, as if to devour the children destined to be burned in honor of that god; of the temple of Ceres and Proserpine; of these and all other temples there remain only insignificant traces, and it is scarcely possible for one without the plan of the city before him to distinguish their sites.

Of the twenty-one Christian churches or basilicas, most of which were either heathen temples, dedicated, like the Parthenon at Rome, to Christian purposes, or were built on the ruins of heathen temples, no vestage now remains, unless it be of the basilica of the Vandal king Thrasamond, situated near the hill of Borge-Geedid. This ruin on the sea coast has served and still serves as a quarry, from which building stones are taken for all the region around. By the side of this basilica, is a vast ruin which Mr. Pellissier believes to be that of the Gargillian baths, where during the reign of Honorius, were held the famous conferences of bishops on the subject of Donatism.

The modern castle of Borge-Geedid (new-castle), is built on the site of the fort taken in 1270, by St. Louis. One of the declivities from the height of Borge-Geedid is covered with the ruins of a stair-case which led by one hundred and twenty or one hundred and thirty steps from the Nova Platea to the water's edge. That height completely overlooks the sea. "Nothing," says Mr. Beulé, "could have been finer than the view from that point. If the spectator turned to the right, he saw old Carthage, with her harbors, her temples, her forum and her acropolis; upon his left and in his rear was the new city, the rich quarter of Magara."

Fifty rods northwest of Borge-Geedid are eighteen magnificent arched cisterns, running parallel to each other and separated one from the other by a thick wall. They are each about one hundred feet long, twenty-five feet wide, and thirty feet deep. They have side galleries extending at right angles, about four hundred and forty feet long, and eight feet wide. At the ends and near the centre of the vast quadrangle formed by these cisterns, are circular basins, formed by the division of the oblong basins. This vast system of reservoirs received only rain water collected by means of inclined planes made of cement around the cisterns, and conducted into them by pipes, pieces of which have been recently found. At the late Universal Exposition, at Paris, was exhibited a large bronze faucet, fastened to the end of a piece of lead pipe, which was recently found in one of the cylindrical reservoirs, at the end of this system of cisterns; and fastened to the wall of the same reservoir, is a narrow stone stair-case which leads to the bottom. This reservoir was discovered during the recent work of excavation and restoration, entrusted to Mr. Gouvet, a skilful French engineer, in the service of the Tunisian government.

It remains for us to say a word about the harbors and necropolis of Carthage. "The harbors of Carthage," says Appian, "were so arranged that the ships passed from one into the other. On the side of the sea there was but one entrance, seventy feet wide, which was closed by means of iron chains. The harbor first entered from the sea was designed for merchant ships, and was provided with numerous hawsers. In the centre of the second harbor was an island, having great quays on its shore, similar to those on the opposite side of the basin. These quays presented the appearance of a series of creeks, which could receive two hundred and twenty vessels. Above the coves on the main land were built some magazines for ship-rigging. Directly in front of each cove were erected two Ionic columns."

The piece of land embracing the site of the ancient harbors is called at the present time El Cram (the fig trees). It is situated south of the Byrsa and northeast of the Goletta. On the part of El Cram nearest Carthage, are the gardens and palace of the Bey's prime minister, General Mustapha Khasnadar. Just before reaching the palace, we pass over ground where were once fitted out proud fleets that swept the Mediterranean. On either side of the gate nearest the palace is a fine granite monolith taken from ruins near by. The villa of General Kheridine is situated on the shore between the site of the ancient harbor and the Goletta. The military (interior harbor) was called *the Cothon* until the Byzantine domination when it took the name of Mandracium. It was ruined as well as the mercantile harbor at the time of the Arab conquest in the latter part of the seventh century. The mercantile harbor has been partially filled up and converted into a garden where, instead of a forest of masts and the hurly-burly attendant upon loading and unloading vessels, are now witnessed thrifty trees, smiling verdure and the quiet processes of nature. The military harbor, though much encroached upon by the garden, preserves somewhat of its ancient form, and we can still readily distinguish the islet on which for centuries waved the flag of the Carthaginian admiral, and the old and new entrances to this harbor are clearly seen. Mr. Beulé has had the good fortune to settle through his explorations the history and topography of this double harbor, so many times controverted through levity or ignorance.*

The necropolis of Carthage was situated in the northeast part of the city enclosure. Thousands of dwellings for the dead, now appearing but simple holes in the ground, may still be seen on that barren and desolate hill which contrasts sadly with the smiling gardens of Camart, near by. The tombs are constructed like those of ancient Syria, the cradle of the Carthaginians. A rectangular subterranean room, which was arched and reached by steps, constituted the body of the tomb, around which were made several places large enough each to receive a dead body. All the tombs had the same general form, differing

---

* Along the sea-shore for a great distance may be seen the foundations of ancient wharves. Here and there a pier extended out into the sea, and the outlines of these piers are readily determined. The docks where the vessels were probably charged and discharged were, according to appearances, protected from the sea by an immense wall or breakwater which has been demolished together with the wharves, and the docks have been filled up with *debris*. A few yards from these wharves and running parallel with them are the Herculean foundations of an extensive building. The masonry and the arches which occur at stated points and were doubtless passages to the docks, are in a good state of preservation and are pronounced by some competent judges to be of Punic construction. St. Augustine, in one of his discourses, delivered in a church near the sea-shore, complains that his services were disturbed by applauses from the theatre near by. As I wandered over these grounds with the engineer referred to, the probable sites of the church and of the theatre were pointed out. Where the theatre stood are now but shapeless ruins and Arabs were carrying off the foundations of the church for building stones. The harbors described by Appian and the docks here referred to were sufficient to accommodate five hundred vessels.

only in size and ornament. Each human being had simply his spot of earth, and now, after the spoliations of many successive generations and races of men, and the ravages of jackals and other animals, it is impossible to distinguish the final abodes of the rich from those of the poor, of the powerful from those of the weak. It is thus that death is a great leveller, abolishing all the fortuitous distinctions observed in life. The tombs were generally of masonry, though some of them were dug into the solid rock, and it is probable that they had inscriptions on metal or marble, which have all disappeared. Each body was shut in by a stone slab, to prevent its violation; but this precaution had no power to overcome the cupidity, curiosity or ignorance of the races and generations that have succeeded the Carthaginians. We will, however, express the hope that science may yet explore the ancient necropolis of Carthage.

We come now to see that little remains of the ancient city; its men have returned to dust; its power is gone except that which results from its history; we search the ground in vain for satisfactory proofs of its glory and splendor. Only vestiges and fragments of monuments mark the spot where once stood the mistress of the sea and the commercial metropolis of the world. But these remains, pitiful though they be, serve as memorials and souvenirs of the greatness which the name of Carthage recalls. If we reflect that from the fall of the Roman empire, Tunis, Pisa, Genoa, Constantine and many other cities have by turns or at times disputed for its ruins, transforming them into simple marble and stone quarries (and this quarrying is still going on), open to the pillage of the whole world, we shall be less astonished to see so little of that city which according to the most moderate calculation was fifteen miles in circumference, and had from 800,000 to 900,000 inhabitants. If any one further observing that this immense pillage was exercised for centuries, mainly upon Roman Carthage, which was built, as it were, upon the ruins of Punic Carthage, enquire how it happens that comparatively nothing remains of Punic Carthage, which after all could not have been pulverized by the vengeance of Rome, the reply is plain; unquestionably vast ruins of that primitive Carthage are still buried under heaps of rubbish, accumulated by twenty conquests and the lapse of as many centuries, and perhaps they will some day be exhumed and brought to light. The facts in the case and the discoveries recently made fully justify this belief.

Before quitting this point of land where the rival of Rome lived and disappeared; where the intellectual capital of Africa, and perhaps of the entire Roman world in the fourth century, made more noise than the city of Hannibal itself, let us pause a moment for contemplation on the summit of the Byrsa, and mark quite around us the site and its horizons.

To the east, the view opens upon the azure gulf, reflecting an illuminated sky which once gilded the façades of Roman or Punic temples. Half submerged upon the shore are enormous blocks of masonry, the *debris* of ancient quays. Thither the peaceful and silent waves of which Virgil speaks,* gently roll, and expending their force seem regretfully to retreat, with soft undulations, into the immense sea which is displayed between cape Zebib and cape Bon, those two videttes of the gulf of Carthage. To the south, in the midst of thriving trees and rich verdure, is the old cothon, withered and shorn of its fair proportions. Still in its centre is the famous islet encircled with silvery water. Here are vestiges of the temple of Baal, and there is the site of the forum, where Bomilcar was one day honored as a king, and shortly afterwards crucified as a traitor. The *Tænia*,† the strategic point of Censorinus, stretches out towards the south. In front, Hammam-el-Lif, Gebel-Rasas and Corbus raise their volcanic and angular peaks, and partly behind them, on the right, some light clouds crown the summit of Zaughan, the highest mountain in Tunisia. To the west, the historic isthmus of Carthage extends between the lagunes of Soukra and the lake of Tunis, which seem ready to force the narrow strips of land which separate them from the sea. Yonder, towards the southwest, is Tunis, the White, backed upon her hills, and in the plains which from Tunis widen out into the delightful oasis of Ariana, behold there, under the olive trees which cover it and the palms which from point to point overlook it, one of the most famous battle-fields of history! The great nations of the world have there mingled their blood, and the victims of their struggles have lain together for centuries in the fraternity of death and oblivion. Agatho-

---

* Æquora tuta silent. † The neck at present called the Goletta.

cles, Regulus, the Gordians, the Vandals, the Byzantines, St. Louis, Charles V., and Barbarosa have in their turn won victories or suffered defeats. Glory and war have not in the wide world a place better consecrated to their honor by the insensate rage of the sword. To the north, in fine, the Byrsa overlooks the valley of the actual Marsa, the ancient quarter of Megara, the richest part of Carthage, with its vast and opulent villas, recalled by the beautiful gardens of to-day; then Mount Khawee, covered with violated sepulchres, and sorrowfully rising by the side of the oasis of Camart; still beyond is the sea with which the Bagrada pours its yellow waters laden with sand, which has utterly changed the face of the coast. Finally we have before us a magnificent panorama; a land inexhaustibly fertile and blooming with verdure, in spite of its abuse and abandonment; its hills with graceful contours; its mountains majestic, on the borders of a sparkling sea, which seems smilingly to display its empire and its immensity, under a heaven where the benediction of God would invite the good will of men. But the men of ancient Carthage, having been only merchants, prevented its becoming the Queen of the World, and it is not the actual Tunisians who will better understand the predestination of their country.

Utica, like her sister Carthage, was at an early period so completely destroyed that few traces remain of her former greatness. At the Arab village of Bou-Shahter are some vestiges of that city which is ever remembered as the scene of the tragic end of Cato. In exploring the site of this ancient town, we find towards the southwest the ruins of an aqueduct built like that of Carthage with cement and small stones. This brought the water from mount Cashbeta, which is situated seven miles to the southwest. By the side of this ruin is a system of six ancient cisterns which have a rectangular form and are parallel to each other. They are at the present time partially filled with dirt and rubbish, and serve as a shelter for the flocks and herds of the rude natives. On the north, is the site of an elliptical amphitheatre, from which all the mason-work has disappeared. After crossing in the same direction a ravine and a plain, we come to the site of the ancient acropolis of Utica, now marked by no clearly defined ruins. At the foot of the acropolis, is a small semicircular hill on one side of which was built a theatre. Further on are some remains of an immense edifice, and near by are the *debris* of a temple or Christian basilica of which little remains but broken columns. We know that a canal ending in the sea once passed through the centre of the city. This canal has been filled up and but feeble traces remain of the quays and of the constructions that lined them. Pursuing our course, we arrive at a great circular basin now nearly filled, in the centre of which are the remains of a wall. Here was the ancient *cothon* or military harbor and these are the sole remains of it above ground. The mercantile harbor has utterly disappeared in consequence of the accumulation of sand and soil brought down by the waters of the river Majerda. Mr. Daux, the distinguished engineer in the service of the French emperor, has been enabled by means of excavations and accurate measurements to draw a most interesting plan of the ancient city.

In like manner, ancient Hadrumetum, the most renowned Phœnician colony of Byzacium, and in later times noted as the landing place of Cæsar in his African campaign, and still later as the seat of a Christian bishop, has now only insignificant traces of its former greatness and importance. The city actually standing on its site is called Susa and the extensive region around it the Sahel. The researches of Messrs. Guérin and Daux, especially of the latter, who has drawn elegant maps of the ancient and of the modern city have verified the locality of Hadrumetum, showing its extent and traces of its ancient cothon. They also have brought to light ruins of important edifices, fortifications, cisterns and sepulchral mouments. In the month of August, 1862, I saw there a tomb just after its discovery. The Roman mosaics in its floor would compare favorably with those of Pompeii. Within the walls of the modern city are many ancient cisterns, one of which is sustained by twelve columns and is still well preserved and in actual use. In passing through the streets of Susa, we find many columns attached to modern constructions, and these are especially noticeable at the corners of mosques and important public buildings. A similar observation might be made in regard to Tunis and all cities in the neighborhood of important ruins.

Moving from Susa in a southerly direction and leaving to our right lake Cairwan whose waters sparkle in the distance, we traverse a desert plain which extends from north to south between the lake and the sea, and soon come in sight of an immense edifice, which appears larger as we approach it, and is at length seen to be a colossal amphitheatre, situated in the centre of the miserable Arab village of El-Gem. This monument is twenty miles from the sea, and stands on the site of ancient Thysdrus or Colonia Thysdriana, forming a long ellipsis which runs from east to west; its greater axis is 489 feet, and its smaller 407 feet; the arena is 295 feet long, and 197 feet wide, and the wall is 66 feet thick, leaving galleries 60 feet wide. The building had above the ground four stories, each of which was supported by 64 arches, separated from each other exteriorly by half columns, with beautiful Corinthian capitals. The upper story has now nearly disappeared, but the whole building must have been about 100 feet high, and its circumference is more than 1,200 feet. It is built of beautiful, well-jointed blocks of sandstone, and must have presented a truly imposing sight, with its circular walls opened to receive the air and light. Its long and high galleries, with broad stair-cases, which served as seats for the spectators, have either disappeared or are in a ruinous state.

At the western extremity of the long axis is a breach in the wall, which enables us to see clearly the interior of the amphitheatre, and this great gap in the building is enlarged year after year by Arabs, who appear to regard this structure mainly as a quarry for their convenience. They carry off its hewn stones, columns, and various carvings, and use them in the construction of their rude dwellings or in walling up their wells. Thus by the hand of man and the effects of time, various arches and passages have been so broken down or injured that it is now difficult to ascend to the summit of the amphitheatre.

It is probable, as Mr. Guérin observes, that the demolition of the staircases began at the period of the Arab conquest in the year 689, A. D., when the Berber heroine, Damia, surnamed Kahenna, transformed this amphitheatre into a veritable fortress, for the defence of the national liberty. Under her orders all the arches of the lower stories were walled up on the outside, to exclude the soldiers of Hassan-ben-Naman, and prevent the injurious effects of their weapons on the interior.

A large opening was made into the western side of this amphitheatre, by order of Mohammed Bey to prevent his insurgent subjects from following the example of Kahenna and turning this gigantic edifice into a fortress. There is under the arena a subterranean passage, with an arched roof, which is now so encumbered with earth and rubbish that it cannot be explored for any considerable distance. A persistent tradition attributes the construction of this passage to Kahenna, who, it is asserted, while besieged here, had thus an underground communication with her friends on the coast. But we are inclined to the opinion that this subterranean passage was confined to the arena, and was made for the service of the amphitheatre. African traditions are no more to be trusted than those which belong to the Holy Land. It is easier to exercise the imagination and yield unquestioning faith than to acquire knowledge by careful investigation and research.

The construction of the amphitheatre of El-Gem is ordinarily attributed to the emperor Gordian, the Elder, who was here proclaimed emperor in the year 236 A. D., but we have on this subject no incontestible proofs. The grandeur and magnificence of this building are rendered more striking by the misery and desolation that surround it. Like the Coliseum at Rome, of which it is the rival and almost the contemporary, it seems to speak, with that silent eloquence which belongs to great historic ruins, of the centuries of events that have succeeded each other at its base. It is a proud witness which, though mutilated by generations of men, bears a distinct record of their deeds. The product of Roman civilization in its decline, it still shows such marks of grandeur as make us forget the aberrations and follies of the royal people. Often 80,000 spectators assembled within the amphitheatre of Thysdrus and rent the air with deafening shouts and applause. Its galleries were thronged to witness the feats of gladiators from abroad or the heroism of Christian martyrs given over as food for the wild beasts. At a later period, a company of Berbers and of Greeks, who took shelter in this arena with the last hope of Christian Africa, fell under the sword of the victorious Saracens. Various reflections are awakened by the sight of these colossal ruins. The shades of night add a mournful solemnity to the solitude, and the light of the moon lends a mysterious influence which we fully appreciated on two of the three nights we spent at this place.

This amphitheatre marks well the last halt of Roman civilization upon the frontier of the ancient African world. Tunisia contains no archælogical monument that can be placed in comparison with it; and in the rest of the ancient western empire, the Coliseum at Rome alone surpasses it in grandeur and historic interest.

At Monastir (ancient Ruspina) are found few traces of antiquity. Mr. Daux has, however, been enabled to identify the camp-ground of Cæsar, who after his failure to take Hadrumetum, fortified his camp at Ruspina. In the Kuriot isles, which are opposite to Monastir, are some ancient cisterns and artificial grottos. At Lempta, a little way from Monastir, are found the important ruins of ancient *Leptis Parva*, a considerable city in the time of Carthage, and later, under Roman rule, the seat of a Christian bishop. These ruins cover a space of four miles in circumference, and contain vestiges of an aqueduct, traces of a quay near the sea, and in the water are visible the outlines of an extended pier.

Following the shore towards the east, we speedily arrive at cape Dimas (Thapsus), and find some of the piers extending out into the ancient harbor. As for the city which was once a great centre of Carthaginian commerce, and is especially memorable for the victory gained there by Cæsar over Scipio and Juba, it is all gone save the ruins of a vast amphitheatre, of a large reservoir and of an aqueduct. At Media are found traces of the ancient harbor and of a necropolis which Mr. Guérin regards as Phœnician. This is known to have been the site of a considerable town and the centre of much commerce. Media contains some old cisterns with arched roofs whose masonry is in a good state of preservation. Here is found an opening into a vast subterranean apartment, which tradition represents to be one end of the underground passage of which we spoke in describing the amphitheatre at El-Gem.

Seven miles from Media we find the scanty ruins of Selecta, ancient Syllectum, which was the first stopping place of Belisarius in his march from his landing point at Caput Vada to Carthage. Near this spot are traces of the city of Justinapolis, founded upon the site of the Byzantine camp, in honor of the successful landing and subsequent victories of the imperial legions, which, under Belisarius, resulted in the overthrow of the Vandal power in Africa, 534, A. D.

At Sfax are a few vestiges of Roman constructions, but in some surrounding villages are important ruins. At Messallah are remains of an amphitheatre 600 feet in circumference, and further north, at Bathnia Casser-Essas, are some ruins two miles in circuit. In the environs of Bir-Koum-Maken, north of Sfax, are ruins three miles in circuit, including some enormous masonry of a large theatre; two vast cisterns, and a triumphal gate much disfigured. At Hoonga, on the route between Sfax and Gabes, are the ruins of ancient fortifications, and of an immense edifice which appears to have been a Christian basilica.

At the mouth of the brook Tarf-el-Ma, which empties into the gulf of Gabes, are the ruins of an ancient city. At Gabes are found scattered over several hills the ruins of ancient Tacape, among which are cisterns and broken columns, and Mr. Alphonse Alkan, vice consul of France at that port, has recently found embedded in a modern construction, an inscription showing conclusively the identity of Gabes and Tacape. In the island of Gerba, ancient Meninx and Lotophagitis, are the ruins of a fortification and of a hall of justice, with columns and statues scattered over considerable extent of ground. There are also cisterns in a good state of preservation, and a part of the old causeway or bridge, connecting the island with the main land, is still visible on the southern side of the island.

In the Gereed and especially in the principal oases, are found many Roman ruins, such as cisterns, reservoirs and marble monuments of various kinds. Gafsa, ancient Capsa, abounds in fragments of inscriptions. On the banks of the river Semha is a Roman mausoleum yet in a good state of preservation. It is built of hewn stone and ornamented with pilasters which have Corinthian capitals. This edifice was once surrounded by a wall whose foundations are still apparent. On one side of this mausoleum is an epitaph recording the virtues of Urbanilla, a rich and benevolent Roman lady. Near by are some ruins on the *henshir* (farm) of Sidi Aishe. They are the remains of an aqueduct and many sepulchral monuments, two of which are well preserved; but the tombstones on the *henshir* Oum-er-Rhir are much more important.

At El-Hammam, north of Feriana, is a gigantic

edifice with niches for statues which have long since disappeared. Judging from the halls, which were once arched over, and from the devices on the mosaic pavements, this building was used as a bathing establishment.

A hundred yards distant upon elevated ground is a wall built with hewn stones without cement, and near by are the ruins of a theatre of which little remains but the outside wall and some steps. Proceeding in the same direction across a field covered with *debris*, we come to an immense enclosure 420 paces long and 180 wide. The walls, which are of an extraordinary size, are broken down and immense blocks of masonry are thrown about as if by some convulsion of nature. In the opinion of Mr Guérin, here was once a fortress containing several edifices. Near by are also the ruins of numerous buildings whose materials are of an extraordinary size. Ruins and *debris* are scattered over an area three miles in circumference. Not even the name of the ancient city is known, though Mr. Guérin supposes it to be Telepta, which was a Roman colony and at one time the seat of a Christian bishop.

North of Telepta, at Cassreen, are the ruins of ancient *Colonia Scillitana*, among which is a superb mausoleum, 13 feet high and 10 feet square. It is covered with inscriptions, two of which are veritable poems; one contains 90 hexameter verses, and the other 20 elegiac verses, but neither have any literary importance. It was consecrated to the memory of a Roman family, the chief of which was a certain Titus Flavius Secundus. Another mausoleum of less

RUINS OF SCILLIUM AND THALA.

importance, consecrated to Petronius Fortunatus and
his family; a mutilated triumphal arch with two
inscriptions, one of them revealing the name of the
city; five enclosures containing considerable monuments, one of which appears to have been a Christian
basilica, and some tombstones complete these important ruins. We have spoken, in connection with the
church at Carthage, of the Scillitan martyrs who were
greatly venerated and whose memory was long cherished throughout Christian Africa.

Proceeding 35 miles in a northwesterly direction
from Cassreen, we arrive at Thala, a town of 1,200 inhabitants, built on the site of an ancient city which
must have been very large, since its ruins extend over
an area of several miles in circumference, and among
them are found numerous tombstones and a beautiful
mausoleum built of huge blocks of marble, but at
present containing no inscriptions. Mr. Guérin hesitates to adopt the opinion of Sir Grenville Temple,
that this city is the Thala mentioned by Sallust.
Thala was a great and opulent city where Jugurtha
collected his treasures and his family, and fled, after
being overpowered by Metellus. It seems to us that
the identity of the name and the importance of the
ruins prove sufficiently the identity of the city. Mr.
Guérin's hesitation arises from the fact that according
to Sallust, Metellus had in beseiging that city to
transport water 50 miles distance across a desert
country. But on the one hand, Sallust may have
been mistaken in regard to the distance or may have
exaggerated the distance to magnify the difficulties
and honors of Metellus's campaign; and on the other

hand, it is quite probable that the river Hydra had not at that period the same importance as at present and was dry while the seige of Thala was in progress, a condition to which the streams of that country are often reduced.

But the ruins of Hydra are much more important. These are situated 12 miles in a southwesterly direction, and are on both sides of the river Hydra, but principally on the left bank. On the right bank are some admirable ruins of a long Roman road which is paved with large flag-stones and leads to a small triumphal arch, which has been stript of its inscriptions and upper layer of stones. Upon the left side of the river we find:—1. A great triumphal arch nearly twenty feet wide. This is entered by two porticos extending to the right and left and supported by Corinthian columns. This arch served as a monumental entrance to the city and was dedicated to the emperor Septimius Severus in the year 195 A. D., as indicated by a beautiful inscription still seen. All around it are huge stones belonging to a wall which was built at a later period, and this enclosure served for a long time as a fortress. 2. A semicircular construction which was probably once a theatre. 3. The ruins of four Christian basilicas, as shown by the fragments of inscriptions, among which is the monogram of Christ. 4. Three beautiful mausoleums, the largest of which is 30 feet high. 5. A road paved with large flag-stones and having vestiges of tombs on each side of it. 6. Two tall columns much defaced. 7. The walls of several houses built with hewn stones; and one of these houses is so well preserved that its interior arrangements are readily recognized. 8. The walls of the citadel with three gates, one of which opens upon the remains of a bridge once thrown across the river Hydra; the citadel enclosure is two-thirds of a mile in circumference and contains vestiges of several towers which, with one exception, were all square. 9. A great number of tombstones, huge masses of ruins without definite character, fragments of inscriptions, etc. Hydra is according to Mr. Guérin, the ancient Ammedera, which was the seat of a Christian bishop and was enlarged, fortified and embellished by Justinian during the first half of the sixth century. It was especially renowned for a victory which Mascerzil, the lieutenant of the emperor Honorius, gained over the usurper Gildon, near the river Ardalio, now called Hydra. Mr. Davis, on the contrary, offers a strong argument to prove that this is Casæ Nigræ, noted as the residence of Donatus, who led in the opposition to the established church.

Travelling five hours in a southeasterly direction, we come to the important ruins of Sbiba, the ancient *Colonia Suffetana*, spread over several hills and consisting principally as follows: Of an immense construction, probably once used as a bathing establishment; a rectangular enclosure having large stones and immense masses of mason-work; a beautiful semi-circular fountain, once decorated with columns and statues; the walls of a building which was probably once a Christian basilica and has at present thirty-six Corinthian columns; the walls of another building which was probably used for the same purpose, and numerous mutilated inscriptions, among which is one showing the ancient name of the city, *Colonia Suffetana*. This city was under the protection of Hercules, and afterwards in the Christian period was the seat of a bishop, gaining at one time much celebrity by the martyrdom of sixty of its inhabitants.

Again proceeding 18 miles in a southeasterly direction, we find upon the right bank of a river of the same name, Sbaitla, ancient Suffutela. Besides the remains of a beautiful arched bridge which served also as an aqueduct, and underneath which is an inscription showing that this construction was dedicated to the emperor Verus, we find among these ruins a vast wall enclosing three temples; a beautiful triumphal arch at the extremity of the city; a fine road leading to vestiges of buildings whose character is not easily determined, and tombstones and shapeless *debris*. It is a well authenticated fact that the patrician Gregory, the Byzantine governor of the African province, resided at Suffutela, and after a battle of three days duration was defeated with his 120,000 soldiers by the little army of Abd-Allah-ben Sayad, the lieutenant of the calif Othman, in the year 647, A. D.

It is impossible for us to notice within our prescribed limits all the ruins scattered over Tunisia. Mr. Guérin's VOYAGE ARCHÉOLOGIQUE, two large volumes, octavo, contains 536 inscriptions with notices of ruins without number, and yet fails to enumerate all that are worthy of attention. However, to complete a brief sketch in accordance with our general plan, we now proceed to point out a few of the most important ruins found in the northern part of the regency, aside from those of Carthage and Utica already noticed. At Bizerta and Beja, we find considerable traces of monuments and inscriptions. In the last named city, we learn from an inscription on a stone fastened into the exterior wall of a mosque, that this building was once a Christian basilica. Kef has vestiges of a temple of Hercules; remains of a palace and of a Christian basilica, and an antique fountain which still supplies the city with water. A little way from Kef, at the henshir of Lorbes, ancient Colonia Zares, are many columns supposed to be milestones, bearing the names of Marcus Aurelius, Nerva, Trajan, and Hadrian, and there are also numerous fragments of inscriptions upon broken stones. At the henshir Mest, ancient Musti near Teboursuk, are the ruins of a beautiful triumphal arch and many inscriptions. Also near Teboursuk are other inscriptions, and in the town itself are some remains of the ancient Byzantine fortifications, built by the prefect Thomas, under the reign of Justin II, together with many inscriptions having the names of the emperors and pro-consuls.

Ten miles from Teboursuk are the magnificent ruins of Dugga, formerly called Tugga. This is at present a miserable place of 300 inhabitants, while it must have been once, judging from the extent of its ruins, an important city. We must name a beautiful mausoleum which is built of hewn stone and once had upon one of its faces the famous bilingual (Punic and Libyan) inscription, whose interpretation caused many controversies among the oriental scholars of Europe. The inscription was engraved upon an enormous block of marble which was firmly fastened into the wall of the mausoleum, and in an effort to remove it, under the orders of Sir Thomas Reade, late British consul-general at Tunis, the monument itself was nearly demolished. Among the *debris* are still seen fragments of some remarkable alto-relievos and statues. The bilingual inscription is now in the British Museum, and as to its interpretation we have the interesting assurance that:—"Docti certant, et ad huc sub judice lis est." The other antique remains of Tugga, are:—A temple with six beautiful upright columns; upon the frontispiece of this temple is carved a gigantic eagle, probably designed to represent Jupiter to whom the building was consecrated; some remains of another less important temple; those of a theatre; of a triumphal arch; of a citadel; of baths and mausoleums; and several fountains, cisterns and mutilated inscriptions.

Four hours from Teboursuk upon the borders of Ain Tunga, we find the extensive ruins of the ancient Municipium Thignica, among which are a Byzantine citadel with the bases of several towers. We find among the rubbish different inscriptions belonging to the period of Marcus Aurelius and Commodus. The other ruins are a temple; a triumphal arch in a good state of preservation; the walls of a circular building which appears to have been a theatre and vestiges of a Christian basilica. At Testour upon the Majerda, are few or no antique ruins, but some inscriptions found there prove that it is the ancient Bisica Lucania. At Mejez-el-Bab, also upon the Majerda, we find numerous antiquities, including a triumphal arch, 12 cisterns, numerous vestiges of a wall along the banks of the river and, among different inscriptions, a fragment which gives an idea of the ancient magnificence of this city. Mejez-el-Bab is the ancient Membressa; it was celebrated in the early Christian period for the number of its martyrs, and became subsequently the seat of a bishop. At Tebourba, which is also upon the Majerda and is the ancient Tuburbo Minus, are vestiges of an amphitheatre and some unimportant ruins. One old-looking mosque is called the mosque of Jesus and, according to Arab tradition, stands on the site of a Christian temple.

It remains for us to say a few words about the ruins around the city of Tunis and the mountains of Zaughan. At Mohammedia we find very long pieces of the ancient aqueduct of Carthage. In this vicinity three sepulchral inscriptions of Christian bishops were found in 1850 and removed to the Catholic church at Tunis. The ruins of Oudena, ancient Uthina, extend over an area nearly three miles in circumference, and contain, besides enormous antique walls, the remains of an amphitheatre, a theatre, an aqueduct, and of an arched bridge together with numerous cisterns. The monumental character of these ruins gives a good idea of the importance of the ancient city of whose history little is known.

From the river Melian to Zaughan, we find detached pieces of the great aqueduct of Carthage; at certain points, these ruins are a mile long and serve as picturesque land marks along the road to Zaughan, the most elevated mountain group in the regency. Arriving at the little city of Zaughan, situated on a hill near the foot of the mountain of the same name, we enter a triumphal gate, built in the Roman period, of beautiful cut stones. Its arch is 14 feet wide and its buttresses are 10 feet square. It was once ornamented with two statues, the niches for which are on each side of the entrance. Upon the key-stone of the arch is a triangular figure resembling the letter A, and under it is a crown of oak leaves euvironing the word AVXILI.—LIQ. This inscription is over the representation of a ram's head with a superb pair of horns. Some writers infer that this city was dedicated to Jupiter Ammon, while others think that the ram's horns indicate abundance. Scattered about the city are broken columns and capitals belonging to another period of civilization.

A mile and a half southwest of Zanghan, at the base of a precipitous mountain crag, we come to the ruins of an ancient temple, erected over one of the sources that used to supply the aqueduct of Carthage and now supplies the aqueduct of Tunis. These picturesque ruins are composed of a rectangular sanctuary at the end of which we distinguish the remains of an altar and a niche where probably once stood the statue of a god. On the sides of a double gallery in the form of a horse-shoe, are 24 arches supported once by 26 columns which have long since disappeared and are said to be now in the mosque of Zaughan. Between the galleries and the sanctuary is a broad open terrace elevated above a basin which is reached by stone steps now in a dilapidated condition. A subterranean canal led to this basin the abundant living waters from an inexhaustible source, which by means of pipes refreshes and enriches the neighboring gardens, and also by means of an aqueduct, constructed in the modern underground style, supplies the city of Tunis and its environs with water as it did Carthage 16 centuries ago. The aspect of this ancient monument is rendered more interesting by the solitude of the place and the magnificence of the scenery of which we attempted to give some idea in our notice of Zaughan.

We now conclude this long and yet very superficial chapter on the antiquities of this country. To specify, describe and explain all these ancient ruins, would require a great work in which the art of designing should come to the aid of observation and learning; in other words, would require more time, labor and expense than are consistent with the object and plan we have in view.

CHAPTER VII.

Government.—Administration of Justice.—Army.—Navy.—Finances. Public Instruction.—Benevolent Institutions.—Revenues and Burdens of the State.

THE Bey of Tunis is, like all Mussulman sovereigns, the absolute master of his kingdom, from whom emanates all religious and civil authority; he is the administrator of the public revenues; the supreme judge of all disputes; and, in short, *he is the State*, in the full extent of the expression. It is readily understood that such a concentration of power must involve abuses, wrongs and disorders when it resides, as it too generally does, in the hands of a man ill-prepared for the vast responsibilities devolving upon him. Where the sovereign is intelligent, capable and upright, this autocracy is not only admissible in principle; it has sometimes positive advantages; for the administration not being complicated, as elsewhere, it is easy for the sovereign to superintend and direct all departments of it; and officers of all grades, not being able to count on the thousand evasions and delays of bureaucracy, are careful to conduct in such a manner as not to draw upon themselves the all-powerful hand that can reach them without obstacle.

But neither the intelligence nor the uprightness of the sovereign, however marked, can always be a sufficient guaranty; since the force and morality of every government depend not so much on the personal worth of one man, as on the collective wisdom of the State. Whatever be the capacity and ability of a chief magistrate, if he do not feel himself controlled by the nation and responsible to it; if he be not restrained from wrong doing and mal-administration by other laws than those of his own conscience and reason, his government is a perilous one for his country. It has a defect that should cause us to look to the future with dismal forebodings, even were the sovereign the most complete and worthy incarnation of his people, and his people the foremost nation in the world. Now, as Mussulman peoples and princes are far from realizing this condition, it is easy to infer the real situation of this country. A degenerate and debased people have rulers who, if superior to themselves, govern apparently without any sense of their responsibility to either God or man.

The Bey appoints officers; levies taxes; disposes of the fortune and honor of citizens; cuts short their disputes at a final appeal; exercises his authority, unlimited in all respects, over everybody and everything, and this according to his good pleasure or his momentary caprice and the undulating and diverse impressions of a spirit ordinarily closed to every other idea than what pertains to himself.

With such a system, the various institutions intended to regulate the relations between citizens are illusory; and first, the tribunals; for from the office of a justice of the peace to that of the president of the supreme religious tribunal, all devolves on the Bey, who is supposed to understand all the cases and to whom all may be carried by appeal; who is the great judge or rather the only judge, the living, acting law; and all this without any preparation or other guide than good sense, which he often lacks; without other counsel than that of the servility that surrounds his tribunal as well as his throne; without other prospect than assured obedience to his sentence, which in his own eyes, as in those of his people, is fatally just, necessarily applicable, irrevocable, infallible and permanent.

The Bey without being a jurist,—and this is not his sole want,—is the sovereign universal judge of all the affairs, and almost all are brought before his tribunal. He regularly sits two days a week, three hours at a time, *to do justice*, according to common parlance, and in his delicate and difficult duties, he is aided, if we credit the popular theory, by light and wisdom from on high. This is certainly a convenient explanation, and we see not upon what other hypothesis he could decide cases in ten minutes or half an hour that would occupy our courts successive days and weeks. On court days multitudes of litigants and interested people crowd around his audience hall, where door-keepers serve as police, introducing plaintiffs, defendants and those arraigned for crime in a stated order, and promptly conducting them out of the court room as soon as their case is finished. All decisions are at once enforced, and condemned criminals sometimes start for the galleys or gallows as the last word of their sentence drops from the lips of the Bey. Plaintiffs, defendants and persons accused of misdemeanors or crimes appear before the throne, explaining their case themselves, or, if they choose, employing an advocate to explain it to the Bey, who listens in majestic silence and with admirable patience. The procedure would, however, hardly command respect among us; for it consists in a single hasty explanation of facts supported by testimony if there be any. The Bey, after listening, proposes questions himself, and reflects a moment, and then renders a definite decision, from which there can be no appeal. Sometimes, when a case is very complicated or important, the verdict is deferred to another session of the court, so that his Highness may have time for reflection and consultation. But the justice of the Bey is in all cases prompt, giving his subjects less annoyance and more satisfaction than the verdicts of the dilatory and corrupt tribunals that prevailed under the constitutional regimen. The Bey probably decides more cases at each session of his court than any European or American tribunal decides in a week.

The Tunisians have the greatest confidence in the justice of the Bey. It is very rare that persons defeated or condemned offer any protest or complaint. When they feel aggrieved, they are wont to console themselves, repeating: "This is all! It is thus our sovereign judge decides!" It is true, litigants have not the wearisome delays and vexatious legal processes that characterize European and American courts, and they are spared the loss of much time and expense. But we think this expeditious and summary method of deciding grave questions causes inconveniences and dangers much more serious than delays and the sacrifices which result from them. Suppose, what is hardly possible to take place, that the sovereign judge who must learn at a single sitting many different matters touching the question at issue, should preserve a mind so calm, clear and well balanced as to incline him to seize on the strong points of the case and strip the truth of its false garb; still even then, there would not be sufficient safeguard for the justice of his sentences; for in this extreme precipitation he is always in danger of committing errors despite his best efforts to the contrary.

In principle, civil as well as criminal justice is in the hands of the cadi, except political cases which directly interest the prince. But now the cadis rarely try cases except where religion is directly concerned. They have the power to imprison and bastonade. This last kind of punishment is administered in the following manner: The sufferer lies upon his back. His feet are then fastened with a cord to a stick and kept at a convenient height by two servants, while the person, charged with the execution of the sentence, inflicts on the soles of the feet the prescribed blows, varying from 20 to 1,000. The force of the blows depends mostly on the officer, whose humanity has degrees of tenderness corresponding to the generosity and wealth of the sufferer. Sometimes the bastinado is applied not only upon the soles of the feet, but upon the thighs. The bastinado ordered by the cadi is always less severe than that ordered by other magistrates; for, according to a curious usage, the officer is then allowed to wield his rod only with a loaf of bread under his arm, in such a way that, being restrained in the use of his arm, he cannot employ much force.

The cadis have for assistants lawyers and notaries. Superior to the cadi is the *medjles*, or religious tribunal, presided over by the mufti and composed of doctors of the law. For religious affairs of great importance, there is the supreme tribunal of the *Schara*, of which the Bey is *ex-officio* the president, but whose decrees do not always depend on him, notwithstanding his sovereign authority, for this tribunal is always composed of the most influential and revered religious dignitaries, and the Bey professes to scrupulously conform to their standard of orthodoxy.

The penalties for crimes and offences are, besides the bastinado, fines, imprisonment, forced labor and death. The Tunisian prisons are hideous, being dark, damp, and alive with vermin. The unfortunate creatures condemned to the galleys or old slave pens, at the Goletta, have this advantage over ordinary prisoners, that, being occupied during the day on the works of the port, in the open air, they are confined in the foul enclosures only during the night. The different kinds of capital punishment are: hanging, for ordinary malefactors; beheading, for persons of a certain rank, guilty of violent crime or of sacrilege, and shooting, for soldiers. Ahmed Bey introduced, twenty years ago, this last usage, contrary to Mussulman traditions, which admit only beheading and hanging. Adulteresses were by law sewed into bags and drowned. The place of these executions was the little island of Shickla, in the lake of Tunis. Exile on one of the Kerkenna islands was first substituted for drowning on Shickla; and later, that mode of punishment was discontinued, and no substitute provided; the law of God, however, in regard to adultery, appears to be in full force at Tunis, with penalties more terrible than drowning or exile.

In general at Tunis, as throughout the orient, justice is understood to be an article of commerce, always in the market; and the success of a litigant or the fate of a criminal often depends on his fortune; the Mussulman law itself countenances this transaction, authorizing compensation in money even for murder, provided the relatives of the victim consent to it. In spite of all this, however, we believe that heinous crimes and offences are not so numerous in Tunisia as the wretchedness and ignorance of the people and the bad organization of justice would lead us to expect.

Since 1858, a municipal commission, charged with the government of the city of Tunis, has had the powers of a tribunal for the decision of all questions coming under its jurisdiction, and for the oversight and regulation of important interests relative to the houses, streets and lands of the city, and the distribution of the water. The prefect of police holds also a kind of correctional court, whose object is to punish petty offenders and settle disputes arising from diverse causes, which are reported by police officers or freely submitted by the parties interested. We hardly need say, that neither the municipality nor the prefect of police can render a decision which may not be carried by appeal before the Bey. It is not rare, then, to see, in the ante-rooms at the Bardo, the same throng of litigants and offenders that a few days before crowded the court of the municipality or the hall of the prefect. But the appeal to the Bey becomes exceedingly difficult when the condemned party has been shut up in a Tunisian prison, which, like the devouring Acheron of mythology, rarely gives up its prey. This is the more to be regretted, as, in general, it is not so much for crime that they are punished as for being too poor to bribe the judge or his subordinates.*

Tunisia is divided for administrative purposes into many districts, the chief magistrates of which are called *kaids*.† Once the kaids took their districts on shares, or paid the government a certain sum for unrestricted power. Besides the sum agreed on, the kaids had to send to the Bey, from time to time, considerable presents in gold and in the products of the country. At the present time, though appointed by the Bey and receiving their salary from him, they keep up the system of presents which are the habitual return for all favors, and especially for those received from Mussulman sovereigns; but it is the district governed, and not the official, that supports the system, where the kaid has naturally full authority. The old Roman pro-consuls have in this country

---

* See Appendix L, for illustrations of Tunisian tribunals and justice.

† The kaids are of two kinds: those of the cities and those of the tribes. The former reside ordinarily in their respective districts, while the latter are often officers of the Tunisian court, who delegate their power to lieutenants, rarely appearing in the district under their jurisdiction.

worthy successors, and the actual Sallusts run no risk, like the historian, of being recalled from their posts; for, more fortunate than he, they have no austere and incorruptible senate to sit in judgment on their acts.

The kaid is in his district the civil governor, chief of police, judge in all kinds of cases, and receiver of customs. He has under him lieutenants, who take charge of subdivisions of his district. The cities have magistrates subject to him, called *sheiks-el-belad*. According to ancient usage there could be only one sheik in each city, but in large cities at the present time are several officers with this title. Each trade has also a chief, styled the *amin*, who exercises over its members a certain authority. The towns, villages and sub-divisions of the tribes are governed by sheiks appointed by the Bey, though nominated by the kaid. They depend either on the *halifa* (lieutenant) of the kaid or on an *oukeel*, who is a superintendent inferior in office to the halifa. A certain number of policemen are under the orders of the kaid and of his agents. Also the commanders of the irregular troops, who are called *kaias*, are associated with the kaid as a guard, and sometimes they render him important aid. There are in the regency of Tunis four *kaias*, whose residences are at Gabes, Cairwan, Bizerta and Kef. The last named·*kaia* is the most important of all, and governs directly or by his lieutenants all the tribes in the western district.

It was under the reign of Ali Bey, in 1830, that the first military reforms were introduced at Tunis. The sovereign of this little country wished, like the Sultan and Mohammed Ali of Egypt, to have an army organized in European style, thinking thus to acquire genuine prosperity and power. The incurable mania to play the soldier that prompted the reörganization of the army is doubtless one of the principal causes of the present financial disorder in the country. Ahmed Bey, during the eighteen years of his reign, spent for the realization of this project large sums of money laid up by his predecessors, and imposed upon his country new burdens. His successor, Mohammed Bey, disbanded the regular troops. Though this was a measure of economy that greatly benefited the agriculture of the country then in a declining state, it was nevertheless an imprudent act; for it disarmed the government in the presence of a dissatisfaction that had already begun, and which finally resulted in an extensive rebellion in 1864, under the reign of the actual Bey, Mohammed Essadek. The latter, after putting down the insurrection and strengthening his authority, again organized a regular army. But, unfortunately, he paid little attention to the wretched state of the country, restoring the system of Ahmed Bey without his means of maintaining it. Thus the debts and burdens of the country were increased, while the agricultural products and available resources were diminished.

The effective regular force consists of 22,500 men.*

---

* The statistics are thus given by the late Mr. Cubisol: REGULAR ARMY.—Five regiments of infantry, 15,000 men; two of artillery, 6,000; one of cavalry, 500; marines, 1,000; total, 22,500 men. IRREGULAR ARMY.—Koulouglis (troops of Turkish origin), 6,000 men; Zouaves, 2,000; Spahis, etc., 4,500; total, 12,500 men. Whole number belonging to the regular and irregular army, 35,000 men.

The arms of the soldiers are generally of an inferior kind and in bad order; for they are mostly refuse arms purchased at different times of European speculators at exorbitant prices, and are allowed by the shiftless soldiers soon to rust and become unfit for use. The costume formerly adopted was that of the French troops of the time of Louis Philippe, grotesquely modified and awkwardly worn; the costume now in use is more in accordance with the habits of the men, and resembles that of the French zouaves. The colors of the turban and of the sash vary according to the arms, but are never gaudy. The jackets and pantaloons are blue, with the sleeves and backs trimmed and ornamented with red, to indicate rank. The uniforms of the officers have gilt trimmings and embroidery. The gaiters or leggins of the soldiers are leather, and those of the officers cloth. Though it is the rule to wear shoes, gaiters and stockings, the soldiers are ordinarily seen bare-legged and slipshod. I hardly need say that the Tunisian army is not distinguished for tidiness and discipline. The soldiers being the victims and involuntary instruments of despotism demonstrate none of the spirit and ambition of freemen.

The mode of recruiting the army is peculiar. Superior officers make tours of observation. Arriving at any particular locality, they give orders for all the young men to appear before them, selecting whomever they choose. The people try in various ways to avoid this tax levied by caprice upon their blood. Entreaties, intrigues, sacrifices and open resistance are employed to save their sons from the army. I knew one Mussulman who had such a horror of the army that, to keep his two sons out of it, he never exposed them to seizure until they were twenty years old, when they passed from the paternal roof to service in foreign consulates. Boys are sometimes sent out of the country with this object in view. The duration of service is, like recruiting, submitted to the decision of capricious officers. The compensation allowed is exceedingly small, and is rarely paid when it is due. Arms, food and clothing are subject to speculations very injurious to the service. In fine, the actual army is so *demoralized* that it could hardly stand fire in the face of a single battalion of efficient soldiers.

This, however, does not prevent the country from having 28 major-generals and 26 brigadiers. There are naturally fewer colonels. This is a singular fact, but is easily explained. Most of the colonels have performed military service, while most of the generals have reached their dignities at a single bound, or simply by wearing for a short time the epaulets of a colonel. It is true that these generals are not regarded as military men, but they have, nevertheless, the rank and enjoy the honors. There are some of them who once sponged the marble floors of the Bardo, or were employed in cafés or barbers' shops at Tunis, and who by means of a few years service, in no way heroic, were decorated with the *grand cordon* and with the double or triple star of massive silver, as insignia of the general's office. Their history is no secret; it is even circulated in all its scandalous details; and yet these men are treated with reverence, simply because they are the favorites of the Bey.

Among the *irregular troops* are:—1. The Turks and their descendants, called *koulouglis*. 2. The zouaves,* who came originally from Algerine Kabyle tribes, and are disposed to maintain their character as French subjects. 3. The Oussellatians, whose former home was about Mount Oussellat. In ordinary times, they are scattered over the regency, and engaged in various kinds of labor. They are united periodically on fiscal expeditions. 4. The Drids, described on the 247th page. 5. The *spahis*, who are Arab horsemen, especially attached to the government. They ordinarily reside with the tribes to which they belong and where they enjoy special privileges. Though rarely united together, they are always ready to march. 6. The *hambas*, who are a select body of *spahis* attached to the person of the Bey, whose orders they bear. In case of foreign war, the Bey could call together, besides the forces already named, contributions from all the tribes in the regency, which would amount to a very large body of troops.

As to the navy, Tunisia, which was, only half a century ago, a formidable power, committing great depredations upon European commerce, has now but very few ships, and even these few, though purchased at exorbitant prices, are not all kept in running order. They are armed with 44 cannon, and manned by 1,000

---

* This term has come into general use in Europe and America to designate a kind of troops distinguished by their dress, weapons and mode of warfare.

marines. The navy officers, like those of the land force, make quite a show on paper. They consist of one vice-admiral, two rear-admirals, four captains of vessels, and numerous captains of frigates, and lieutenants.*

Public instruction is more than languishing in Tunisia. Apologies for schools are found at the corners of streets, in miserable rooms, where antiquated masters make up in whipping for their want of skill in teaching. They attempt to give only elementary instruction, and fail in that. The pupils learn to repeat in a singing tone many phrases from the Koran, and to write a few words, after which their studies are completed. Those who are destined for service in the mosques or to act as jurists or secretaries, study under the direction of teachers in the mosques, which contain, as did the churches of the middle age, schools for superior instruction. But their studies are ordinarily limited to the Koran and its commentators, and to some vague principles of grammar. Those who aspire to become *tolbas* or *oulemas*, undertake reading and writing the text of the Koran. There are several ways of reading the Koran, based

---

* List made out in 1867: One screw frigate, 16 cannon, 300 horse-power; 1 screw advico, 6 cannon, 150 horse-power; 1 wheel steamer, 4 cannon, 180 horse-power; 1 screw steamer, 4 cannon, 160 horse-power; 1 wheel steamer, 6 cannon, 140 horse-power; 1 screw steamer, 6 cannon, 120 horse-power; 1 screw steamer, 2 cannon, 70 horse-power; 2 screw steamers, 25 horse-power each. There is an arsenal at the Goletta, very badly furnished, though directed by skilful European engineers, who are not responsible for its inefficiency. To give an idea, we will simply say that this establishment figures in the budget for three-fourths of the sum devoted to the navy, which costs one-sixth of all the revenue of the state. There is not a maritime power in the world that, all things considered, spends so large a proportion for its navy as the regency of Tunis.

upon the methods of some renowned theological doctors who had peculiar ways of reading certain words, of articulating certain consonants, and of giving pious inflections and modulations of the voice at certain points. To know and practise these modes of reading is in the eyes of Mussulmans a great accomplishment. Grammar, theology and law have their place in the course of study. A knowledge of the law is acquired by studying legal commentaries favorable to this or that sect, and the traditional accounts of Mohammed. The elements of arithmetic, geography, geometry, astronomy and prosody have a place among their studies, but are little understood by modern Mussulmans, who are only slightly acquainted with discoveries made since the middle age. The state does nothing to aid public instruction, or to organize and extend it. The small expenses incurred at Tunis are, as we have elsewhere explained, covered by pious legacies and by certain revenues entrusted to the mosques.

Of efficient charitable institutions there is great deficiency at Tunis. There is only one Mussulman hospital, and that is unworthy of its name, being so organized and managed as often to aggravate disease rather than allay its ravages. Some mosques and zawias do, however, furnish lodgings and distribute food and clothing at certain seasons of the year. Though the state make no sacrifices for these objects, it could and should better superintend and direct the management of the large endowments entrusted to its care for the support of beneficent institutions. It could and should see that the proceeds of funds consecrated to beneficence are appropriately applied. In the city of Tunis alone the net income of charitable foundations amounts annually, as I am informed, to $40,000, which, properly used, would accomplish incalculable good. But, painful to relate, most of this sum is either pocketed by dishonest agents or foolishly expended, and very little of it actually goes for the relief of distress and suffering.

The streets of Tunis are meanwhile thronged with ragged and hideous beggars, many of whom are wretchedly diseased, and all of them, though Mussulmans, call upon Christians for bread. These poor creatures evidently have more faith in the charity of Christians than in that of their co-religionists, though the latter are, according to their creed, the saints of the Lord, and the former accursed infidels.

To describe the financial condition of the government, is a task from which we involuntarily shrink. We will, however, try to give some idea of the mode of collecting and disbursing the public revenues, and of the sources of wealth and the causes of poverty. Grain crops are taxed 10 per cent. on arbitrary estimates, in regard to which great injustice is practised. Olives are divided into three classes, and taxed 20, 30 or 45 per cent. Commercial establishments and articles sold are also taxed. Cattle are subjected to a heavy duty. The manufacture and sale of tobacco is a government monopoly, yet Europeans sell it without hindrance. The custom house is let out like a farm, at so much a year, or on shares. While the import tax is very light, the export duty is so heavy on many articles as to prevent legitimate trade, and induce smuggling. A poll tax of $4.50 on each man was established for years, when it was suddenly doubled, and became one of the leading causes of the rebellion in 1864, since which time the rule has been to impose as heavy a tax as possible. The inhabitants of the interior of the regency suffer most from official exactions and extortions, while those of Tunis and other large cities fare better, though they are not without grievances. Besides the direct taxes and revenues from monopolies, the state has numerous domains, forests, mines, and salt lakes, which it might turn to account.

Nothing can be more irregular and confused than the mode of collecting the revenues, unless we except the mode of spending them. Outside the large cities, the taxes are collected by sheiks and *oukeels*, appointed by the kaids, who are the general receivers; but there are on the one hand, many subjects who are either so poor that they cannot pay the sums demanded of them, or so indignant at official wrongs that they will not; and on the other hand, there are many publicans who seek not so much to replenish the public treasury as to accumulate fortunes for themselves, and thus the country is oppressed with taxes without the government's receiving corresponding advantages. Of the sums collected, probably not half reaches the public treasury, and not half of that is expended for the legitimate purposes of the government. The revenue of each district is put into the hands of its respective kaid, who either sends it directly to Tunis or puts it into the hands of the Bey of the Camp, when the latter makes his annual or biennial tour with a view of overawing the tribes and collecting imposts.

The expeditions of the Bey of the Camp take place; the first at the end of the winter, in a southerly direction to Tozer, where this officer remains several months; the second takes place at the end of summer; the body of the army generally stops at Beja, while the governor of Kef visits, at the head of a strong detachment, the tribes of the west, and collects large sums of money and quantities of provisions from the defenceless creatures scattered over his district. When the Bey of the Camp sets off from the capital, his army presents the appearance of an immense caravan, composed of several hundred elderly Turks panting under the weight of their ancient armor; of a thousand horsemen, most of them Drids; of 2,000 zouaves; of several batteries, and throngs of servants in charge of numberless cattle for food, and beasts of burthen, such as mules, donkeys and camels, loaded down with baggage. The departure of the camp is always a jubilee attended with extraordinary noise and confusion. Soldiers celebrate the day by the occasional discharge of their guns; horsemen show off their steeds; donkeys bray; cocks crow; women and children shriek; donkey-men and camel-drivers shout; bagpipes, drums and French horns utter forth their strange notes, and in the midst of these discordant sounds are now and then heard words of command from officers who think of order amidst this admirable confusion.

When this motley force halts, the camp is arranged in a circular form, according to oriental custom. The tents of the infantry are placed in regular order on the exterior circumference of the circle; the tent of the commander-in-chief is put in the centre, and around this are first the tents of the principal officers, and around these last are the tents of the scouts, messengers and guards, called *hambas* and *spahis;* and the Drids have a stated place a little farther from the centre of the circle. The signal for the departure of the camp each morning is not a discharge of musketry or cannon, but such a furious and discordant beating and blowing of musical instruments as might drive the most ferocious animals frightened from their dens. The prince rides in the centre of his escort to the sound of Arab music, which is less harsh and cruel than that of the Turkish band. Before him marches the chief of his guard, with three subordinates and some magnificent horses, led by grooms, and behind him are the standards. After the staff of the Bey, comes the rest of the army, without fixed order, men, horses, mules, camels, donkeys, cattle, wagons, cannon, and even women and children on camels' backs, all moving on helter skelter, amid the most discordant cries of men and beasts. The scene is such as we might fancy to have been witnessed at the departure from the ark of Noah, with a greater variety of the human kind and fewer species of animals. The Bey of the camp is invested during his expeditions with extraordinary powers, even over life and death.

But these expeditions, instead of accomplishing their object and bringing to the coffers of the state the sums desired, often fail even to cover the large expenses which they incur; and yet almost always the unfortunate tax-payers contribute more than they ought. This belongs to the system of pillage and waste that characterizes the administration; vast sums are collected by this system and lost by bad calculation and dishonesty. The money naturally *sticks* to those persons that handle it, and thus the chances of its reaching the general treasury are diminished in proportion as intermediate agents are increased. The government is unfair in its dealings with its subjects, plundering those whom it should protect in their industrial pursuits. The subjects are naturally indignant, paying back the evil that they receive with interest. There is thus a competition between the two parties to outdo each other in the commission of violence and wrong, and both are necessarily injured and enfeebled. For several years past, the two expeditions of the Bey of the camp have not sufficed; at intervals, detachments of the army have gone forth under experienced generals to strip the defenceless tribes. They may temporarily relieve the public treasury; but they at the same time bring it into a more hopeless state, by destroying its resources in the future. It is a touching Arab proverb that "armies leave in their track only weeping eyes."

The revenues are variously estimated from 3,000,000 to 6,000,000 dollars. Under a judicious system fairly administered, we think the revenue might be tripled with much less hardship than is now experienced. At present, there is no proof that the money collected is appropriately applied. Collectors, clerks, cashiers and treasurers of all grades are not duly looked after and controlled. All these officers of the government are either badly paid or not paid at all, and yet they acquire in a little time great riches, which, however, do not prevent their having debts after the example of the government, and, like it, also neglecting to pay them.

The government is overwhelmed with debts, and appears scarcely to concern itself about them. Worse still, it goes on increasing them, either by contracting new ones or leaving the old ones to be augmented with interest. Who can say how it spends its meagre revenue, since on the one hand, misery is frightful, and the unfortunate inhabitants of the interior are reduced to extremities; and on the other, it does not pay its coupons when they are due; it leaves its paper protested on the markets of Europe, and even at Tunis, and, discounting a future that does not belong to it, obtains credit and delay, indefinitely renewed by promising to pay in so many months or years the sum that is due at the moment, augmented by such or such interest. And how will it pay? The process is easy. It will issue paper representing the value of the olive crop of such a future year, which may, of course, turn out like the maid's pot of milk, as has repeatedly been the case in years past.[*]

[*] For estimate of the revenues and expenses of the state, see Appendix M.

CHAPTER VIII.

The Israelites in Tunisia.*

IN Africa, as elsewhere, this race, at the same time obstinate and supple, yielding and firm, changing in appearance but remaining unchanged in its essential elements, the elder branch of the human family, intermingles with the other races without being confounded with them, and is distinguished from them by particular characteristics always and everywhere the same. Jewish features are peculiar and expressive. The face indicates intelligence and

---

* Mr. Noah, himself a Jew, in his book written more than a half century ago, estimates the number of Jews in Tunisia at 60,000, and in all the Barbary States at 700,000. He says the Jewish exiles from Spain and Portugal found in Fez, Algiers, Tunis and Tripoli great numbers of their brethren originally from Judea, some of them doubtless descended from the Canaanites who fled from Joshua and settled in Mauritania Tingitana. Rev. William Fenner, who has enjoyed unusual means of information, has furnished the following table of the Israelitish population: SEAPORT TOWNS.—Tunis (the capital), 32,000; Goletta, 200; Soliman, 100; Nabel, 600; Susa, 3,000; Monastir, 500; Media, 400; Ksoor-es-Sef, 50; Shebba, 30; Sfax, 5,000; Gabes, 2,000; Gerba (island), 7,500; Porto Farina, 25; Ras-Gebel, 100; Bizerta, 400. INLAND TOWNS.—Gereed (oases of), 3,000; Kef, 500; Beja, 350; Mater, 80; Testour, 250; Medjez-el-Bab, 25; Tebourba, 50; Mukneen, 400; Zaughan, 50; Nomadic Jews scattered among the various tribes of the interior, 3,000. Seaport towns, 51,905; Inland towns, 7,705; total, 59,610.

shrewdness tinged with melancholy, and in its ever-varying expression are shown great power of language and a natural, insinuating eloquence, which have served the Jew in the greatest straits for centuries. For, reduced by the hatred and oppression of all nations to efface or belittle himself, and resolved by family instinct and national pride to finally triumph in his views and interests, he understands how to gain by circuitous ways places which he could not take by assault. In other words, he dissembles, humiliates and even degrades himself, excites pity, causes disgust, wins confidence, and thus finally succeeds in reaching all posts to which he aspires. This is especially true in commercial and financial affairs. In this country, the Jew is the life of business.

It is a tradition that a part of the Jews of North Africa have been established there since the destruction of Jerusalem by Titus; but very many came from Spain and Portugal in the fifteenth and sixteenth centuries. They occupy there, as formerly in Europe, separate quarters, called *haras*, a word which belongs to antiquity, and means stables or unclean places. The streets are there narrow, dark, damp and dirty. The houses are many of them in a ruinous state, small and badly aired. Numerous and sickly families are often crowded into these unhealthy habitations, and there multiply in suffering and wretchedness. In the rainy season, liquid mud deluges these quarters, and penetrates into many of the houses, which are below the level of the ground. Of late years, however, the new municipality has done much to improve the sanitary condition, and introduce light and air into this quarter. Good new houses are now rising on points where but recently were squalid ruins crowded with wretched tenants.

The custom which formerly prevailed of closing the gates of the *harras* at night was discontinued many years since at Tunis, where several times these unfortunate people, unable to escape, fell a prey to the flames; and their distresses were more than once aggravated by the uncharitableness of Christians as well as Mussulmans, who, influenced by religious animosity, neglected to come to their relief. But since the reign of Ahmed Bey, it is only the mass of the Israelitish people that live in the *harra*. Families in easy circumstances, especially if they are of European origin, select elsewhere their dwelling, and from the top of their palatial mansions look out on the entire city.

We have seen an essay, entitled, "The Jews our Lords." It was a suggestive satire, setting forth in a clear light a remarkable truth. In the midst of our industrial and commercial activity, where capital and prices absorb attention, it is certain that influence and success attend speculative and financial genius, of which no people possess so great a degree as the Jews. They are engaged in almost every important speculation, and have, in proportion to their population, more eminent business men than any other people on the face of the globe, for the simple reason that each one aims at business and depends upon it. In this country nothing is done without the Jews. From the management of the finances of the state down to the humblest private speculation, all is in their hands. Christians and Mussulmans affect to despise and hate them, especially the latter, and yet neither could succeed without them. They are, in all the administrations of the government, the general treasurers and financial agents, and, encountering fearful obstacles and a malicious espoinage, they show as much skill and sagacity in business as in avoiding conviction and punishment when guilty of fraud and mal-administration. They are in general suspected and accused by everybody; but they care not for this, and feeling themselves to be a necessary part of the machinery of the government, they shrink from no encounters to maintain their position.

To gain as much money as possible in very little time and at any sacrifice, is the prevailing ambition of the Israelites of this country. Most of them are traders, and all aspire to be such. A few only engage in other pursuits, while waiting for a chance to indulge their besetting propensity. Almost all the trade with Marseilles, Leghorn and other ports, is in their hands, either directly, by the number and importance of their mercantile houses, or indirectly, by their brokers, courtiers, and exchange agents, whose services are indispensable in all commercial and financial operations, and who usually serve in this humbler sphere only until they can appear as merchants in their own names. Showing wonderful tact and fitness for this kind of service, they never fail to take care of their own interest and make sure of their profits, whatever may happen to their employer.

Besides their position as commercial brokers, the Israelites occupy there, as in all the Levant, places that are sometimes very lucrative, as courtiers, in the different consulates. They know how to acquire consideration, and to become in some important consulates the confidents of the consuls themselves even in political affairs. For, corruption playing everywhere, and especially in Africa and the orient, a considerable part in human affairs, the Jewish courtier is found at the outset fully prepared for peculiar service by his love of money, natural shrewdness and freedom from conscientious scruples. It is thus that such men, without moral worth or dignity of character, gain the absolute confidence of their chief, the agent of this or that great nation, and become not only the men for all situations, but virtually the directors, acting in the name of the consul, and consequently of the government and people represented by him, disposing of the rights and interests of subjects, and compromising, in the eyes of the local government, from whose jurisdiction they have broken away, the influence of the European legation and colony whose scourge and dishonor they are, and quietly and with impunity amassing for themselves, by various measures, under the protection of a noble flag, great fortunes to be compared only to their unblushing pretensions and arrogance.

We include under the name of European Jews those who recently came from Europe and have European habits, and also those who claim to be of European origin, though their customs and appearance are altogether Tunisian. Neither are dependent on the Bey, but on their respective consuls. All put the highest estimate on this advantage, so much

the more appreciable as once every Jew, without
regard to his nationality, was a subject of the Bey,
exposed to various insults and extortions on the part
of Mussulmans. They were all restricted to a particular costume, traces of which remain at this day;
a blue turban with a red cap and a dress of a sombre hue. Ill luck to them if they dared sometimes
infringe this rule, and so far forget social proprieties
as to wear, for example, the *sheshia*, appropriated to
Mussulmans, or some garment of bright colors, especially if it were red, consecrated to the pilgrims of
Mecca, or green, the color of the religious nobility.
The Leghorn Jews alone were authorized to wear a
little white cotton cap. And this privilege is said to
have sprung from a tyrannic freak of a Bey, who,
seeing a cargo of these white caps brought into port
as a prize by one of his corsairs, and not knowing
what use to make of them, compelled the Leghorn
Jews to purchase them on his terms. The Jews
advanced the money, and enjoyed in return the right
to ornament the chief of this singular purchase, who
swore thenceforth in the native costume as well as
in the European; but in fine, it was the beginning
of a privilege, and a conquest over the prejudices of
their tyrants. These restrictions are at this time
removed by law. European Jews dress like other
Europeans, and native Jews much like Mussulmans.
They wear the *sheshias*, though in time of excitement,
prejudice is manifested against this practise, and they
put on gay colors as if to challenge opposition; and
if they abstain through prudence from open provocation by putting on green and red turbans, which

are the consecrated colors of Islamism, they sometimes have their sashes, handkerchiefs and shoes of these colors, which insult Mussulmans feign not to see, in order not to be compelled to avenge it.

The Jewish subjects of the Bey are subjected to a state tax in return for the privilege of opening their synagogues and schools. This is a relic of the ancient tribute imposed on infidels in Mussulman countries. But in our day, the Tunisian government shows itself in general very moderate towards the Jews, who are much disposed to seek European protection, and whom the consuls are inclined to defend in the name of humanity.* As the sons of Abraham escape from the persecutions and crying wrongs to which they were subjected in other times, they gradually lose that trembling heart which once characterized them everywhere, and especially at Tunis, and assume the bearing and character of men.†

Let us now enter into some details in regard to the manners and customs of this interesting people. And first, of their persons. Their complexion is in general a mixture between lead and white; black hair; of medium size; face intelligent, but, contrary to that of the Arabs, indicating more cunning and less haughtiness. Their air is brisk and business-like, and their movements are, as it were, insinuating and sinuous in the crowd, as in life and business. Their

---

* See Appendix N, for further information on this subject.

† Mr. G. L. Ditson, in "The Crescent and French Crusaders," says that "the Jews were formerly held in great contempt in Algiers, and even a Mohammedan child could smite them with impunity; but now they are fully protected in all their rights of citizenship; they flourish like Barbary figs; they reap golden harvests in the commercial world, and their women are the most richly dressed of all who walk the streets."

face has a smile without warmth and joy; their body inclines forward in the attitude of deference, and at the same time of attention; they keep their hands in front, and in their many gestures never extend them in a large circle nor raise them to the height of their faces, making what are called in physiognomy concentric instead of eccentric movements; for the first indicate supplication, and the concentration of the soul upon itself under the ascendency of a superior influence; while the second express contrary dispositions, which are not habitual with the Jews. Such is in brief their portrait. The tone of their voice, drawling, mellifluous, nasal, whining, wholly from the head, and never from the chest, together with a cruel, bantering tone and manner, adopted according to circumstances, are other essential traits.

Their habitual tongue is a corrupt Arabic mixed with Hebrew, Italian and Spanish words. Many can read Hebrew, but speak it with difficulty. In writing Arabic, they generally employ Rabbinic-Hebrew characters, which are very unlike the Hebrew alphabet. These characters are employed by all the Jews of North Africa. This very remarkable fact serves to illustrate and confirm the persistent and traditional repugnance of the Jews to being confounded with other peoples, and their tendency to distinguish themselves by some peculiar traits, and to Hebraize, so to speak, every thing they have been forced to borrow from nations that surround them, in order to preserve, at least in what is essential, their ineffaceable national physiognomy.

There is scarcely a city in the interior of the country which has not some Jews among its inhabitants. These people are found even in the oases of the Sahara and in the mountains of the west. They are often seen in the Arab or Kabyle nomad tribes, speaking the same language and wearing the same costumes as those tribes, with two exceptions; the men have, instead of the Arab head-dress, a piece of cloth wound around their head, or a black turban, and the women refrain from tattooing themselves like the Mussulman women; for tattooing is strictly forbidden in the Jewish law. Nomadic Jews are also found maintaining an existence distinct from the Arabs, and while they preserve some distinctive Jewish traits, they appear in general just like Arab bedouins.

In 1837, the great Algerine tribe of the Hanensha, living on the confines of Tunisia, had more than two hundred Jewish tents, whose chiefs fought by the side of the Arab chiefs with long, slender guns trimmed with silver. Afterwards, in consequence of difficulties, one hundred and fifty tents emigrated into the Tunisian Gereed, where they are still established.

These Jews share in general the life and labors of the tribes; work either on their private account or for the tribe with Arab farmers; are there, as everywhere else, supple, insinuating, active, and very skilful in adapting themselves to all the interior necessities of life, and yet maintaining with inviolable fidelity the obligations and usages which spring from their religious law, and which constitute their true typical physiognomy in all countries and at all times. They furnish, however, but few cultivators of the soil. They are in general pedlers and traders of some kind.

They are expressly excluded from two or three Kabyle tribes in order to prevent competition in some flourishing branch of industry. They are led by their industrial and commercial enterprise into the centre of Africa, where they trade in gold dust, and have co-religionist correspondents established at various points in the Tunisian and Algerine Gereeds, and in the oases of the desert as far as Soudan.

These peculiarities belong to the Israelitish race, which has never been confounded with any other. The creed of the Jews, by separating them from other nations and imposing upon them a distinct life, has produced what we now witness—peculiar traits and characteristics indelibly stamped upon the race. From Moses, their great law-giver, the levites and rabbis have continued his theocratic office, more or less disguised, according to times and circumstances, but always persistent and unshaken in their faith. National kings were only their docile instruments or their adversaries, soon to fall. Foreign oppressors never found in the Jewish priesthood anything but the most implacable hostility. In short, the levites, who are to-day the rabbis, have been from the first and in diverse experiences the soul of the Jewish nation. From the taking of Jerusalem and the dispersion of the Jews to the four corners of the earth, they have played a perilous and touching part as shepherds of that unfortunate and scattered people. They have held on through tears and blood to the old religion of their fathers and to the traditions, usages and superstitions of their ancient national life. Better than the Greeks and Romans, who, when exiled from their native soil, carried with their household gods the image of their country, the Jews, through the agency of the rabbis, have borne, so to speak, that country itself in their hearts, and at each halt in their march and in the midst of other strange or hostile peoples, have formed a society similar to that of their original country.

The religion and political system of the Jews, constituting a part of the Bible record, are so well understood as to need no explanation here. Pure monotheists, they are more clearly distinguished from Christians than Mussulmans; for the latter admit to a certain point the mission of Jesus; while Jews recognize no other mission than that of Moses, and if they needed to be confirmed in this exclusiveness, they would have only to say to themselves that the mission of Moses is the sole one which all believers in revealed religion recognize without reserve, and that this is at the outset a great presumption in favor of its excellence. The Mosaic books constitute for the Jews a universal code, designated under the name of *Tara*, the law. The other religious books have not so practical a character, though they are the object of religious respect. In general terms, they are called the prophets. This distinction is indicated in the gospel. *The Law and the Prophets* constitute the holy books. But it is the books of Moses, containing the law, that are shown for the veneration of the faithful in the synagogues, where they are kept locked up in a box which answers as their ark of the covenant. It is by means of these books that the rabbis teach the sacred Hebrew tongue. It is from these books that they draw all their civil and religious rules. Dogmas, religious duties, marriages, circumcision, indications in regard to food permitted or forbidden, essential laws in social and domestic relations,— each thing is there found explained in detail or in general terms.

The rabbis, faithful to their office, watch over and direct the people, counsel, admonish, blame and condemn them. At certain calamitous periods, they impose upon them penances or the observance of public ceremonies; they protest against certain offences which appear to them to draw down the wrath of heaven, and as often as it is in their power, they chastise offenders, or at least bitterly reproach them in open synagogue. The synagogues of Tunis are very numerous, but are in no respect remarkable. Outwardly, they can scarcely be distinguished from other buildings. Within, besides the inhabited part and that for the school, they contain for worship square halls without any decorations except numerous lamps, which hang from the ceiling, and a case or tabernacle in which is preserved the roll of parchment containing the law, a chair for the rabbi and stools or benches for the congregation. All the religious ceremonies of the Jews consist in chanting certain verses from their scriptures and prayers regulated by their ritual, which naturally vary according to circumstances. At the end of the ceremony, the law is borne in procession, receiving marks of respect from the assembly. As among most oriental people, females do not sit with the men in their religious assemblies. The men, whatever be their costume, keep their heads covered. At the great annual fast in commemoration of the destruction of the temple at Jerusalem, the Israelites are bound by usage not to go out except with their feet bare, or at least with nothing on them but cloth slippers. At the feast of the Tabernacle, in commemoration of their sojourn in the wilderness, they build in their houses rooms or tabernacles with boards covered with myrtle and palm branches, and there assemble in the light of symbolic lamps to repeat their prayers and take their meals. At the feast of the Passover, they live for fifteen days on unleavened bread. At all the feasts for rejoicing or expiation, food or money is gratuitously distributed to all their poor, who, though very numerous, are effectively cared for. The system of almsgiving, or rather of taxation for the poor, is very creditable to the Jews, tending at the same time to prevent the prevalence of suffering and the nuisance of beggars.

The Jews of Tunis are divided into two communities, one of which is called the Portuguese community, because it was founded by rabbis of that nation, or sometimes simply Barbary Jews, and the other the Leghorn community, so named on account of its origin. Each of these communities has its rabbis, treasuries, system of almsgiving, schools and slaughter houses. Besides abstaining from certain forbidden meats, the Israelites must submit to the most careful inspection even those meats that are permitted. Thus the least weakness, such as an incipient wart or wen appearing on a healthy animal, has the effect to render that creature unclean and unfit for food. The throat of the animal must also be cut in a certain way. Also, only special levites can practice or direct the grave operation of cutting the throat of lawful animals and fowls, from the ox down to the chicken and dove.

All wild game is in general forbidden as food on account of its usual violent death; pork is an 'abomination; butter cannot be employed unless it be prepared in a certain way. This last condition applies also to wine and cheese. This is the reason why in all great Jewish centres there are special butchers and provision agents. All these obligations in regard to the manner of living explain why the Israelites generally avoid eating with gentiles. They regard these last as in principle unworthy of such intimacy with the people of God. All but their own co-religionists are uncircumcised and unclean. Mussulmans, it is true, do not fully justify these reproachful epithets, but they have no particular merit, since, while adopting the distinctive sign of the chosen people, they reject their religion. Polygamy is permitted, but the men have only four wives. It is, however, but very little practised, even among the native Jews.

Tunisian Jewesses have a costume very similar to that of the Mussulman women; but it is in general more flowing, shows better taste in regard to its combination of colors, shape and materials, and, in fine, renders the Jewesses more attractive and graceful, especially as we are permitted to see their faces. Embroidery in gold and silver, broad necklaces composed of gold rings, numerous finger rings, artificial coloring, powdering the eyes with *koheul*, anointing the

JEWESSES AND THEIR ATTRACTIONS. 497

eyebrows with a kind of cosmetic, are all regarded as essential to a beautiful toilet. Also married ladies must have such a head dress as will conceal their hair. In general, Jewesses have good features, but are far from being beautiful according to our standard; for their faces, though not ugly, betray their great want of intellectual culture, and indicate their purely material life. Also many of them acquire, even in their youth, formidable proportions, which contrast strangely with the delicacy of their faces and the elegance of their hands and feet. Divorce is authorized, provided one of the two parties brings before the rabbi a reasonable cause. If the cause be pronounced insufficient, the wife alone has to suffer; for the husband can marry again in accordance with the law of polygamy.

The Jews have at Tunis a large cemetery, situated just out of the city. It is but partially fenced, and, besides a few beautiful monuments, contains many marble slabs, and innumerable brick or cement coverings to graves, kept as white as chalk. It is a rule that a dead body cannot remain in a house after the setting of the sun, unless the death occur on Friday night, in which case the interment takes place as soon as the sun goes down on Saturday. The Jews manifest their grief like the Mussulmans, by making a great noise and turning their houses into bedlams. During epidemics, however, the government usually interferes to prevent these noisy demonstrations. The mode of interment is also peculiar. The corpse is first well washed. It is then wound in a white sheet, which is sewed together in such a way as to prevent any part of the body from being seen, and inclosed in a white wooden coffin, which serves for all persons, and belongs to a fraternity piously devoted to the service of the dead. The coffin is then borne upon the shoulders of some members of this fraternity, who are designated in turn, and cannot refuse to serve even in case of pestilence. The nearest relative goes at the side of the coffin, holding on to a ring situated near the head of the deceased. Since attending the burial of the dead is regarded as a meritorious act, funeral processions are usually large, and they go on increasing till they reach the cemetery. There they halt in the court of an edifice devoted to this use, and have a short service, expressing their resignation to the will of Jehovah, "Lord of life and death." Then proceeding to the grave prepared beforehand, after a prayer the body is let down upon a bed of slaked lime. The procession then withdraws by the same way, the members of it always making a contribution for the poor as they pass off.

European Jews do not conform to all these usages, but rather imitate the European custom in regard to the shroud and coffin as well as in their mode of expressing grief. Also, some of their number bury their dead in Christian cemeteries, though they always conform to the Jewish ritual.

It is easy to understand the contempt which Mussulmans have for Jews, and especially for dead Jews, by remarking that in all their contemptuous and profane expressions the idea of the Jew stands out foremost. Thus the most insulting remark one Arab can make to another is to liken him to a Jew, as, "You are fit to join a tribe of Jews." "Let me become a Jew!" is a common imprecation employed to attest the truth of some affirmation. "O, the Jew!" is an exclamation often applied not only to a mean man, but to an ugly beast.

This vindictive animosity is justified in the minds of Mussulmans by the thousand and one vexations to which the Jews subjected Islamism in its cradle, and by the perfidious character which has always distinguished them in their relations with true believers. A curious expression of this popular sentiment is found in the following legend, which is still current among the Arabs:

The Jews of the present day, says this legend, are not regularly the descendants of Adam, but only a progeny sprung from a dead branch of the Adamite stock. In fact, one day, by the permission of God, a camel spoke miraculously, attesting that God alone is God and Mohammed is his prophet. The Jews stoned the beast, and then rose in arms against the prophet, who so terribly defeated them that their women alone survived, together with decrepit old men and children at the breast. This impious race appeared then on the point of being exterminated from the earth, and surely this great benefit would have come about if God had wished it. But by the permission of God, it happened thus: The women in tears came before Mohammed, lamenting the extermination of their husbands. "Go," said he, "upon the field of battle. Each one of you recognize your husband and remain at his side during the night.

God is powerful and wise." It happened thus that from dead men and living women was formed in process of time an abject and abominable race, which is none other than the actual Jews.

The marriage ceremonies observed by native Israelites are peculiar and interesting. The family of the bridegroom and that of the bride make the contract of marriage, which must be legalized by a public notary. In this contract must be written:—1. The day on which the couple will be united as husband and wife. 2. The dowry which the wife brings to her husband, and the gift, if there be any, which the husband makes to his wife. 3. The sum of money to be paid by either party that shall break the engagement. This sum is generally equal in value to eleven pounds and five shillings, English money.

A few days before the marriage, the nearest relatives of the bride dye the hair of her head black, with the gall-nut, prepared after the manner of the Arabs. This coloring must take place, even though the hair of the bride be of itself beautifully black and glossy. Then, on the following day, they lead the bride to the bath, accompanied by her female friends. There, as she sits, an old woman begins to sing her praises. The singing is usually accompanied by several Moorish instruments, played by women and blind men. They then take the bride into an inner room, where the old woman attends to her toilet according to the fashion of the country. While this operation, which lasts several hours, is going on, the other women, from time to time, repeat in a very loud singing tone the well known popular interjection of joy: ri, ri, ri.

The following day, a great dinner is given in the house of the bride, who, however, instead of joining in the festivities of the occasion, is gaudily dressed and seated upon an elevated divan to receive the felicitations of the guests. The day previous to that of the marriage, all the friends and relatives being present, the parents of the bride bring out all her clothes and jewels, and show them to two rabbis, who make a note of all the things and send them to the bridegroom. On the evening of the marriage, the bridegroom, accompanied by all his relatives and friends, goes to the house of the bride, where he finds her sitting and veiled. Once there, the bridegroom goes near her and gives her, in the presence of all his friends, the wedding ring, on which their names are marked. Immediately afterwards a rabbi gives the pair the nuptial blessing.

The religious ceremony being over, a great supper begins, which lasts generally till after eleven o'clock. A little before midnight, the bride is conducted out of her own house to that of the bridegroom. This transfer of the bride is performed through the streets, with the greatest show of lights, singing, playing upon musical instruments, dancing, and many repetitions of the syllable ri, ri, ri. Meanwhile the bridegroom waits for his bride in the first room of his own house, near the door, and as soon as she comes in, he treads on her right foot, saying to her these words, from the 3d chapter, 16th verse of Genesis: "Thy desire shall be to thy husband, and he shall rule over thee."

To conclude this chapter, which though incomplete

in regard to details,* gives some idea of an interesting branch of the human family in a strange locality, we will say a few words in regard to the prevalent means of instruction. Education, meaning the development and training of the human faculties, is scarcely known among Tunisian Jews. Instruction, which is, properly speaking, only a means of education, is but feebly sustained. The rabbis have the charge of children in halls connected with the synagogues. To learn the Hebrew text and read it, while chanting and marking the cadence with the body, and to know how to write the Arabic language with the Rabbinic-Hebrew characters, constitutes the whole programme of these Rabbinic establishments. The elements of useful knowledge receive no attention. The foreign languages, natural science, geography, history and arithmetic are ignored, though in this last named branch Jewish children scarcely need instruction; for they are *born* calculators. Yet these schools are very picturesque. Almost all are upon the ground floor, and some, especially in the old synagogues, are kept

---

* We have to omit at this point numerous details illustrative of Jewish life in Barbary. To have children is the great desire of all classes. On the island of Gerba, a wealthy Jew told me, apparently with a view of enjoying my sympathy, that though he had three wives, he had no children, and he added that he was upon the point of taking a fourth wife, with the hope of leaving some one to maintain his name and inherit his property. A poor Jew, who had already six children, repeated to me the 3d verse of the 128th Psalm, as expressive of his idea of the Lord's blessing: — "Thy wife shall be as a fruitful vine by the sides of thy house; thy children like olive-plants round about thy table."

The ceremony of loosing the shoe, as described in Deuteronomy 25th chapter, 5th and following verses, is gravely kept up, though it can now be witnessed only where the Jews are permitted, as in Tunisia, the free exercise of their civil and religious rites.

in rooms that are like cellars. They have for furniture a cupboard where master and pupils crowd confusedly together their books and papers; several willow seats; one or several small low tables, around which are, resting upon mats or badly seated upon narrow benches, a multitude of pupils who though poorly clad, are generally quick witted and intelligent. The aged master, inspiring awe by the gravity of his face, his long beard and picturesque slovenliness, is enthroned upon a stool, or oftener seated cross-legged upon a mat, with a low table before him, and his shoes or rather slippers at his side; his pupils leave their shoes at the door. He holds majestically upon his knee a large reed, which serves as his sceptre and wand of office. Nothing is more comic than the scenes enacted in the presence of this antiquated dominie. From winks and nods and diverse manifestations of attention and curiosity to expressions of astonishment, foreboding an outburst of passion, we observe anger, pride; pleasure, pain; grief, exultation; victory or defeat, successively depicted on the faces of the assembled group. No artist's pencil could adequately represent the amusing scenes occasionally witnessed in these school rooms. We are happy, however, to report that there are manifest indications of improvement in the modes of teaching and training children in these Rabbinical schools.

As to the European Jews, they provide their children, especially their boys, better means of instruction. While their daughters are still much neglected, their sons constitute three-fourths of the pupils in the Italian college, one-third in the Catholic school and the entire number in the Protestant school. It is just to remark in this place, that the European Israelites, though they by no means attain the full stature of a vigorous manhood, merit an honorable notice. As a general thing, they understand the exigencies of the times, entertaining some elevated ideas and taking part in progressive movements. It is desirable, however, that the Israelites (not to speak of the Christians) of Europe and America, who show an elevated and enlarged spirit in promoting the interest of Judaism throughout the world, and who have already founded schools and charitable establishments in the orient and in Africa, should turn their attention towards the numerous and interesting body of their co-religionists established in the regency of Tunis. There are many wants to be satisfied, much service to be rendered to humanity, and, in a word, great good to be done. The Tunisian Jews on the one hand possess good intellects and are quick to learn, and on the other they are heartily united to other Israelites, so that their more advanced brethren of Europe and America could hope gradually to regenerate them, securing for them by means of sympathy, aid and protection important intellectual, moral and material advantages which they do not yet possess, and which alone can draw them out of their semi-barbarous state and prepare them for the free air and sunlight of civilization and universal brotherhood, regardless of country, race or creed.

CHAPTER IX.

The Europeans in Tunisia.—Relative Importance of their Colonies and Influence.—Foreign Representatives at the Tunisian Court.

THE number of Europeans established in the regency of Tunis is estimated at 25,000, most of whom reside in the capital and in the maritime cities. A majority of them have taken up their abode in this country within comparatively few years. Some families, however, have resided there for several generations. The European subjects of any one nation, considered in their collective capacity, are called, without regard to propriety of language, a *colony*. Thus there are said to be several European colonies, of which the Italian colony, composed largely of Sicilians and Jews, is the most numerous. Next in numerical order is the English colony, which is composed almost exclusively of Maltese. The Maltese and Sicilians belong in general to the lower classes. The French colony is the third in point of numbers, and comprises a few Christians, many Jews and several thousand Algerine Mussulmans. The other enlightened powers have there but few subjects.

The Europeans are mostly devoted to commercial

and mechanical pursuits. It is only within a few years that a certain number of them have been engaged in what are properly termed the liberal professions. The wholesale merchants constitute the élite of the European colonies, assuming to be a kind of aristocracy. Their haughty airs and the sensitiveness of their presumed inferiors occasionally give rise to some ludicrous scenes which are amusing to impartial observers. The European society of Tunis resembles that of some dwarfed European city. Idlers and gossipers are sufficiently numerous. Ignorance and presumption go hand in hand, and jealousy and malignity combine to give them power. All this is seen with various shades of national and individual character. Intellectual and moral training is much neglected. The range of thought and of subjects for conversation is limited, and personal rivalries and contests occasionally occur. Enterprises for the common good, which are not numerous, have thus much to encounter. We must say, however, that as the relations of Tunis become intimate with Europe, the Europeans established there resume their original character, acquiring European virtues and rising above African vices. Their mental vision is enlarged and a step taken towards civilization. Unfortunately there, as everywhere else, the desire to become rich, that eternal *auri sacra fames* of the poet, seems to be the dominant passion of European society in general and of the Jewish element in particular, and its gratification is checked by no scruples about the means. We can attempt no description of this low ambition fomented by pride, excited by jealousy and encouraged by scandalous examples of success and enormity. The financial situation of the Tunisian government is most unfortunate for the country, opening an unlimited field for unprincipled adventurers and swindlers. Many of this class arrive from Europe and remain only long enough to effect their objects by the aid of confederates in the city and at the court of the Bey. This mania for making money is probably the more apparent because it is not counteracted by the refining influence of the fine arts.

France, England, Austria, Italy, Spain, Holland, Belgium, Sweden, Portugal, Denmark, Prussia, Monaco, and San Marino among the powers of Europe, and the United States among those of the New World, have there official agents clothed with the title of consuls-general or simply of consuls. Most of these officials have a diplomatic character. Direct representatives of their government to the Bey, and magistrates and judges over their respective fellow citizens, they fulfil various functions, sometimes acting the part of ministers plenipotentiary, expounding and enforcing international laws, and sometimes appearing as police officers, restraining and punishing the wayward.

The government of the Bey has no authority or control over the Europeans who reside there, enjoying the benefits of the country and often doing it much mischief without sharing the burdens of taxation that are imposed upon the natives. This altogether exceptional position or privilege, sanctioned and confirmed by the treaties of all nations, has been insisted on to obviate the insecurity to which Mussulman justice would expose Europeans, and to prevent such difficulties as would naturally result if the Europeans were subjected to Mussulman jurisdiction. But it is just to say that this privilege which, when Europeans are the objects of it, is very considerable, becomes a flagrant abuse and injustice when extended, as is notoriously the fact, to a class of persons called protegés, who, on account of some questionable service or of some judicious presents, succeed by virtue of consular omnipotence, in throwing off their allegiance to the Bey and taking shelter under a flag which is not theirs, and which protects them in violation of international law and in disregard of official honor.

From time immemorial, the consulates have enjoyed the rights of asylums or rather of *houses of refuge*; that is, when natives of the country, pursued by officers of justice, cross the threshold of a consulate, their persons become inviolable. The consul may then interpose his friendly offices, to moderate the sentence of the fugitive if he be guilty or to save him from punishment if he be innocent. In principle, this usage is not without serious objections; but as it contributes to the prestige of the Christian powers, the consuls maintain it voluntarily and for the most part content themselves with hindering or mitigating the abuses to which it can give rise. Each consulate has a kind of guard of honor composed of native janissaries, whose number varies according to the importance of the colony. These janissaries, who are inappropriately called *dragomans* (interpreters) and are substantially little more than servants, often assume an importance which is but too real in most of the affairs entrusted to them. Their intrusion gives occasion to scandalous traffics, and it is not unusual to see them in their character as subaltern tyrants affect an odious autocracy over unfortunate natives who fall in their way.

The consuls are received at the Bardo with great pomp and parade when they appear officially in uniform, and they are always in their private visits the objects of marked courtesy and attention. Theoretically, the consuls are equals in their relations to the Bey, all having the same treaty stipulations, but practically there is a great difference in their standing and influence. The consuls of France and England are, it may well be believed, received with more marked attention than their colleagues of Monaco and San Marino, though the latter are supported with high sounding titles and set off with decorations and showy uniforms. Twice a year (on the Great and the Little Bairam), the Bey has a public audience in presence of all his court, resplendent with gilt ornaments and decorations of various kinds, in the Hall of the Throne, where in a standing posture he receives all the agents of the different powers who are introduced to him now in the order of their arrival. Formerly the consuls of France and England were received before all the others. They at length, however, had a dispute in regard to who should be received first, when it was finally decided between them and afterwards between their colleagues that in future all the consuls should be received in the order of their arrival at the Bardo.

Before being introduced to His Highness, the Bey, the consuls are received in a body by the Prime Minister, who showers upon them honeyed words and with bows and smiles endeavors to put them into a good humor for the more formal reception which forthwith takes place in the large hall. This is a rare sight, resembling doubtless other analogous assemblies, but it borrows some striking peculiarities from the country and the character of the court. In proportion to the importance of their posts or their personal vanity, the consuls crowd forward, or drawing back put on an air of impassible dignity. While waiting together in full uniform set off with decorations, it is not a little interesting to observe the physiognomy of the different personages. All the attractions of ribbons, badges, gilt uniforms and a retinue of gaudily dressed attendants, assuming airs of importance and feigning gracious smiles or virgin modesty, are simply ludicrous, where underneath this covering are seen with the mind's eye personal and national vanity and corruption. The Prime Minister, General Mustapha Khasnadar, who possesses a superior physique and is an extraordinary man, entering the hall with a beaming face, salutes this assembly and then, after bandying compliments with the Catholic Bishop, goes from one consul to another, exhausting the resources of language for complimentary phrases, and displaying such charming politeness and courtesy as are not common even in European circles. In the Hall of the Throne, the ministers and principal officers of state are drawn up in a line, when as each consul enters, the Bey gravely advances some steps towards him, indicating by the number of his steps his appreciation of the consul's importance, and offers his hand which the latter takes and presses, bowing at the same time.

It is scarcely thirty years since the Beys at these receptions remained as stationary as the god Terminus, usually in a sitting posture, and instead of offering their hand open to be taken and pressed, held it up closed to be kissed on the back by all the European representatives without distinction. Some consuls protested against this custom, and Mr. Thomas D. Anderson, United States consul in 1816 and 1817, left his post rather than conform to it. After the capture of Algiers, the French government supported their consul, Mr. Schwebel, in taking decided ground against this usage. In his first audience, he took and pressed the hand which the Bey held out for him to kiss. The Bey, starting back, expressed his astonishment and displeasure. The consul replied that according to his instructions, he was to treat the Bey of Tunis just like a European prince, and that when a European prince offers his hand, it is the usage to press it, bowing. The kissing of the hand from that time ceased to be a court requisition and the consuls were thus relieved from the necessity of conforming to a custom which even an elaborate despatch now in the American consulate at Tunis, written by John Quincy Adams while secretary of state at Washington, could not invest with favor. It is reported, however, that some consuls who prized their manhood less than court favor, expressed regret at the change and privately for years afterwards observed the ancient usage.

The intrepidity and success of the Americans at Tripoli and Algiers; their appearance in the waters of Tunis; the ever-memorable expedition of Lord Exmouth; the battle of Navarino, and especially the conquest of Algiers by France, have greatly elevated the position of consuls and Europeans at Tunis. The court of the Bardo and the Tunisian people are at this time very humble in the presence of those flags, most of which they once treated with contempt. Forty years ago, the consuls were insulted in the streets with impunity. A Danish consul, though a friend of the Bey, saw his son who was then a mere lad exposed to the bestial passions of some Turkish soldiers, and the only satisfaction which he could get was the promise of the Bey that he would search for the culprits, who, as a matter of course, were never found. As to Europeans who had no official position, they had to suffer daily insults and indignities. In meeting any Mussalman of whatever grade, it was their duty to yield him the walk and salute him with a bow. The dead, far from being respected, received on their way to the grave insolent manifestations of ill-will and contempt. Funeral processions were sometimes pelted with stones and besmeared with filth. We need not say how much worse still was the condition of the Jews, even of those who were known to be Europeans. They had to submit to every insult without any show of opposition or displeasure through fear of losing their lives, with which Mussulmans did not hesitate to trifle.

But now how changed are the times! At the least insult offered to a European citizen or even to a mere protegé, the consuls require explanations and apologies from the local government, some of them showing a quarrelsome disposition by converting police difficulties into international questions. In 1859, the prefect of police and the admiral at the Goletta went in full uniform to the French consulate to apologize for some punishment imprudently inflicted on several Algerine-French subjects, and in 1865, the Prime Minister performed a like humiliating task in presence of Baron Saillard, envoy extraordinary of the emperor of the French. In 1857, when the Bey, after due process of law, took the life of a Jew, who was one of his own subjects, a terrible outcry was raised, and the French squadron of the Mediterranean appeared in the waters of Tunis, and under the influence of this demonstration, a constitution was devised for the regency and promptly accepted.

As to Christians in general, they have more the air of being masters of the country than the Mussulmans themselves. The rôles which these parties formerly played towards each other are now completely changed, and we may occasionally see the cane of a "Christian dog" laid upon the saintly back of a "Mussulman believer." Though retaliation is plainly contrary to the gospel and to Christian civilization, its existence at Tunis cannot be denied. Europeans, remembering the oppressions and wrongs which they once suffered at the hands of the Mussulmans and seeing now opportunities for revenge, yield to their passions and become in their character lik the vile Mussulman oppressors whom they affect to despise. The Jews also now raise proudly their heads and look boldly in the face their late tyrants. Sometimes they defy their power with a ludicrous and cruel affectation. Whenever there is a public demonstration of Mussulman humiliation, the Jews never fail to be present with every expression of joy. Thus when the high Tunisian functionaries had to resort to the French consulate to make humble apologies, multitudes of Jews could not forego the pleasure of witnessing the visits and manifesting their interest.

Most of the Christians residing in Tunisia belong to the Roman Catholic church, whose chief is Monseigneur Sutter, styled Bishop of Rosalia and Apostolic Vicar of the Mission of the Capucins at Tunis. This monastic order has constituted the Tunisian mission since 1624. There are twelve friars at Tunis and several at points along the shore for conducting the worship which has at Tunis a church and several chapels, and a church at each place where there is a Catholic population.*

There are in the regency twenty-five or thirty European doctors, two-thirds of whom reside at the capital. Most of them are Italians and well off in life. Some of them are scientific and skilful practitioners, and half of them are in the service of the Bey, either as surgeons of the army or as doctors of the court. There is not a single native physician of any standing, and the local medical art is scarcely

* For statistics in regard to churches, schools and masonic lodges, we refer our readers to Appendix J. In Chapter V, 298th and following pages, will be found some notices of amusements and popular life at Tunis.

represented except by a few Jewish quacks whose ignorance and pretension are their sole recommendations to favor.—The fine arts of Europe are represented there by a few barely respectable painters and photographers and by several amateur pianists and musicians, mostly Italians, whose concerts would hardly delight a refined audience; but Tunisians are not hard to please, as their ears are accustomed to the shrill discords of the Moorish bands. However, at the great balls and receptions which are given from time to time by consuls and other European personages, the music is often very respectable, and in general the dancing is very good. It is true that the pleasure of these balls consists mainly in music and dancing; the conversation amounts to little or nothing; though each of these balls excites much curiosity and is for a week beforehand a subject of animated conversation, especially among the ladies, constituting always a grave event among invited Europeans, who are all accustomed to regard themselves as belonging to the fashionable circles.

It has been remarked that balls are rarely popular where a fondness for display does not prevail. At Tunis some weakness of this kind is undeniable. Ladies are mainly concerned, not to acquire the refinement and culture most prized in the best circles of life, but to understand the arts by which they may show off their charms in the ball room, and their husbands and fathers are often greatly exercised to know how they shall pay or prevent extravagant bills. There are few cities in Europe where a certain style of extravagance is more apparent than at Tunis. Ladies, lacking the means and inducements to acquire a good education, too generally occupy themselves in adorning their persons with silks, jewelry and brilliants. In their toilette, the best taste is not displayed in the selection and arrangement of their ornaments. In their desire to shine, they too often try to imitate, equal or surpass each other without regard to condition and means.

Of all the European nations France is, beyond question, the most influential at Tunis. This is readily explained by the contiguity of Algeria and Tunisia, without speaking of the priority of influence and action which France has had in Mussulman countries since the period of the crusades. French influence is naturally counteracted, if not balanced, by British influence. For some years past, Italy and Spain have been taking an active part in Tunisian affairs. Italy possesses, in fact, important interests there, having more subjects than any other nation. Spain, since her war with Morocco, has been tormented with an ambition to regain her Castillian prestige over these shores. One curious result of this desire to acquire importance is the naturalization *en masse* of numerous Jews claiming to be of Spanish origin, but established in the regency and recognized as subjects of the Bey for a long time; and what is more remarkable still, most of them are the descendants of Jews banished from Spain in the fifteenth and sixteenth centuries. The consul of Austria enjoys much personal influence, and the nation which he represents has always been popular at Tunis, notwithstanding the collisions of the old German empire and Hungarian kings with the Ottoman sultans.

WAY OF PROMOTING CIVILIZATION.

In general, there is not remarkable harmony of action or nobility of purpose among the consuls. They are courteous in their intercourse with each other and punctiliously observe the rules of etiquette, but a resort to schemes and intrigues in the name of diplomacy too often shows their want of elevated ideas as men, and of a right appreciation of their representative and diplomatic office. In this way, the country and the world are losers; for if instead of divergent efforts for personal or partisan purposes, the consuls were unitedly to exert their energies for great objects tending to the triumph of civilization, their influence would be irresistible, and the country would be the first to be benefited. Wherever a great common good is evident, it is the duty and honor of all men who acknowledge their common parentage, laying aside narrow and personal considerations, to think only of the means of realizing it. Once let it be accomplished, and each one will perceive that his private interest is better served than if the interest of all had been sacrificed for him. In political and social science as in the ordinary discussions and conduct of life, it is only by rising above selfishness and seeking the good of all, that each member of the human family can infallibly secure the highest allotment of earth and heaven.*

* For list and notices of consuls, see Appendix O.

CHAPTER X.

General Considerations on the Present Condition of Tunisia compared with the Past, and Inferences in regard to the Future.

IN terminating these studies, so extended though still incomplete in regard to details, it may not be uninteresting to resume and put in relief some general conclusions to be drawn from the facts to which our attention has been directed. This country was predestined to enjoy a varied and remarkable history by reason of its geographical position, natural resources and salubrious climate. Under different governments and passing through various vicissitudes, it was generally flourishing and prosperous until the end of the Roman domination. Two centuries later it somewhat revived, and again, under the Arab princes of the middle age, it acquired much consideration. At the end of the fifteenth century, i. e., of the Turkish domination, decay set in and became progressive and irresistible; and it has since gone on increasing, with the exception of some brief periods of comparative prosperity, until to-day the distresses of the country seem almost to portend the approaching agony of death.

This "Africa ferax," renowned at an early period of the world for its rich and productive soil appears now pitifully exhausted and sterile, and we behold it awaiting in sadness supplies of provisions from less fertile countries which it once served from its generous and superabundant granaries, and which, were it in the hands of an intelligent and progressive people, it could again feed and supply from its luxuriant harvests. A very small part of the territory is cultivated, and no where are witnessed skill and an ambition to improve the soil. The laborers, discouraged, famishing and almost stupefied by destitution and want, scarcely find protection in the hot season from the burning sun that dries up, cracks open and calcines vast regions once covered with waving grain, fresh verdure and flourishing towns and cities; and in the wet season are much exposed to drenching rains that, once falling on beautiful plantations, fertilized the soil, which they to-day thoroughly soften and mellow, producing broad gullies which in many places are the sole passage-ways through districts at a former period provided with Roman roads. Over the whole extent of this ancient line of highways, which once formed an extensive system of circulation and a means of activity and prosperity, are now met only ruins, whose imposing grandeur is put in bold relief by the desolation of the surrounding country and by the pitiful aspect of some inhabited points, which we meet after long intervals in our journey across entire provinces devastated and laid waste. In the most important cities, wretchedness stares us in the face; parts of them are dilapidated and depopulated; houses are crumbling and falling to the ground, and everywhere are indications of negligence, poverty, suffering and incurable shiftlessness and despair.

Under the Roman empire, the population in this province was estimated at 15,000,000 souls, while at the present time it does not exceed 2,000,000. In the last years of Carthage, the little city of Leptis Parva, situated on the eastern shore, paid the metropolis an annual contribution equal to one-tenth of the actual revenue of the entire regency. This revenue to-day scarcely amounts to $5,000,000, whereas under happy auspices ten times this sum might be readily raised.

Still sky and land are unchanged. It is always the same firmament of sapphire bounded by magnificent horizons, with an imposing sea that always comes with the same cadence to caress the shores; but often touching and dashing upon ruins of ancient moles and edifices. The landscape has lost none of its grandeur and harmonious proportions; nor have the mountains, rising abruptly and standing boldly forth, refused their refreshing shades and unfailing supplies of living water. But most of these waters now flow off uselessly down precipices and ravines, while once they formed fertilizing streams, carrying the blessings of a luxuriant vegetation over a wide extent of territory. The land has not lost its productive power, but the hand of man and the plow have failed to perform their part, cultivating only here and there a meagre spot, while an immense area, dying of thirst, is spread out invitingly before laborers also dying of famine. As to the trees, if not mutilated and stript, left to themselves and exposed to the scorching rays of the sun for centuries, they decay, and falling, gradually disappear, like the men. The very forests of the north and west wither and dwindle from the exhaustion of vital force which the axe of the woodman comes no longer to renew, or from the ravages of fire sent from heaven or set by imprudent and shiftless beings who only look upon the distant scene in stupid wonder and admiration.

Thus it is not nature that is wanting to man, but man to nature. The regency of Tunis, like most Mussulman domains, is a beautiful country, deplorably peopled and encumbered by a government more deplorably administered. The inhabitants are indolent and apathetic, benumbing their intellect and beclouding their vision by laziness and inactivity, and allowing themselves to be overpowered and enervated more and more without any effort to withstand or counteract the enfeebling influence of the climate. *Withstand* or *counteract!* How could they? They are ignorant and superstitious fatalists. For centuries bound under the blows of an unfeeling destiny and a cruel despotism, they have acquired a kind of stupid resignation, submitting themselves without reserve to the will of God and *the powers that be*, without thinking that neither *the powers that be*, nor God himself could, humanly speaking, make them prosperous and happy without their own coöperation.

Of this central power, facts already stated give some idea. Arbitrary, without other thought than to persist to the end in its exhaustive system of mutilation and bleeding, and so blind in its measures of extortion, waste, injustice and tyranny as not to see that this unhappy country is reduced to extremity, and that, regardless of the interest of the government alone, some measures must be devised for ameliorating its condition and retarding if not preventing, its complete devastation and ruin.

People and government are incurable if left to themselves. To save Tunisia, to gradually raise her up from her fearful prostration and insensibly heal and regenerate her, requires time and the persistent efforts of earnest, progressive men. Two distinct plans for the accomplishment of this object have been suggested and urged by their respective advocates: political and diplomatic action on the one hand; and moral influence on the other. But in my opinion, each of these plans involves the other. Diplomacy without morality as its basis is a swindle, and a morality that does not reach and regulate diplomacy needs another name.

At this time, the different civilized powers compete with each other for influence, and draw in different ways the government which, despite its understanding of the needs of the country, perceives that the rivalry of the nations that desire to take its place or control its counsels, can only prolong its existence and adjourn its fall. Nay, more, it perceives that the personal interest or vanity of European agents tends to the same end as national rivalry; and thus it encourages this personal weakness and turns it to its account. To some consuls it pays exorbitant interest without always advancing the principal when it is due; upon others, it showers decorations and honorary titles, worth what they cost the recipients, provided, however, manhood and independence are not bartered away; and still others it benefits *sub rosa*, by giving to their agents *fat* contracts for some governmental supply or enterprise. We mean merely to indicate the kind of difficulties that stand in the way of reform and improvement in this country. They are local and foreign, moral and material, religious and secular, personal and official. If the Bey were to be asked by the consuls collectively or individually, in their official or in their private capacity to reform his system of administration, we can readily imagine his reflections if not his words. As he thought of national jealousy, diplomatic (?) intrigues, and greed, vanity and obsequiousness manifested by foreign nations and their agents, he would be tempted to call out, "physician, heal thyself." But however great these weaknesses may be and however formidable the difficulties, we will not fail to recommend a higher plane of action and more elevated considerations.

Instead of rivalry and selfishness, let there be union from a community of interest among the great progressive powers of the world. Let those who have the honor to represent civilization in this sombre, though still renowned and important quarter of the globe, be faithful to their mission, demonstrating publicly and privately the manhood and character that constitute national strength and glory. Let them with civilization in view unite on a plan of action that shall not involve a direct intermeddling with the local government. Instead of seeking the aggrandizement of this or that nation, or personal interest, let civilization be the watchword attended by justice, humanity and universal progress. Let diplomacy, instead of being degraded by the tricks and evasions of charlatans, be elevated to the dignity of a profession, with honesty and fair dealing as its basis and the public good as its object. In this way, the consuls would become, instead of supple tools or tricky partisans blinded and blown about by wind and wave, the dignified and honored agents of civilization and the promoters of humanity and universal progress. Instead of being members of this or that clique and protectors of adventurous speculators and hucksters, they would take a higher position and have a wider sphere of influence and better associations, becoming protectors of men and promoters of justice and truth. In this way alone, we believe, they can become the respected and trusted counsellors of the Bey and his court, restraining by their presence injustice, violence and wrong, and encouraging every good tendency and worthy aspiration. With such an appreciation of their office and of their moral and diplomatic powers, they would diffuse light and knowledge without resorting to threats or calling for the display of material force. Such representatives, counselled and sustained by their respective cabinets, would prove efficient monitors to the government which would speedily understand that shameful abuses lead to the inevitable destruction of the country, and finally to foreign intervention as a natural consequence of insufferable troubles; as when a house is on fire, all rush thither regardless of law, to extinguish the flames, or save and plunder from the exposed premises.

I once heard an intelligent Mussulman remark that "foreign nations and their representatives look upon Tunis much as birds of prey are wont to turn towards some inviting repast; the former having no settled policy but to keep each other away, and the latter guided mainly by personal interest or vanity." If this statement, which I did not attempt to refute, be correct, there is not much encouragement for the Bey to undertake reforms, though he is a man of kindly nature and generous sentiments. He can do little more than employ king-birds and kites to watch the persistent eagle, and amuse and satisfy the foxes and wolves as best he can. Who can blame him for some folly in such a plight? I cannot. His course is without dignity, but he is terribly beset. The eagle's claws are upon him, and the lion's growl is within hearing, and the offspring of both bird and beast constantly prey upon his life. If with such teachings and experience, the Bey did not show decidedly predatory instincts, it would seem to me astonishing.

I am persuaded that if the members of the Tunisian government were practically assured that the interest and policy of the great powers were not to dispute with each other for the possession or profits of their country, but by coöperation to elevate it and bring it up by degrees to a level with the nations that have a right to live because they labor, prosper and progress; if they could know that the representatives of the great powers, instead of entertaining rival personal and national schemes, were bound to act together for the promotion of civilization and humanity, they would begin to reflect, and soon this oligarchy with the rapacious claws of despotism would falter, review its course, face about and march onward in the line of progress; or, too weak to take this decisive step, would yield its place to braver and more worthy men.

I am persuaded that if the great powers of the world seriously wished to ameliorate the situation of this country, they could and would succeed. Acting harmoniously, their counsel in favor of all practical and practicable reforms would come with authority. No hybrid constitution and no awkward imitation of the institutions belonging to countries far advanced in the career of progress would need to be suddenly imposed upon Tunisia while she is in her present state. To prepare the way for progress, pressing evils should be promptly removed or diminished, and in proportion as they disappear, effective measures should be introduced to secure the good results in view. And here we especially recommend the saying of the great Sully, while minister of Henry IV, that "agriculture and pasturage are the two teats of the state." These almost exhausted sources of the material life of this nation should be opened anew. Agriculture should be encouraged by restraining the violence and injustice of taxgatherers, and the cultivators of the soil should become attached to their grounds by enjoying the fruits of their labors. They

would soon redouble their efforts, exhibit more skill
and intelligence in their modes of tillage and culture,
and bring back life and verdure to a vast region
whose fertility is not exhausted but only temporarily
suspended for the want of the nurturing hand of
man. Improvement in the breeds of horses, sheep
and cattle would follow as one of the many benefits
resulting from the revival or rather resurrection of
agriculture. The production of articles of every sort
needful for man would follow in the order of their
importance. Many foreign products would be introduced and acclimated; for we believe the climate
and soil are admirably adapted to the various productions of the two hemispheres on a grand scale. Commerce would gradually revive; the country would
regain some of its strength; and then we might
begin to think of more resolutely pursuing measures
for its cure and for the definite recovery of its energies. We could also extend the means of moral and
intellectual culture through schools, benevolent institutions, journals, books and countless other contrivances readily suggested; and thus light and hope
would be gradually diffused and the influences of
genuine civilization would come to bear sway where
now mere dead dogmas and stupid formularies are
pertinaciously held in the name of Moses, Christ
and Mohammed.

But suppose the natives should resist this transformation, and the actual system of government and
administration be found with its roots in the very
entrails of the country afflicted with the incurable
malady of races and peoples composed of such incon-

gruous and discordant elements that nothing could save them; still there would always remain to the civilized powers of the world the honor of having attempted to fertilize by their influence and benevolent action the ancient germs of material and moral prosperity of this land, better consecrated by the blood, virtues and immaculate glory of the primitive church, than even by the grandeur of Carthage and the domination of Rome.

The time will perhaps come when on the very site of the city of Dido, commanding the two basins of the Mediterranean, whose point of union it will constitute better even than in ancient times, will arise a new city, inheriting the prestige of the ancient metropolis and balancing the past with the future; a city having commerce, industry, activity and intelligence, and worthy to be ranked among the the capitals of universal civilization, and to be accounted in history as one of the milestones on the great highway of the human race.*

* See in Appendix P inferences in regard to the political future of the country.

APPENDIX.

(A.) *Extracts from a Journal at Tunis.*

SEPTEMBER 14, 1814.—This morning Mr. Oglander, the British consul, and Mr. Sielvos, the French chargé d'affaires, went to the palace at Bardo; the former to protect Captain Ferraro under English colors, and the latter to protect Mr. Ré, a French merchant. The said captain and merchant had a quarrel the day before with certain Jews, who complained to the Bey for having been beaten by the captain and Mr. Ré. A mameluke was immediately sent by the Bey to bring them both to the Bardo; and on all the parties being before the Bey and the two consuls being present, the Bey ordered Captain Ferraro and Mr. Ré in prison and to leave the country in three days, without the said two consuls being able to do anything in their behalf, or countermanding such an order of the Bey!

SEPTEMBER 15.—This being the last evening of Ramadan, the Bey who was surrounded, as is the custom, by all the great men of his court, ordered the signal gun to be fired after sunset for the beginning of the Byram. Coffee then was handed him by a slave. Having taken a sip, he dropped the cup from his hand, fell back and instantly expired without the least apparent struggle; medical aid was immediately administered, but in vain. It was thought at first, that he had been poisoned, but this suspicion was proved to be unfounded by the testimony of his physician, Doctor Gay, who declared that he died of an apoplectic fit.*

Soon after the death of Hamouda Bashaw, his brother Ottoman was called and seated on the throne by all the great men who were present and was saluted as Bashaw Bey of Tunis on that same evening.

SEPTEMBER 16.—Being the Little Byram's day, no visit of the consuls at Bardo, nor the divan or great men of the court, no colors on the consular houses hoisted. This afternoon the body of Hamouda Bashaw Bey was interred in the family tomb at Tunis; after which all the forts fired a salute and displayed their colors, and so did all the consuls.

SEPTEMBER 17.—This morning, all the great men, the divan and the Christian consuls paid their respects to the new Bey, Sidi Ottoman Bashaw

---

* But he was probably poisoned by his Christian secretary, Mariano Stinca. — W. P. C.

Bey, as well as to his eldest son Sidi Salah Bey, the prince hereditary; and everything has passed these three days without the least commotion.

This morning arrived 17 Christian slaves from Bizerta, sent in there by two cruisers of the regency. These unfortunate men are the crews of two fisher boats under Tuscan colors, captured on the coast of Tuscany.

A messenger has been despatched to Algiers announcing the death of Hamouda Bashaw, and the accession to the throne of Ottoman Bashaw, &c.

OCTOBER 7.—A Tunisian cruiser, a Xebeque, arrived, bringing a cutter prize under Roman colors, with eight Christian slaves.

DECEMBER 20.—This evening at about 9 o'clock, broke out a revolution at Bardo against the reigning Bey Sidi Ottoman; Sidi Mahmoud Bey together with his two sons, Hassan and Mustapha and a strong party, assailed Sidi Ottoman in his bed-room, put him to death, and his two sons Salah and Ali escaped from the terrace and throw themselves from the walls of Bardo and came to Tunis, where, finding the gates shut and no party on their side, they ran away to the marine, and there took a boat and sailed to the Goletta the same night. Mariano Stinca the Christian secretary was cut to pieces by order of the new Bey, and at the instigation of the sapatapa, as well as a physician renegade called Mahomet, who was accused of having poisoned the late Bey, Hamouda Bashaw. In this revolution, and during the night, about 20 persons lost their lives.

DECEMBER 21.—This morning at about 9 o'clock Sidi Mahmoud was proclaimed Bey of Tunis through all the streets of the town; the fortresses fired, and the consular houses hoisted their colors, and everything was passed with the utmost tranquillity. The two sons of the reigning Bey, Sidi Hassan and Mustapha, went to the Goletta this morning with a numerous cavalry to overtake the two fugitive princes Salah and Ali; and the latter were beheaded, and their corpses brought to and exposed on the square of El Gaspa all the day, and in the night were buried with their father Ottoman Bey.

DECEMBER 22.—All the consuls assembled and went to Bardo to pay their respects to the new Bey. Mr. Noah declined going, as he was not presented yet.

DECEMBER 27.—To-day the Bey sent his band of musicians to all the consular houses, congratulating them on his accession to the throne by playing their music for about an hour, and after receiving their regalia of 22 maboobs or 99 piastres, they went away. Afterwards the musicians of the divan came to make the same compliment, and they received 25 piastres; also the bawebs, or doorkeepers of the palace, and they received 36 piastres.

DECEMBER 28.—Mr. Noah was at Bardo this morning with Mr. Coxe, and delivered his consular presents to the Bey, the first minister, and to his brother Sidi Ismail Bey, and the two sons of the Bey, Sidi Hassan and Sidi Mustapha; who have all been well satisfied. On the 29th, Mr. Noah paid his visit to the caya, or minister of marine, and delivered his present.

DECEMBER 30.—The Bey set at liberty 32 Neapolitan slaves, as an acknowledgment of their having taken up arms on the night of the revolution in his defence, having previously promised them their liberty should he succeed in getting on the throne.

(B.) *Letters sent on the Visit of the Tunisian Embassy to the United States in 1865.*

Praise to the only God: To the excellency of him who has given distinction to the ministry, who has at the same time ordered and directed its affairs; to the excellency of him who is the glory of eminent ministers; whose renown is universal, and whose character and services are above all praise—Monsieur William H. Seward, minister of state and of foreign affairs of the United States of America: may he always be the head of the ministry and the director of eminent men. Rendering due honor to the distinguished office and to the high character of your excellency, we make known to you that his Highness, our august sovereign, ceases not to entertain for your government an abiding and ever-increasing friendship and regard, the cause of which is, your admirable conduct and your noble policy. His Highness has received the news of the re-establishment of peace and tranquillity in your great country. This news has afforded him unmeasured satisfaction; and sincere friendship makes him share with you the pleasure consequent upon this happy result and great event.

To this end, then, his Highness sends to your government the honorable, the beloved, the elect General Otman Hashem, to express to the President his sincere felicitations, and also to express to the President the heartfelt grief which his Highness experienced at the death of the lamented President, Abraham Lincoln, which sad event wounded all our hearts. We pray God that this may be the end of trials and misfortunes to your beloved country. His Highness also sends with his ambassador his portrait, to serve as a souvenir of his friendship, as stated in his letter.

His Highness looks with confidence to your excellency to arrange for an agreeable reception of his envoy, General Hashem, before His Excellency, the President.

We take this occasion also to inform your excellency that we have found in the conduct of the distinguished among his colleagues, Mr. Amos Perry, consul-general of your government at this court, the best disposition to maintain and strengthen the bonds of friendship which unite our two governments. His (Mr. Perry's) courteous and honorable bearing merits and receives the approbation and the best acknowledgments of his Highness, our august sovereign. We make this statement to bear our testimony in favor of a worthy representative and to show that your choice falls only upon meritorious persons.

May God perpetuate the happiness of your excellency.

Written by the poor before his God.

(Signed), MUSTAPHA,
Major General, Prime Minister and Minister of Foreign Affairs.

TUNIS, the 7th Rabi-el-Tani, 1282 (A. D. Aug. 29, 1865.)

Praise to the only God: To the excellency of the eminent personage whose merits are celebrated and whose renown is universal like the light of the sun which cannot be hidden from the day; to the excellency of him who is the glory of great men—the cream of men of distinction—and whose virtues are above all praise, to our friend Andrew Johnson, President of the United States of America; may he always be exalted, and may his days be ever prospered.

Having rendered due honor to the elevated rank and to the eminent character of your excellency, we inform you that we have heard the agreeable news of the fruitful victory gained by your government, and of the consequent re-establishment of peace and tranquillity in your great country. This news has rejoiced us beyond measure, and has awakened our warmest sentiments of gratitude by reason of the great and sincere friendship which unites our two governments—which friendship has been bequeathed to us as a heritage by our ancestors to become stronger and stronger forever.

We were the more cheered by this news from having shared in the grief of the American people in the loss which they experienced in the death of their late President, Abraham Lincoln, a loss which we keenly felt. This grief would have remained unalterably fixed in our hearts but for the news of the re-establishment of tranquillity in your country, which news comes to moderate and assuage our affliction.

We desire to present to your excellency and to your people our compliments, with expressions of condolence in your affliction and sorrow, and with expressions of felicitation in your prosperity and joy. We despatch our envoy, the honorable, the beloved, the elect, General Otman Hashem to be the interpreter of our sentiments in the presence of your excellency and in your country. We send at the same time with him our portrait as a souvenir of our friendship. May God preserve your excellency and perpetuate your happiness and the prosperity of your illustrious nation.

Written by him who has for your excellency the highest consideration, the servant of God, the Mooshir Mohammed Essadak, Bashaw Bey, Possessor of the Kingdom of Tunis. The 7th Rabi-el-Tani, 1282. (A. D. Aug. 29, 1865.)

[L. S.]

GENERAL HASHEM, referred to in the letters above, died of typhoid fever at Tunis about the close of 1867, much respected and lamented by a numerous circle of friends. He gained much credit in this country for his dignified manners and for the tact and good sense shown in the conduct of his mission. A shrewd observer, he carried home many lessons which he learned in his American tour, and he availed himself of every occasion to communicate his views to his sovereign and to his fellow-subjects. Indeed, so strong were his impressions and expressions in favor of our country, that he was familiarly designated by the Bey and his Prime Minister as *the American*.

Though a warrior by profession, he was in character a peace-loving, pious man, preferring to pass his time repeating prayers to enforcing discipline in military camps. Being a sincere Mussulman, he scrupulously avoided any act that might seem to compromise his religious profession. He refused to accept beautiful bronze bas-reliefs of President Lincoln and General Grant, tendered to him by Governor James Y. Smith of Providence, on the ground that such images were contrary to his ideas, though the Bey and his Prime Minister had no scruples on that point. On entering the chapel of Brown University, and the library of Harvard, he shrank for a moment at the sight of busts and bas-reliefs, lest he might be entering some idolatrous place.

Though in general disposed to place unbounded confidence in the late Consul at Tunis, who accompanied him to this country, and in the honored head of the Department of State at Washington, his suspicions and fears were once thoroughly roused. He passed one Saturday evening with Mr. Seward, and while delightfully entertained by that genial and accomplished man, he showed himself very complacent and deferential. Just before the General's withdrawal, Mr. Seward said: "General, I don't know how you are in the habit of spending your Sundays; but if for curiosity or any other reason you would like to see the inside of a church, I should be happy to furnish you a seat with me to-morrow in St. John's Church." *Katahayric*—thank your Excellency—was the curt response, after which scarcely a word was uttered till the party reached their rooms in Willard's Hotel, when the General, calling his interpreter, with an air of dignity and decision, said: "Mr. Consul, you have always praised your minister, and I am willing to follow his counsel in all but one respect. But as for joining his church, I tell you nay, nay!" During this address, the General placed his right hand on the Consul's shoulder, and looking him sharply in the face, assumed a manner that bespoke excitement and indignation. The reply was a burst of laughter and an assurance that Mr. Seward was trying, not to make a proselyte of him, but to show him a courtesy.

On another occasion, the General's servant, Mustapha, giving much trouble and annoyance and rousing the indignation of the party, was brought before the General to be reprimanded, if not annihilated by one burst of wrath. The party waited in silence, expecting an explosion. The General's face was as dark as a thunder-cloud. But the only words that escaped his lips were, in subdued tones: "I am too angry to speak to him."

In examining our ships of war and firearms, the General showed a lively interest and a thorough appreciation of our workmanship and skill, sometimes expressing emotions of wonder and admiration. When he saw our public schools and other institutions for the promotion of popular education, he exclaimed: "These show how you got your guns and ships of war from the brain. These beat all. Don't expect me hereafter to express astonishment at any thing I may see; I shall not do it."

It is a Moslem article of faith that infidels must be a godless people. General Hashem in common with his co-religionists entertained this sentiment, which was, however, seriously shaken while visiting the charitable institutions of our country. After spending a day on the islands below New York, witnessing the provisions for the relief of suffering and for the well-being of all classes, he seemed deeply moved and among other things said with marked gravity: "A people that are so charitable must enjoy the special favor of God."

(C.) *Ali Ben Radam, a Bedouin Sheik and Leader of the Rebellion of* 1864.

Born among the mountains of the interior of the regency, Ali Ben Radam came to the capital in his younger days, and had for some time a subordinate governmental post. He was of a restless nature, and made many acquaintances and friends as a pious devotee. He also acquired some reputation for his expositions of the Koran. On returning to the interior of the country, he became the sheik of a powerful tribe of Bedouins. There he assumed sanctimonious airs, and professed to have prophetic visions. By ingenious interpretations, the Koran was made to foretell the downfall of the Houssenite (reigning) family at the end of the year of the hegira 1280, (A. D., June, 1864); and the visions of the saints further pointed out Ali as the instrument who was to bring about this event. Ali's acquaintance at the capital, his saintly bearing and indomitable energy acquired for him a commanding influence. He seemed fitted by nature and education for a revolutionist. He complained of excessive taxation and insinuated that the Bey favored infidels (Christians) to the dishonor of the saints. In the course of time, much zeal was enkindled in the breasts of fanatical Mussulmans to witness the fulfilment of the prophecies and interpretations with which they had become familiar.

In the spring of 1864, many restless tribes, imbued with Ali's spirit, yielded to his sway. Persuaded that the Koran predicted great events on that year, they naturally wished to witness the verification of the holy book. Enlisting under Ali, they seemed to imagine themselves acting in accordance with the divine commands. He assumed the leadership of the confederated rebels with the confidence and composure of a man born to rule. His reputation was a tower of strength to his party. Visions of aggrandizement and Moslem glory were repeated with effect.

But the new government was doomed to disappointment and trouble. A squad of hot-headed rebels, impatient of restraint, rushed to action without waiting the word of command and committed murders and robberies of a revolting nature. The flocks and herds of the loyal tribes were seized as a means of warfare, and the capital of the regency was threatened with pillage.

To this course of procedure Ali did not lend his sanction. He protested against these robberies and murders, and was evidently chagrined that his troops did not await his orders and conform to his instructions. The manifestations of his displeasure produced misunderstanding and coolness between him and his subordinates. And finally, he became so disgusted with the lawlessness of his partisans, that he withdrew from them, and came and presented himself, an humble suppliant for mercy, before the Bey. There is no reason to question the sincerity of his motives in taking this step. Robbery and murder he abhorred, and he demonstrated this truth when he appeared at the Bardo. The Bey received him cordially and pardoned him, and, in the hope of securing his services to promote loyalty and good order, loaded him with presents and sent him back to the rebellious tribes. But on his arrival in rebeldom a new difficulty appeared. Ali soon perceived that he could not serve the Bey and the rebels at the same time. The latter had acquired a firm faith in the oft-repeated prophecies and visions of Ali and other saints, and determined that he should either aid in their fulfilment or die at their hands. Ali, not wishing to die thus and then, put himself again at the head of the rebels, turning to their advantage all the knowledge he had acquired on his recent visit at the capital. The war was waged anew; some battles were fought with lead and gold; the rebels, who were not bribed, were routed, and the confederate dynasty ceased in the summer of 1864.

Ali then escaped into the neighboring province of Algeria. There the tribes, being under the rule of the French, could afford him but little aid. His movements were constrained, and in the autumn of 1865, he again entered the Tunisian dominions, where, however, the tribes having been sufficiently entertained with ingenious expositions of the Koran, and with prophecies and visions of Moslem aggrandizement, refused to join any further schemes of his device. In fine, he was taken a prisoner to the Bardo and walled into a dungeon where he died about two years afterwards, despite the earnest efforts of his friends to send him on a pilgrimage to Mecca.

In the summer of 1867, the youngest brother of the Bey rose in rebellion. He, too, was speedily taken prisoner, and ended his life in like manner within less than a year from the time of his incarceration.

(D.) *Chronological List of the Deys of Tunis.*

1, Ibrahim, 1590; 2, Mousa, 1592; 3, Kara Otman, 1593; 4, Yousef, 1610; 5, Ousta Mora, 1637; 6, Ahmed Kodja, 1640; 7, Hadj Mohammed Laz, 1647; 8, Hadj Mustapha Laz, 1653; 9, Hadj Mustapha Karakuz, 1665; 10, Hadj Mohammed Ogli, 1667; 11, Hadj Shaban Kodja, 1669; 12, Hadj Mohammed Menteshali, 1672; 13, Hadj Ali Laz, 1673; 14, Hadj Mohammed Gemal, 1673; 15, Hadj Mohammed Bishara, 1676; 16, Hadj Mohammed Gemal, 1677; 17, Wazoun Ahmed, 1677; 18, Mohammed Taba, 1677; 19, Ahmed Shelebi, 1682; 20, Hadj Bactash Kodja, 1686; 21, Ali el-Rais, 1688; 22, Ibrahim Kodja, 1694; 23, Mohammed Kodja I, 1694; 24, Mohammed Tabar, 1694; 25, Yakoub, 1695; 26, Mohammed II, 1695; 27, Dali Mohammed, 1699; 28, Kawadj Mohammed, 1701; 29, Kara Mustapha, 1702; 30, Ibrahim el-Scherif, Dey and Bey, 1702.

Chronological List of the Beys of the Reigning Family.

1, Houssein Bey, 1705; 2, Ali Bashaw, 1735; 3, Mohammed Bey, 1756; 4, Ali Boy, 1759; 5, Hamouda Bashaw, 1782; 6, Otman Bey, 1814; 7, Mahmoud Bey, 1814; 8, Houssein Bey, 1824; 9, Mustapha Bey, 1835; 10, Ahmed Bey, 1837; 11, Mohammed Bey, 1855; 12, Mohammed Essadak Bey, 1859; Ali, Bey of the Camp and heir to the throne.

(E.) *Baba Ali, a Captain, Pirate and Dragoman.*

UNITED STATES CONSULATE, TUNIS, April 11, 1863.[*]

This photograph will introduce to you Baba (i. e., Father) Ali, familiarly so called, though his full name is Ali Ben Abdallah, the patriarch of Tunisian dragomans, whose life and exploits are set forth in Dr. Davis's "Carthage and Her Remains."

Baba Ali has been head-drgoman in the American Consulate for about forty years, and is now, according to the calculation of those best able to judge, nearly ninety years old. With health unimpaired, a piercing eye, a well-proportioned, sinewy frame, a commanding voice, a firm step, and his dignity braced by an American sword and a good supply of American military buttons, you may imagine Baba Ali, a very consequential personage; and so he is in his own estimation. Assuming a grave and sanctimonious air, and rising to his full height, he frequently tries to impress those around him with an idea of his importance by exclaiming in Italian, "I have been a general of the camp."

Prompt at his post, he guards the door of the consulate from morning till night, unless called upon to march in front of the consul or his family, which office he delights to perform, showing off his magisterial and military airs to the dismay, amusement or inconvenience of men and beasts. "Baalek, baalek, guarda, guarda," he calls out, making a singular mixture of Arabic and Italian, as he warns with his voice and his baton men, dogs and donkeys to clear the way.

From his relations to Tunisian piracy and slavery, the history of Baba Ali becomes interesting. Born on the island of San Pietro, near the

[*] Copy of a letter addressed to the Librarian of the Rhode Island Historical Society, accompanied with a photograph of the veteran dragoman.

CAPTIVE AND CORSAIR.—NEW ENGLAND. 537

southwest coast of Sardinia and early instructed in the doctrines of the Christian church, he was taken a captive when a young man and brought to Tunis, where he was sentenced, like thousands of Christian captives of his time, either to abjure his faith or become a slave. He chose the former course, and was circumcised and designated by another name, according to Moslem custom.

Piracy was at that time one of the most important branches of business in Tunis, and afforded scope for the genius and enterprise of this Moslem convert. In a few years his new name became, according to his own account, a terror in the Mediterranean. As commander of a piratic squadron, he attacked, plundered and destroyed by sea and by land. When this career was finally checked in 1816, by European and American squadrons, our Mohammedan convert went upon shore and was soon clothed with honors and responsibilities in the army. In the course of time, however, our hero, or rather apostate, was compelled by the force of circumstances to lay aside these honors and assume the humbler, though still honorable post of janissary. In this post, however, Baba Ali contrived to gain great credit, not only for energy and efficiency, but withal for sanctity.

Though his physical powers continue sound, his mind is far gone. While imagining himself a General of the Camp, he is often overcome by his propensity to steal, though he has no tact at concealing the articles he takes. But he is believed to be just as much of a saint as ever, praying lustily in the hall of the consulate at the canonical hours.

My Moorish cook Mohammed, who is also described in Dr. Davis's book, is a special object of the old dragoman's care. Mohammed having been to Paris and London and knowing that the English language is spoken at the latter place, asked me the other day very innocently if America was in London. For the quietness of this house, I am obliged to conceal from Baba Ali such heterodoxy as this question implies. A nation that has the tallest mast, the largest flag, and the oldest and best known dragoman must be the greatest nation in the world. This is Baba Ali's creed. The other day, hearing a great noise in the outer hall, I called my Jewish broker for an explanation. His reply was, "Baba Ali is praying."

Mr. Ambrose Allegro, who is nearly of Baba Ali's age, and who entered the American consulate as secretary and interpreter at its establishment under General Eaton in 1799, informs me that Baba Ali has a brother still living who has maintained the religion of his fathers, though at the expense of his liberty, many years at Tunis.

NOTE.—Baba Ali departed this life in November, 1865.

CORSAIRS AGAINST THE NEW ENGLAND COLONIES.—Since concluding the body of this work, Zachariah Allen, LL. D., has called my attention to an important fact showing that remote New England early experienced the effects of Barbary piracy. Morton in his history says that the first cargo from the Plymouth colony, composed mostly of beaver skins, was captured, together with the crew, and sold on the coast of Morocco. William Harris, one of the companions of Roger Williams in Rhode Island, was also captured near the British coast and enslaved at Algiers. The facts in this case are given in Arnold's History of Rhode Island, vol. 1, p. 437. Before our country adopted as a motto: "Millions for defence; not a cent for tribute," we repeatedly paid tribute to Barbary princes. We did not carry into effect the above motto till many years after our gallant war with Tripoli, begun in 1801.

(F.) *Letter on Tunisian Slavery.*

A letter on Tunisian Slavery by General Heussein, addressed to me in November, 1864, may be found in the third volume Diplomatic Correspondence, 1865. It explains the nature of Mohammedan slavery and the motives that led to its abolition. It was written by a Mussulman who loathes slavery, and it contains a touching appeal for the emancipation of the blacks of our country. Liberal minded Mussulmans take decided ground against slavery, attributing to it many of the ills that afflict oriental countries. General Kheredine, also one of the most enlightened men in the regency, has written and spoken in the same strain with General Heussein. They are radicals and progressives, favoring such measures as are calculated to elevate and improve the masses. Want of space is our only excuse for not inserting extracts from the writings of both of these gentlemen.

(G.) *A Strange Animal.*

During my residence in Tunis, I received two letters from gentlemen interested in natural history, containing the following extract from "Shaw's Travels and Observations in Barbary," and requesting information in regard to the accuracy of the statement:

"To the mule, we may join the kumrah, as I think these people call a little serviceable beast of burthen begot betwixt an ass and a cow. That which I saw was single-hoofed like the ass, but distinguished from it in all other respects, having a sleek skin, and the tail and head (except the horns) in fashion of the dam."

In reply, I have to state that I met at Tunis but two persons who had ever actually *seen* the kind of monstrosity referred to above. One of these was my trustworthy servant, Mohammed Bograda, who was born far south in the mountainous part of the regency. He confirms the statement of Mr. Shaw, with one important exception. He says the beast in question is not *serviceable* or useful in any way. On the contrary, when it accidentally and unluckily (as the Bedouins think) appears among the herds, it is regarded with decided disfavor on account of its inveterate propensity to steal milk from milch animals, including sheep, goats, cows, assos and camels. It is now called among the Bedonins the *rawn*, instead of the *kumroh*. Though not in general malicious, it has the habit of striking with its head, or butting every one that approaches it.

(H.) *Measures, Weights and Coins.*

The oil measure is called by the Moors a *metar*, and by the Europeans a *metal*. The metal of Susa contains 24 French litres (large quarts), and that of Tunis one-fifth less. The metal is divided into 2 *kollas*, into 16 *saas*, and into 64 *rebaias*.

The grain measures is the cafis, which contains 533 French litres, and is divided into 16 *weebs*, and each weeb into 12 *saas*, familiarly called *measures*. The *weeb* is then a little more than an English bushel.

The unity of weight is the *artal* or pound, which is of three kinds: the pound *aatari* contains 16 ounces, and is used for weighing groceries; the pound *soukhi* contains 18 ounces, and is used for weighing oil, vegetables and fruit for the table; and the pound *kadari* contains 20 ounces, and is used for weighing all vegetables and coarse articles sold by the quantity. 100 pounds make a *goutar*, or quintal, called an *aatari*, *soukhi*, or *kadari* quintal, according to the kind of pounds of which it is composed. An *aatari* pound is equivalent to a pound avoirdupois. To weigh precious objects, such as jewels, pearls and essences, grains and carats are employed.

The unity of long measure is the *draa*, or cubit, which is of three kinds: The Arab draa is equivalent to .484—the Turkish to .637 and the Andalusian to .667 of a French metre, which contains 39 and 37-100ths English inches.

The Arab draa is used to indicate the dimensions of buildings. The term *mile* is in general use to indicate distances. The Arab mile consists of 3,000 *draas*, and is about the same as the Roman mile, which is composed of 1,614 English yards. In journeying, the distance of a place is generally indicated by the number of hours or days required to reach it.

The monetary unit is the piastre. Though its intrinsic value was formerly only 12 cents, its current value often reached 18 and 20 cents. The money of the country was re-coined a few years since, and the piastre generally passes at a discount.

The piastre is divided into 16 carroubs, and to indicate the fraction of a piastre, the number of caroubs is ordinarily stated.

(I.) *John Howard Payne.*

The information on which the foregoing statement is based was elicited under instructions from the Department of State to use my "best endeavors to trace the papers in question and restore them, if possible, to the relatives of the deceased." Some curious little pictures and private papers, taken to America under pretext of being delivered to the niece of Mr.

Payne, the wife of Rev. Lea Luquer, never reached their destination, having been sold without any consultation with Mrs. Luquer. An album of autographs and of short original pieces in the handwriting of distinguished American and European contemporary authors, was taken from Mr. Payne's effects after his death and subsequently offered for sale in New York city for $700. Two volumes of manuscript intended for publication and containing an extended historical notice of Tunis and of Barbary piracy and slavery, were taken away without any satisfactory explanation and are not yet accounted for. Yet the appraisers of Mr. Payne's effects, and the gentleman who completed the settlement of his estate, testify that nothing of this kind was ever appraised or to their knowledge sold for the benefit of his creditors.

As I have seen "Sweet Home" accredited in an English book to Barry Cornwall, I give the following statement from John Miller, who was forty-six years United States despatch agent at London:

"SIR:—I first published 'Sweet Home' as an interlude in a play entitled 'Clari,' the title page of which is as follows: 'Clari, an Opera in three acts, as first performed at the Theatre Royal, Covent Garden, on Thursday, May 8, 1823. By John Howard Payne, Esq. The overture and music (with the exception of the national airs) by Henry R. Bishop, Esquire. London: John Miller, 69 Fleet street, 1826. (Price two shillings and sixpence.)' I gave Mr. Payne, who was introduced to me by Washington Irving, £50 for the copy-right, and he was to revise the proof.

(Signed), JOHN MILLER.

"*London, Office of the U. S. Despatch Agency, Sept. 19, 1865.*"

EPITAPH.

[U. S. seal.]

IN MEMORY OF

COL. JOHN HOWARD PAYNE,

Twice Consul of the United States of America for the Kingdom of Tunis,
this stone is here placed by a grateful country.

He died at the American Consulate in this city after a tedious
illness, April 1st, 1852.

He was born at the city of Boston, State of Massachusetts, June 8, 1792.

His fame as a Poet and Dramatist
is well known wherever the English language is spoken through his celebrated ballad "Sweet Home," and his popular tragedy
of "Brutus," and other similar
productions.

The monument is an oblong, thick slab of white (Italian) marble lying over the grave, and each edge of the slab is inscribed with a line of poetry, thus:

"Sure when thy gentle spirit fled
To realms beyond the azure dome,
With arms outstretched God's angels said—
Welcome to Heaven's Home, Sweet Home."

(J.) *Ecclesiastical, Educational and Masonic Statistics.*

I am indebted to Father Anselme, who has served for twenty-five years in the Catholic church, most of the time as chancellor to the Bishop, for some valuable statistics connected with the Catholic missionary work in the regency. The number of actual communicants residing in Tunis is represented to be 11,500. There were from 1756 to 1799 (43 years), 201 marriages, 785 baptisms and 993 deaths. From 1833 to 1867 (34 years), there were 6,827 baptisms, 1,390 marriages and 4,136 deaths. The statistics of 1833, as contrasted with those of 1866, show a decided gain by the Europeans, viz.: In 1833, there were 92 baptisms, 18 marriages and 39 deaths; in 1866, 312 baptisms, 63 marriages and 195 deaths. The records of the church were destroyed by the Algerines in 1755, and during the rage of the cholera, in 1832, the records were neglected.

The number of children admitted to the Brothers' School, in 1866, was 346, of which 142 were Maltese, 28 Tunisian Jews, 27 French, 8 Germans, 7 Greeks and 2 Spaniards. The number of children admitted in 1866 into the School of the Sisters of Charity was about 200. The Superior of the Boys' School is a gentleman of liberal culture and appears to be well fitted for his work, and the Sisters of Charity, in their efforts to instruct and train the children committed to their charge, do themselves and their church great credit.

The Italian College is a school recently established under the combined direction of the Italian government and of a committee of the Italian colony. It is provided with a neat and commodious building, and the expenses incurred for its maintenance are shared by the Italian government and the colony. It has 4 teachers, and the number of pupils in 1866 was more than 100. This educational enterprise, together with some patriotic and charitable associations among the Italians, deserves special commendation.

The Greek Church at Tunis has a neat, commodious and beautiful chapel, and two priests and about fifty families are connected with it. Its school has not thus far been regularly sustained in a prosperous condition, and I have not succeeded in obtaining any valuable statistics connected with it. Poor Greek families are said to be remarkably well provided for. Previous to the establishment of the English mission for the Jews, the Greek priests usually attended the funerals of Protestants.

There is no Protestant Chapel at Tunis, but the English church service is read and a discourse given to a very small audience every Sabbath morning at the house of the missionary to the Jews, who is also styled chaplain to the British consulate, though the British consuls have of late years been Catholics. There are two Protestant mission schools which are supported by the "London Society for Promoting Christianity amongst the Jews," and are under the general direction of Rev. William Fenner, missionary and chaplain. The Boys' School was established in 1861, under the charge of Mr. G. B. Gioja, and the Girls' School in 1863, under the charge of Miss Fanny Combe. The statistics of the schools for the years 1865 and 1866 are as follows: Boys' School, 1865, number of children in attendance 28,—23 Jews, 5 Christians; 1866, 33,—26 Jews, 7 Christians. Girls' School, 1865, number of children in attendance 102,—86 Jewesses, 16 Christians; 1866, 126,—106 Jewesses, 20 Christians.

These schools have improved from the time of their opening, and are doing much good, not alone to the children who enjoy their privileges, but to the cause of good education, by exciting a healthy emulation and activity in other worthy institutions of learning. The children of Tunis, unlike most of their superiors in age, are apt to learn, acquiring with great facility a knowledge of several languages and the elements of geography, arithmetic and natural history. I have not great faith in mere preaching as a means of usefulness at Tunis, and think it not enough to substitute Christian formularies for those of Jews and Mussulmans. It is the exemplification of Christian truth and the labors of able, earnest and energetic teachers that are destined to produce the best results. Hence I hope that with preaching for the mature in age, schools and other instrumentalities for training up the rising generation may be efficiently sustained, and encouragement given to enlist and retain in the department of elementary instruction skilful teachers who shall at the same time be accomplished ladies and gentlemen.

FREEMASONRY is an established institution at Tunis and may perhaps be classed among the educational instrumentalities of the place. Denounced by priests, muftis and rabbis, it embraces among its members Christians, Mussulmans and Jews, bringing into fraternal relations those who would otherwise have no intercourse or fellowship. Without definite knowledge of any weaknesses, and with high respect for its positive character, I suspect, however, its dangers are to lose sight of its moral aims in social and festive enjoyment. Its leaders, though liberal and progressive, are not highly educated men. Several lodges have been established there, but the lodge of "Cartagine ed Utica," founded a third of a century ago, was alone efficiently sustained in 1867. In this lodge are active men who take note of passing events and sympathize in the progressive movements of the age.

In Tunis only a few of the most liberal Mussulmans belong to the European lodges, but in the interior of the regency large numbers belong to a masonic fraternity which professes to derive its origin from Egypt, and has a form, a spirit and an aim somewhat peculiar. This fraternity having only three degrees, all its members are either apprentices, companions or masters. Its spirit is decidedly clannish and its aim is local, commercial and political. It acknowledges the existence of one God and has the secret signs of free and accepted masons. These people, striving for political independence, often give the Beys of Tunis much trouble, and claiming the right to control the trade with Central Africa, they rob and murder caravans and travellers. This information, together with a statement of a variety of incidents among these Mussulman masons, is given on the authority of competent witnesses who may be consulted at Tunis.

SANITARY COUNCIL.—I omitted stating in the appropriate place that the consuls, together with two doctors appointed by the Bey, constitute the sanitary council of the regency. In seasons of epidemics, the members of this council are often called together to deliberate in regard to quarantine regulations. The discussions at these meetings become occasionally very animated.

(K.) *Ascent of Mount Zaughan.*

ZAUGHAN, May 1st, 1867.

Away in the wilds of the regency of Tunis, will you let me send my greeting from Africa to the readers of the "Home Weekly?" Far from any Europeans and anything that speaks to us of civilized life, yet we find a strangeness, a *loneness* with nature that may in after years tempt us to look back on our week's stay here with no sad feeling.

Zaughan, itself on the side of a hill, is situated in the midst of mountains that stretch around it as far as the eye can reach, unrelieved by any glimpse of sea. But meeting one at every step there are rivulets and springs which fertilize the soil, and both hills and valleys are covered with a luxuriant vegetation, that only needs the hand of the worker to coin gold as well as beauty.

But these same mountains have given your correspondent the keenest anxiety during two mortal hours, while she wandered, like the "Babes in the Wood," up and down in a most literal sense. Shall I tell you more of our adventure, for adventure indeed it was? For the two days since our arrival here, a precipitous, rocky mountain of about 5,000 feet in height, had tempted me to its ascension, not only for the beautiful view I was sure of having from its summit, but because Guérin, a French writer, had described it in glowing language as something to be accomplished. I, who "had done" half of Europe, could I go away from Africa without a view of the world below me? At last I persuaded my father, and we set out on our expedition, with only one guide. We started in fine spirits, crossing a ravine, and went on for a long time, never minding the nettles and the rocks that would bruise our feet and tear our robes, in spite of thickest of boots and stuff for dresses. Before halfway up the cliff, our very guide gave way, yielding not so much to weariness of distance as to the dread of the overhanging rocks that kept rising high above our heads. Here, so near the desert, it seemed as if we had borrowed the mirage, for at each mount conquered, as we felt ourselves approaching our goal, we saw new peaks and

"Alps on Alps arise."

At last, even a man's feet were wearied beyond endurance, and I went on "just a few steps further," thinking to rejoin my father in a few moments. .But I kept on too far, not thinking that each step in the winding path was taking me further and further, not only from the sight, but from the sound of any living thing. For a moment, as I sat perched on the very pinnacle of the mount, and looked at the beautiful prospect beneath, I could not help a slight feeling of triumph at having conquered these steep rocks, that but a few hours before had looked so frowningly at me.

For miles and miles around there was the undulating land, covered with the fresh spring verdure, and an outline of mountains enclosing this beautiful valley, as if to protect it from the dryness and waste that were only kept from it by Nature's wall. But all this beauty could not keep one from thinking that it would be anything but nice to get lost in these African ravines, and cries were raised only to hear their own echo, and hours were passed that seemed like weeks. The wind blew our voices the wrong way, and each thought the other lost, while springing from rock to rock with a strength that fear alone could give, and fearing, with an almost nameless dread, to find the other fallen down some precipice. The night was coming on fast, and the danger of Bedouins and panthers was very great. But "all's well that ends well," and at last we met, soon after encountering the Kaid, or governor of the place, with a long procession of Arabs, all armed, and seeming so glad to be assured of our safety, that it half atoned for the fright that one must feel at being out till nearly nine o'clock in the mountains of Zaughan.

These are the outward surroundings of a life in the semi-barbarous part of Africa; but if you were to see the house arrangements to which we must submit for one week! Fortunately for our table comforts, we brought spoons and forks, thinking to find knives and other necessaries in the place. But we have learned that knives and chairs are luxuries. The first day a penknife had to do duty for all table matters, with three people to share it. But at last we have contrived to muster three large carving knives, either of which would not, I think, prove unacceptable if presented to an antiquarian society. A "Home Weekly" serves as table cover, and our table would challenge admiration as a sliding plane.

I have been led into this description of our household gods by reading of the *comforts* of a life in New York. By this experience we have learned that one can be comfortable anywhere—even in a bare room. We have so many beautiful flowers with which to make our rooms gay. Roses, pinks, geraniums and oleanders abound here, and with a little art one can hide many a bare spot. HELENA.

(L.) *Tunisian Courts and Justice.*

Notwithstanding the prevalent mode of administering justice, the Tunisians are noted for their litigious spirit and fondness for lawsuits. Mr.

JUDICIAL DECISIONS AND PENALTIES. 545

Noah in his TRAVELS IN NORTH AFRICA, speaks of a dispute between two Bedouins which was referred to Hamouda Bashaw. One Bedouin had several eggs and the other a hen, and they agreed to set the hen to hatch the eggs, and equally divide the issue; but as there happened to be thirteen chickens, they quarrelled about the odd one. The case came before the Bey, and the hen and chickens were taken into the court room. The Bey ordered the hen and chickens to be given to his cook and the litigants to receive each fifty stripes as a cure for their quarrelsome disposition.

In the summer of 1867, a Jewish peddler was in the Mussulman quarter at Tunis, when a Moor seized from him a roll of cotton cloth and concealed it in his house; then stoutly denying that he had taken the cloth, drove the Jew away with curses and blows. Forthwith the Jew and Moor appeared before the governor of the city, one complaining that he was beset and tormented by that miserable Jew, and the other complaining that he had been robbed and beaten by the Moor. The governor, feigning anger with the Jew, shut him up in prison, and while he entertained the Moor with coffee and tobacco, directed a servant to go quietly and report to the wife of the Moor that her husband wanted that piece of cotton cloth. The wife, not suspecting the artifice, promptly sent the cloth. The Jew was then brought forward, and identified his cloth amid many other pieces. The result was that the Jew regained his liberty and his property, while the Moor received fifty stripes and was shut up in prison.

An amusing scene of a politico-religious character was brought before a Tunisian court in the month of March, 1866, which seems to me worthy of note in this place, especially as it illustrates Tunisian jurisprudence. Ignorance, superstition and diabolism were duly represented. Some dignitaries of saintly pretensions having prevailed on the Bey previously to spare the life of Ali Ben Radam, the chief of the late rebellion, a Mussulman woman, encouraged by the success of her lords, volunteered her efforts to promote the interests of the arch rebel.

Though Radam's friends at the outset manifested gratitude for the clemency that spared his life, their tone of feeling was soon changed. They forgot the Bey's act of grace and raised a clamor for the liberation and marked honor of the culprit. Averse to seeing their friend with chains about his ankles employed among the galley slaves on the public works at the Goletta, they prayed that he might be permitted to make a pilgrimage to Mecca. His virtues were pronounced, his saintly character dwelt upon, and a lively interest awakened in his behalf. But the Bey, not believing in the traitor's sanctity, preferred that he should atone for his crimes in close confinement or in some useful occupation, rather than in wandering off to the Holy City.

It was at this stage in the proceedings, after the ordinary means of persuasion seemed likely to prove of no avail, that female genius came to the rescue of the traitor. Rumor, plumed afresh, soared aloft, as when Dido occupied the land, and set afloat reports of an extraordinary character. Taking no account of fancy flights, I give the simple facts as follows: A buxom dame of the Moslem faith, who had passed some fifty years with saintly airs and a reputation none too pure, astonished the credulous world one morning with the announcement of a marvellous scene during the night. Sister Rosaline, familiarly so called, affirmed that the Prophet had appeared to her in person and communicated important truths for the happiness of the Bey and the prosperity of his kingdom. She exhibited her right hand and arm of a lively green color, which, she said, was produced by the Prophet, as a proof of his presence and power. The Prophet told her, she said, that Ali Ben Radam was a saint and must be treated with honor and respect; otherwise a terrible calamity would befall the Bey and ruin the estate of the believers. "The Prophet acknowledged that he had predicted the downfall of the Bey in the year 1280 (1864, A. D.), and this would have taken place, he said, but for the rebellion raised up by Ali Ben Radam, which latter event served as a substitute for the more terrible calamity predicted." It is a Mussulman theory that small calamities prevent greater ones, and in accordance with this idea the believers are wont to thank God for every ill that befalls them, always feeling that it would be a greater misfortune to be excluded from the Mussulman paradise than to suffer temporary troubles.

The announcement made by sister Rosaline, together with the sight of the green hand and arm, created a profound sensation among ignorant and fanatic devotees. Multitudes sought to view the hand on which a miracle had been wrought and to place within its grasp choice gifts as a testimony of their faith. The streets in the vicinity of sister Rosaline's house were blocked up by a fanatical rabble from whose presence sober and well-disposed people were beginning to shrink, when the governor of Tunis, putting on the air of a disciple, sent his carriage with a suite of attendants to the scene of the alleged miracle. Sister Rosaline received the salutations and compliments of the distinguished official with dignity, and entering the carriage drove to the executive mansion with the air and pomp of an honored guest. There she exhibited her hand and displayed her eloquence, appearing greatly gratified with the attentions shown her.

The governor, who at first played the disciple, at length assumed the bearing of a magistrate and suggested the application of some test in regard to the genuineness of the miracle on sister Rosaline's hand. A chemist was called before the company by whose skill all traces of the prophetic green were speedily removed. At this point, Rosaline was told that if the Prophet had desired to honor a woman with his revelations, he would have selected a younger and better person than herself, and if his object were really to release Ali Ben Radam, he would be more likely to succeed by communicating directly with his Highness the Bey, or with his minister. The governor added dryly: "If the Prophet be disposed to visit you in future, he can as readily enter a prison as a house." Upon this announcement, Rosaline was conducted to the municipal tombs, where she speedily recovered from the effects of her vision. Her followers ceased to block up the public ways, and Ali Ben Radam, whose release was the object of all her efforts, was still left in prison.

A LONG SUIT.—STATE FINANCES.

On the 353d and 354th pages will be found a statement, showing that female advocates appear before the Bey in behalf of their sex.

CONSULAR DISPUTES.—The questions most delicate and difficult to be solved are those between consuls, as there are no duly appointed judges or arbitrators in such cases. In 1866, a dispute was settled between the American and Italian consuls, that had continued half a century. It related to the right of the Italian consul to maintain some windows looking into the American court. The Neapolitan consul was the original party enlisted against the American consul. There was repeatedly a sort of border warfare, with an appeal to arms on two different occasions. The controversy was revived in all its fierceness soon after my arrival at Tunis, and was brought to a satisfactory conclusion only after a great amount of time had been spent in collecting testimony, and the Italian ministry duly enlightened in regard to the nature of the case. American rights were thus finally secured and all cause for future difficulty removed.

(M.) *State Revenues and Expenses.*

The most hopeful view of Tunisian finances is the following, presented by the late Mr. Cubisol:

REVENUES OF THE STATE.

Taxes collected on provisions sold at the different markets in the regency,	$1,141,668
Taxes on rents,	551,180
Custom house revenue,	178,808
Taxes on the date trees of the Gereed and Gabes,	310,000
Taxes on the olive trees of the Sahel, Sfax, Gerba and Gabes,	310,000
Taxes on the olive trees of Tunis, Soliman, Menzel, Bizerta, Zaughan, Tebourba and Ras-Jebel,	201,500
Taxes on the above for the throne,	55,800
Taxes for the supervision of the olive trees,	37,200
Tithes of the wheat and barley,	260,400
Poll tax of $4.50 on 300,000 men,	1,350,000
Rent of government lands,	99,200
Taxes for the investiture of 24 kaids and 36 sheiks over territorial divisions,	898,380
Total,	$5,394,136

EXPENSES OF THE STATE.

Regular army,	$1,000,000
Irregular army,	125,000
Arsenal and navy,	375,000
His Highness the Bey,	250,000
The royal family,	125,000

Ministers of state,	125,000
Investiture of kaids, sheiks, etc.,	62,500
Miscellaneous,	437,500
Interest on public debt,	2,400,000
Total,	$4,900,000

According to this estimate, the revenues of the state exceed the expenses by $494,136. This shows well on paper. But the facts of the case are not so agreeable nor so satisfactory to the creditors of the Bey. The expenses of the government never fall below the estimate, while the revenues, being dependent on abundant crops and the loyalty and honesty of the subjects, often fail.

(N.) *Reply to an Israelitish Memorial.*

In the year 1866, the Secretary of the American Board of Israelites sent to the Department of State at Washington a memorial setting forth certain grievances of the Tunisian Jews, and requesting the friendly offices of our government in their behalf. A copy of that memorial was communicated to me at Tunis, recommending such unofficial aid as I could render. Appended will be found the substance of my reply to that communication.

The condition of the Jews of Tunis is a subject of decided interest to me and has received much attention during my residence in this place. I have thrown what influence I have possessed in favor of the broad principles of civil and religious liberty alike for Jews and Gentiles. On receiving the memorial of the American Israelites, I placed a copy of it before the Bey. I did this, not in an official way, but as it were to show my good will by giving the government an opportunity to make its own explanations. Addressing me as a friend, the Bey replies: "The American Israelites are mistaken in regard to the treatment which their co-religionists receive here. No odious discriminations are made by law, and we call you to witness that our court and the important officers in our kingdom are fully represented by Jews. Jews are among our doctors, bankers and confidential advisers, while they are relieved from service as soldiers and are not burdened with taxes."

I have not yet found a Jew or a Christian prepared to controvert this statement of the Bey, though I have invited to my office some of the most intelligent and respectable Jews residing here, and have conversed upon the subject with most of my colleagues. The statement of the American Board of Israelites is pronounced by all parties to be inaccurate and unjust in its reference to the Tunisian government. I believe the impression to be general if not universal here, that the treatment of Jews is fair if not generous. Jews are permitted to have their own tribunals in all matters between each other; and my most experienced colleagues assure me that more complaints are brought to their knowledge against arbitrary and tyrannical rabbis, than against Mussulman officials.

It is probable that Jews are occasionally ill-treated or denied justice by Mussulman officials; so also are Mussulmans occasionally and often ill-treated by their co-religionist officials with but little chance of redress; whereas the Jews have, besides their friends in the government, strong supporters in every consulate and vice-consulate in the regency. Jews and Christians were once slaves here, but this state of things no longer exists. The tables are now completely turned. Jews and Christians now occupy places of responsibility and power. Jews are the brokers, bankers, money lenders and merchants of the regency; and when they combine, they can make the Bey tremble on his throne.

The Bey has not the power to enact, nor would he dare try to execute, any such injustice as is laid to his charge by the American Israelites. There are influences here more powerful than his religion to regulate his conduct towards his Jewish subjects. He knows that the Jews, though they may be despised by him, have able friends, not only here, but throughout Christendom, to advocate and sustain their civil and religious rights; and therefore he is inclined as a matter of policy to deal gently and justly with them. The Bey is aware that a single case of downright injustice towards a Jew may involve him in serious trouble, while he knows a hundred cases of injustice towards Mussulmans may pass unnoticed. No legal decision is made by the government against a Jew, however unjust his cause, which is not carefully scrutinized and often followed by a wholesale misrepresentation of the facts. Nay, some foreign Jews, supposed to be employed here for political and partisan purposes, appear to have little else to do than sending forth to the European press garbled statements and exaggerated accounts of the Bey's treatment of Jews. It is but just, however, to say that this course of conduct is generally discountenanced by the respectable Israelites of Tunis.

My conviction is that moral action is needed more than politics or diplomacy to elevate the condition alike of Jews and of Gentiles in this regency. Jews, Mussulmans and Christians here appear to me in one respect very much alike. Their religion consists in dogmas to be quarrelled about, rather than in a spirit of love and good will to be lived and breathed.

There are here Bedouin or Nomad Jews as well as Mussulmans, living in tents and wandering from point to point with their flocks and herds. On my recent visit to Gerba, I saw several villages of Jews whose only fear seemed to be,—not of the Tunisian government, but of those who cast aside its jurisdiction, as was done during the late insurrection. When the government is strong they are best protected, and they are brutally robbed and their lives endangered only in times of revolt, when the functions of the government are suspended.

(O.) *Consular Officers at Tunis.*

UNITED STATES.—Joseph Ettienne Famin, a French merchant, was the agent of the United States at Tunis from May, 1796, till March, 1799.

William Eaton was the first consul of the United States for the city and kingdom of Tunis. He began his services in March, 1799, shortly before signing the treaty of peace with the Bey of Tunis, and continued them till March, 1803. General Eaton on leaving Tunis, visited the United States and returned the following year to the Mediterranean, where he performed a most brilliant military feat. Hastily collecting a body of Mussulmans and Christians in Egypt, he marched across the desert of Barca, took Derne and menaced and frightened the reigning Dey of Tripoli, who, finding that he was to be encountered by land as well as by sea, speedily demanded terms of peace. Consul Lear, encouraged by naval officers who were jealous of the land force, yielded to this request, and the Tripolitan war was thus terminated, much to the disgust of Eaton, and in violation of the compact with Hamet Bashaw, the rightful ruler of the country, who coöperated with Eaton in this remarkable expedition. The honor of our flag was, however, vindicated, and the usurper, Joseph Bashaw,* was humiliated. America, then in her infancy, struck the first effective blow against the Barbary Corsairs, and the account of that enterprise, in connection with which the name of Eaton, as well as that of Decatur, must ever be honored, now constitutes one of the brightest pages in our nation's history. General Eaton died in April, 1811, aged 49 years.

George Davis, a surgeon in the navy, was charged with the duties of the office in March, 1803, and continued till August 17th, 1805.

James Dodge, also a surgeon in the navy, received his first commission from Commodore Rodgers, August 17th, 1805, and died in the consulate, November 22d, 1806. His remains are in the Protestant Cemetery at Tunis.

Charles D. Coxe, from November 22d, 1806, till December 14th, 1814; was transferred to Tripoli.

M. M. Noah, from December 14th, 1814, till September 21st, 1815. Left Ambrose Allegro in charge. He wrote an interesting book of travels and became subsequently distinguished as a politician and journalist. Died 1851, aged 66.

Thomas D. Anderson, from December 21st, 1815, till 2d of January, 1818. The account of his difficulties encountered in consequence of his refusal to kiss the Bey's hand is very interesting.

Charles Folsom, from January 2d, 1818, till October 19th, 1819. Vice Admiral Farragut pursued his studies a considerable time under Mr. Folsom's charge at Tunis. Mr. Folsom is still living at Cambridge, Mass.

Townsend Stith, from the 19th of October, 1819, till the 16th of August, 1823. Left Ambrose Allegro in charge.

Samuel D. Heap, a surgeon in the navy, from January, 1824, till April

---

* The son of his successor, the last Dey of Tripoli, who was driven from his throne in 1838, resides at Tunis, a pensioner on the bounty of the Bey. He owes no good will to either Turkey or England, and has slight hopes of ever returning to his native land. He is of a social nature, though saddened by his experience as an exile.

21st, 1825. Signed a treaty with the Bey of Tunis on the 24th of February, 1824.

Charles D. Coxe, from April 21st, 1825, till September, 1826. Transferred to Tripoli, where he died.

Samuel D. Heap, from September, 1826, till March 1st, 1842.

William B. Hodgson, from March 1st, 1842, till May 5th, 1842. Left W. R. B. Gale, an American merchant, in charge.

John Howard Payne, from the 11th of May, 1843, till the 15th of September, 1845. Left Joseph Gaspary, American agent at the Goletta, in charge.

Samuel D. Heap, from the 20th of October, 1845, till the 30th of June, 1851.

John Howard Payne, from June 30th, 1851, till his death in the American Consulate April 1st, 1852. His remains are in the Protestant Cemetery at Tunis. Left Joseph Gaspary in charge. (See notice on page 539.)

Samuel D. Heap, from April, 1853, till his death in the American Consulate on the 2d of October, 1853. His remains are in the Protestant Cemetery at Tunis. Lewis Ferrière, English Vice Consul, and David Porter Heap were successively charged with the duties of the office.

William Penn Chandler, from the 17th of July, 1854, till the 30th of August, 1858. Left David Porter Heap in charge.

John Merritt, from January 20th, 1859, till the 27th of June, 1859. Left Nathan Davis, an English subject, in charge.

George W. S. Nicholson, from the 8th of October, 1859, till the 6th of July, 1862.

Amos Perry, from the 6th of July, 1862, till the 10th of September, 1867. Left Charles Cubisol, agent at the Goletta, in charge.

Gwin Harris Heap, from the 14th of November, 1867.

In the course of about seventy years America has had sixteen different consular officers at Tunis. Messrs. Coxe and Payne were each twice appointed consul, and Dr. Heap four times. Three of these sixteen consular officers, viz., Messrs. Dodge, Payne and Heap, Sr., died in the consulate and have monuments erected over their remains in the Protestant Cemetery at Tunis.

Several other appointments were made at different times, and one consul arrived at Tunis only to find himself superseded and his successor in possession of the archives.

FRANCE.—The consulate that has been the longest established at Tunis is that of the French. This contains the original treaty signed in 1270, shortly after the death of St. Louis, and many other documents of great interest, as shown in the invaluable work of Mr. Rousseau, repeatedly referred to in these pages. The full list of French consular officers from 1583 to 1855 is given in Mr. Rousseau's book.

1855, Leon Roches, Consul-General and Chargés d'Affaires.
1863, De Beauval, " " " " "
1865, De Bellecourt, " " " " "
1867, De Botmilieu, " " " " "

CARTHAGE AND TUNIS.

GREAT BRITAIN.—The consulate of England was established with the treaty in 1662, though it appears from monuments in the Protestant Cemetery that British consular officers resided at Tunis at an earlier period.

1804, Sir Richard Oglander, Agent and Consul-General.
1822, Alexander Tulin, Esq.,   "   "   "   "   (ad interim).
1824, Sir Thomas Reade,   "   "   "   "
1849, Sir Edward Baynes, .   "   "   "   "
1855, Richard Wood, Esquire,   "   "   "   "

SPAIN.—Treaties were made at an early period between Spanish princes and Tunis. When the first consulate was established in the Spanish name does not appear on record at Tunis, the old official documents having been long since removed to Spain. Independent of the Spanish domination (1535—1570) Spain was for a long time a leading Christian power at Tunis.

Spanish Consuls-General and Chargés d'Affaires from the treaty of Paris, 1792:

1792, Suchita; 1796, Guillen Buzaran (Ignacio) left in charge.
1796, Soler (Jayme); 1798, Guillen Buzaran (Ignacio) left in charge.
1800, Soler (Arnoldo) left in charge.
1802, Guillen Buzaran (Manuel Ventura).
1802, Noguera.
1804, Sequi; 1808, Soler (Arnoldo) left in charge.
1811, Soler (Arnaldo); 1816, Soler (Pedro) left in charge.
1817, Soler (Pedro); 1821, Soler (Carlos) left in charge; 1827, De Ossa left in charge; 1828, De Lesseps left in charge; 1832, Deval left in charge.
1832, Rizzo (Juan Bautista); 1847, Rizzo (Felipe) left in charge.
1847, De Malagamba; 1858, Rizzo (Felipe) left in charge.
1859, De Barros; 1861, De Fortuny left in charge.
1862, Romea; 1864, Alvarez Perez left in charge.
1864, De Navarro.

SWEDEN AND NORWAY.—The first treaty of peace and commerce between Sweeden and Tunis was concluded by Mr. Logie, Swedish consul at Algiers, in 1736, since which time there have been seven consular officers, as follows:

Rönling, from 1737 to 1759.
Ferner, from 1760 to 1764.
Molinari, from 1764 to 1779.
Charles Tulin, (Senior) from 1779 to 1808. He was succeeded by his eldest son.
Charles Tulin, (Jr.) from 1808 to 1832. Was appointed in 1829 Consul General for Sweden and Norway. Was succeeded by his brother.
G. A. Tulin, from 1832 to 1864. Was charged by the Prussian government to represent Prussia at the Court of Tunis. Was succeeded by his eldest son.
Charles Tulin, from 1864.

Tulin, father and two sons, occupied the Swedish consular mansion 85 consecutive years.

ITALY.—The consulate of Naples was established in 1816 and that of Sardinia in 1822. The Italian consulate general, embracing all Italy with the exception of the province of Venice, whose consulate was given up about the beginning of this century, was established in 1860. Its agents and consuls-general have been as follows:

1860, F. Mathieu.
1861, E. Fasciotti.
1862, E. Bensa.
1863, F. Gambarotta.
1866, G. Luigi Pinna.

AUSTRIA.—G. G. Merlatto, appointed consul-general in 1850.

HOLLAND.—The consulate of Holland was established with the treaty in 1662. The office of consul has been held by the highly respected family Nyssen, for nearly a century. Mr. Charles Nyssen is now the consul, and also the agent of Russia.

The consulate of Denmark was established in 1751, and that of Belgium in 1839. Mr. Charles Cubisol represented these two powers at Tunis for many years up to the time of his death in 1868. Mr. William Schmidt was appointed commercial consul of Portugal in 1864; Dr. Abraham Lumbroso, consul-general and diplomatic agent of San Marino in 1865; and about the same time Mr. Charles Cubisol was *sprinkled* with decorations and inducted into a like high-sounding office to represent the Prince of Monaco. The republic of San Marino is represented by an Italian *baron*, and has a bigger flag at Tunis than the United States.

(P.) *The Political Future of the Country.*

Just as I was leaving Tunis, after having endured the heat of the summer of 1867, and breathed a noxious air that brought cholera and death to thousands around me, I received from an eminent diplomatic source a pointed inquiry, whose definite answer, which was then confidential, implied on my part some insight into the future. Though not a prophet, nor the son of a prophet, I embraced my privilege as a Yankee and *guessed*.

Since then, I have seen no reason to change my views. As the great ship canal across the isthmus of Suez progresses under French auspices, Tunis, centrally situated on the great highway between the canal and the ocean acquires a new importance which the French people and government are not slow to appreciate and turn to their account. They see on the Tunisian coast better harbors and a richer soil than are to be found in their Algerine possessions, and they evidently mean to bring them under their control. Instead of being animated by a chivalrous spirit and a desire to diffuse the blessings of civilization, they seem disposed to take advantage of the weakness of this government to extend their power and increase their territorial possessions. Despite his graceful air and comely looks, the French eagle is savagely rapacious; and now the British lion, which seeks the gratification of his own appetite, is powerless to restrain the soaring and plunging movements of this keen-eyed bird. The American eagle, distrustful of both the bird and beast that hovered and prowled around his western domains in the season of his exposure, contents himself with simply noting passing events. The inquiry and reply were as follows:—

WHAT IS TO BE THE POLITICAL FUTURE OF TUNIS?

This question is often put, and gives rise to a variety of speculations and answers. Frenchmen apparently regard Tunis as the supplement of Algeria. Englishmen see here an important source of supplies for Malta, and Italians claim special consideration on account of their language and customs, which have to some extent prevailed here from the Roman period to the present time. Italy has the largest colony here; England has the most pressing need of supplies for Malta; but France has the greatest force at hand to control the country.

Politically, too, France has the most intimate relations with Tunis. From the beginning of the war against Algiers, the French have been near neighbors of the Bey, and much of the time have been patronised as his special friends. On one occasion they prevented the Ottoman fleet from an organized effort to get control of this government. They have employed the full range of diplomatic arts to introduce and keep up intimate relations between the two countries. The French consul at length acquired a leading, not to say controlling, influence with the Bey. He was consulted, and his aid was regarded as needful to the success of all important enterprises. French subjects were invited to fill places of emolument and trust, and to them were given the most important contracts, such as establishing telegraphic communication between different parts of the regency, making loans to the government almost on their own terms, and introducing water into the city and its environs from the mountains of Zaughan.

With French influence thus strongly established and recognized, in the year 1864 a French consul with little experience in the country attempted to inaugurate a new line of policy, boldly treating the Bey as a French vassal by interrupting his vessels in his own waters, demanding the dismissal of some of his ministers, and recommending other important changes in the government. Not being able to execute this line of policy without resorting to force (from which measure the consul did not shrink), and giving serious offence to other nations, the French government withdrew this consul and has since sent other officers who have pursued a more conciliatory course. Still, during their administration, the Bey has been made to feel the arbitrary power of the French government.

When the Bey was relieved of the presence of the offensive consul, it was regarded as a victory on his part and was so proclaimed abroad. But

I believe France took this step both because she did not wish to encounter the displeasure of other nations and especially because she was not disposed unnecessarily to have another religious war similar to that waged in Algeria. But her ultimate purposes in regard to this country are scarcely to be questioned. While she watches it with a vigilant eye lest it escape her irritating touch, she sees that gentleness is in general better than harshness. Feeling secure of her plunder, she can afford to await the maturity of plans of slow development.

If the French were to take forcible possession of the regency, other nations might protest, and Mussulmans might massacre and plunder. The seizure could be made and the country held. Difficulties would, however, naturally arise in regulating many complicated affairs while encountering the hatred of Mussulmans and the ill-will of Europeans. In view of all the facts in this case, France decides to await the progress of events. Her experience in Algeria and in Mexico probably serves as a warning. Her legitimate influence as a powerful neighbor of the Bey is great, and she has but to persist in the maintenance of apparently friendly relations, and seize every petty occasion to assert her presumed authority, to secure present advantages and a final triumph.

Tunisia is destitute of the elements of life and progress which alone can long save her from falling an easy prey to a stronger power. The policy of her adoption leads directly to ruin. Instead of being judiciously taxed to secure a revenue, a considerable part of the country is annually overrun by an army, pillaging and plundering in the name of the government, and the poor Arabs are fast becoming so miserable and so desperate in their misery as to demand rather than repel foreign intervention; and consuls, who exerted their utmost energy to overcome French intrigues during the late rebellion, are now apparently disposed to menace the Bey with French intervention to induce him to pay his debts, the responsibility of which rests heavily upon some of them. While the Bey pays fifty thousand francs a year to a French subject to promote his interests at Paris, the interests of the French government at Tunis are believed to be gratuitously watched and promoted by both French and Tunisian subjects who are ever near the Bey.

I am, then, persuaded that this country will at length come under the acknowledged protection and control of France, if not with the consent and approbation of other nations, probably without violent opposition. Such at least is the manifest tendency of affairs at the present time, notwithstanding a species of state-craft employed to produce a counter result. The malady is too deeply seated to be overcome by empirics in the name of diplomacy. The Gallic eagle, already scenting the prey, prepares to clutch it, despite the lion's growl and all the shrieks and howls that may be raised as he enjoys his repast.

(Q.) *A Day at Carthage and Tunis.*

(COPY OF A LETTER.)

TUNIS, April 20, 1867.

As I have read the chatty letters in the "Home Weekly," from Paris and New York, I have thought that a second letter, from even such an out-of-the-way place as Tunis, might not prove unreadable. It is our very *out-of-the-wayness* (don't look too carefully in Webster) that adds a zest to the life otherwise so dull. The great things seem small, and the small things great, as seen through our Eastern spectacles. Will you put on the glasses—let them be of rose-color—and the seven-league boots, to visit with me, for just one day, my Eastern home? See, as we approach the Goletta, the port of Tunis, how the blue waves of the Mediterranean dash against the shores of Dido's ancient home. There are but few ruins of Carthage remaining, but those few are well worthy of the sight-seer's attention. Cisterns are there of such a size, that one feels fairly lost inside, and, though very ancient, yet in excellent preservation. There we find a ricketty old ladder, that tempts the courageous to descend only to have an *underground* prospect. Shall we try it? The first round makes us shiver, but, after that, we go bravely on, and are repaid by finding bits of the little jars that the ancients used as drinking cups. Here the water used to come, not by aqueducts or pipes, but fresh from the Giver's hand, as poured out from the heavens. A little further on we come to the tombs, where they are constantly excavating the beautiful jewelry, of every kind, that so far outshines the best efforts of the present day. But, after all, the spot that most attracts us is the very summit of the hill, crowned by the little chapel, built in honor of St. Louis. Here is a view so beautiful, that we can but feel tempted to wish we could stay always and feast our eyes.

However, this lingering over beautiful scenery will not bring us to Tunis, and we have yet something to see there. After a drive of ten miles we alight, and go at once to the bazars, which are full of curious sights and sounds. From beautiful Nature we see the reverse picture—Nature in man left without cultivation; and fortunate will it be for you if you keep your good temper in all the pushing and screaming. Let us avail ourselves of one of the consular janissaries, who will scream "*Balek! balek!*" (take care), till you begin to wonder if that one word constitutes his whole dictionary. "*Balek*," however, aided by the stick, is very effective.

As you are a stranger, you must want to buy, and fifty people will soon be around you, pressing upon you all their wares, and in the jewelry bazar there are really very rare and costly things for sale. By dint of shouting in an unknown tongue, and gesticulations that remind you that "all their bones do shake," you are at last tired out, and you move on to the clothing bazar, followed by the disappointed looks of your fifty friends. Here are the gayest colors, in the choicest silks and wools, woven together to make

www.ingramcontent.com/pod-product-compliance
Ingram Content Group UK Ltd.
Pitfield, Milton Keynes, MK11 3LW, UK
UKHW020749101125
8855UKWH00001B/2